To:
know
the
truth
about
ISLAM

Exposing the Truth about the Qur'an

THE REVELATION OF ERROR

VOL. 1 OF 2

The Stories of the Prophets
by Usama K. Dakdok

Exposing the Truth about the Qur'an, Volume 1

Copyright © 2013 Usama Dakdok, Venice, Florida
Published in 2013 by Usama Dakdok Publishing, LLC
P.O. Box 244 Venice, FL 34284-0244

All rights reserved. No part of this book may be reproduced, stored in a retrieval system, or transmitted in any form or by any means – printed, electronic, mechanical, photocopy, recording or otherwise – without written permission of the copyright holder.

For copyright information:
Usama Dakdok Publishing, LLC
P.O. Box 244
Venice, FL 34284-0244

All scripture quotations, unless otherwise indicated, are taken from the New King James Version®. Copyright © 1982 by Thomas Nelson, Inc. Used by permission. All rights reserved.

ISBN: 978-0-9824137-6-0

Dewey decimal system number: 297, Islam

Published in the United States of America

Contents – Volume 1

Ch.	The Story Of:	Page
-	Guide for Readers	vi
-	Introduction	3
1	Creation	9
2	Adam	43
3	Idris (Enoch)	62
4	Noah	64
5	Houd	81
6	Saleh	92
7	Abraham, Lot, Ishmael and Isaac	101
8	Midian and Shoaib	166
9	Joseph	176
10	Job	247
11	Za Al Kafel	259
12	When All People Perished Together	262
13	The Companions of the Rass	263
14	Yassin	266
15	Jonah	271
16	Moses	283
17	Joshua	374
18	Al Kadar (The Green Prophet)	385
19	Elijah	392

Guide for Readers of This Book

1. Scripture taken from the New King James Version ®. Copyright © 1982 by Thomas Nelson, Inc. Used by permission. All rights reserved.
2. Qur'an verses are quoted from *The Generous Qur'an; An Accurate, Modern English Translation of the Qur'an, Islam's Holiest Book,* by Usama K. Dakdok, 2nd printing (Venice, FL: Usama Dakdok Publishing, LLC, 2009).
3. Order of the text follows Ibn Kathir's book, *Stories of the Prophets* - this explains the somewhat erratic and occasionally repetitious nature of the content.
4. Frequent mention is made within the text of Mohammed or Muslim scholars copying from the Bible. In Mohammed's time the collected books of the Bible were not readily available in one document as we know it today and relatively few people had possession of actual manuscripts. While Muslim scholars writing in the following centuries no doubt had access to, and leaned heavily on, many of these manuscripts, it is more likely that Mohammed heard many of the scriptures recited verbally while on his various trading trips and that he got other information from his first wife's cousin, Waraka Ibn Nawfal, reportedly a heretical priest or monk familiar with much of the Old Testament manuscripts and some of the New Testament manuscripts, and who probably helped Mohammed create some of the Qur'an. Mohammed's frequent misspelling of names as well as the confusion of people and facts further suggests that he obtained much of his information verbally from others.
5. References are made to people being asked to **"revert"** to the original religion (Islam). Islam teaches that everyone is born Muslim, but some are taught by their parents to follow other false religions. Therefore if one leaves another religion to become a Muslim, they **revert** rather than **convert** to Islam.

6. Definitions of:

Terms used as part of a name:

'Abd	"Servant (slave) of"
Abu	"Father of"
Al	"The"
Bin	Colloquial term for "Ibn" (son of)
Bint	"Daughter of"
Ibn	"Son of"
Oom	"Mother of"

Other terms frequently used in text:

Allah	Used in text for the god of the Qur'an, who has no son; is also the word used in the Arabic Bible for God, who is the Father of our Lord and our Savior, Jesus Christ.
Ayat	Plural of the word "ayah." It literally means signs or miracles and is often used to refer to the smallest units of the Qur'an; equivalent to "verses." Depending on context, it might also mean proofs, evidences, verses, lessons, revelations, etc.
Gabreel	An angel described in the Qur'an. Not spelled the same way in Arabic as the archangel Gabriel of the Bible.
'Iblis	Literally the Devil; Satan which is also known in Arabic as Shaytān.
'Isa	The name used in the Qur'an which Muslims falsely claim to be Jesus' name; actually in Arabic the correct translation of Jesus' name would be Yasua from Joshua in Hebrew, meaning "savior."
The People of the Book	A term used to designate Christians and Jews.
Surah	A portion of revelation; a division of the Qur'an corresponding essentially to "chapter."

DEDICATION

To my father who served the Lord for 62 years. A man who lived a godly life, he raised sons and daughters for the kingdom of God. I am proud to be one of his children. If it were not for my father, I would not be in this ministry.

I praise God for him, for he was also a godly husband married to my mother for 52 years. She was a godly woman who served the Lord with my father all those years of marriage and raised her children to fear God and to love the Lord Jesus Christ and one another. If it were not for my mother, I also would not be involved in this ministry. My parents taught me to love the Muslim - that's why I wrote this book - and to expose the truth about the Qur'an, which Muslims believe to be a holy book.

Because Muslims generally do not know the Qur'an, they grow up blindly believing in it. My prayer is that as my dear Muslim believers read this book, they will discover the truth - that the Qur'an is a counterfeit to the Holy Bible. My prayer for Christian believers is that, as they read and understand this book, they will be equipped to effectively reach out to Muslims with the truth of the Gospel.

A special thank you to my brothers and sisters in Christ – without your hard work, dedication of time, and laborious efforts this book would not have been possible. I really appreciate all you have done for me, for The Straight Way of Grace Ministry, and most importantly for the Kingdom of our Lord and our Savior, Jesus Christ.

Thank you, Mom & Dad.
From a loving and grateful son,
Usama K. Dakdok

INTRODUCTION

On my first trip to Indonesia in 2002, the Lord gave me the opportunity to sit with a Muslim Yemeni man. Although the airplane was nearly full, the seat next to that one man just happened to be empty. I asked my colleague to pray for the man, saying, "Perhaps the Lord will give me an opportunity to share the Gospel with him."

I noticed that the man was reading the Qur'an in Arabic. When I sat next to him, I asked him if he would read louder so that I could hear what he was reading. The portion he was reading contained the story of Abraham. I asked him, "Do you understand what you are reading?" He answered, "Yes." When I asked him some questions concerning the story though, he could not come up with any responses. "But," he said, "we can easily find the answers for these questions. We simply need to read the interpretations of Muslim scholars."

He was obviously a businessman; he certainly was not an imam. As the conversation went on, I shared that I was a Christian student at a theological seminary. At the end of the trip, he generously gave me a book which I still hold dear and which I will be referencing as I pen this book. It is called *Stories of the Prophets* by Ibn Kathir.[1]

Several years later, I was flying from Dallas, Texas, to Orlando, Florida. A friend and I arrived at the airport ninety minutes earlier than necessary. The friends who dropped us off at the airport suggested that we spend time in a coffee shop, but we decided not to do this. I said, "Perhaps the Lord will give us an opportunity to minister to a Muslim person."

We had just spent two wonderful days in Dallas where we taught other Christians how to minister to Muslims. As a matter of fact, my topic had been "Using the Qur'an as a Bridge to Reach Out to Muslims with the Gospel." Amazingly, the first person we met was Namaan, a Muslim man from Pakistan, who worked for American Airlines. He was happy when he found

---

[1] Ibn Kathir, *Stories of the Prophets*, Abo Al Fida Ishamail Ibn Kathir Al Kurashi Al Damashce (Beirut: Dar Al-Arab Heritage, 1408 AH, 1988).

out that my name was Usama and that I was an Egyptian. With a big smile on his face, he said: "Masha Allah, Masha Allah! What a marvelous name! If I ever have a son, I will name him Usama."

I asked him if he loved the name Usama, and he said, "Yes." I whispered in his ear, "Usama bin Laden?" He nodded his head and said, "Absolutely."

As my friend and I ministered to him for over an hour, he changed the subject about fifteen times. We discussed many doctrines and beliefs of the Christian faith and Islam. I challenged him to answer some simple questions about the stories contained within the Qur'an. I offered him some of the answers from the Bible. He tried to tell me that all Muslim scholars know these answers. I responded, "No, that's not true, for I have read many of the Muslim scholars' interpretations, and they do not know because neither the Qur'an nor the hadith mentions anything concerning the details in the stories of the prophets."

Then I shared with him that I had studied and read *Stories of the Prophets* by Ibn Kathir. With a serious look on his face, he asked, "You read this book by Ibn Kathir?" I said, "Yes." He replied with surprise, "And you're still a Christian?" I said, "Yes. As a matter of fact, the more I read what Ibn Kathir wrote, the more I hold dear to the Christian faith and the Bible. I discovered that Ibn Kathir was going in circles and fabricating interpretations for many of the verses of the Qur'an, trying to help Mohammed and Allah by trying to create some sense from the stories of the Qur'an." At this point, we exchanged email addresses because we had to leave to catch our flight.

Can a Muslim who reads the Qur'an and the interpretations of the Qur'an by Muslim scholars really understand the Qur'an? When we ask relevant questions like who, why, where, when, what, and how concerning any topic of any portion of revelation (the Qur'an), Muslims alway reply with the verse in the Qur'an which states: *O you who have believed, do not ask about things which, if they were revealed to you, it would be harmful to you* (Qur'an 5:101).[2]

What a way to understand the Qur'an! Just don't ask questions because, if you ask, perhaps you won't find an answer. On the other hand, if you do find the answer and it contradicts the teaching of the Qur'an, then perhaps you will become an infidel (unbeliever).

Christians, on the other hand, are encouraged to ask questions and seek further understanding, which is one of the primary reasons that we have Bible study classes. In them, we can investigate and search for answers to all kinds of questions, and these answers are in the Word of God. Perhaps the greatest problem that Muslims face is the necessity to believe in a book, which in many cases they have not read, but whether they have or not, they simply cannot understand. As it is even written in its own pages, no one can even interpret it, except Allah himself! You can read this in Qur'an 3:7 where it says: *[7]He is who has sent down on you the book; some of its verses are decisive. Those are the mother of the book and others are ambiguous. So those whose hearts deviate, so they will follow what is ambiguous of it, desiring the sedition and desiring its interpretation, and no one knows its interpretation except Allah. And those deeply rooted in knowledge say, "We believed in it, all of it from our lord." But none will remember except those who have understanding.*[3]

Those with "understanding" believed in all of it (the Qur'an) without knowing its interpretation! What a statement! *How can a person believe in something without understanding it?*

As I travel all over the world and meet with Muslims, I point out some of the hateful and barbaric verses throughout the Qur'an, such as verses calling for the death of non-Muslims, like Christians and Jews, those who criticize Islam, or those who become apostates (those who renounce the religion of Islam). Their answer is that my claim is false, and they always

---

[2] Usama K. Dakdok, trans., *The Generous Qur'an: An Accurate, Modern English Translation of the Qur'an, Islam's Holiest Book,* (Venice, FL: Usama Dakdok Publishing, LLC, 2009). Note: all Qur'an verses will come from this translation.

[3] *The Generous Qur'an*

quote to me some of the early Meccan verses such as (109:6): *⁶To you your religion, and to me is my religion.* When I tell them that Islam is spread with the sword, their answer is that this is not true; this is a lie, for the Qur'an says (2:256): *No compulsion in religion.*

When I quote to them from among the many violent verses of the Qur'an, not unsurprisingly, they respond that I am taking the verses out of context. When I quote the full verses, including the verses before and after, they insist that the translation must be wrong. Then when I quote them the same verses from several different translations (and note that these are by Muslim scholars who have the approval of Al-Azhar University of Cairo, Egypt), they tell me there are many accurate meanings of the words of the Qur'an which can only be understood in Arabic.

Finally, when I read the Qur'an to them in Arabic, they say, "Sorry, we don't know Arabic." Whenever I ask them to show me any unabrogated verses in the Qur'an which teach love or peace, they come with the answer of "I am not a scholar; I don't know." What an endless cycle of ignorance and complacency! These types of followers are blind zealots and can be even more dangerous than native Arabic speakers who are Muslim from birth.

Notice that even though these Muslims may not know very much about the Qur'an, they memorize early Meccan verses to defend their religion. For those who understand the Doctrine of Abrogation (basically, when in conflict later verses supersede earlier verses) and then knowingly still use the early Meccan verses, I refer to this type of people as deceivers. Some of them, however, do not know the Doctrine of Abrogation, and so they are merely the deceived ones, victims of a faith who are encouraged to never question.

Muslims are not the only ones who are (1) using rationale that is difficult to follow, (2) stating their beliefs ardently, and (3) expecting compliance without allowing thoughtful inquiry. Many people in the United States today speak loudly concerning the freedom of religion. Although I have lived in the United States for over twenty years, I had never heard such bold insistence concerning freedom of religion until fairly recently. Historically, the opposite has been true; many oppose this freedom for Christians and Jews by causing the removal of any expressions of worship outside the church building or synagogue. For example, many insist on removing the Ten Commandments from public buildings and eradicating prayer from schools.

You may wonder why these people are speaking out now about the freedom of religion. *Is it because they want Muslims to take over America?* That is what they are allowing to happen, even though they may not even realize it. They promote the right of Muslims to build a mosque at Ground Zero and another one where Flight 93 went down in Pennsylvania, as well as mosques all over American airports. They allow Islam to be taught in the public schools, they facilitate Muslim prayer rooms in our school buildings, and Muslims openly teach about Islam in our state universities.

On the other hand, these same people who are now crying out "freedom of religion" seek to intimidate Christians with legal action when they express their faith. While Christians cannot pray in Jesus' name over meals and Jews, until recently, were not served kosher meals in our military branches, Muslims are allowed to perform Islamic prayer five times a day and practice Islamic law (sharia) in their daily lives and are given lawful (halal) meals, such as where no pork may be served.

People must realize that they must act intelligently regarding freedom of religion. If they really knew the history of Islam, the words of Allah in the Qur'an, and the teachings of Mohammed in the hadith, they would realize that America is currently on the road to destruction as accommodations are implemented in the name of tolerance, even acceptance. They need to realize that the Muslims' way of life is highly regimented by Islamic law and their practices threaten to permeate every aspect of American freedoms and our way of life, not just in the array of religious practices. The religion of Islam will demolish freedom of religion and every other personal freedom that we have historically enjoyed in the United States.

The current political climate, coupled with my education, knowledge, and experience of Islam in my home country of Egypt, influenced me to write this book after I had completed a literal English translation of *The Generous Qur'an*.[4] I will follow the order of topics set forth in Ibn Kathir's book which, although it differs greatly in form and content from the Bible, is largely based on it. That will be my mission, which is to help the reader to compare the Qur'an, the hadith, and the Muslim scholars' writings with the original and true accounts that are readily found in the Bible.

We will be discussing the following: creation, the stories of the prophets, and the Muslim assertion that the prophethood story ended with Mohammed. We will respond to such teachings with the words of the Holy Bible, the standard of faith for Christians.

Many Muslim scholars who have had deep knowledge of Islam, some of whom even served as imams and professors in Al-Azhar University and other universities around the world, have become Christians. They have something in common which astonished me when I first discovered it. They reported that they had become Christians because they studied the Qur'an and discovered the falsehoods and the errors in it as they read the Bible. They saw the light and truth of the original account, not as it was copied and corrupted in the Qur'an. That realization led me to use this same kind of scholarly approach to write this series of chapters investigating the Qur'an and compile it together as *Exposing the Truth about the Qur'an: The Revelation of Error*.

---

[4] I use the title *The Generous Qur'an*, for my translation of the Muslims' holy book, which is a literal and correct translation for the title *Al Qur'an Al Kreem*.

The Story of Creation

When and how did God create the universe? Where was Adam created, and where did he live? Were there any creatures called the "jinn" created by God? Are angels male or female? Were all things created in pairs? Which was created first, the heavens or the earth? Is it true that God created the universe in only six days? Why did God create humans? What was life like in the beginning? Did people live for hundreds of years in the beginning of creation? These questions will guide our investigation into how everything and everyone came to be.

Both the Holy Bible and *The Generous Qur'an*[1] talk about creation and the One who created the universe, humans, angels, animals, plants, stars, and other heavenly bodies. (The Qur'an also talks about beings called the *jinn*, but the Bible does not.) Muslims claim they worship the same god as Christians and Jews, but if you take a closer look at creation according to the Qur'an and compare it to creation according to the Bible, you will conclude that the God whose creation is described in the Bible is not the Allah whose creation is described in the Qur'an.

According to Islam, in general, everything except Allah was created. In some hadith[2] written by Muslim scholars, Mohammed was said to have given more detail than all that had been written previously in the Qur'an, concerning creation. We will explore the verses about creation in the Qur'an, with its interpretations by Muslim scholars, as well as the quotations of the hadith, and compare this with the inspired Word of God, the Holy Bible. We will follow the sequential order of the Qur'an, that is, Qur'an 1 through Qur'an 114, rather than the order of Mohammed's claim of receiving the verses of the Qur'an in Mecca and Medina.

Even though many of the verses and ideas of the Qur'an were repeated throughout its pages, we will do our best to include all of the related passages. Mohammed spoke of Allah and creation in over two hundred verses in the Qur'an, and since much of the material is repetitious, our intent is simply to expose the most blatant misusages

---

[1] Usama K. Dakdok, trans. *The Generous Qur'an: An Accurate, Modern English Translation of the Qur'an, Islam's Holiest Book* (Venice, FL: Usama Dakdok Publishing, LLC, 2009). All Qur'anic verses will come from this translation.

[2] hadith, the sayings of Mohammed

of information originating in the Bible, as well as other distortions and discrepancies which are found in the Qur'an. You will also notice that completely fabricated information has been added.

Qur'an 2:21 contains simple advice for people to serve their creator, their lord: *[21]O you people, serve your lord who created you and those who were before you, perhaps you may fear.* Also, in Qur'an 13:36 which says: *[36]And those to whom we have given the book, rejoice in what has been sent down to you. And some of the parties deny a part of it. Say, "Surely I am only commanded to serve Allah and not to partner with him. To him I do call, and to him my return."* Then, in 39:11: *[11]Say, "Surely I am commanded to serve Allah, devoted in the religion to him."*

Ibn Kathir wrote a lengthy narrative about creation before telling the stories of the prophets since, obviously, prophets must be created before they exist. Again, we will respond only to the most relevant sections, but the reader can read it in its entirety in *Stories of the Prophets*.[3]

The Creation of the Throne

A primary difficulty concerning Muslim scholars' interpretations of the account of creation is the inconsistency among them. For example, Ibn Kathir stated that before the creation of the heavens and the earths (yes, plural), nothing had been created.[4] However, immediately after this, he stated that others said before the creation of the heavens and the earths, there were other created things.[5] It was written in Qur'an 11:7: *[7]And he is who created the heavens and the earth in six days. And his throne was on the water...*

In his speech he stated that Imran Ibn Hasseen said, "Allah was and before him there was nothing and his throne was on the water. And he wrote in the reminder everything. Then he created the heavens and the earths."[6] *Are God's throne and the water created things?* If so, then according to Muslims, there were created things before God created the heavens and the earths. Mohammed stated in a hadith that before Allah created the heavens and the earths, Allah created his throne on the water.

---

[3]Ibn Kathir, *Stories of the Prophets*, vol. 1, Abo Al Fida Ishamail Ibn Kathir Al Kurashi Al Damashce (Beirut: Dar Al-Arab Heritage, 1408 AH, 1988).
[4]Ibid., 9.
[5]Ibid.
[6]Ibid., 9.

What was created first? Muslim scholars disagree. For example, Ibn Jarir and Ibn Al Jawzi and others stated that Allah created the pen before he created "all these things."[7] Mohammed was quoted in the hadith as saying, "The first thing Allah created was a pen. Then Allah commanded the pen to write from this hour until the day of resurrection; the pen will continue to write." Mohammed also stated that Allah wrote down the measurements for creatures before he created the heavens and the earths some fifty thousand years *later*. That is why Allah created the pen before the actual creation. However, Ibn Jarir and others stated that Allah created the water before the throne: "If Allah's throne sat on the water, then Allah did not create anything before he created the water."

However, Ibn Jarir also stated that Mohammed Ibn Isaac said that the first thing Allah created was the "light and the darkness, and he separated between them, so Allah made the dark black night, darken, and he made the light day bright and translucent." He also stated that after Allah created the pen, he created the chair. Then he created the throne and then the air and then the darkness and then the water. Then he put his throne above the water, and he ended his theory with the general statement, *and Allah knows best*, which is a mantra often employed by Muslim apologists when the facts do not line up or when the Qur'an contradicts itself.[8]

The Description of the Chair (Throne)

The throne is described in the following verses in the Qur'an. In 40:15: *[15]The highest in degrees, the possessor of the throne…*; in 23:116: *[116]So Allah is exalted, the king, the truth. There is no god except him, the lord of the generous throne;* in 27:26: *[26]Allah, there is no god but him, the lord of the great throne*; in 85:15: *[15]the possessor of the glorious throne*; and in 39:75: *[75]And you see the angels going around the throne, praising with their lord's praise, and he judges between them with the truth. And it was said, "The praise be to Allah, the lord of the world."* The description continues in 40:7: *[7]Those who carry the throne, and all those around it, praise with their lord's praise. And they believe in him, and they ask forgiveness for those who believed: "Our lord surrounds everything in mercy and

---

[7]Ibid., 10.
[8]Ibid., 11.

The Revelation of Error

knowledge...." Then in 69:17: *[17]And the angels will be on its sides, and eight will carry the throne of the lord above them on that day.*

These verses concerning the throne of Allah contain several of the following adjectives used to describe the throne: the generous throne, the great throne, and the glorious throne. Also, we can read that angels praise the lord going around the throne, and the throne was carried by eight angels.[9]

When Mohammed asked his companion about the distance between the heavens and the earth, Ibn Kathir said they said, "Allah and his messenger know best."[10] Mohammed answered him this way:

> Between them the distance of traveling five hundred years, and between the heaven and the following heaven the distance of traveling another five hundred years, and the thickness of each heaven is another five hundred years, and above the seventh heaven, a sea between the bottom of it and the top of it, as the distance between the heaven and the earth. Above that are eight angels, the distance between their knees and their hooves, as the distance of what is between the heaven and the earth. Then on their back is the throne, the distance between the bottom and the top of the throne, as is the distance between the heavens and the earth, and Allah is above that. And nothing of all the work of the sons of Adam is hidden from him.

Information in the Qur'an shows that the distance between the throne and the seven earths (that is not a misprint, yes, *seven* earths) is so great, it would take fifty thousand years to travel between each one, and the width of the throne, as Ibn Kathir stated, is also fifty thousand years.[11] It is written in Qur'an 70:4: *[4]The angels and the spirit ascend to him in a day; its duration was fifty thousand years.*

What about the chair which Allah sits on? Qur'an 2:255 states the following: *[255]Allah, there is no god but he, the living, the qayyūm,[12] slumber does not take him nor sleep. To him what is in the heavens and what is on the earth. Who is he that can intercede with him except by his permission? He knows what is*

---

[9]Ibid., 11.
[10]Ibid., 12.
[11]Ibid.
[12]self-subsisting, non-Arabic word of Syriac origin

between their hands[13] *and what is behind them, and they cannot surround[14] anything out of his knowledge except by what he wills. His kursiy[15] reaches over the heavens and the earth, and keeping them does not burden him. And he is the high, the great.*

The word *kursiy* in this verse is understood by many to be his bed, but it is actually his throne. Ibn Abbas stated that the chair is a place where Allah puts his foot, and no one knows the dimension of the throne except Allah. Ibn Abbas also stated if all the seven heavens and the seven earths were flattened and then attached to each other, they would not be the width of the chair.[16]

The Guarded Board

Ibn Kathir stated that Mohammed said, "Allah created a guarded board from white pearls. Its pages were made of red ruby; its pen was from light. Its written word was from light. To Allah in it, 365 moments every day, he creates and brings provision, gives death, and gives life, he gives honor and disgrace, and he does whatever he wills."[17] Following this, Ibn Abbas stated, "In the beginning of this guarded board: There is no god but Allah alone. Islam is his religion. Mohammed is his servant and his apostle. So whoever believes in Allah and accepts his promises and follows his messengers, he will enter into the garden (paradise)." The length of this guarded board, according to Ibn Kathir, is like the distance between the heaven and earth, and its width is like the distance between the east and the west. All of Allah's creation is recorded in writing upon the guarded board.

The Creation of the Heavens and the Earths and What Is Between Them

In Qur'an 2:29, Mohammed claimed that Allah said that he created all the things on earth first; then he created the seven heavens: *[29]He is who created for you all of what is on the earth, then went straight to the heaven, so he made them seven heavens. And he is knowledgeable of all things.* This is also seen in verse

---

[13]now before them
[14]comprehend
[15]throne, non-Arabic word of Aramaic origin
[16]Ibid., 15.
[17]Ibid., 16.

65:12 wherein Mohammed claimed that there are seven earths: *¹²Allah is who has created seven heavens and the same number of earths. The divine command comes down through them all so that you may know that Allah has might over all things and that Allah indeed surrounds all things in knowledge.*

As we continue to read the order of creation of what was created first, almost all the verses in the Qur'an teach that the heavens were created first, as shown in 2:164: *¹⁶⁴Surely in the creation of the heavens and the earth, and in the changing of the night and the day, and in the fulk[18] which run in the sea with what is useful to people, and what Allah has sent down from the heaven of water so he gives life by it to the earth after its death, and he scattered in it from every creature, and in the change of the winds and in the clouds that are made to be subservient between the heaven and the earth, are signs to people who understand.*

Notice that throughout the Qur'an sometimes the earth is written as singular and other times as plural. This scene is repeated in the following verses: Qur'an 3:190-191; 6:1, 73, 101. Qur'an 3:190-191 states: *¹⁹⁰Surely in the creation of the heavens and the earth and the change of the night and the day are signs to those who have understanding. ¹⁹¹Those who remember Allah when standing and sitting and on their side, and they think of the creation of the heavens and the earth: "Our lord, you did not create this in vain, praise be to you. So save us from the fire torment...."*

In Qur'an 6:1, 73, 101: *¹The praise be to Allah who created the heavens and the earth and made the darkness and the light. Then those who became infidels set up equals[19] with their lord. ⁷³And he is who created the heavens and the earth, with the truth and a day he says, "Be," so it will be. His word is the truth and to him the kingdom. A day the trumpet is blown, the knower of the unseen and the seen; and he is the wise, the aware. ¹⁰¹The inventor of the heavens and the earth, how can he have a son when he has no female companion? And he created everything, and he is the knower of all things.* (Also, see 7:54; 9:36; 10:3; 11:7; 14:19, 32; 15:85; 16:3; 17:99; 18:51; 21:16;

---

[18]ships, non-Arabic word of Greek origin
[19]false gods

25:59; 27:60; 29:44, 61; 30:8, 22; 31:25; 32:4; 36:81; 38:27; 39:5; 40:57; 41:9-12; 42:29; 43:9; 44:38; 45:22; 46:3; 50:38; 57:4; 64:3; 65:12; and 79:27-32.)

From the previous verses, one would surmise that Allah, the god of Mohammed, created the heavens first and then created the earths. This contradicts, however, as we showed earlier in Qur'an 2:29, the teaching that the creation of the earths was before the creation of the heavens, which is supported by the following verses in Qur'an 41:9-12: *⁹Say, "Have you become infidels in him who created the earth in two days, and you make partners with him? That is the lord of the worlds." ¹⁰And he made in it stabilizers on top of it, and he has blessed it. And he measured in it provisions in four equal days to those who ask. ¹¹Then he turned to the heaven, and it was smoke. So he said to it and to the earth, "Come willingly or grudgingly." They said, "We come willingly." ¹²So he completed them seven heavens in two days and revealed to every heaven its affair...*

Another proof that, in Mohammed's account according to Ibn Kathir, the creation of heaven took place *before* the creation of the earth is found in the following verses, in Qur'an 79:27-32: *²⁷Are you a stronger creation, or the heavens he built? ²⁸He raised its height, so he leveled it. ²⁹And he gave darkness to its night and brought forth its light. ³⁰And after that, he flattened the earth. ³¹He brought out from it its waters and its pastures ³²and the mountains he established.*[20]

Notice the details of creation in the previous verses: Allah created the earths in two days, he created the *stabilizers*, or mountains, in four days, and then he completed the seven heavens in two days. In other words, the verses show that the heavens were created after the earths and this entire process took eight days (2+4+2=8). This, of course, conflicts with the number of days Mohammed said Allah used to create the heavens and the earths. Several other verses point to a six-day creation. Several examples are found in the following Qur'an verses:

7:54: *⁵⁴Surely your lord is Allah who created the heavens and the earth in six days; then he sat on the throne. He covers the night [with] the day, he pursues it swiftly, and the sun and the moon and the stars are subservient by his command. Is it*

---

[20]Ibn Kathir, 17.

The Revelation of Error

not to him the creation and the commands? Tabārka[21] Allah, the lord of the worlds.

10:3: *[3]Surely your lord is Allah who created the heavens and the earth in six days; then he sat on the throne arranging the affair. There is no intercessor except after his permission. This is Allah your lord, so serve him. Do you not remember?*

11:7: *[7]And he is who created the heavens and the earth in six days. And his throne was on the water, that he tests you, which of you does the best work. And if you say, "After death you will surely be raised again." Those who became infidels will surely say, "This is nothing but obvious sorcery."*

25:59: *[59]Who created the heavens and the earth and whatever is between them in six days; then he sat on the throne, the merciful, so ask about him, the knower.*

32:4: *[4]Allah who created the heavens and the earth and what is between them in six days; then he sat on the throne, you have no friends or intercessors without him. Do you not remember?*

50:38: *[38]And indeed, we created the heavens and the earth and what is between them in six days, and no weariness touched us.*

57:4: *[4]He is who created the heavens and the earth in six days, then sat on the throne. He knows what penetrates into the earth and that which comes out of it and what comes down from the heaven and what goes up in it, and he is with you wherever you are. And Allah is seeing what you do.*

Did Allah create the world in six days or eight days? How long was each day? Once again, Muslim scholars who interpret the Qur'an disagree about the number of days Allah used to create the heavens and the earths, without knowing which was created first. Ibn Abbas and Mujahid and Al Dahak stated that each day of creation is equal to one thousand years of what we count, but other Muslim scholars disagreed and stated that the days were twenty-four hours long.

Ibn Kathir stated that Ibn Jarir said that Mohammed Ibn Isaac said, "The people of the Talmud (the Jews) said the first day Allah created was Sunday. The people (Christians) of the Ingeel (the Gospel) said that Allah began the creation on Monday. We Muslims

---

[21]blessed, non-Arabic word of North Semitic origin

Chapter 1

believe that the apostle of Allah, Mohammed, said that it began on Saturday."[22]

First of all, Christians do not say that God began creation on Monday; this is a false statement. According to the Bible, God created the universe in six days, and He ceased from His work on the seventh day, which is Saturday, the Sabbath, as it is consistently stated throughout the Bible. Accordingly, God commands to keep the Sabbath day holy, for on it He ceased from His work. The obvious conclusion is that the first day was Sunday, not Saturday, as Mohammed claimed. This claim can be inferred clearly in the meaning of the words in the Hebrew language. The word Sunday or **Yom rishon** means *the first day*. The word Sabbath or **Shabbat** means *to rest*.

Abu Horyrah, who was a senior companion and contemporary of Mohammed, said the apostle of Allah, Mohammed, took him by the hand and said, "Allah created the dirt on the Sabbath day, the mountains on Sunday, the trees on Monday, the hated things on Tuesday, and the light on Wednesday. Then Allah spread the beasts on Thursday. Finally, Allah created Adam on Friday afternoon. He was created in the last hour of Friday, between the afternoon and the evening."[23]

Ibn Kathir disagreed and stated, "This is a strange saying because this order of creation misses the creation of the heavens. Besides, this shows the creation took place in seven days rather than six days." One can see here the irreconcilable conflict among Muslim scholars and in the hadith concerning creation.

Ibn Kathir stated that Ishmael Ibn Abd Al Rhaman said that Mohammed said, "Allah's throne was on the water, and he created nothing from all that he created before the water, so when he desired to create creatures, he brought forth smoke from water. The smoke was raised up above the water. He went above the smoke and called it heaven. Then he made the water hard which became one earth. He divided the land into seven earths in two days – Sunday and Monday. Then he created the earth above a whale [al nōn]."[24] That is why Allah said in Qur'an 68:1, *^{1}N,*[25] *[I swear] by the pen and what they write.*

---

[22]Ibn Kathir, 17.
[23]Ibid., 19.
[24]Ibid.
[25]an Arabic letter without meaning

The Revelation of Error

Ibn Kathir quoted Ishmael Ibn Abd Al Rhaman who stated, "And the whale was in the water. And the water is above the *sfat* [a smooth rock], and the sfat is above an angel. And the angel is above the rock. And the rock is in the wind. And it is the rock which Lokman[26] mentioned as being neither in the heaven nor on the earth. The whale moved and became agitated, and then the earth shook. So Allah put mountains on the earth so it would stay still."[27] This account of events may not make sense to the English reader, but it actually makes even less sense in the original Arabic.

Ibn Kathir continued by saying on Tuesday Allah created the mountains and everything good upon them. On Friday Allah created the trees, the water, the cities, the construction, and the destruction. He split the heaven, and it was one piece so he made it seven heavens. This took two days, Thursday and Friday. Allah called Friday by that name because it was the day when he gathered the heavens and the earths. He revealed to each one of them its command. Then Ibn Kathir said that Allah created in every heaven its creatures, such as the angels and the seas and the mountains and everything else. *Only Allah knows.* Then he beautified the heaven with the stars, making it as an ornament and saving it from all of the devils. After Allah created all that he loved to create, he then sat on the throne.

When you read this chaotic account of creation, do you wonder how Muslims who call themselves scholars could have believed such disorder and confusion? Although the early Muslim scholars did not know the complete account of creation from the Bible, they obviously used what information they did have and then embellished the stories which had been passed on to them from Mohammed's followers. All this disorder is the result of ignorance of the true Creation as it is written in the Genesis account which will be discussed later in this section.

The Creation of the Seven Earths

When I meet and talk with Muslims all over the world, I point out to them the errors in astronomy contained in Mohammed's stories of the creation of seven earths, as stated in Qur'an 65:12: *[12]Allah is who has created seven heavens and the same number of earths. The divine command comes down through them all so that you*

---

[26]may refer to the wise Lokman of Qur'an 31:12-13
[27]Ibn Kathir, 19.

Chapter 1

may know that Allah has might over all things and that Allah indeed surrounds all things in knowledge.

Usually, these Muslims immediately reject my point by stating that the Qur'an does not contain this particular information or that I have misinterpreted the verse. However, when you read the interpretation of the same verse by all accepted Muslim scholars, they are all in agreement. Yes, Allah created seven earths, and each of them is flat. In the hadith, Mohammed repeated his so-called *divinely-revealed* assertion that there are seven earths.

A Muslim man named Rashad translated the Qur'an into English in 1991. He claimed in his translation that Allah said the earth was created in the shape of an egg. Muslims and those who believe the earth is flat were insulted. Rashad was stabbed thirty-seven times in the chest and died in his mosque in Arizona. *Should he have agreed with Muslims and their Qur'an that the earth is flat and there are seven earths altogether, or should he have done exactly what he did— misrepresent the Qur'an to make it consistent with modern science and the Bible?*

Ibn Kathir stated that even though all Muslim scholars agreed there are seven earths, they disagreed on whether they are stacked on top of each other or spaced apart.[28] Most agree there are spaces between them. Mohammed said that there are seven hundred years of travel between each earth and the successive one, and there are five hundred years of travel between each heaven and the following one. Mohammed explicitly assured Muslim followers that there are seven earths and seven heavens.

The claims of Muslim scholars are so varied and extensive that we will not spend needless time delving into all the minute details. Many of Mohammed's statements are rambling and without sound basis. For example, Mohammed said, "After Allah created the earth, it began to move; so he created the mountain so it stabilized, so the angels were wondering about such a thing. So they asked Allah, 'Is there anything stronger than the mountain?' He said, 'Yes, the iron.' They asked Allah, 'Is there anything stronger than the iron?' He said, 'Yes, the fire.' Then they asked him, 'Is there anything stronger than the fire?' He said, 'Yes, the wind.' So they asked him, 'Is there anything you created stronger than the wind?' He said, 'Yes, the son

---

[28]Ibid., 20.

of Adam. He does charity with his right hand, and he hides it from his left hand.'"[29]

Abu Horyrah stated that Allah created the dirt on the Sabbath day, which plainly contradicts the Bible, for nothing was created on the Sabbath according to Genesis and other passages. Muslim scholars stated, as Ibn Kathir explained in his book, that Allah completed the creation in six days and the last day he created was Friday.[30]

Muslim scholar Qatadah stated that the Jews have knowingly lied concerning the *rest* on the seventh day after creation. His explanation concerning the statement was "it was easy for Allah to create, and he was not tired to do so…"[31]

We read in Qur'an 10:4: *[4]To him you will all return. Allah's promise is true. Surely he began the creation; then he repeated it so that he may reward those who believed and did good deeds with fairness...*

Some scholars, like Abu Hatem and Ali Ibn Abu Talib, explained that the term *repeated*, in the above verse relating to creation, is referring to the stages which a man goes through to become human from a *nutfah* to a creature. Nutfah refers to the two fluids, the white one which comes from the man's backbone, which is the sperm, and the yellow fluid, which comes from just above the woman's breast, according to the teachings of the Qur'an and the hadith, from which Muslims believe babies are conceived.

On the other hand, Al Tabari stated that Ibn Abbas and others stated that the word *repeated* refers to the different stages man goes through from health to sickness. Still others said it was different kinds of colors and languages.

In Sahih Al Bukhari, Al Bukhari stated, "Allah said he began his creation and repeats it."[32,33] According to Al Bukhari and in Al Tabari's interpretation of the previous verse and other verses throughout the Qur'an concerning the heavens and their structure, the repetition refers to how the earth will bring forth what is in it from the

---

[29] Ibid., 23.
[30] Ibid., 20.
[31] Ibid., 23.
[32] Sahih means *correct*. Bukhari is a great Muslim scholar who collected the sayings of Mohammed, and he chose less than 2 percent of them. This is why Muslims highly respect his writing and believe in all the statements he declared that Mohammed said to be true.
[33] Sahih Bukhari, Hadith 3190-3194.

dead.³⁴ Also, Al Bukhari related this to the animals on the earth concerning their sleep and their feeding habits.

Ibn Kathir wrote that Ibn Jarir and Ibn Abbas talked about the seven heavens and the seven earths.³⁵ Their writing is considered proof that there are seven earths, each above another as are the heavens. They and others taught that for every one of the seven earths, there was an Adam, like the Adam of earth, as well as a Noah, an Abraham, and an Esau. Ibn Abbas stated, "If it is spoken to you with an interpretation to this verse, you will become an infidel and your infidelity will be that you will not believe it." Apparently, Ibn Abbas realized that actual understanding of the teaching would lead to the knowledge that it was all a farce, which would cause unbelief or *infidelity*.

Concerning the distance between each of the earths and the distance between each of the heavens, Ahmed Al Tarmaze stated that Abu Horyrah said that the distance between every heaven to another is five hundred years. Interestingly, other scholars say it is seven hundred years. Likewise, the distance between each earth is five hundred years…*or is it seven hundred? Was he traveling at the speed of a camel or the speed of a man walking?* In Mohammed's lifetime there were no cars, planes, or space shuttles. Other scholars like Al Tarmaze and Ibn Abbas stated that the distance is seventy-two years. Their explanation considers the speed of a person walking. The reader will soon discover that key numbers always vary with early Muslim scholars, even as the numbers differ throughout the Qur'an.

Let us examine the interpretation for the *lift up ceiling*, or heaven, in Qur'an 21:32: **³²*And we made the heaven a kept ceiling, and they turn away from its signs.*** In Mujahid's interpretation, he stated that this proves that the heavens are not spherical above the earth because *ceiling* in the Arabic language cannot be spherical, only flat.

Throughout the previous hadith (3195-3198), Mohammed stated that there are seven heavens and seven earths. He also stated this throughout the Qur'an, for example, in 65:12: **¹²*Allah is who has created seven heavens and the same number of earths. The divine command comes down through them all so that you may know that Allah has might over all things and that Allah indeed surrounds all things in knowledge.***

---

³⁴Sahih Bukhari, Hadith 3191-3198.
³⁵Ibn Kathir, 23.

The Creation of the Seas and the Rivers

Throughout the Qur'an, Mohammed repeated himself concerning the seas and the rivers. For example, in Qur'an 16:14-18: *^{14}And he is who has made the sea subservient to you so that you may eat of its tender meat and take from it ornaments to wear them, and you see the ships sailing through it, and that you may seek of his bounty, and perhaps you will be thankful. ^{15}And he threw the stabilizers on the earth, so that it does not move with you, and rivers and ways, perhaps you may be guided. ^{16}And marks and by the stars they are guided. ^{17}Is he who creates like he who does not create, do you not remember? ^{18}And if you would number the grace of Allah, you could not count it. Surely Allah is forgiving, merciful.*

Also, in Qur'an 35:12: *^{12}And the two seas are not equal. This is fresh, sweet, pleasant for drink, and this is salty, bitter. And from each you eat tender meat and take forth ornaments for you to wear, and you see the ships sailing in it so that you may seek from his bounties. And perhaps you may give thanks.* Finally, in 42:32-34: *^{32}And among his signs are the jawar^{36} in the sea like aālam.^{37} ^{33}If he wills, he will cause the wind to stay still. And it lies motionless on its back, surely in this are signs to every patient, thankful. ^{34}Or he destroys them because of what they earned, and he pardons toward much.*

Similar verses are repeated throughout the Qur'an. The common message is that Allah made the seas and the rivers subservient to men; from them they bring ornaments, and from them they eat soft meat. One of the common errors throughout the Qur'an is that Mohammed calls the rivers *seas*. We see this in Qur'an 55:19-20: *^{19}Run the two seas to meet. ^{20}Yet between them is a barrier which they do not overpass.*

Muslim scholars like Ibn Kathir wrote that the two seas are the salty seas and the fresh seas are the rivers. One of the unusual statements also written by Ibn Kathir was "Allah created the seas and the rivers, and the seas which surround the earth and all that grow next to it are salty to taste and bitter."[38] He stated that this was the wisdom of Allah: to keep the air healthy. If the fruit of this plant was

---

[36] running ones, Muslim scholars claim this means ships
[37] banners, Muslim scholars claim that in this instance it means mountains
[38] Ibn Kathir, 25.

sweet, the air would be bad and the weather would be rotten. All the animals would die on the earth, and it would cause the destruction of the sons of Adam. *Where are these plants? Which Muslim can show us some salty-tasting fruit of plants by the sea?*

Some consider the following verse, Qur'an 25:53, as a great proof of Mohammed's prophetic ability: *[53]And he is who mixed the two seas, this is fresh, furāt,[39] and this salty and bitter, and has put a barrier between them and forced repelling.*

However, the knowledge of the separation between fresh water and salt water was not a new discovery. Pliny the Elder, the noted Roman naturalist, senator, and commander of the Imperial Fleet in the 1st century AD, observed this peculiar behavior of fishermen's nets in the Strait of Bosporus near Istanbul. Pliny deduced that surface and bottom currents were flowing in opposite directions. He provided the first written documentation of what is now called the *estuarine circulation*. Additionally, it can be shown from simple logic that fresh and salt water do eventually combine. If they did not, there would be huge oceans of fresh water continually flowing out of every major river. Simple studies show that fresh water flowing out from rivers slowly mixes with salt water and becomes increasingly salty over time and distance until it reaches equilibrium with the normal salt levels of the greater body of water. The speed of this changeover depends on temperature as well.

In the following passage, Muslim scholars introduced two different interpretations of Qur'an 52:6-8: *[6]And by the thrown sea, [7]surely the torment of your lord is imminent. [8]There is not any who can avert it.* In the first interpretation, it is the sea which exists below the throne of Allah. This body of water is above the seven heavens. It is the sea from which the rain will come on the day of resurrection, and by it their bodies will come to life from the tombs. The second interpretation is that it is the general name of all the seas on the earth.

Ibn Al Khattāb stated that Mohammed said that three times every night the sea comes before Allah asking permission to cover the earth, but Allah stops the sea from doing so.[40] Qur'an 5:96 states: *[96]Lawful for you the catch of the sea, and its food is enjoyment for you and to the travelers...* This contradicts the teachings of Moses in the

---

[39] sweet river water, non-Arabic word of Akkadian origin
[40] Ibn Kathir, 25.

Bible, which Muslims claim to believe, referring to it as the book of Torah. In the Torah many sea animals are forbidden to be eaten. Also, notice how Allah speaks to the sea and the sea speaks to the water and the water speaks back to Allah. This occurrence is only one of the many strange things found in the Qur'an.

Another hadith by Mohammed tells that Allah created a thousand nations. Six hundred of them supposedly live in the sea and the remaining four hundred on the land. Amazingly, he asserted that even the animals have their own nations and prophets, and they will be resurrected and judged. He told us that the first nation which will perish is the locusts. The number of types of creatures is completely wrong, which demonstrates that Mohammed was ignorant concerning the enormity of biodiversity on the planet. *With errors such as this one, can Mohammed even be considered a prophet of God?* Hardly. The National Science Foundation's Tree of Life project estimates that there could be anywhere from five million to one hundred million species on the planet, although scientists have only identified about two million.[41] According to Qur'an 6:38: *[38]And there is no creature on earth or bird that flies with its wings, but nations like you. We did not neglect anything in the book. Then to their lord they will be gathered.* *Is this true? Are all of the birds, bugs, animals, and other creatures going to be resurrected and judged before Allah?* What a strange concept!

One of the astonishing statements concerning the nature of heaven and earth is found in Qur'an 21:30: *[30]Or have not those who became infidels seen that the heavens and the earth were a solid mass, so we parted them, and we made every living thing from the water? Do they not believe?* This description by Allah of the nature of the heavens and the earth is amazing. Ibn Kathir explained that Allah separated between the heavens and the earth until the wind blew and the rain came down, and then the spring rain swelled the rivers and refreshed the animals. A similar misunderstanding exists in Qur'an 21:32 on the part of Allah and Mohammed, and perhaps Angel Gabreel, in how Allah described the heaven as a ceiling: *[32]And we made the heaven a kept ceiling, and they turn away from its signs.* *How could this be a divine revelation, for all scientific observations show clearly that heaven is*

---

[41]"Tree of Life Project," National Science Foundation, accessed December 28, 2011, http://www.nsf.gov/funding/pgm_summ.jsp?pims_id=5129.

an "empty" space with billions of galaxies floating in that space? We will talk about the three different heavens when we talk about the biblical account of Creation from the Bible.

What Was Created on the Earth of Mountains, Trees, Fruit, and Plains
Numerous verses in the Qur'an indicate a six day creation. For example, in Qur'an 7:54: *[54]Surely your lord is Allah who created the heavens and the earth in six days; then he sat on the throne. He covers the night [with] the day, he pursues it swiftly, and the sun and the moon and the stars are subservient by his command. Is it not to him the creation and the commands? Tabārka[42] Allah, the lord of the worlds.* See also 10:3; 11:7; 25:59; 32:4; 50:38; and 57:4.

All these verses contradict the passage in Qur'an 41:9-12 which clearly teaches that creation took eight days: *[9]Say, "Have you become infidels in him who created the earth in two days, and you make partners with him? That is the lord of the worlds." [10]And he made in it stabilizers on top of it, and he has blessed it. And he measured in it provisions in four equal days to those who ask. [11]Then he turned to the heaven, and it was smoke. So he said to it and to the earth, "Come willingly or grudgingly." They said, "We come willingly." [12]So he completed them seven heavens in two days and revealed to every heaven its affair. And we adorned the world's heaven with lamps and kept. This is the measure of the dear, the knowing.* Not only does this verse clearly teach that creation took eight days, but it also contradicts many of the verses of the Qur'an by stating that Allah created the earths first, then he created the heavens.

Now we come to the question of the nature of the heavens and the shape of the earth as Mohammed described them in the pages of the Qur'an. In Qur'an 22:65, Mohammed described heaven as if it is a structure which Allah holds in his hand to secure it from falling down and crushing those who are living on earth. Qur'an 22:65 declares: *[65]Do you not see that Allah has made subservient to you what is on the earth and the ships run in the sea with his command? And he holds the heaven so that it will not fall on the earth except with his permission. Surely Allah is with the people, compassionate, merciful.* Also, the following verse, Qur'an 31:10,

---
[42]blessed, non-Arabic word of North Semitic origin

The Revelation of Error

supports the premise of the verse above by showing that Allah created the heavens without any columns, which proves that Mohammed literally believed that heaven is like a ceiling, a solid structure: *[10]He created the heavens without columns, you see it, and he threw stabilizers on the earth lest it should move with you. And he scattered in it of every creature. And he sent down water from the heaven, so we grow plants in it from every generous pair.*

What is the condition of the earth? Does it move? According to the last verse, Mohammed assured his followers that the reason Allah created the stabilizers, or mountains, was to secure the earth so that it might not rotate or shake. You can see this also clearly in Qur'an 16:15: *[15]And he threw the stabilizers on the earth, so that it does not move with you, and rivers and ways, perhaps you may be guided.* Then, in Qur'an 21:31: *[31]And we made stabilizers on the earth, lest it move with them, and we made ways between them on it, perhaps they may be guided.*

Another great error concerning the physical creation is when Mohammed described the earth as being flat. We see this clearly in the following verse, Qur'an 15:19: *[19]And the earth, we <u>spread it out</u> and tossed on it stabilizers, and we planted in it from every weighted thing.* Also, in Qur'an 50:7: *[7]And the earth, we have <u>spread it out</u> and have thrown the stabilizers on it and have caused plants to grow in it, from every beautiful pair.*

Another error about the universe concerns the nature of the moon in Qur'an 10:5: *[5]He is who has made the sun bright and the moon a light and has ordained its stations so that you may learn the number of years and the reckoning. Allah did not create this except with the truth. He expounds on his signs to a people who know.* Mohammed claimed that the moon is not a natural satellite reflecting the sun's light, but it produces light of its own and has its own stations. See also verse 71:16: *[16]And he made the moon in them[43] light, and he made the sun a lamp.* This contradicts the Bible which clearly states that the moon does not produce light of its own as written in Job 25:5: **[5]***If even the moon does not shine, and the stars are not pure in His sight.*

---

[43] the seven heavens

Chapter 1

The Creation of the Heavens and Their Signs (Wonders)

Ibn Kathir,[44] in his explanation concerning the stars, stated that the stars in the first heaven were created for the following three reasons: first, as an adornment to the first heaven; second, as missiles to throw against the satans; and third, as guidance for travelers. This is supported by the verses of the Qur'an, such as in Qur'an 67:5: *⁵And indeed, we adorned the heaven of the world with lamps[45] and made them to be missiles for the satans, and we prepared for them the torment of the blaze.* Again in Qur'an 6:97: *⁹⁷And he is who has made the stars for you so that you may be guided by it in the darkness of the shore and the sea. Indeed, we expound on the verses for people who know.* See also Qur'an 15:16-18 and 41:12.

Qur'an 55:5 provides this information: *⁵The sun and the moon are in calculation.* In his explanation of the meaning of *calculation*, Ibn Abbas stated that the sun and the moon travel in a route and never leave their tracks. On the other hand, Mujahid stated that the sun and the moon travel as a grindstone does in a circle.[46] These scholars and the Qur'an are in agreement that the sun and moon travel around the earth on their own orbits but never catch each other.

Mohammed was quoted in Qur'an 13:2: *²... You see it, then he sat on the throne, and he made the sun and the moon subservient, each traveled to its named time. He arranges the affairs. He explains the verses; perhaps you may be certain of meeting your lord.* Mohammed asked Abu Zer, "Do you know where the sun goes when it sets?" He answered, "Allah and his messenger know best." Mohammed responded, "It goes until it worships under the throne and then it asks permission to leave, and when it receives permission and when its worship will not be accepted any longer, it will be commanded to 'return from where you came.'"[47] Mohammed also stated in the Qur'an that the sun sets in a muddy spring, which causes the darkness of night. An example is found in Qur'an 18:86 which states: ... *⁸⁶until when he reached the setting of the sun, he found it set in a muddy spring, and he*

---

[44] Ibn Kathir, 32-33.
[45] stars
[46] http://quran.Al-islam.com/Page.aspx?pageid=221&BookID=14&Page=238, accessed January 18, 2012.
[47] Sahih Bukhari, Hadith 3199, 4802, 4803, 7424, and 7433.

found a people by it. We said, "O Za Al Qarnain, either that you torment them or that you do good to them."

The Creation of the Galaxy and the Rainbow

Ibn Kathir stated that Ibn Abbas said that Heraculius wrote to Maawyah and proclaimed that if there was any proof of Mohammed being a prophet, "he must tell me an answer for some questions."[48] So he asked questions about the galaxy, the rainbow, and a land which had not seen the sun except for one hour. So Maawyah came with these questions to Mohammed. When Mohammed heard these questions, he said, "I never thought till this day that someone would ask me these questions." Ibn Abbas said then that Maawyah folded the letter and sent it to Ibn Abbas. So he wrote to him, "As for the rainbow, it is to save the people of the earth from drowning. As for the galaxy, it is the door of heaven which the earth comes from. As for the land which saw the sun for one hour, it is the land of the sea which was open for the Children of Israel."

Obviously, Muslims believe that these are three great answers from Mohammed, but there are errors in his answers. The rainbow did not save people on earth from drowning, but it was a sign of a covenant which God established with Noah and his descendants after him. As God told Noah in Genesis 9:12-13: *[12]And God said: "This is the sign of the covenant which I make between Me and you, and every living creature that is with you, for perpetual generations: [13]I set My rainbow in the cloud, and it shall be for the sign of the covenant between Me and the earth."* The second error of Mohammed's answer is that the galaxy is the door of heaven which earth comes from, but a galaxy is made up of billions of stars.[49]

In the third error concerning the land which saw the sun for one hour, Mohammed answered with "it is the land of the sea which was open for the Children of Israel." The error is that the nearly 3 million Israelites who crossed the Red Sea did not cross the sea by day but by night, and it took them all night long, not one hour. In Exodus 14:21-22: *[21]Then Moses stretched out his hand over the sea; and the Lord caused the sea to go back by a strong east wind all that night, and made the sea into dry land, and the waters were divided. [22]So the children of Israel went into the midst of the sea on the dry ground,*

---

[48] Ibn Kathir, 41-42.
[49] *Webster's New World Dictionary*, 2nd college ed., s.v. "galaxy."

and the waters were a wall to them on their right hand and on their left. We know from the Bible that when the morning appeared, God commanded Moses to stretch his hand over the sea so that the water returned to its original place, drowning all of the pursuing Egyptians. There was not an hour of time for the Egyptians to escape as some may assume. (See Exodus 14:24-27.)

Ibn Kathir rejected the hadith which stated that Mohammed said, "O Moaz, surely I am sending you to the People of the Book, and if they ask you about the galaxies which are in heaven, say to them it is the saliva of a snake which is under the throne."[50] The obvious reason Ibn Kathir rejected this hadith was because it was erroneous. His denial of this hadith would be understandable if we did not find other similar errors in the teachings of the Qur'an. However, this is not the case, as we see in the following verses, Qur'an 13:12-13: *[12]He is who shows you the lightning fearing and hoping and brings up the heavy clouds. [13]And the thunder praises with his praise, and the angels, for fear of him. And he sends his thunderbolts, so he smites with it whom he wills while they dispute concerning Allah. And he is severe in prowess.* So how did Mohammed understand the nature of the thunder in this verse? He understood thunder to be an angel who worshiped Allah. This is a huge error, and if this error exists in the Qur'an, obviously many other errors exist in the hadith.

For example, Ibn Kathir said that Imam Ahmed said that Mohammed said that Allah created the cloud and he "made it speak the best speech and he makes it laugh the best laugh."[51] Moses Ibn Obadiah said that "the speech of the cloud is the thunder and its laugh is the lightning." From such statements, one could hypothesize that these were just simple people who were ignorant of simple facts. Another hypothesis is that the Qur'an and the hadith are simply books full of error. Notice that in Islam, Allah's word in the Qur'an and Mohammed's sayings in the hadith do not use metaphorical language, as in the case of the Bible. Therefore, when Allah says the "angel of the cloud" or the "angel of the wind" that is what he meant. When Allah said that the ants or birds speak and make specific statements,

---

[50] Ibn Kathir, 41.
[51] Ibid., 42.

The Revelation of Error

that is what he meant. So when Mohammed said that the cloud spoke, that is exactly what he meant.

The Creation of Angels and Their Description

In Islamic theology, angels are considered to be beautiful creatures, and each is able to appear in various forms. The Qur'an addresses angels in 19:64; 21:19-20, 26-29; 37:164-166; 40:7-8; 41:38; 42:5; and other verses.

According to Mohammed, angels were created before people. Throughout the Qur'an, we read that angels and the prophets are to be believed in, as seen in Qur'an 2:285: *^{285}The messenger believed in that which had been sent down from his lord. And the believers all believed in Allah and his angels and his books and his messengers. We do not differentiate between any of his messengers. And they said, "We heard and obeyed. Your forgiveness, our lord. And to you is the final return."*

You will discover many contradictions as you read Mohammed's sayings in the hadith and compare them with what is written in the Qur'an. For example, Mohammed said, "Angels are created from light and jinn are made of fire and Adam was created as was described to you."[52] However, on the other hand, in Qur'an 38:76, Satan, supposedly one of the angels, refused to worship Adam and said that the reason was that he was better than Adam. As he says: *^{76}He said, "I am better than him. You created me from fire, and you created him from mud."* We must ask the following question: *Are angels made of light or fire, or perhaps, was Satan an angel or one of the jinn?* We might also ask if the jinn really exist.

Angels also do many other functions, according to Mohammed. The angels say the *amens* for those who pray. They also call to those who are waiting for prayer. It is also their job to curse any woman who refuses to be with her husband in bed.

Angel Gabreel is called by many names throughout the Qur'an, such as the faithful one or even the holy spirit. In the hadith, Anis stated that the Angel Gabreel is the enemy of the Jews.

A lengthy but very important hadith concerning the Angel Gabreel and Mohammed's famous trip to the seven heavens will be discussed in more detail in the section on Mohammed but must be

---

[52]Sahih Bukhari, Hadith 53 and 2960-2996.

shared briefly here.[53] Mohammed claimed that he was cleansed with water and filled with wisdom, transported from Mecca to Jerusalem, and then to the first heaven by a white mule. In the first heaven he met with Adam. He moved from heaven to heaven, meeting with different prophets, like Joseph and Moses, along the way. When he arrived at the seventh heaven, he was commanded to pray. After negotiating with Allah about the number of times to pray per day, Allah agreed to lower the requirement down to only five daily prayers.

Gabreel was the angel who supposedly gave Mohammed the verses of the Qur'an. During the month of Ramadan, it is said that Gabreel came to Mohammed in different forms, sometimes in the form of a man named Dhyah[54] and sometimes as Ibn Kalefah Al Kalby. He appeared another time in the form in which he was created.

He supposedly had six hundred wings, and the distance between each wing was said to be the distance between the east and the west. This postulation in itself is a great error because if the distance between the wings of the Angel Gabreel is as the distance between the east and the west, then this would make the Angel Gabreel infinite since the east and west are opposite directions which never meet.

Mohammed saw Angel Gabreel in his massive created form twice.[55] Each time Gabreel tutored him.[56] In a strange hadith given by Mohammed to Ibn Abbas, concerning the size of angels, it was said, "Allah had an angel, and if he was asked to devour the heaven and the earths with one piece of bread, he would do it with one dip. Seven hundred years is the measurement of traveling between an earlobe and a shoulder of an angel."[57]

Although the Qur'an mentions four particular angels in many places, only two are mentioned by name. First, there is Gabreel. Scholars disagree about his role, but some say he descended from heaven "with a guidance." Mika'il (counterpart of the biblical archangel Michael) is responsible for the provision of nourishments for bodies and souls. Another angel, whom Muslim scholars claim is named Israfeel, gives the victory and the rewards. He is also

---

[53]Sahih Bukhari, Hadith 3207, 3430, and 3878.
[54]Ibn Kathir, 43.
[55]Ibid., 44.
[56]Sahih Bukhari, Hadith 3220.
[57]Ibn Kathir, 48.

described as one of the carriers of the throne and will blow on the horn three times. The first is called the terrifying blow, causing great panic; the second is the shocking blow, which causes people to die; and the third is to call people back to life, the resurrection blow. As for the fourth angel, the Qur'an never mentions his name, nor does the hadith; he is simply called the angel of death. Notice it is a singular name, as if it is one angel; some scholars call him 'Azraeel. As usual, Ibn Kathir eluded the identity question with his statement, *Allah knows best.*

Then, astonishingly, on the next page of his book, Ibn Kathir stated that, "The angels of death come to the men, according to his work; if he was a believer, his angel will come to him in a white face, with white clothes, with good spirits. And if he was an infidel, so was the opposite of that. I seek refuge from the great Allah from this."[58] One must ask a question here. *Is the angel of death a single angel or are there many of them?* Then the statement follows again that *Allah knows best.*

Abu Horyrah stated that angels do not enter a house with a picture or a statue or even a dog in it.[59] He also said that Mohammed said that angels will not be around people with a dog or bells. Also, there are always two angels with every man, one on the right hand and one on the left hand, to write down all his good deeds and to write down all his evil deeds. Qur'an 50:17-18 states that: *[17]When the two receivers[60] meet, one sitting on the right and one on the left, [18]he will not say a word, except that a watcher is prepared, present by him.* Also, Mohammed stated that everyone has a companion of the mysterious jinn, as well as a companion of the angels. So they asked him, "Even you, O apostle of Allah?" He said, "Yes, even me, but Allah has helped me, so he will not command me except what is good."

Although there are many myths in the writings of Muslim scholars and the sayings of Mohammed, the prophet of Islam, concerning creation, I decided to highlight and respond to the main points. We end with a lengthy hadith by Abu Horyrah about Angel Israfeel:

---

[58]Ibid., 51.
[59]Ibid.
[60]recording angels

Chapter 1

Abu Horyrah said that the apostle of Allah said that when the Angel Israfeel is commanded to blow the horn of destruction, he will destroy the people of the heavens and the earth, except those whom Allah desires not to die.[61] So, behold, they are all dead. Then the angel of death came to Allah and said, "O lord, the people of the heavens and the earth are dead, except what you wished." Then Allah will say (and he knows who stays alive), "So who's still living?" Then the Angel Israfeel will say, "You are the living who never dies. And the carriers of your throne are still alive. And Angel Gabreel and Angel Mika'il are still alive." Allah will say, "May Gabreel and Mika'il die." So Allah causes the throne to speak. So Angel Israfeel will say, "Gabreel and Mika'il died." So Allah will say, "Silence! So surely I described the death to everyone who was under my throne." So they both died. Then the angel of death will come to the mighty Allah and will say, "O lord, indeed Gabreel and Mika'il died." So Allah will say (and he knows who stays alive), "So who is still living?" So the angel of death will say, "You are the living who never dies. And the carriers of your throne are still alive. And I am still alive." So Allah will say, "May the carriers of the throne die!" Then they will die.

Then Allah will command the throne, and it will take the horn from Israfeel. Then the angel of death will come, and he will say, "Indeed, the carriers of your throne are dead." So Allah will say (and he knows who stays alive), "So who's still living?" So he will say, "You are the living who never dies. And I am still alive." So Allah will say, "You are a creature of my creation. I created you when I desired, so die!" Then he died. There would be no one living except Allah. He is Allah the one of, the absolute. He does not birth, neither was he birthed, and there is no one equal to him. He was the end as he was the first.

Will the throne of Allah be hanging in the air after the eight angels die? Who will carry the throne? What was the purpose of this hadith?

---

[61] Ibn Kathir, 51.

The Preference of Angels Over Humans

Ibn Kathir stated that there were many disagreements among those who discussed the preference of angels over humans.[62] Since neither the Qur'an nor the hadith gave clear answers, the door was left open for different opinions of who is considered to be greater, men or angels. Ibn Asakir said that Umar Ibn Abd Al Aziz said that no one is more honorable to Allah than the honorable children of Adam. He proved his point by quoting Qur'an 98:7: *[7]Surely those who believed and did good deeds, those are the best of the creatures.* On the other hand, Arak Ibn Malik said that no one is more honorable to Allah than his angels. They are the servants of his house and his messengers to his prophets, and he proved his point with Qur'an 7:20: *[20]So Satan whispered to them to show them what was hidden from them in their nakedness. And he said, "Your lord has not forbidden you from this tree except that you become angels or that you become immortal."*

Umar Ibn Abd Al Aziz said to Mohammed Abd Kaab, "What are you saying, O Abu Hamzah?"[63] He said that, indeed, Allah honored Adam, and "he created him by his hand, he breathed into him from his spirit, he caused the angels to worship him, and he made the prophet and the messengers from his descendants whom the angels visit." Umar Ibn Abd Al Aziz agreed with him in this opinion. The weakest proof of what he said is found in Qur'an 98:7: *[7]Surely those who believed and did good deeds, those are the best of the creatures.* Umar Ibn Abd Al Aziz said that this verse does not pertain exclusively to humans because angels also believe in Allah.

He additionally stated, concerning the mysterious jinn, that Allah stated in Qur'an 72:13-14: *"'... [13]And that when we heard the guidance, we believed in it, so whoever believes in his lord, so he will fear neither stinginess nor perversion. [14]And that some of us are Muslims, and some of us are deviators.' So whoever becomes Muslim, so those are aimed to the right way."* He said that the best proof of this situation was what Osman said, which was more accurate, that when Allah created the garden (paradise), the angels said, "O our lord, make this for us so we may eat from it and drink from it for you created the earth for the sons of Adam." And

---

[62]Ibid., 59.
[63]Ibid.

Allah said, "I will not make the good for the descendants of what I have created by my hands like the one of whom I said, 'Be' so he was."

By comparison, just what does the Bible teach about the relationship between angels and humans? The Bible gives a clear answer. In Psalm 8:4-5, the Scripture asks: *What is man that You are mindful of him, and the son of man that You visit him?* A clear answer follows in verse 5 which states: *⁵For You have made him a little lower than the angels, and You have crowned him with glory and honor.* These verses plainly teach us that man was created lower than the angels, but at the same time the Scripture states that the angels were created to serve man.

The Creation of Jinn and the Story of Satan

Many statements have been given by Muslim scholars concerning Satan. When you consider all of them, you find that the scholars are in chaos and conflict over the nature of their information. Some connect Satan ('Iblīs, also Shayṭān) to the jinn, while others do not. Some seek to connect Satan to angels. As usual, in dealing with this problem, they conclude *and Allah knows best*. Ibn Abbas stated that Mohammed said, "After Allah created everything and he sat on the throne, he made Satan the king of the world, and he was one of the tribe of angels called the jinn.[64] Satan became proud because Allah gave him such a kingdom. Satan stated that Allah gave it to him because he was better than all of the angels."

Here we find that, not only is Satan a member of the jinn, but he was also an angel. This demonstrates the depth of confusion on the part of Mohammed who did not appear to know, or at least could not keep straight, the difference between angels and jinn. It is the opinion of many that these mythical jinn do not actually exist, except perhaps in Mohammed's imagination. Mohammed Ibn Isaac stated that Ibn Abbas said that Ibn Jarir said, "Satan's kingdom is on the sea." It is claimed that he also has an army. Muslim scholars disagree as to whether he was an angel and then changed to Satan, or if he was ever an angel. Qatadah stated that Satan was the leader of all of the angels of the first heaven. However, on the other hand, Al Hasan Al Basri said that he was not among the angels at all and was never with them; rather, he was the root of the jinn as Adam was the root of humanity.

---

[64]Ibid., 60.

The Revelation of Error

After Allah finished creation, he sat on his throne, and he made Satan over the kingdom of the earth. Ibn Abbas said that Mohammed said that the jinn used to be a tribe of angels, so-named because they were the doorkeepers of the *jannah,* or garden.[65] Satan was also a gatekeeper, so he said, "Surely Allah gave me this because I am better than the rest of the angels." Al Dahak said that Ibn Abbas said, "When the jinn vandalize on the earth and when they shed the blood, Allah sent Satan to them and with them a troop of angels, so they fought them and kicked them out of the earth and sent them to the islands of the seas."

Ibn Abbas said that Satan's name before he committed his sin was Azazeel, and he was among the people who lived on earth. He was a great jihadist among the angels, and he was more knowledgeable than all of them. He was among the group that was called the jinn. He was one of the honorable angels with four wings, according to Ibn Abbas and Ibn Jarir. Notice the wrong name, Azazeel, is given to Satan; according to the Bible, he is an angel called Lucifer (Isaiah 14:12).

One of the strangest things Muslim scholars claim about Satan is that he has both male and female sexual parts.[66] Al Qurtobi said that Satan had a male sexual part in his right thigh and a female sexual part in his left thigh and that he made love to himself every day. He produced ten eggs per day, and each egg had seventy male and female satans!

Bukhari stated that there are many reasons why the scholars believed that Satan was called by the name 'Iblis. Possible reasons are that he was hopeless from Allah's mercy or that he was evicted from the garden and cursed. However, it should be noted the Qur'an mentions his name before any of this occurred.

There are many bizarre hadith regarding Satan written by Bukhari.[67] A disturbing example is that Satan urinates in the ear of those who do not pray. Other hadith describe Satan's role concerning himself and his army.

Many verses throughout the Qur'an also mention the jinn. Muslim scholars have taught that they are a class of supernatural creatures, between men and angels in importance, and that they were

---

[65]Ibid.
[66]http://quran.Al-islam.com/Page.aspx?pageid=221&BookID=14&Page=299, accessed January 18, 2012.
[67]Sahih Bukhari, Hadith 3268-3295.

created by Allah about two thousand years before Adam. Some of the jinn are said to be Muslims, but according to most reference sources, the jinn are nothing but Islamic mythology.

A good example of this teaching can be found in Qur'an 6:130 where Mohammed asks: *[130]"O assembly of the jinn and the humans, have not messengers come to you from among yourselves relating my verses to you and warning you of the meeting of this your day?" They said, "We bore witness against ourselves." And the world's life deceived them, and they bore witness against themselves that they were infidels.*

Further proof that some jinn are Muslims is found in Qur'an 46:29: *[29]And when we turned a company of the jinn toward you, they listen to the Qur'an. So when they arrived there, they said, "Listen." So when he finished, they returned to their people warning them. [30]They said, "O our people, surely we have heard a book revealed after Moses, confirming what is between his hands, guide to the truth and to a straight way."*

Hadith 3296 assures that jinn-like humans will be punished or rewarded at the time of the resurrection: "For Mohammed says, 'The voice of the caller to the prayer by jinn and by humans will not be heard except it will be witness to it on the day of resurrection.'"

The Account of Creation from the Bible

We have traveled a portion of our journey together toward learning what the Qur'an and the hadith teach concerning creation. Some may feel that it was a waste of time, because as I have said earlier, no Muslim scholar can clearly explain anything concerning the writings of their book, the Qur'an, or the sayings of their prophets. The greatest proof of my assertion can be summed up in two of their own often-used phrases. The first is the phrase with which they open their interpretation: *scholars disagree.* Then there is the phrase with which they close: *Allah knows best.* I believe these are words of resignation which simply mean *NO ONE KNOWS.*

Now we will look at what God knows, which is divinely inspired by the one true God in His real and holy words: the Bible. Notice that the writings of Genesis 1 and 2 are short and to the point, without ambiguity. They are also without contradiction. They give a true account of what took place, although considerable opposition has been offered by Muslim scholars and atheists, as well as some who even claim to be Christians.

We will now summarize the book of Genesis and outline the account of Creation contained in its first few chapters. As usual, readers are encouraged to read the entire account. The Bible is completely different from the Qur'an, as the Bible is well organized and also written with sufficient detail to make it easily understood without the need to fill in numerous blanks.

The story begins in the first two chapters in the book of Genesis where the Scripture states in Genesis 1:1: *[1]In the beginning...* What a wonderful way for God to start speaking to man. It is like God saying, "I am telling you the truth all the way from the very beginning. Before there was anything, there was 'Elohim' (a plural form of a Hebrew word meaning god or gods), whose Spirit moved over the waters and whose Word created the heavens and the earth." The story unfolds in Genesis 1:1-3. Even though the earth was void with no form and was dark, "I AM" (God) spoke the words, "Let there be light," and there was light. He called the light day and the darkness night, and it was good. This was the first day.

According to Christian understanding of the nature of God, as He describes Himself in His word beginning with Genesis 1, He is a triune God; that is, God is three Persons but one God. The Hebrew word *Elohim* in verse 1 is a grammatically singular or plural noun, depending on how it is used, for *god* or *gods* in both modern and ancient Hebrew language. As the plural for *El* or *Eloh*, it could literally be translated in English as *Gods*. God the Father is spirit, as Jesus taught that no one has seen the Father. God is spirit, and whoever worships Him worships in "spirit and truth." God the Holy Spirit, as we read in Genesis 1:2, ***moved upon the face of the waters***. The third Person of God is His Word, as seen in Genesis 1:3: ***[3]Then God said...*** This statement is repeated in verses 6, 9, 14, 20, 24, and 26. These words describe the six days of creation.

God's spoken Word (Jesus) created the entire universe. Internal proof of this assertion is found in John 1:1-3 and 14: ***[1]In the beginning was the Word, and the Word was with God, and the Word was God. [2]He was in the beginning with God. [3]All things were made through Him, and without Him nothing was made that was made.... [14]And the Word became flesh and dwelt among us, and we beheld His glory, the glory as of the only begotten of the Father, full of grace and truth.*** The Jesus that we Christians worship is the Word of

Chapter 1

God who became flesh. We Christians do not believe that Jesus is just a good man, just a good teacher, or just a good prophet that was made a god.

We believe He is the God who created all things and then humbled Himself to become a man, as it is written in Philippians 2:5-11: *⁵Let this mind be in you which was also in Christ Jesus, ⁶who, being in the form of God, did not consider it robbery to be equal with God, ⁷but made Himself of no reputation, taking the form of a bondservant, and coming in the likeness of men. ⁸And being found in appearance as a man, He humbled Himself and became obedient to the point of death, even the death of the cross. ⁹Therefore God also has highly exalted Him and given Him the name which is above every name, ¹⁰that at the name of Jesus every knee should bow, of those in heaven, and of those on earth, and of those under the earth, ¹¹and that every tongue should confess that Jesus Christ is Lord, to the glory of God the Father.*

Notice Mohammed's complete misunderstanding of the doctrine of the trinity from the beginning to the end of the following verse in Qur'an 4:171: *¹⁷¹O People of the Book, do not exaggerate in your religion and do not speak against Allah, except the truth. Surely the Christ 'Isā, son of Mary, is only a messenger of Allah and his word, which he cast to Mary, and a spirit from him. So believe in Allah and his messengers, and do not say, "Three."*[68] *Cease; it is better for you. Surely Allah is only one god. Praise be to him that there would be to him a son. To him what is in the heavens and what is on the earth, and Allah is a sufficient guardian.*

Jesus is God and can do all things, including becoming a man. However, He cannot sin because He is holy. If we look carefully into the life of this "human," we discover that He lived a perfect, sin-free life, and therefore must be God. No one else who has ever walked the face of the earth has lived a perfect, sin-free life. In Colossians 1:15-17: *¹⁵He is the image of the invisible God, the firstborn over all creation. ¹⁶For by Him all things were created that are in heaven and that are on earth, visible and invisible, whether thrones or dominions or principalities or powers. All things were created through Him and for Him. ¹⁷And He is before all things, and in Him all things consist.*

---

[68] the Trinity

These and many other passages throughout the Bible show not only the divinity of Jesus but that all things were created by Him. Further discussion on these passages will be included later, but now we will refocus our attention on the biblical account of the Creation as recorded in Genesis.

Creation was accomplished in six actual days; this assertion is accepted by Christians with no guessing, no suggestions, and little disagreement among conservative Christian or Jewish scholars. God knows what He did, and He told us exactly what He did, when He did it, and how He did it.

This is what took place in the early history of the earth. In the beginning, people lived long lives because the condition of the earth before the flood was completely different from the conditions today. Life on earth would have been similar to living in the midst of a water bubble, for the earth was surrounded by water which stopped many harmful rays from the sun. These rays advance aging and cause cancers and other diseases. Notice also that there was no summer, winter, spring, or fall. Earth had a perfect environment year-round. There was also no rain. (See Genesis 2:5.) The first rain will be discussed in the story of Noah.

Another important fact concerning life on earth in the beginning was that men and animals were vegetarians. As it is written in Genesis 1:29-30: *[29]And God said, "See, I have given you every herb that yields seed which is on the face of all the earth, and every tree whose fruit yields seed; to you it shall be for food. [30]Also, to every beast of the earth, to every bird of the air, and to everything that creeps on the earth, in which there is life, I have given every green herb for food"; and it was so.* Then in Genesis 9:3, God gave man permission to eat meat: *[3]Every moving thing that lives shall be food for you. I have given you all things, even as the green herbs.* Notice also that the weather changed drastically after the flood, as it is written in Genesis 8:22: *[22]While the earth remains, seedtime and harvest, cold and heat, winter and summer, and day and night shall not cease.*

On the second day of creation, God made the firmament to divide the waters; some water was above the firmament while other water was under the firmament. God called the firmament *heaven* (Genesis 1:6-8).

On the third day of creation, God separated land from the water on the earth. He also caused vegetation to grow on the land (Genesis

1:9-13). On the fourth day, God created the sun, moon, and stars and put them in the second heaven (Genesis 1:14-19). An important point that must be made here is that the moon, according to biblical understanding, does not produce light as stated by Mohammed, but only reflects the light of the sun. The book of Job states this in 25:5: **[5]Behold even to the moon, and it shineth not; yea, the stars are not pure in his sight.** When you read Scripture, the Holy Bible, you notice there are only three heavens. The first heaven is the skies around the earth where birds fly as written in Genesis 1:20: **[20]Then God said, "Let the waters abound with an abundance of living creatures, and let birds fly above the earth across the face of the firmament of the heavens."** The second heaven is that which a psalmist referred to as the heaven of the stars, moon, and planets, and which we commonly refer to as space. We read this in Psalm 8:3: **[3]When I consider Your heavens, the work of Your fingers, the moon and the stars, which You have ordained.** The Apostle Paul, in 2 Corinthians 12:2-4, wrote about being called up to the third heaven, which he referred to as paradise: **[2]I know a man in Christ who fourteen years ago, (whether in the body, I do not know, or whether out of the body, I do not know, God knows) such a one was caught up to the third heaven. [3]And I know such a man, (whether in the body or out of the body, I do not know, God knows) [4]how he was caught up into Paradise...** The Bible never mentions seven heavens or seven earths as the Qur'an states throughout its pages. The Bible states that there are only three heavens.

Also, note that the one earth of the Bible is spherical, not flat, as taught throughout the pages of the Qur'an. Isaiah 40:22 states: **[22]It is he who sits above the <u>circle</u> of the earth, and its inhabitants are like grasshoppers, who stretches out the heavens like a curtain, and spreads them out like a tent to dwell in.** The Arabic translation of the word *circle* in this verse in Isaiah is *ball* and is pronounced as *korah* in the Arabic language.

On the fifth day of creation, God created all the living creatures in the water and the sky. God blessed, as always, and commanded the creatures to reproduce and fill the earth (Genesis 1:20-23).

On the sixth day, the Bible teaches the creation of all the beasts of the earth. So it was. The question we must ask here, just to remind ourselves of the description of the creation of heaven and earth, is this. *How did God create the entire universe?* The Bible says that God spoke it all into existence. *How much time is required for God to speak, to command creation into existence?* The answer is *no time at all.* Now here is an important point. God instructed the earth to bring forth every living creature after its *kind* (Genesis 1:24-25). Finally, He created the ruler of all the earth, the one who would have dominion over all the rest of creation. God created Adam and his wife Eve (Genesis 1:26-28).

We have now summarized the first six days of creation. *But what about the seventh day?* In Genesis 2:2-3, we read that God ended His work and rested. He also blessed and sanctified the seventh day. Notice the Bible does not say God was tired from His work and so rested on the seventh day as Muslims have written and taught. Muslims look at the Bible's Genesis account of creation and make fun of the word *rested* and ask ridiculous questions such as the following question: *How does Allah get tired?*

The Bible states that God rested from His work after He ended His work. It is a very common expression used in the Old Testament when something *stopped from continuing* that something *rested from whatever was happening.* A good example can be found in Joshua 11:23 where, when peace came upon the land, it is written that ***the land rested from war.***

In conclusion, from a study of Muslim writings to this point, we discover an excessive level of confusion, contradiction, and error concerning creation as it is described in the Qur'an, hadith, and interpretations of the Muslim scholars. If Muslims would remove the distorted lenses of Islam and objectively read and restudy this information, especially when it is compared to the solid teachings of the Holy Bible, the true words of God, not only would they recognize all the previous errors, but they would also discover the truth of the Word of God concerning the account of creation. I hope and pray as we continue our research into the creation of Adam, as it is written both from a Muslim perspective and the Judeo-Christian perspective, that those who seek to know the truth will find it, and it will set them free.

2. The Story of Adam

The Qur'an first mentions Adam in Qur'an 2:30-39. Let us begin with verses 30-33: *³⁰And when your lord said to the angels, "Surely I am placing on earth a kalefah."¹ They said, "Will you place in it those who will vandalize in it and shed the blood, and [while] we nusabah² with your praise and extol your holiness?" He said, "Surely I know what you do not know." ³¹And he taught Adam³ all the names and then set them before the angels, so he said, "Inform me the names of these, if you were truthful." ³²They said, "Praise be to you. We have no knowledge except what you have taught us. Surely you are the knowing, the wise." ³³He said, "O Adam, inform them of their names." So when he informed them of their names, he said, "Did I not say to you that I surely know the unseen of the heavens and the earth, and I know what you reveal and what you were hiding?"*

While reading the above passage, you probably noticed the scattered style of writing which is common throughout the Qur'an as it addresses a hodgepodge of topics. There is not one portion of revelation in which Mohammed claimed to receive a revelation from Angel Gabreel on one specific story, except for Qur'an 12 where Mohammed wrote exclusively about Joseph. The other accounts were scattered throughout the book and contained somewhat different information. Adam is actually mentioned in Qur'an 2:30-39; 3:33-34, 59; 4:1; 5:27-32; 7:11-35, 172, 189; 15:26-44; 17:61-70; 18:50; 19:58; 20:55, 115-126; 36:60; 38:67-88; 49:13; and 50:50.

Mohammed's style of writing a story uses one of three different methods. First, he mentions the name of someone whom he claimed to be a prophet, and you see this name spread all over the Qur'an without any details. Second, the name of an alleged prophet will be mentioned along with one to four verses providing very limited information. The third method is to include ten or more verses including the name in an incomplete story. This third method is what I refer to as the long story. This will be seen throughout the Qur'an.

---

¹viceroy, non-Arabic word of Berber/Syriac origin
²praise, non-Arabic word of Aramaic/Hebrew/Syriac origin
³Adam, non-Arabic word of Hebrew/Syriac origin

The Revelation of Error

In Qur'an 2:30, Allah, speaking to the angels, stated that he was about to create a *kalefah* or viceroy. *Why was Allah informing his angels of the matter? Was he asking permission?* In response, the angels asked Allah a question, which indicated that they were knowledgeable of the future. In Qur'an 2:30: [30] ..."*Will you place in it who will vandalize in it and shed the blood, and [while] we nusabah*[4] *with your praise and extol your holiness?*"....

The Creation of Adam

Allah created Adam. *How did he create him? What condition was he in? How did it all begin?* Mohammed taught that Adam and his wife, whose name was not mentioned in the Qur'an, were created in heaven, not here on earth. Mohammed taught that Allah sent his Angel Gabreel to bring to him some of the dirt of the earth, but when he was about to reach out to the earth to take some of its dirt, the earth said, "I seek refuge from Allah that you may not shame me by reducing me by taking some of my dirt."[5] Therefore, Angel Gabreel left earth and went back to heaven empty-handed. Allah then sent another angel, Mika'il, and the same thing happened.[6]

Allah then sent the angel of death. The earth spoke to him, "I seek the refuge of Allah," but the angel of death said, "I also seek the refuge of Allah, and I will not disobey Allah's command." He took out of the earth three piles of dirt (red, white, and black) which he took back to heaven. Allah took this dirt and mixed it together until it became mud. He left it a while until it became clay. Then he shaped it and left it again until it became potter's clay, as it is written in Qur'an 55:14: [14]*He created the human from clay like the fakhkhār.*[7]

Allah created Adam by his hand so that Satan would not be proud.[8] Ibn Kathir stated that Allah made him a human, and he became flesh from clay.[9]

Allah began on Friday, and forty years later the angels walked by him. They were scared of him, and Satan was the

---

[4] praise, non-Arabic word of Aramaic/Hebrew/Syriac origin
[5] I do not know what language, but perhaps it was the Arabic language. A famous song in the Middle East has the phrase "the earth speaks Arabic."
[6] Ibn Kathir, *Stories of the Prophets*, vol. 1, Abo Al Fida Ishamail Ibn Kathir Al Kurashi Al Damashce (Beirut: Dar Al-Arab Heritage, 1408 AH, 1988), 96.
[7] potter's clay, non-Arabic word of Syriac origin
[8] If Allah had made him by his word or simply speaking him into existence, then Satan would have achieved more dignity than Adam.
[9] Ibn Kathir, 97.

Chapter 2

most frightened one. Satan walked by Adam and hit him, and his body made the sound of potter's clay. Satan said: "I will go through what you create." Satan entered Adam's mouth, and he came out of him from his buttocks. Then Satan said to the angels, "Do not be afraid of this. Your Allah is absolute, and this one is empty. If I were asked to go against him, I would demolish him."

After that, Bukhari wrote that Allah breathed into Adam from his spirit, first through his gills. (Since man does not have gills, perhaps the writer meant his *nostrils*, as it is written in the Bible.) When Adam sneezed, the angel told him to say, "Praise to Allah." So Adam said, "Praise to Allah." Allah then said, "Your lord forgave you."

Because Adam was made from different colors of dirt, the sons of Adam were also different colors. Some were red, some were black, and some were white. Bukhari also stated that Allah asked Adam to go to someone (we don't know to whom) so he might say the greeting, "Al salam alycom," which means *peace be upon you*. When he said that, they said to him, "And peace be upon you too, and the mercy of Allah and his blessings."

Then Ibn Kathir stated that Allah told Adam, "This is your greeting, and this is the greeting of your descendants."[10] Notice that no one had used such a greeting until Mohammed said this greeting to his followers. Then Adam asked Allah, "Who are my descendants?" Then Allah said, "Choose one of my hands, O Adam." He said, "I choose your right hand, my lord, and both your hands are right, my lord." So Allah spread his palm and showed Adam's descendants, and they were lights in his hand. One of these lights was a small light.

Adam saw one of the lights and said, "O lord, who is this?" He said, "That is your son David." Then Adam asked, "So how long will he live?" Allah said, "Sixty. I made to him sixty." So Adam asked Allah, "O lord, give him from my age that he may live a hundred years." So Allah did that, and he brought a witness for that. So when it was time for Adam to die, Allah sent the angel of death, and Adam said, "Didn't I have another forty years?" The angel said, "Didn't you give it to your son David?" So Adam denied this, and his descendants also denied it. This is only one of many different stories concerning the creation of Adam.

---

[10]Ibid., 98.

The Revelation of Error

According to Muslim scholars, Adam was sixty cubits tall. Each cubit measured close to fifty centimeters which made Adam roughly thirty meters or ninety feet tall.[11] His width was only seven cubits. Rather than a linear decrease in the height as Mohammed asserted, scientific research has shown that height is an indicator of overall health and economic well-being.[12] The height of mankind has decreased and increased in response to climate and overall environment. For example, men from the early middle ages were nearly as tall as modern people. Studies of burial sites in northern Europe dating from the ninth to the nineteenth centuries indicate that average height declined slightly during the twelfth through sixteenth centuries and hit an all-time low during the seventeenth and eighteenth centuries. Northern European men had lost an average 2.5 inches of height by the 1700s. However, that loss was fully recovered in the first half of the twentieth century and is now surpassed. The height of the tallest man in modern history is 8 feet, 11.1 inches (272 centimeters).[13] It is doubtful that Mohammed ever saw anyone taller than that.

The ridiculous assertions about creation continue with the claim that Adam's hair was like the head of a palm tree. His hair pulled a tree out of a garden.[14]

These questions still plague me: *where, when, and how was Adam's wife created?* Muslims cannot explain until they read the Bible which, by the way, gives her name, Eve. Mohammed said she was made from a crooked rib. Mohammed said, "Do good to them (women). If you try to correct them, you break them."[15]

Allah made a surprising request to his angels which contradicts the nature and the character of the true God (for He is a jealous God and His word in Scripture teaches that He alone is to be worshiped) when Allah commanded the angels to worship Adam in Qur'an 2:34: *³⁴And when we said to the angels, "Osjodo*[16] *to Adam," so they*

---

[11]Ibid., 99.
[12]http://researchnews.osu.edu/archive/medimen.htm, accessed March 10, 2012.
[13]http://en.wikipedia.org/wiki/Robert_Wadlow, accessed March 11, 2012.
[14]Ibn Assaka, *A Summary of the History of Damascus,* part 4 (*n.p.*: Dar Alfakr, *n.d.*), 222.
[15]Sahih Bukhari, Hadith 3331. The same hadith also exists in Sahih Muslim, Hadith 1460-1468. This hadith clearly shows that the value of women in Islam when the statement that they are made out of crooked ribs mean there is no good in them and no hope of fixing them. Men must live with them as they are.
[16]worship, non-Arabic word of Aramaic origin

all worshiped except 'Iblis.[17] *He refused and became proud, and he was among the infidels.*

Here I would like to demonstrate the inconsistency within the Qur'an concerning the response of Satan to Allah when he refused to worship Adam. For example, in Qur'an 7:12: *[12]He said, "What has hindered you that you did not worship when I commanded you?" He said, "I am better than him. You have created me from fire, and you created him from mud."* Also, in Qur'an 17:61, he said: *[61]"Will I worship him that you have created of mud?"* These quotes from Satan are quite different, although the Qur'an is to be taken literally. *Which were the actual words of Satan to Allah?*

What does the Bible state about the creation of the first man and woman? How were Adam and Eve created? In Genesis 2:7 we read: **[7]And the LORD God formed man of the dust of the ground, and breathed into his nostrils the breath of life; and man became a living being.** Notice that God did not send any angel to bring dirt to heaven, and the earth did not speak; but the Lord God Himself formed Adam and breathed into his nostrils the breath of life. God made him a living soul. Adam was in the Garden of Eden which is on earth, not in heaven as Mohammed and scholars erroneously interpreted.

According to Genesis 2:10-14, a river came out of the Garden of Eden which divided into four rivers: the Pision River which surrounded the land of Havilah, the Gihon River which surrounded the land of Cush, the Hiddekel River which goes east of Assyria, and the Euphrates River. Also, many trees in the garden were pleasant to the sight and very good for food. Two very important trees were in the midst of the garden. One was called the Tree of Life, and the other was called the Tree of Knowledge of Good and Evil.

God put Adam in the garden to tend it, and He advised Adam to eat from all the trees of the garden except the Tree of Knowledge of Good and Evil, for God said to him that if he ate from it, he would surely die. Although God throughout Creation made the statement that it was good, after He made Adam He said it was not good for Adam to be alone without a helper. In Genesis 2:18: **[18]And the Lord God said, "It is not good that man should be alone; I will make him a helper comparable to him."** Then God brought all the animals and the birds that He had made before Adam, and Adam named all of them.

---

[17] devil, non-Arabic word of Greek origin

God did not teach Adam any names as Mohammed stated in the Qur'an. Adam made up the names for all these creatures. God noted that Adam did not have a helpmate, and so God caused Adam to sleep. God took one of Adam's ribs, and from this rib God made a woman. He brought her to Adam, and because she was bone of his bone and flesh from his flesh, he named her woman. Genesis 2:24 ends with this statement, that a [24]***man shall leave his father and mother and be joined to his wife, and they shall become one flesh.***

Adam and Eve were naked in the garden, and they were not ashamed. Notice they did not have any clothes or feathers, and they did not lose their clothes, as we will later see that Mohammed and his scholars claimed. They were created naked, lived in the garden naked, and were not ashamed.

A conversation took place in the garden on earth between Satan and Eve. According to Scripture, the serpent was the most cunning of all the creatures God made. It came and spoke to Eve and asked a very deceptive question. "Did God say that you should not eat from every tree in the garden?" As we just read earlier, Satan knew that God had not made this statement. He only commanded them not to eat from the Tree of Knowledge of Good and Evil. When Eve answered the serpent's question about the tree which was in the middle of the garden, she added to God's original command, not to touch the tree. She said that God had told them not to eat from it or touch it for if they did, they would die. *Did God say not to touch it?* Clearly not. God simply instructed them to not eat of that tree.

Carrying on a conversation with Satan was not a very smart thing for Eve to do, for he realized that she was weakening; and the serpent said to the woman, "You will not die." He continued by stating that if they ate from this tree, their eyes would be opened and they would become like gods knowing good and evil. Then Eve looked at the tree and saw that it was good for food and desirable to look at. She ate and then gave to her husband who ate with her. Yes, their eyes were opened, and they now knew they were naked. They tried to do everything to cover their nakedness, but their sewn fig leaves did not last. When they heard the voice of the Lord God, they hid from His face.

The Lord God called unto Adam, "Where are you?" Adam replied, "I heard your voice in the garden, and I was afraid because I was naked. I hid myself." Then God asked him, "How did you know that you were naked? Did you eat from the tree that I commanded you not to eat from?" Then Adam blamed Eve, and Eve blamed the serpent. God cursed the serpent and gave the promise that the seed of the woman would crush the head of the serpent and that the serpent would bruise his heel.

This prophecy was the first one in the Bible concerning the coming of our Lord and Savior, Jesus Christ, the seed of Virgin Mary. The punishment on Eve was severe, for she would have multiple sorrows, pain in pregnancy and at childbirth, and a desire for her husband who would rule over her. As for Adam, the earth was now cursed because of him. With sorrow he would eat from it all of his days. It would not always bring fruit for him as it was supposed to; rather, it would bring to him thorns and thistles, and now he must sweat to produce bread until he returned to the earth. Then Adam called his wife Eve, for she was the mother of every living human.

This event was not the end of the story, for God then provided coats of animal skins for Adam and his wife. Death took place on earth for the first time, as God sacrificed animals so that he could remove their skins to cover the nakedness of Adam and Eve, which had resulted from sin. This skin was not artificial, but true animal skin. Since Adam and Eve sinned and ate from the Tree of Knowledge of Good and Evil, God said in Genesis 3:22:

[22]*"...Behold, the man has become like one of Us, to know good and evil. And now, lest he put out his hand and take also of the tree of life, and eat, and live forever."*

Because God did not want Adam and Eve to live forever in sin, he cast them out of the Garden of Eden so that they could not eat from the Tree of Life. They were cast out to the east of the garden. A cherubim with a flaming sword stood blocking the way to the Tree of Life.

What about the inconsistency of who Satan is? Notice that Allah said to the angels (and again I emphasize, *the angels*) to worship Adam. *Is Satan an angel, or is he a jinni?* If Satan is not from the angels, the conclusion is that he did not disobey Allah, simply because he is not an angel. As it is shown in Qur'an 18, verse 50:
…he was from the jinn…

Where was the garden in which Adam and his wife lived? According to Muslim scholars and the Qur'an, it is in heaven which is not the true place as we explained in the true biblical account. This is

The Revelation of Error

shown clearly in Qur'an 2:35: *[35]And we said, "O Adam, askon[18] you and your wife in the garden and eat from it plentifully wherever you will, and do not come near this tree so that you will be of the unjust."* This story is repeated throughout the Qur'an in 4:1; 7:11-25, 189; 15:26-44; 17:61-65; 20:115-126; 38:71-88; 49:13; etc. Also, in Qur'an 2 is a description of the temptation of Satan and the fall of Man and how Adam fell from the garden in heaven to earth.

<u>Allah's Command, Satan's Temptation, and the Fall of Adam</u>
After Satan refused to worship Adam, the Qur'an teaches that he was kicked out of the garden, which Mohammed, as well as a majority of Muslim scholars, believed was in heaven.[19] No doubt, Allah kicked Satan out of heaven when he refused to worship. In Qur'an 7:13: *[13]He (Allah) said, "So get down from it. So it was not for you to be proud in it, so get out. Surely you are of the lowly."* Allah commanded Satan to get out of heaven and descend from it because Satan disobeyed his command. In Qur'an 7:18: *[18]He said, "Get out of it despised, driven away."* Also, in Qur'an 15:34: *[34]He said, "So get out from it, so surely you are stoned."* Notice that as Mohammed continued to repeat the story in the pages of the Qur'an, he rewrote the statements of Allah and others by using different words. The words of the Qur'an are not consistent. *Which one of the previous sentences were the actual words that Allah spoke?*

Even though Mohammed stated that Satan was kicked out of the garden in heaven in Qur'an 7:20-22, Satan was still in the garden to tempt Adam and his wife to eat from the tree. In Qur'an 7:20-22: *[20]So Satan whispered to them to show them what was hidden from them in their nakedness. And he said, "Your lord has not forbidden you from this tree except that you become angels or that you become immortal." [21]And he swore to them: "Surely I am an adviser to you." [22]So he brought them down with pride. So when they tasted the tree, their private parts appeared to them, and they began to cut and glue together leaves of the garden on them.[20] And their lord called to them: "Have I not*

---
[18]dwell, non-Arabic word of Greek/Syriac origin
[19]Ibn Kathir, *Stories of the Prophets,* 83.
[20]their private parts

forbidden you of this tree, and I said to you, 'Surely Satan is your obvious enemy'?"

    Notice that Satan in the previous verse was speaking to Adam and asking him to show him the tree of immortality. That is nonsense. As we have seen in the Genesis account, Satan was talking to Eve, not to Adam, and he did not ask her to show him the tree of immortality but actually asked her the question: "Did God say that you should not eat of every tree of the garden?" In Qur'an 20:120: *^{120}So Satan whispered to him and said, "O Adam, will I show you the tree of immortality and of the kingdom that will not perish?"*

    In his interpretation, Ibn Kathir addressed how and where this took place.[21] He said that it was acceptable that Satan met with them in the garden as he walked through it, not as if he was living there, but visiting. He was kicked out of it, but Ibn Kathir stated that he was visiting. Additionally, he stated that Satan whispered to them while he was standing at the gate to the garden, or perhaps he was below the heaven when he whispered to them. Ibn Kathir ended his interpretation as all Muslim scholars usually do, with the statement, *and Allah knows best.* He, like others, did not know how this happened.

    The problem here is the Qur'an teaches that the Garden of Eden was in heaven and that Allah cast Satan out of heaven because he refused to worship Adam. Since Mohammed erroneously stated in his Qur'an that Satan talked to Adam and Eve after he was cast out of heaven, Muslim scholars tried to find a solution for the error. That is why they came up with the fabrication above, saying that Satan was passing by, visiting, or whispering from outside the door of the garden. None of the above fabrications are sensible.

    In Qur'an 2:36-39, we find Mohammed ended the story of Adam and his wife's removal from the garden, which he said was in heaven, by stating that Allah cast them down to earth. The final punishment for those who would not follow the guidance of Allah was that they would be the companions of the fire forever: *^{36}So Shaitān[22] made them fall from it, so he got them out from where they were. And we said, "Get down. You will be enemies to one another, and you will have on earth a dwelling place and enjoyment for a*

---

[21] Ibn Kathir, 85.
[22] Satan, non-Arabic word of probable Abyssinian origin

The Revelation of Error

while." ³⁷So Adam received words from his lord, so he tāba²³ toward him. Surely he is the tawwāb,²⁴ the merciful. ³⁸We said, "Get down from it, all of you, so either guidance will come to you from me, so whoever follows my guidance, so no fear on them, and they will not grieve. ³⁹And those who became infidels and denied our āyat,²⁵ those are companions of the fire; they will abide in it forever."

This is what I would call an extreme shortcut of telling the story. *Can anyone read these three verses and tell me how Adam fell into sin? Was it he or his wife who fell first, and what did they really do?* We know from verse 35 that Allah said to them not to draw near to this tree. *What tree? Is this really what the Bible said? Did the Bible say not to eat of the tree or not to draw near to the tree?* No such information is in these three verses. In verse 36, Allah said to them to come down to earth which meant they were really up in heaven. After all, they were up in the garden in heaven where they were created.

In verse 37, Adam received words from his lord. *What words? Would simply receiving words from Allah fix the problem?* What a wonderful and clear word of Allah the Qur'an is. However, one could say, "Perhaps in the following verses, in other parts of the Qur'an, there will be more details." For example, the story is recorded in 7:20-25. Let's begin with verses 20-21: *²⁰So Satan whispered to them to show them what was hidden from them in their nakedness. And he said, "Your lord has not forbidden you from this tree except that you become angels or that you become immortal." ²¹And he swore to them: "Surely I am an adviser to you."* At the end of the last book in the Bible (Revelation), the Bible clearly commands that no one can add to, or take away from, the prophecies in the Bible. As we can see here and throughout his writing, Mohammed, in his Qur'an, took away from the Bible and also added a great deal to the Bible. The Bible in Revelation 22:18-19 clearly states that if any man adds to the prophecies of the Bible or takes away from the words of the Bible, God will remove that man's part from the book of life and the holy city and from what is written in the Bible.

---

[23] relented, non-Arabic word of Aramaic origin
[24] relenting
[25] verses, non-Arabic word of Syriac/Aramaic origin

Chapter 2

Perhaps one will say Mohammed took away and did not mention some portion of the story because it was not important. Perhaps he added information which was important and would help the Muslims to understand the action and the story at a deeper level. However, that was not the case in the stories of the Qur'an. Let us have a closer look at Qur'an 7:20-21 above. As it is written in the Qur'an, Satan whispered to Adam and his wife so that he might show to them their private parts. What a strange statement. When one reads the interpretation of Muslims who are called scholars, he will discover the chaos of the situation, for as usual they will disagree, *and Allah knows best.*[26]

What clothes were Adam and his wife wearing before they tasted the tree? By the way, one must ask another question. *Did they eat from the tree, or did they taste it?* Add to that the words of Satan concerning why Allah forbade them from eating from the tree. He said in Qur'an 7:22 that Allah forbade them because they would become angels or live forever. **[22]So he brought them down with pride. So when they tasted the tree, their private parts appeared to them, and they began to cut and glue together leaves of the garden on them.**[27] **And their lord called to them: "Have I not forbidden you of this tree, and I said to you, 'Surely Satan is your obvious enemy'?"** They tasted the tree, not the fruit of the tree, and they became naked and glued the leaves of the garden upon themselves. Then Allah asked them the question, "Have I not forbidden you of this tree?"

Wow! It is amazing that *Allah asks questions*! Muslims reject the Bible as the true word of God because they find in it that God asks questions. They claim that if God is all-knowing, He should never ask questions. Sadly, they do not understand that when God asks questions in the Bible, it is not because He does not know the answer. It is simply because He wants us to know that we have sinned against Him, and He is giving us the opportunity to repent. However, Muslims have no objections to Allah asking questions throughout the Qur'an.

Qur'an 7:23-25 states: **[23]They said, "Our lord, we have been unjust to ourselves, and if you do not forgive us and have mercy on us, we will surely be of the losers." [24]He said, "Get**

---

[26]Ibn Kathir, 85.
[27]their private parts

down. *The one of you is an enemy to the other, and you will have on earth dwelling and enjoyment for a while."* ²⁵*He said, "In it will you live, and in it will you die. And from it you will be brought out."* Once again, the Qur'an clearly states that they confessed that they had done wrong. They sought the forgiveness of Allah, and then Allah sent them down to earth where he commanded that they would live in it, die in it, and be brought out of it on the day of resurrection. Still, questions remain concerning the fall, how the temptation took place, and the true conversations between Satan and Eve, and then between God and Adam and Eve. These questions have not yet been answered.

The story is repeated once again in Qur'an 20:117-120: ¹¹⁷*So we said, "O Adam, surely this is an enemy to you and to your wife. So do not [let him] get you out of the garden, so you will be in misery.* ¹¹⁸*Surely you will not be hungry in it, neither will you be naked.* ¹¹⁹*And you will not be thirsty in it, neither will you feel the heat of the sun."* ¹²⁰*So Satan whispered to him and said, "O Adam, will I show you the tree of immortality and of the kingdom that will not perish?"* Notice in verse 120 Satan whispers to him, meaning Adam, but back in Qur'an 7:20, Satan whispered to *them*, meaning Adam and his wife.

One must ask some questions. *Did Satan whisper to Adam, or did Satan whisper to him and his wife? What was Satan whispering about?* The Qur'an stated that Satan said, "Will I show you the tree of immortality and of the kingdom that will not perish?" *Did Adam really not know the location of the tree?* Then in verse 121 they ate from the tree, and their nakedness was shown to them. Qur'an 20:121 states: ¹²¹*So they ate from it, so their nakedness appeared to them, and they began to cut and glue together leaves of the garden on them.*[28] *And Adam disobeyed his lord, so he was seduced.* Adam repented, as it is written in verses 122-124: ¹²²*Then his lord chose him, so he relented on him and guided.* ¹²³*He said, "Go all of you down from it; each of you is an enemy to the other. So whatever guidance comes to you from me, so whoever follows my guidance, so he will not go astray nor be in misery.* ¹²⁴*And whoever will turn away from my reminder, so surely to him a life of hardship. And we will gather him blind on the resurrection day."*

---

[28] their private parts

What about the inconsistencies of Allah's statement after the fall of Adam? Notice in the following three passages taken from Qur'an 2, 7, and 20, a question must be asked. *Which statement is truly what Allah said?* We need to examine the following three passages carefully because each account is different. They cannot all be right, for the conversation only happened one time.

Notice in Qur'an 2:36, 38: *[36]...And we said, "Get down. You will be enemies to one another, and you will have on earth a dwelling place and enjoyment for a while..." [38]We said, "Get down from it, all of you, so either guidance will come to you from me, so whoever follows my guidance, so no fear on them, and they will not grieve."*

In Qur'an 7:24: *[24]He said, "Get down. The one of you is an enemy to the other, and you will have on earth dwelling and enjoyment for a while."*

In Qur'an 20:123-124: *[123]He said, "Go all of you down from it; each of you is an enemy to the other. So whatever guidance comes to you from me, so whoever follows my guidance, so he will not go astray nor be in misery. [124]And whoever will turn away from my reminder, so surely to him a life of hardship. And we will gather him blind on the resurrection day."*

The Sons of Adam

The story of Cain and Abel is copied from Genesis 4 in the Bible. However, key details are missing. *Who are the brothers? What were the sacrifices? Who killed whom?*

Qur'an 5:27 states: *[27]And recite to them the news with the truth of the sons of Adam when they each offered an offering, so it was accepted from one of them and not accepted from the other. He said, "Surely I will kill you." He said, "Surely Allah only accepts from the fearer.* Here Ibn Kathir, in his interpretation, like many other scholars, was able to come up with names for the two sons of Adam, but their prophet Mohammed was not.[29] This accounts for the scholars' confusion in the title of their interpretation, Kabeel and Habel, but as we will see shortly, the real names given in the Bible were Kaieen (not Kabeel), which is translated as Cain in English, and his brother Abel.

---

[29]Ibn Kathir, 104.

The reason given by Muslim scholars for the trouble between Cain (or Kabeel, as they mistakenly called him) and Abel was that Abel desired to marry the sister of Cain, and he was the elder.[30] The sister was beautiful, and he desired to keep her for himself and not to give her to his brother. Adam commanded him to give her to his brother as a wife, but he refused. So Adam commanded him to offer a sacrifice, and Adam went to Mecca to perform the Hajj. Adam required the heavens to watch over his sons, but the heavens refused. Then he asked the earths and the mountains, but they refused. However, Cain agreed to watch over his brother. When they offered their sacrifices, Abel offered a sacrifice of fat sheep, and Cain gave from the unhealthy plants. So the fire came from heaven and took the sacrifice of Abel and left the sacrifice of Cain who then became angry and said, "I will kill you so you will not marry my sister." And he said, "Surely Allah accepts from the fearer."

Now, let us consider the killing of one of the sons of Adam. In Qur'an 5:28-30 these words are recorded: *[28]If you stretch your hand against me to kill me, I will not stretch my hand to you to kill you. Surely I fear Allah, the lord of the worlds. [29]Surely I desire that you will bear my sin and your sin so that you will become among the companions of the fire, and that is the reward of the unjust." [30]So his soul persuaded him to kill his brother. So he killed him, so he became of the losers.*

How did Cain kill Abel? In his book, Ibn Kathir gave us different interpretations.[31] He wrote that Abu Jafar said that Adam was watching the sons when they offered their sacrifices, and he saw that the sacrifice of Abel was acceptable but not the sacrifice of Cain. So Cain said to Adam that his sacrifice was accepted "because you prayed for him, and you did not pray for me." He secretly threatened his brother. One night, Abel was delayed in his shepherding, so Adam sent his brother Cain to see why he was late. When Cain went to Abel, he said to him, "It was accepted from you, and it was not accepted from me!" So Abel said, "Surely Allah only accepted from the fearer." Then Cain became angry, and he struck Abel with an iron that was with him. So thereby Cain killed Abel. Obviously, these Muslim scholars were not aware that iron was not available since it was not developed until about 1200 BC. Then others said, "Surely he

---

[30]Ibid.
[31]Ibid., 105.

killed him with a rock. He threw it on his head while he was asleep." While others said, "No, he strangled him with a strong strangling, and he bit him as the predators do so he died." *Only Allah knows best.*

In the story about the burial of the deceased brother, the reference to the raven apparently comes from chapter 21 of a Jewish book, *Pirke Rabbi Eleazar*,[32] which tells of the raven coming to show Adam, not the brother, how to bury his son as seen in Qur'an 5:31:

³¹So Allah sent a raven which searched on the earth to show him how he might bury his brother's body. He said, "O woe is to me. Am I unable to become like this raven, so I will hide my brother's body?" So he became of those who regret.

The interpretations of this verse, according to Ibn Kathir, were many.[33] Some said when Cain killed his brother that he carried him on his back one year. Others said that he carried him on his back a hundred years, and he was still the same when Allah sent the ravens. After he saw the raven bury the other raven, he was sorry that he would have to do such a thing, but he did just like the raven and buried his brother.

As was Mohammed, so were his scholars, for Mohammed copied from the Bible many stories without any details. Also, his followers copied the stories either with little changes or sometimes exactly as written. A good example of this was when Ibn Kathir listed the descendants of Adam as literally as if he were copying Genesis 5.[34] I wish he were alive today so I could simply ask him the question which I offer to my Muslim friends: *how and where did Ibn Kathir come up with this knowledge of their names and their ages?* Neither Mohammed nor his Angel Gabreel or even Allah knew anything about these people: Seth, Enos, Cainan, Mahalaleel, Jared, Enoch, Methuselah, Lamech, Noah, Shem, Ham, and Japheth. One could go on and on because so much has been written about Cain and Abel, but that is enough for now.

Mohammed stated that 104 books descended from heaven. Fifty of them were descended on Seth, son of Adam. The Bible never mentions such a thing, for the first writing we know of was the book of Job. Second were the writings of Moses. Before that, there was no written Scripture.

---

[32]*Pirke Rabbi Eliezer ben Hyrcanus* (*Seder Rav Amram,* ed. Warsaw, 1865).
[33]Ibn Kathir, 106.
[34]Ibid., 107-108.

The Revelation of Error

The True Story of the Sons of Adam from the Bible

In Genesis 4, Adam knew Eve, and she conceived a son whom they called Cain who became a farmer. Then she conceived again and had another son who became a shepherd. They named him Abel. This account is in the first two verses. Notice that the amount of information in these two simple verses does not require any fabrication as is the case with the writings of the Muslim scholars. Here we know their names (which Mohammed forgot to mention), we know which of the brothers was older, and we know what their occupations were.

In verses 3-4, the Bible describes a very important event: the offering unto the Lord. One may ask how Cain and Abel knew of such an event, and the obvious answer is they had learned it from their father and mother as there were no uncles or aunts or neighbors. Cain offered from the fruit of the land; Abel offered from the best of the flock. *So what was God's reaction to the two offerings?* The Bible clearly states that He accepted the offering of Abel but rejected the offering of Cain. The reaction of Cain was anger as we see in verse 6.

What can we learn up to this point? Since Adam's sin, sacrifices were being offered. Men may offer many different kinds of sacrifices, but the only accepted sacrifice by Almighty God is the blood sacrifice. He made an offering of an animal on behalf of Adam and Eve after the fall when they ate from the Tree of the Knowledge of Good and Evil, and He covered their nakedness. Adam and Eve tried to cover their nakedness with fig leaves (the work of man), but that did not solve their problem. Therefore, God intervened through the provision of an animal sacrifice, the blood to serve as atonement and the skin to cover their nakedness.

Here we see that Cain tried to do the same thing, for he worked hard, sweating, but he chose from the fruit of the land as a sacrifice (work of man), and it was rejected. In Hebrews 9:22: ***For without shedding of blood there is no forgiveness of sin.*** This is why God offered Jesus Christ, His Son, as a sacrifice for all mankind. Anyone ***who believes in Him will not perish but will have eternal life (John 3:16).***

Did God know why Cain was angry? The answer is *yes,* for He is the One who refused Cain's offering. *Why did God ask him why he was angry?* He only asked in an effort to reach out to the lost, angry man that He might reconcile him to Himself, and that is why God said to him, as written in Genesis 4:6-7, that if he did well, it would be accepted. If he sacrificed correctly (the sacrifice of clean animals), his offer would be accepted as it was with his brother Abel. On the other hand, if he did not offer the right sacrifice, there is a sin which lies by the door and his desire of this sin would rule over him.

What was God talking about here? He was talking about the sin of the first murder on earth. In Genesis 4:8, we read about a conversation which took place between Cain and his brother Abel when they were together in the field, and Cain rose up against his brother Abel and killed him. Once again, God was reaching out to Cain in order to restore him to Himself, so He asked him the following question: "Where is your brother Abel?" God's question offered a great opportunity for Cain to confess his sin; instead, he foolishly lied by saying, "I do not know." Then he dared to ask God the question, "Am I my brother's keeper?"

Again, I am amazed that Muslims who read the Scripture today are quick to reject the Bible as the Word of God. They say, "If God is all knowing, how can He ask questions?"

Obviously, this passage will prove the false interpretation of such Muslims, for as we saw already in verse 7, God is telling Cain what he hid in his heart, the murder of his brother. God knew before time that this would happen. God's answer to the deceptive question of Cain, "Am I my brother's keeper?" was written in verse 10: "What have you done? The voice of your brother's blood is crying out to me from the ground." Here we see that God knew what happened to Abel. The crime scene was well known to the God who knows all things!

In conclusion, Cain was cursed upon the earth, which opened its mouth to receive the blood of Abel, and the earth was cursed by no longer being as capable of producing its fruit as it previously had. Cain then would wander on the earth. Confession took place, but it was too late because the blood had already been shed, not the blood of the true sacrifice but the blood of the brother. Cain said, "My sin is greater than I can bear. I will live lost on the earth, and everyone who sees me will kill me." But the Lord answered that if anyone were to kill Cain, retribution would be taken out on him sevenfold. Then the Lord once again showed mercy to Cain by setting a mark upon Cain so no one who found him would kill him. This is written in Genesis 4:11-15.

The Scripture provides additional information which is not known to Muslims. We read in verses 16-22 that Cain went out from the presence of the Lord and dwelled in the land of Nod which is located east of Eden. He knew his wife and had sons. Cities were built, and the land was populated. Some who lived in tents worked as herders of cattle, and some were musicians who played the harp, flute, and the drum.

The Death of Adam

The Qur'an does not mention anything concerning Adam's death. All that we know is written by some Muslim scholars in the hadith of Mohammed.[35] For Mohammed said that when Adam was about to die, he made a covenant with his son Seth and taught him the hour of the night and the day. He taught him the worship of all these hours. Mohammed stated also that he taught him that the flood would take place. Ibn Kathir stated that the children of Adam were all demolished except for Seth, *and Allah knows best.*[36] He also stated that Adam died on Friday. The angels came with spices and brought a coffin from the garden from Allah. They comforted his son Seth. Ibn Isaac said, "The sun and the moon eclipsed for seven days and seven nights" (as if mourning Adam's death).

When Adam was about to die, he craved to eat from the grapes of the garden, so his sons went about to get them for him. They met with the angels, and the angels asked them, "What do you desire, O sons of Adam?" They said, "Our father craves to eat the grapes of the garden." So they said to them, "Return." They took his spirit and washed him and mummified him. Angel Gabreel prayed over him, and all the angels were behind him. Then they buried him, and they said to Seth, son of Adam, "This is the way of life concerning your death and those who come after this." This story points out a very significant error on the part of those Muslim scholars who maintain that the garden was in heaven, for this is clear evidence that the garden where Adam and Eve lived was on earth rather than in heaven. *If the garden were in heaven, how would the sons of Adams be able to go up to the garden in heaven to retrieve the grapes for their father?*

Scholars disagree on where Adam was buried and the number of years he lived. Ibn Abbas and Abu Horyrah stated that he lived a thousand years. Ibn Kathir stated that this does not disagree with what is written in the Torah where it is stated that Adam lived 930 years

---

[35]Ibn Kathir, 110.
[36]Ibid., 111.

Chapter 2

(Genesis 5:5) because there was doubt about what was written in the Jewish writings. We can respond to the disagreement with the truth which is in our hands (according to Mohammed and Muslim scholars), which is kept from any corruption. Ibn Kathir also stated that the 930 years (solar years) is acceptable considering that this could include the other years which he lived in the garden. In lunar years, this would be 957 years. According to Ibn Jarir and other Muslim scholars, when we add the forty-three years he lived in the garden in heaven before coming to earth, the total number is a thousand years.

As for the years which Adam gave to his son David, this will be discussed in detail in the story of David. So much has been written about Adam that, in my personal opinion, this is ridiculous information from Mohammed and his scholars; for the sake of time, we will stop here.

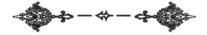

3. The Story of Idris (Enoch)

The name Idris is used in the Qur'an to refer to Enoch of the Old Testament book of Genesis. Mohammed made up the name, and he is mentioned in the Qur'an in only four verses, and these verses offer very little information. He was identified as a friend and prophet, and he was raised in a high place as it is written in Qur'an 19:56-57: *[56]And remember in the book Idris,[1] surely he was a friend, a prophet. [57]And we raised him to a high place.* In Qur'an 21:85 we can read: *[85]And Ishmael and Idris[2] and Za Al Kafel,[3] all were among the patient.*

In his book, Ibn Kathir claimed that Mohammed came from the genealogy of Idris, and he was the first of the sons of Adam who received the prophethood after Adam and Seth.[4] Ibn Isaac stated he was the first to write with a pen, and he lived with Adam 380 years. It is puzzling how Ibn Kathir came up with this knowledge since there is no basis for it (or *any* number recorded) in the pages of the Qur'an. Moreover, any such information in the hadith is widely disputed. Ibn Kathir stated that Ibn Jarir said that the higher place mentioned in Qur'an 19:57 was ascension into the fourth heaven.[5]

> A friend of the angel of Allah carried Idris between his wings up to the fourth heaven where he met with the angel of death coming down. So the angel of death said, "Where is Idris?" The angel's friend said, "Here he is on my back." The angel of death said, "I was sent to take his spirit in the fourth heaven. So I have asked, 'How can I take a spirit of someone who lives on earth from the fourth heaven?'" So he took his spirit.

Allah was attributed with the statement in the Qur'an, *we raised him to a high place.* Ibn Abbas said he was lifted to the sixth heaven and died there. Al Hassan Al Basri said he was lifted to the garden. Others said that he was raised up in the days of his father Mahalaleel,

---

[1] wrong name, he meant Enoch, non-Arabic word of Greek/Syriac/Arabic origin
[2] wrong name, he meant Enoch
[3] wrong name, he meant Isaiah
[4] Ibn Kathir, *Stories of the Prophets*, vol. 1, Abo Al Fida Ishamail Ibn Kathir Al Kurashi Al Damashce (Beirut: Dar Al-Arab Heritage, 1408 AH, 1988), 112.
[5] Ibid., 113.

Chapter 3

and Allah knows best. Still others claimed that he did not live before the days of Noah but that he lived in the days of Israel (Jacob).

One must ask a question here. *What does the Bible teach concerning the Prophet Idris?* First of all, the name Idris, for this man, is not mentioned anywhere else. Mohammed made up the name because the real name is Enoch. He was not the son of Mahalalel (the correct spelling is found in Genesis 5:15). Mahalalel was his grandfather. His father's name was Jared. Enoch had a son by the name of Methuselah when he was sixty-five years old, and he had many sons and daughters after Methuselah. He lived 365 years, and the Bible said that he walked with God and *was not* because God took him, just as it is written in Genesis 5:18-24.

This so-called story of the Prophet Idris is a very good example of how Muslim scholars can fabricate an interpretation from a few words or verses of the Qur'an by simply copying copious information from the Bible and applying or misapplying it to whatever information they have in the Qur'an. All that we know about Idris from the Qur'an is contained in two simple verses, Qur'an 19:56-57, which simply state there was a man by the name of Idris who was a friend and prophet whom Allah lifted up to a high place. That is literally all that is written in the Qur'an. Then Ibn Kathir and his scholars in their interpretation (fabrication) told us the real name, how he related to Mohammed, how many years he lived, that he was a great writer with a pen, how many good deeds he performed, how he was taken to the fourth or perhaps the sixth heaven riding on the back of a godly angel, and how the angel of death took his spirit to heaven. They know all this information from these two simple verses of the Qur'an, but they do not know when he lived on earth, who his real father was, or even whether he lived before Noah or lived in the days of Israel. *Do you agree with me that their interpretation is pure and simple fabrication?*

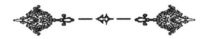

4 The Story of Noah

The story of Noah is told or at least his name is mentioned in the Qur'an forty-three times in forty-three verses. Qur'an 71 is called the Book of Noah and is primarily about Noah.

In some of these locations, only his name is listed, without any details, as one of the prophets whom Allah sent; then sometimes there is just a short passage and other times a lengthy passage as in the following verses: 3:33; 4:163; 6:84; 7:59-64; 7:69; 9:70; 10:71-74; 11:25-49, 89; 14:9; 17:3,17; 19:58; 21:76; 22:42; 23:23; 25:37; 26:105-122; 29:14-15; 33:7; 37:75-82; 38:12; 40:5, 31; 42:13; 50:12; 51:46; 53:52; 54:9; 57:26; 66:10; and 71:1-28. Although his name exists in forty-three locations, and even if one studies all that has been given by Allah in the Qur'an and all that is written in the hadith by Mohammed, one cannot answer some of the simple questions concerning the life of Noah or the life of the people of his time.

The first question one must ask is this: *who was Noah?* The answer cannot be found from the reading of the Qur'an or the hadith, but amazingly, Ibn Kathir gave us the genealogy of Noah.[1] He wrote that Noah was the son of Lamech who was the son of Matashalech, which is the wrong name (he meant Methuselah), son of Knok (he meant Enoch) whom Mohammed wrongly called Idris, son of Yard, which is the wrong name (he meant Jared), son of Mahalaleel, which is the wrong name (he meant Mahalalel), son of Caineen, which is the wrong name (he meant Cainan), son of Enos, son of Seth, son of Adam. Now a question must be asked. *Where did Ibn Kathir find all of these names of genealogy which are almost correct in the number of generations and pronunciation?* The only answer is that there is no place except in Genesis 5. Notice that the only differences between the Genesis record and his genealogical listing are minor spelling errors in the Arabic language.

He continued by saying that Noah was born 126 years after the death of Adam. *How did he come up with this date?* He must have read Genesis 5. There, one will find the ages of every one of these

---

[1] Ibn Kathir, *Stories of the Prophets*, vol. 1, Abo Al Fida Ishamail Ibn Kathir Al Kurashi Al Damashce (Beirut: Dar Al-Arab Heritage, 1408 AH, 1988), 114.

fathers and when they birthed their sons. There, and only there, can one find the age when Adam died. When you subtract the difference between when Noah was born and the day Adam died, you will find it was 126 years. Adam was 130 when he had his son Seth. Then add to that the ages of the ancestors of Noah, 105 + 90 + 70 + 65 + 162 + 65 + 187 + 182, and the total of these years is 1,056 years. Adam died at the age of 930. When we subtract the age of Adam at death from the year that Noah was born, 1,056 – 930, we find that Noah was born 126 years after the death of Adam.

Ibn Kathir continued to make fun of the Bible, considering it to be false when he said that the People of the Book said that the days between Noah's birth and the day when Adam died was 146 years. No, nothing in the Bible talks about 146 years, but it was 126, as we have just shown above.

In Sahih Bukhari, Ibn Abbas said that between Adam and Noah are ten centuries and all of them were Muslim.[2] *Did you read what I just wrote?* They were all Muslim. In other words, Adam was Muslim, Noah was Muslim, and, yes, all the generations between them were Muslim. This reminds me of the hadith, which is repeated by many Muslim scholars, where Mohammed said that when Adam was walking in the garden, he saw the written statement in the sky which was made of light which said, "There is no God but Allah and Mohammed is his messenger."[3] Then Adam asked Allah, "Who is Mohammed?" The response of Allah was: "Because of Mohammed, I created you." Wow! That is why Adam was a Muslim. He believed in Mohammed. Therefore, all the people who lived between Adam and Mohammed were believers in Islam. Some may say that the word Muslim means those who surrender or submit, meaning that they surrendered to Allah. The answer is *no*; they were literally believers in Mohammed.

One of the stranger statements of Ibn Kathir is that the generations before Noah were different than the generations of our days because people's life spans were longer then.[4] According to that, the distance between Adam and Noah was thousands of years, *and Allah knows best.* On the same page, he tells us that the time between Adam and Noah was 1,056 years, which is the difference between

---
[2]Ibid., 114.
[3]Ibid., 92.
[4]Ibid., 115.

when Adam was created and Noah was born. He contradicted himself by telling us that there were thousands of years between them. Obviously, he was confused because he knew that people lived nine hundred or so years, but he could not measure the length between those people and the following generations. Muslim scholars also disagreed on the age when Noah was sent to be a prophet. Some said he was 50 years old, others said he was 350 years old, while even others said 480 years. The real answer is in the Bible, as we will disclose later.

How long did Noah live? According to Qur'an 29:14-15: *[14]And indeed, we sent Noah to his people, so he stayed among them a thousand years less fifty. So the deluge seized them, and they were unjust. [15]So we delivered him and the companions of the ship, and we made it as a sign to the worlds.* He stayed with his people 950 years before the flood took place. In his interpretation, Nassir Ibn Ali stated that Noah was sent to his people when he was 350 years old and that he lived with them one thousand minus fifty years. Then he lived 350 years after that. Let us add these numbers: 350 + 950 + 350 = 1,650. Wow! He was an old man. According to the Bible, the number was a lot less, and we will find out how old Noah actually was when he died.

One of the statements which Mohammed repeated throughout the Qur'an was that Allah saved Noah and the companions of the ship; obviously, Mohammed did not know who the ones were who were saved on the ship. Qur'an 7:59-64 is the first time where Mohammed mentioned more than just Noah's name. *[59]Indeed, we sent Noah to his people, so he said, "O my people, serve Allah. You have no god other than him. Surely I fear for you the torment of a great day." [60]The leaders of his people said, "Surely we see that you are in obvious error." [61]He said, "O my people, there is no error in me, but I am a messenger from the lord of the worlds. [62]I deliver to you the messages of my lord, and I give you advice. And I know from Allah what you do not know. [63]Or do you wonder that a reminder came to you from your lord upon a man from among you to warn you and that you may fear and perhaps you may receive mercy?" [64]So they denied him. So we delivered him and those who were with him in the ship, and we drowned those who denied our verses. Surely they were a blind people.*

Chapter 4

One of the amazing things concerning the words of his speech to his people is that, when compared to other prophets' words to their people, it is what we call in the modern way of typing on computers *copy and paste*. It contains the exact words which other prophets used to talk to the people. This is the style of Mohammed's wording throughout the Qur'an. From reading a passage such as Qur'an 10:71-73, one can compare the wording: *[71]And recite to them the news of Noah when he said to his people, "O my people, if my dwelling with you was big,[5] and my reminding you of the verses of Allah, so on Allah I depended. So gather your affair and your partners; then do not let your affair be a burden on you. Then come to me and do not wait. [72]So if you turn away, so I have not asked you for any wage. My wage is only on Allah. And I am commanded to be of the Muslims." [73]So they denied him. So we delivered him and those who were with him in the ship, and we made them viceroys. And we drowned those who denied our verses. So see how was the end of the warned.*

Also, see Qur'an: 54:9-17: *[9]Before them the people of Noah denied, so they denied our servant and said, "Demon-possessed and rebuked." [10]So he called to his lord, "Surely I am overcome, so help me." [11]So we opened the doors of heaven with swift water. [12]And we caused the earth to gush springs, so the water met according to the preordained measure. [13]And we carried him on planks and nails. [14]Sailing before our eyes, a reward to who was an infidel. [15]And indeed, we left it a sign. So is there any who remember? [16]So how was my torment and my warning? [17]And indeed, we made the Qur'an easy to remember. So is there any who remember?*

When you study such passages and others not mentioned here concerning Noah in the Qur'an, you will notice it is the same story, just repeated. Perhaps one or two words were changed. You may wonder why Allah or Angel Gabreel repeated the story over and over again in the Qur'an. Not only is the story repeated over and over, but it is not a complete story. It is just a short version of the story. All that we learn from these verses is that Noah was sent to his people with the message to worship Allah or serve Allah, but his people did not believe in him. They called him a lost person. "No," he argued with them, "I am a messenger from Allah, the lord of the worlds," which

---

[5]bothersome

The Revelation of Error

is, according to the Bible, Satan. (The God of the Bible never describes Himself as the lord of this world, but the Bible clearly states that the god or the lord of this world is Satan. See 2 Corinthians 4:4.) So they denied him, and Allah saved him and those who believed in him.

Notice in the previous passage that the ship was made with planks and nails. According to the Bible, as well as oral and written history, that is not true because the boat was constructed with pegs. Noah did not use nails to put the ship together.

One of the strange short passages concerning Noah's wife is found in Qur'an 66:10, which directly contradicts the true account of the Bible, for Mohammed mistakenly tells us that Noah's wife and Lot's wife were admitted into hell, as it is written in the following verse: *[10]Allah set forth an example to those who became infidels: the woman [wife] of Noah and the woman [wife] of Lot. They were under two of our good servants, but they betrayed them. So they did not benefit them anything against Allah, and it was said, "Enter the fire with those who are entering."*

Someone may say that we need to read some of the other locations in the Qur'an where the long detailed story of Noah is given. Then I would ask a question. *If there are long passages in the Qur'an about Noah, why are the other locations simply bits and pieces spread throughout the Qur'an?*

Another important question needs to be asked. *Why are some of the important details in the story inconsistent? For example, what was the response of Noah's people when he advised them to serve Allah rather than whatever else they were worshiping?* Qur'an 7:60 states: *[60]The leaders of his people said, "Surely we see that you are in obvious error."* In Qur'an 11:27: *[27]So the leaders of those who became infidels from his people said, "We do not see you except a human like us, and we do not see any who follow you except they are the lowliest of us at first thought. And we do not see that you have any favor over us, yet we think you are liars."* According to Qur'an 23:24-25: *[24]So the leaders of those who became infidels among his people said, "What is this except a human like you, who desires to be preferred over you. And, if Allah willed, he would send angels. We did not hear of this from our ancient fathers. [25]He is only a man in whom is jinn, so watch him for a time."* Qur'an 26:111 states: *[111]They said, "Will we believe in you, and your followers are the lowliest?"* Then in

Chapter 4

Qur'an 71, which is the Book of Noah, in verse 7, notice what they did: *⁷And surely whenever I called them so that you may forgive them, they put their fingers in their ears and covered themselves with their clothes and persisted, and they were proudly proud.*

Noah is one of the prophets to whom Mohammed devoted an entire portion of revelation. It is Qur'an 71, consisting of twenty-eight verses. Also, another long passage is Qur'an 11:25-49. We will use these two lengthy passages to tell the story of Noah as described in the Qur'an. Since Qur'an 71 was set apart to tell the story of Noah and was even named the Book of Noah, one might expect it to have more details of his story; but the fact is, Qur'an 11:25-49 includes more details of the story of Noah when compared to the account of Noah in the Bible, Genesis 6-11. If the entire story of Noah were collected throughout the Qur'an into one passage to tell all Allah told Mohammed through his Angel Gabreel, even Muslim scholars could not answer some of the simple questions which are answered in Genesis 6-11. *For example, who was Noah?* Yes, Muslim scholar Ibn Kathir gave us his ancestry, but the question is this: *where did he get this information, as we have questioned earlier?*

But can Muslims tell us who Noah was, without reading the Genesis account? For sure, the answer is *no*. *When was Noah born, and how long did he live? When did he die? Who were the people in his family? When were they born? Who were the people he was sent to? Was there any description of the ship which he built, such as the material with which it was built, dimensions, and time needed to build it? What about the length of time it rained, the duration of the flood, or where the ship came to rest?*

Yes, the Qur'an says the ship rested on Mt. Jūdī, a mountain in Mesopotamia near Mosul. However, that is obviously the wrong name, as we will see in the biblical account. There are many other questions, and the answer from those who are called Muslim scholars is simply *Allah knows best*.

Let us look first to the Book of Noah, and we will add to it the missing information from Qur'an 11. Then we will compare what has been given in the Qur'an with the Genesis account in the Holy Bible.

Qur'an 71:1-4 states: *¹Surely we sent Noah to his people: "That warn your people before a painful torment comes to them." ²He said, "O my people, surely I am to you a plain warner. ³That serve Allah and fear him and obey me. ⁴He will forgive you some of your sin, and he will delay you to an appointed time. Surely when the appointed time of Allah comes, it will not be delayed, if you were knowing."*

Allah sent Noah to his people, although we do not know who they were, to warn them of a painful torment. I thought he was supposed to warn them that they would drown. *What is a painful torment?* He commanded people to serve Allah and obey him. He promised them that Allah would forgive some of their sin. *What about the rest of the sin that Allah will not forgive? Also, what is the punishment of the sin that Allah will forgive? Who will pay for the sin which Allah will forgive?* No sin should be forgiven without a punishment for God is just, as He said in Hebrews 9:22: ..."**Without shedding of blood there is no remission [of sin].**" God teaches that the wages of sin is death (Romans 3:23). Noah also promised his people that Allah will delay them to an appointed time. *What does Allah mean by that?*

According to Qur'an 71:5-9: *⁵He said, "My lord, surely I have called my people night and day. ⁶So my call did not increase them except flight. ⁷And surely whenever I called them so that you may forgive them, they put their fingers in their ears and covered themselves with their clothes and persisted, and they were proudly proud. ⁸Then surely I called to them publicly. ⁹Then surely I announced to them, and secretly I gave them secrets.*

Here Noah was speaking to Allah, telling him that he called on his people, and his calling did not cause them to believe but rather to go further away. They refused to even hear his preaching, and they were proud. In many ways he tried to lead them to Allah, but they rejected his words. Noah sought forgiveness from Allah, the forgiver. In the following verses, 10-19, Noah preached to his people as he explained to them how Allah is the creator and he created the seven heavens, which is the wrong number according to the Bible.

In verse 15, he taught that the moon which Allah created is a light; this is also an error. In verses 16-17, the people came out of the earth, and they will return to it. In verse 19, the earth is flat, which is another error. See these teachings for yourself in Qur'an 71:10-20:
*¹⁰So I said, "Ask forgiveness of your lord, surely he was forgiving. ¹¹He will send the heavens above you with abundance.*⁶ *¹²And he will aid you with money and sons, and*

---
⁶rain

he will make gardens for you and will make rivers for you. *¹³What is [the matter] with you that you do not hope to Allah a reverence, ¹⁴and indeed, he created you in stages? ¹⁵Have you not seen how Allah created seven heavens one above another? ¹⁶And he made the moon in them[7] light, and he made the sun a lamp. ¹⁷And Allah planted you from the earth plants. ¹⁸Then he will return you into it[8] and bring you forth a bringing forth. ¹⁹And Allah spread the earth out for you ²⁰so that you may walk in it along spacious ways."*

In the following five verses, Noah once again was speaking to Allah, explaining the state of frustration and how they refused to worship Allah but actually worshiped their gods, Wadd and Sowah and Yaghuth and Ya'uq and Nasr. Muslim scholar Ibn Jarir stated that these were righteous people who lived between the days of Adam and Noah and that they did have followers who were guided by them.[9] When these righteous people died, their companions who were guided by them, made pictures of them, but others said statues. But when these companions died, a new generation came after them, whom Satan deceived, telling them that their ancestors were worshiping them. These pictures or statues used to bring the blessing of rain and other blessings, so people continued to worship them until Mohammed's days.

Other scholars like Ibn Abu Hatem said that Aroah said that these five people were sons of Adam and that Wadd was the oldest.[10] Not only did the people of Noah worship these gods, but they also led others astray. As Noah said, in the end of 71:24: *"...And [my lord], do not increase the unjust except in error."* This was an astonishing statement, for this described Allah in a very ungodly way. *How can a god increase those who are lost into an even deeper error?* As is written in the following passage, they were drowned and entered the fire of hell, obviously without finding any relief from the punishment of Allah as seen in Qur'an 71:21-25: *²¹Noah said, "My lord, surely they disobeyed me, and they followed those who did not increase him their money and son except in loss. ²²And they deceived a big deception. ²³And they said, 'Do not forsake*

---
[7] the seven heavens
[8] the earth
[9] Ibn Kathir, 120.
[10] Ibid.

The Revelation of Error

your gods and do not forsake Wadd nor Sowah nor Yaghuth and Yahuk and Nasr."[11] *²⁴And indeed, they led many astray. And [my lord], do not increase the unjust except in error." ²⁵Because of their sins they were drowned, so they were admitted into the fire, and they did not find for themselves a helper without Allah.*

Finally, in Qur'an 71:26, Noah is asking Allah not to leave any infidels on earth. This is another strange statement, for he knows the flood killed everybody. *So how can Allah leave some infidels on earth after he killed everybody?* His fear was that if Allah left some of these infidels on earth alive, they might lead the believers astray as written in verse 27. In verse 28, Noah is asking forgiveness for his sin, his parents' sin, and for the sin of all believers who enter his house as written in the following verses: *²⁶And Noah said, "My lord, do not leave any infidel dwellers on the earth. ²⁷Surely if you leave them, they will lead your servant astray, and they will not beget except wicked infidel. ²⁸My lord, forgive me and my parents and believers who enter my house and the believing men and believing women, and do not increase the unjust except in destruction."* From the previous verses, we can assume there were many believers who fled the flood with Noah, *but is that true?*

Now, let us look at the final passage which comes from Qur'an 11. We will not look at the entire passage but just the verses which are not duplicated in the verses from Qur'an 71 discussed above. In verses 27-30, it is written as follows: *²⁷So the leaders of those who became infidels from his people said, "We do not see you except a human like us, and we do not see any who follow you except they are the lowliest of us at first thought. And we do not see that you have any favor over us, yet we think you are liars." ²⁸He said, "O my people, have you seen that if I were with a proof from my lord and he has given me mercy from himself, so it was hidden from you, can we force it on you while you hate it? ²⁹And, O my people, I do not ask you money for it, that my wage is only except on Allah. And I will not drive away those who believed, surely they will meet their lord. But I see that you are an ignorant people. ³⁰And, O my people, who will give me help against Allah if I drive them away, do you not remember?"*

---

[11]Some scholars state that these are pagan Arab gods.

Chapter 4

These verses show the rejection of Noah by the people of Noah because of two reasons. First, Noah was just a human; second, Noah's followers were the lowliest of the people. Noah explained that he did not want any reward or wages. He could not drive the lowliest away from his ship because, if he did so, they would complain to Allah.

The length of time which Noah disputed with his people is mentioned in Qur'an 11:32: *[32]They said, "O Noah, indeed, you have disputed with us, so you dispute much with us. So bring on us what you promise us, if you were of the truthful."* Ibn Kathir stated that the length of this time was 950 years; and he wrote that, although it was a long time, just a few believed in him.[12] He also explained that when the sons of the infidel people grew up, their parents advised them never to believe in Noah as long as they lived.

Here is a description of the ship which Noah built in Qur'an 11:36-38: *[36]And it was revealed to Noah: "That none of your people will believe except those who have believed, so do not grieve at what they were doing. [37]And make the ship by our eyes and our revelation. And do not speak to me about the unjust, surely they will be drowned." [38]And while making the ship, whenever leaders of his people passed by, they scorned him. He said, "If you scorn us, surely we will scorn you as you scorn.* What ship? What size? What was it made of? What was the shape of the ship? Did it have any windows? Did they enter through some doors or from the roof?* Obviously, Muslims cannot know unless they read the account in Genesis.

Who was on the ship? So far, Noah and his people, who were from the lowliest of the society, were on board. In Qur'an 11:40, we discover that the water rose, and then Allah asked Noah to take two of every pair. *Is this what really happened in the Bible? Or, perhaps there was a period of time after everyone was on the ship and then the flood took place.*

Ibn Abbas said the first to enter the ship were the birds and the last to enter was the donkey. According to Ibn Kathir, Satan entered hanging on its tail.[13] Ibn Kathir continued saying that when Noah carried with him on the ship a pair of each animal, his companions said, "How can we not be troubled and all the animals not be troubled when the lion is with us." So Allah made the lion sick with fever.

---

[12]Ibn Kathir, 123.
[13]Ibid., 128.

The Revelation of Error

This was the first fever on earth. Then his companions complained about the rat. They said that it would contaminate the food and supplies. Then Allah caused the lion to sneeze. A cat came out of him, and the rat hid from the cat.

It was also written that Noah was told to take two of every pair, four elephants, four cows, four sheep, four doves, four dogs, and four pigs (perhaps some Muslims would say pigs were made later when Allah cursed some of the Jews to become pigs in Moses' days). *Isn't that two of every pair?* Obviously, there is something wrong here. That would mean he would take four of every kind. You will get the answer when we read the Genesis account.

Muslim scholars disagree about the number of people who were with Noah on the ship. Ibn Abbas said there were eighty persons with their wives, but Kaab Al Ahbar said there were seventy-two people. Others said there were ten. Still others said that there was Noah and his three sons and four wives, with the wife of his son Yam. This final opinion is not acceptable since the verses of the Qur'an say that there was a group of people, who were not his family, who believed in him. Amazingly, this is the closest answer to the facts of the Bible.

As for the wife of Noah, the mother of his five sons, Ham, Shem, Japheth, Yam, whom the People of the Book call Canaan, and Aaber, it is said that she died before the flood because of infidelity. Some say that perhaps she became an infidel after that. What chaos and disagreement about almost everything! Ibn Kathir stated that it was said that Noah's three sons, Ham, Shem, and Japheth, were born after the flood.[14] Then Ibn Kathir corrected this information by stating this was not true because Ham, Shem, and Japheth were in the ship with Noah. This shows the level of chaos concerning the knowledge of Noah by Muslim scholars.

It was also said that Ham had sexual relations with his wife on the ship. Noah cursed him and called on Allah to cause his child to be disfigured. As a result, Ham's wife had a black child who was named Canaan, son of Ham, the grandfather of the Sudanese people.[15]

Then Allah asked Noah to take on the ship with him all his family, except the one who Allah said would not be saved. The story continues in Qur'an 11:39-41 with Allah speaking: *[39]So you will know who will receive torment, it will shame him and will dwell*

---
[14]Ibid., 132
[15]Ibid.

on him, a lasting torment." ⁴⁰Until when our command came and the tannūr[16] *gushed up.*[17] *We said, "Carry in it from every pair two and your family, except against whom the word has already gone forth, and those who believed." And no one believes in him, except a few. ⁴¹And he said, "Embark in it. In the name of Allah, its sailing and its anchoring. Surely my lord is forgiving, merciful."*

One of the astonishing verses concerning Noah's story is verse 40 which says: ...except *against whom the word has already gone forth. Who was Allah talking about?* The answer is Noah's son, as we read in verses 42-43: *⁴²And it*[18] *sailed on with them amid waves like mountains. And Noah called to his son, and he was apart: "O my son, embark with us and do not be with the infidels." ⁴³He said, "I will take refuge to a mountain that will secure me from the water." He said, "No one will be secure today from the command of Allah except him on whom he will have mercy." And the waves passed between them, so he was among the drowned.*

The ship moved in the water which was like a mountain, meaning that the water was really high and the waves were high as well. I can only imagine the conversation between Noah and his son, as Noah called to his son, "O my son, come be with us. Do not be with the infidel." However, the foolish son said to his father, "No, I will take refuge on top of the mountain." Then the waves came between him and his father, and he drowned. Of course, for Muslims who have never read the Bible, that is what happened. That must be it! After all, the Qur'an says so. One must ask a question. *Who was this son? Did he have a name?* Such a foolish son must be known.

In his interpretation, Al Qurtobi said that Noah's son was riding on a horse which he liked when he saw the water rising.[19] He announced it to his father Noah, and his father asked him to come and ride with him on the ship. But as the waves came between them, he drowned. Al Qurtobi also stated that others said he took for himself a house, made of glass, so that he might save himself from the water. He lived inside the house, urinating and defecating until he drowned

---

[16]oven, non-Arabic word of Persian or Akkadian or Aramaic origin
[17]like froth on milk
[18]the ship
[19]http://quran.Al-islam.com/Page.Aspx?pageid=221&BookID=14&Page=226, accessed October 17, 2011.

The Revelation of Error

in that. However, others said he sought refuge on Mt. Sinai. Still, no one knows, so far, who this son was. Muslim scholars also stated that Noah's son died because he was a product of adultery.[20] This is based on Al Tabari saying that in Ali's reading of Qur'an 11:42, the reference to Noah's son as *her* son rather than *his* son indicates that Noah had not fathered this son. Also, Noah's wife was said to be an infidel. Therefore, neither Noah's wife nor son survived the flood.

In the interpretation of Muslim scholars of Qur'an 66:10, the wife of Noah betrayed him, but they all insist that it was *in the religion,* not sexually, as an attempt to deny that the prophet's wife committed adultery. However, they forget that Prophet David committed adultery, as we will see in his section. Also, Mohammed committed adultery, as we will see in his section. The conclusion we must draw is that the Qur'an says Noah's wife did commit adultery. *Can Muslims not see the confusion of their own scholars?*

The story of Noah is recorded in Qur'an 11:44-49: *[44]And it was said, "O earth, swallow up your water," and "O heaven, desist." And the water abated, and the command was fulfilled. And the ship sat on the Jūdī,[21] and it was said, "Away with the unjust people." [45]And Noah called on his lord, so he said, "My lord, surely my son is of my family, and surely your promise is true. And you are the wisest of the judges." [46]He said, "O Noah, surely he is not of your family, surely he did what is not good. So do not ask what you have no knowledge of. Surely I preach to you, lest you become of the ignorant."*

[47]He said, "My lord, surely I seek refuge in you, that I ask you of what I do not have knowledge. And unless you forgive me and be merciful to me, I will be of the losers." [48]It was said, "O Noah, go down with peace from us and blessings on you and on nations who are with you. And nations, we will give them enjoyment. Then we will afflict them with a painful torment." [49]This is some of the news of the unseen; we reveal it to you. You did not know it, neither your people before this, so be patient. Surely the end is to the fearer.

Although Ibn Kathir did not provide interpretation for these verses in his book, *The Stories of the Prophets,* he went into great

---

[20]http://quran.Al-islam.com/Page.aspx?pageid=221&BookID=14&Page=238, accessed January 19, 2012.

[21]mountain in Mesopotamia near Mosul, non-Arabic word of possible Syriac origin

Chapter 4

detail in his own interpretation.[22] The following is a summary of that interpretation. Allah said that he flooded all of the people of the earth except the companions of the ship. Allah commanded the earth to swallow its water, which came from it, and the water was gathered to it. He then commanded the heaven to cease the rain. All the people of the earth, except the companions of the ship, were destroyed. Allah took the ship to Mecca, and the ship circled around the Kaaba for forty days.

Then Ibn Kathir said that Allah took the ship to Mt. Jūdī where it rested. Noah sent the raven and later the dove, which came back to him with an olive leaf, and she had mud on her feet. *Where do you suppose Ibn Kathir came up with this information, since it does not exist in the Qur'an?* Noah asked Allah for his drowned son, for Allah is the wisest of the wise. He told Allah, "You promised to save my family." Allah responded, "He is not of your family. That is why I told you before that some of your family will not make it." Allah went on to say that the drowned son was not really his son. Opinions differ, but some say he was the son of adultery while others say he was the son of Noah's wife. Allah caused the water to recede slowly, and Noah took off the cover of the ship. Noah got out of the ship when Allah said, "Come down with our peace." *Once again, where did this information come from?*

The Lifetime of Noah According to the Bible

Now, let us look into the true account of Noah as is written in Genesis. The genealogy of Noah can be found in Genesis 5. I encourage the reader to read the entire chapter. He was Noah, son of Lamech, son of Methuselah, son of Enoch, son of Jared, son of Mahalalel, son of Cainan, son of Enosh, son of Seth, son of Adam. It is amazing that the Bible can give us not only the true genealogy of Noah but also the ages of each one of these ancestors. We can find in the Bible the genealogy from Adam, with the dates, to our Lord and Savior Jesus Christ. This brings us to the conclusion that from the time of Creation, the earth and heaven have only existed for around six thousand years.

According to the Bible, God called Noah to build the ark when he was five hundred years old. He had three sons, Shem, Ham, and

---

[22]http://quran.Al-islam.com/Page.aspx?pageid=221&BookID=11&Page=226-227, accessed December 16, 2012.

Japheth (Genesis 5:32). Because the evil of men was great and all the thoughts of their hearts were wicked all day long, the Lord was sorrowful in His heart that He had made man. Therefore, He made the decision to remove man along with all the creatures of the earth (Genesis 6:5-7).

Did God destroy all creatures and all men? The answer is *no*. In Genesis 6:8, the Bible says that Noah found grace in the eyes of the Lord, and God spoke to him, asking him to build an ark. He told Noah exactly how it was to be built and from what it was to be constructed. The ark had to be built from gopher wood. He had to coat it inside and outside with pitch. The Bible also gives the following dimensions: the length of the ark to be three hundred cubits, the breadth to be fifty cubits, and the height to be thirty cubits. It also says there would be a window above, the door was to be set in the side, and it must contain three stories. Neither Mohammed nor Allah his god knew anything about this blueprint given to Noah.

God made a covenant with Noah and his family. He asked Noah to take with him a male and female of every creature, birds, cattle, and creeping things after their own kind (Genesis 6:19-20), not four (two pairs) as Mohammed claimed. God said to take seven of every clean animal (Genesis 7:2-3). Noah also took food for himself and all those who were in the ark. Again, I encourage the reader to read the entire story in Genesis 5-11. Notice, the story is not repeated throughout the Bible but is told completely in this one location.

Who were the ones saved in the flood? It was only Noah and his family. Eight people were saved from the flood. The Qur'an states that it was Noah and his people. One may say the people were his family, but that is not true according to Qur'an 11:27 as quoted earlier: [27]*So the leaders of those who became infidels from his people said, "We do not see you except a human like us, and we do not see any who follow you except they are the lowliest of us at first thought. And we do not see that you have any favor over us, yet we think you are liars."* In other words, the people told Noah that those who followed Noah were the lowliest.

According to Qur'an 66:10, as we discussed previously, Noah's wife was not a believer and drowned. And of course, *Allah knows best*. However, the Bible states that she was one of the eight who was saved from the flood. The eight people were Noah, his wife, their three sons, and their three daughters-in-law.

What about the time from the completion of the ark to the beginning of the flood? According to the Qur'an, the rain began when Noah and his people were gathering the animals, but completely different information is given in the Bible. Noah and his family had one full week before the beginning of the rain. This all took place when Noah was six hundred years old.

How long did the rain last? Mohammed did not know. According to the Bible, the rain lasted forty days and forty nights (Genesis 7:12). The water went higher than all the mountains, and all flesh and every bird, cattle, creeping thing, and all people who lived on the earth died (Genesis 7:22). The water prevailed above the earth 150 days, and then it began to recede slowly (Genesis 8:3). *Where did the ark come to rest?* According to Qur'an 11:44, the ship set down on Mount Jūdī. However, the Bible gives a completely different answer. It came to rest on Mount Ararat (Genesis 8:4) as discovered by archeologists.

Forty days later, Noah sent out a raven which flew back and forth until the earth began to dry. Then he sent out a dove which came back because she could not find a place to rest her feet. Seven days later he sent the dove out again. This time she returned with olive leaves in her beak. Finally, one week later, he sent her out again, but this time she did not come back. That is when Noah removed the cover of the ark. He knew that the earth was dry. God spoke to Noah asking him and his family to come out of the ark with all the creatures, birds, and creeping things so that they could be fruitful and multiply on the earth.

The first thing Noah did after coming out of the ark was to build an altar to the Lord and to offer a sacrifice from the clean beasts and birds to the Lord. This is a very important part of the story which Mohammed purposely chose to ignore. God blessed Noah and his family, and He allowed them to eat every living creature on earth. This was the first time men began to eat animals' flesh (Genesis 9:3). Before that time, God did not allow people to eat animals; mankind and animals were vegetarians according to Genesis 1:29-30.

Why did Noah curse his son? Who was this son? Muslim scholars give us the wrong name and wrong reasons as we read that Ham had a black son as a result of the curse because he had a sexual relationship with his wife on the ship. First of all, I do not see any reason for Muslim scholars to consider any of Noah's sons having a sexual relationship with his own wife on the ark to be a sinful act. It was not a sin to do so. Second, choosing a black color as a result of a curse as

Muslim scholars and Mohammed always do is despicable and racist towards me and my people from Africa. It is amazing how Muslims in the West lie to blacks by trying to convince them that Islam respects them and rejects slavery. However, the opposite is actually true, for even the word *abd* in the Arabic language is used for both the color black and for a slave. Throughout the Qur'an Allah allowed Muslims to have slaves, and so did Mohammed throughout the hadith.

What about the true story? Why did Noah curse his son, Ham? We read this in the true account of Genesis 9:20-27. We encourage the reader to read the entire account in the Bible. Noah planted vineyards and then drank from the wine. He became drunk and was naked in his tent. Ham *saw* the nakedness of his father and told his brothers outside of the tent. Shem and Japheth covered their father without looking at their father's nakedness. When Noah woke and discovered what had happened, he cursed Ham's son, Canaan, to be a servant to his brothers, but he blessed Shem and Japheth.

How long did Noah live? The Bible states that Noah lived 350 years after the flood, and the total years of his life were 950. Then he died (Genesis 9:28-29). As for the children of Noah and their descendants and their journeys and the change of the languages, the entire story can be found in Genesis 10-11. We encourage the reader to read the entire story.

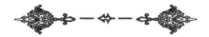

The Story of Houd

The story of Houd is written throughout the Qur'an although there is no specific information of who Houd was or who his people, the people of Ad, were or where they lived. Mohammed inserted this story in the following passages of the Qur'an: 7:65-72; 11:50-60; 23:31-41; 26:123-140; 41:15-16; 46:21-25; 53:41-55; 54:18-22; 69:6-8; and 89:6-14. I do not believe there was a prophet named Houd simply because if he had existed, the Bible would surely have told us about him. Moreover, no historical or archeological evidence exists to show that either the man or the location ever existed. Muslims have attempted to provide proof of them, but what they have done is to copy a fraudulent picture, alter it, and assert that this is one of the people of Ad which shows men to be over fifty feet tall.[1] The photo's caption states that the people of Ad lived from 70,000-7000 BC. Muslims claim that they were the ones who built the pyramids. In reality, none of the Egyptian mummies are taller than six feet or are older than 4000 BC.

Who was Houd? In Ibn Kathir's writings, he stated that Houd was Ibn Salak, (he apparently meant Salah), Ibn Arphaxaz (he apparently meant Arphaxad), Ibn Shem, Ibn Noah.[2] Ibn Kathir then contradicted himself by stating that Houd was Eber, Ibn Salak, Ibn Arphaxaz, Ibn Shem, Ibn Noah. In another opinion, Ibn Kathir said that Houd was Ibn Abd Allah, Ibn Rabah, Ibn Al Jarood, Ibn Ad, Ibn Aos, Ibn Aram, Ibn Shem, Ibn Noah. As you can see above, three sets of names are given, and not one Muslim scholar can come up with a credible genealogy of Houd.

Here is the question we must ask again. *What source did Ibn Kathir use to come up with these names?* All that he said was "Houd came to his people." No extra information was given. The obvious answer is that, although he misspelled some of them, these names can be found among the descendants of Shem as written in Genesis 10:20-31. Ibn Kathir, however, described who the people of Ad were and where they lived. Ibn Kathir stated that they were Arabs who lived on

---

[1] David Emery, "Giant Skeletons Found in Middle East," About.com Urban Legends, accessed March 2, 2012, http://urbanlegends.about.com/ library/bl_giant_skeleton.htm.
[2] Ibn Kathir, *Stories of the Prophets*, vol. 1, Abo Al Fida Ishamail Ibn Kathir Al Kurashi Al Damashce (Beirut: Dar Al-Arab Heritage, 1408 AH, 1988), 138.

a sand mountain in Yemen from Aaman to Hadra. They used to live in tents which had huge pillars. According to Qur'an 89:6-7: *⁶Have you not seen how your lord did with Ad? ⁷At Iram,³ that with columns,* Ibn Kathir stated that these are the first (people of) Ad. Ibn Kathir also stated that this city of Iram used to be a city which moved in a circle around the earth. Sometimes it was in Sham, sometimes it was in Yemen, sometimes it was in Hijaz, and sometimes it was in other places. He then wrote there was no proof of such a thing.

The Correct Hadith of Ibn Haban stated that there were four prophets who were Arabs: Houd, Selah, Shoaib, and Mohammed.⁴ This is strange, for Mohammed claimed that he was the only prophet who came to the Arab people and that no one came to his people before him. Here we come to another disagreement among Muslim scholars.⁵ Some said Houd was the first man to speak the Arabic language. Others said his father was the first one who spoke it; however, others said Noah was the first one. Finally, others said Adam was the first one who spoke Arabic.

I have a question. *Why were Allah and the angels not the first ones to speak the Arabic language?* Ibn Kathir stated that Ishmael was the first man who spoke the classic Arabic, and he learned it from those neighbors who used to visit him and his mother.⁶ Ibn Kathir continued by saying that the people of Ad were the first ones who worshiped idols after the flood. They used to have three idols: Sada, Samoda, and Hera. That is why Allah sent to them their brother Houd.

The following passage gives the long story of Houd.⁷ Ibn Kathir explained that the people were infidels and rebellious Arabs. They were worshiping idols. Therefore, Allah sent a messenger, a man from among them calling them to worship Allah alone. If they obeyed him, Allah would forgive them and give them the good of this world. If they did not obey him, Allah threatened them with the punishment of this world and the world hereafter. That is what is stated in Qur'an 7:65-66: *⁶⁵And to Ad, their brother Houd said, "O my people, serve Allah. You have no god other than him. Do you not fear?" ⁶⁶The leaders of his people who became infidels said, "Surely*

---

³non-Arabic word of undetermined origin
⁴Ibn Kathir, 138.
⁵Ibid., 139.
⁶Ibid.
⁷Ibid., 142.

we see that you are unsound of mind, and we surely think you are of the liars."

Ibn Kathir stated that the people of Ad thought it was a foolish thing when Houd asked them to leave their idols, which they believed were helping them, and instead insisted they worship Allah alone, for they did not believe that Allah had sent him at all. Houd's response was to defend himself by explaining that the situation was not what they thought, that he was indeed faithful without lying, and he had not added or taken away to cause any misunderstanding, disagreement, or worry. This is described in the following verses of Qur'an 7:67-70:
[67]He said, "O my people, there is not unsoundness of mind in me, but I am a messenger from the lord of the worlds. [68]I deliver to you the messages of my lord, and I am to you a faithful adviser. [69]Or do you wonder that a reminder came to you from your lord upon a man among you to warn you? And remember when he made you viceroys after the people of Noah and increased you in tallness of stature? So remember the favors of Allah, perhaps you may prosper." [70]They said, "Have you come to us that we may serve Allah alone and leave what was our fathers serving? So bring to us what you promise us, if you were of the truthful."

Ibn Kathir interpreted Qur'an 7:70 by stating that the response of the people to Houd was a careless one.[8] They refused to leave the gods which their fathers and their relatives worshiped. They also challenged Houd by saying, "If you are truthful, then bring the torment and the punishment you claimed upon us." He replied to them, "You deserve the uncleanness of the idols and the anger of Allah to be upon you for you worshiped idols who you and your fathers carved and named."[9]

"Allah did not give any authority. If you refuse the truth and continue in the vanity, the torment of Allah will fall on you." This was Ibn Kathir's interpretation of Qur'an 7:71: *[71]He said, "Indeed, vengeance and wrath fell on you from your lord. Do you dispute with me in names that you and your fathers named them which Allah did not send it down with authority? So wait, surely I am with you among those who wait."*

---

[8]Ibid., 144.
[9]Ibid., 145.

The Revelation of Error

    As for the punishment from Allah, it was given in Qur'an 7:72: *⁷²So we delivered him and those who were with him with mercy from us, and we cut off, to the last, those who denied our verses. And they were not believers.* This theme is repeated in Qur'an 11:58-60: *⁵⁸And when our command came, we delivered Houd and those who believed with him with a mercy from us, and we delivered them from a thick¹⁰ torment. ⁵⁹And this was Ad. They disbelieved in the verses of their lord and rebelled against his messengers and followed the command of every powerful stubborn. ⁶⁰And they followed a curse in this world and on the resurrection day. Is it not surely Ad became infidels of their lord, except away with Ad, the people of Houd.* Then in Qur'an 23:41: *⁴¹So the shout seized them with the truth, so we made them as scum. So away with the unjust people!* Also, Qur'an 26:139-140 continues by saying: *¹³⁹So they denied him, so we destroyed them. Surely in this is a sign, and most of them were not believers. ¹⁴⁰And surely your lord he is the dear, the merciful.* As for the exact description, Ibn Kathir referred to Qur'an 46:24: *²⁴So when they saw it coming straight for their valleys, they said, "It is a passing with rain." Yet, it is what you are hastening with, a storm, in it is a painful torment.*[11]

    Ibn Kathir said that this was the beginning of the torment. They were in a drought and seeking water. When they saw the heavens with a cloud, they thought water was coming, but instead it was a torment. That was why Allah said, "That is what you were hastening to which is the falling of the torment." Ibn Kathir said that interpreters said that "Allah withheld the rain for three years. This was difficult for them, so they sought help from Allah for the sake of his sanctity and the sanctity of his house which was known at this time."

    That is why it was said that the people of Ad sent seventy men to bring them a drink from Mecca.[12] They met with a man by the name of Maawayah, and they stayed in his house. They lived in his house for an entire month drinking wine. Because of the lengthy time they stayed, he experienced financial hardship trying to take care of them, but he was embarrassed to ask them to leave. That is why he wrote poetry to them to politely ask them to leave. Then they remembered

---

[10] great
[11] Ibn Kathir, 145.
[12] Ibid., 146.

why they were there. They stood up to ask Allah to send rain to the people. Allah sent three clouds—white, black, and red. Then a voice came from heaven saying, "Choose for you and your people one of these clouds." Then he said, "I choose the black one; it is heavy with water." Then Allah said, "You choose dust (destruction), and no one will be left in Ad, neither a father nor a son."

The people of Ad who were in Mecca were not harmed; they were the ancestors of the people of the second Ad. A severe storm brought destruction to Ad for seven nights and eight days. As for Houd and the believers who were with them, it was said that they were separated from the storm, and so they were not harmed. It only softened their skin and brought pleasure to their souls. As for the people of Ad, the storm hit them with big rocks.

A similar story to this one is repeated.[13] Ibn Kathir said that, in a similar way, maybe the second Ad was destroyed. Maawayah said for the second Ad that the cloud had lightning, but for the first Ad it was just a storm. The result was that the people of Ad became like tree stumps with no heads. This is shown in the following verse in Qur'an 54:20: *[20]People will be uprooted as if they were cut palm tree stumps.* That was because the storm came to some of them and carried some of them upside down; and when they dropped from the wind, their heads were smashed as they were dropped upside down, head first. They were headless bodies. The same message is repeated in Qur'an 41:16: *[16]So we sent on them a tempestuous wind for unfortunate days so that we might make them taste the shameful torment in the world's life. And the torment of the hereafter is more shameful, and they will not be helped.* The message is repeated in Qur'an 54:18-22: *[18]Ad denied. So how was my torment and my warning? [19]Surely we sent a roaring wind against them in a day of continued misfortune. [20]People will be uprooted as if they were cut palm tree stumps. [21]So how was my torment and my warning? [22]And indeed, we made the Qur'an easy to remember. So is there any who remember?* Notice here that the punishment of the people of Ad was one day which contradicts what was written previously and will be explained in more detail in the following writing of Ibn Kathir which taught that it was seven nights and eight days.

---

[13]Ibid., 147-148.

The Revelation of Error

Now let's look at the following verses in Qur'an 51:41-42: *⁴¹And in Ad, we sent the barren wind on thom. ⁴²And it did not leave anything as it came over, except it made it like decay.* Ibn Kathir once again described this storm as "barren; it did not bring clouds, and it did not cause the trees to be pollinated for nothing good came from it, only destruction."

Almost the same story is repeated in the following passage in Qur'an 11:50-60. Verse 50 states: *⁵⁰And to Ad, their brother Houd said, "O my people, serve Allah. You have no god other than him. That you are only forgers.* Ibn Kathir interpreted this verse by stating that Houd spoke to the people, asking them, "Do you have any mind to differentiate or understand that I call you to the truth? Your instinct should tell you it is the religion of truth which Allah sent to Noah."[14] Houd told them, "Here I am, and I do not ask you for my wages, for my wages come from Allah which has the harm and benefit" as is written in the following verse: *⁵¹O my people, I do not ask you a wage for it, for my wage is only from him who created me. Do you not understand?*

Qur'an 11:52 continues: *⁵²And, O my people, ask forgiveness of your lord, then repent to him. He will send down the heaven on you with abundant and increase you power over your power, and do not turn away, criminals."* Here the Prophet Houd encouraged his people to turn to Allah and seek forgiveness for their sin, so he would bless them with the rain from heaven and make them a powerful people.

Ibn Kathir interpreted the following two verses defending the people of Ad, for they had said to Houd:

> You have not brought us any miraculous thing to make us believe in you. We will not leave our idols just because of your words. For you do not have evidence, and we think you have become crazy. We believe our gods struck your mind and made you crazy.

Then we read in Qur'an 11:53-55: *⁵³They said, "O Houd, you have not brought us proof. And we will not abandon our gods at your word, and we are not believers in you. ⁵⁴We say that some of our gods have smitten you with evil." He said, "Surely I witness Allah. And surely I witness that I am innocent of what*

---

[14]Ibid., 142.

you partner [55]*without him, so all of you together scheme against me, then you will not be delayed.* Ibn Kathir said that here Houd challenged the people of Ad and declared his innocence from their gods for they do not benefit nor harm.

Ibn Kathir interpreted the following verses by explaining that Prophet Houd was proven as the servant of Allah and his messenger. He also proves that the people were foolish in their service to other gods than Allah. Then Houd explained that he would depend on and trust in Allah, and he would be oblivious to all other creatures and would not depend on them or serve them. Qur'an 11:56-57 states: *[56]Surely I depend on Allah, my lord and your lord. There is not a creature except he takes it by her forelock. Surely, my lord is on a straight way. [57]So if you turn away, so indeed, I have delivered to you what I was sent with to you. And my lord will raise a successor nation other than you, and you will not harm him anything. Surely my lord is a keeper over all things."*

Sometimes the Qur'an continues to tell a story without any specific names, but Ibn Kathir would select a passage and use it as if it concerned some specific prophet. A good example of this is Qur'an 23:31-41 which some scholars claim to refer to the people of Houd. However, others claim they were the people of Themoud for whom the punishment in verse 41 was the shout which seized them, while the people of Ad were punished with a storm. Ibn Kathir stated that it could be that both of them came together, the shout and the wind.

When we read Qur'an 23:31-40, we discover that the verses do not give details about whom these verses were written. Verses 31-32 read: *[31]Then we raised up after them another generation. [32]So we sent to them a messenger from among them: "That serve Allah, you have no god other than him. Do you not fear?"* Ibn Kathir stated that the people of Ad thought it was unlikely for Allah to send a human messenger and this way of looking at the prophet was foolishness to the people in the early days and even in this day.[15]

Looking at verses 33-34, once again these verses are very general and could fit any people groups on any piece of land at any time: *[33]And the leaders of his people, those who became infidels, and they denied the meeting[16] of the hereafter, and though we give them plenty of enjoyment in the world's life, said, "This is*

---

[15]Ibid., 143
[16]Day of Judgment

The Revelation of Error

just a human like you. He eats from what you eat from and drinks from what you drink. ³⁴And if you obey a human like yourselves, then surely you will be losers.

Ibn Kathir interpreted verses 35-40: *³⁵Does he promise you that if you die and were dust and bones, you will be coming out? ³⁶Far away, far away is what you promised. ³⁷This is only our life of this world: we die and we live and we will not be raised. ³⁸He is just a man who forged lies against Allah, and we will not believe in him." ³⁹He said, "Lord, help me for they denied me!" ⁴⁰He said, "In a little while, they will surely become regretful."* He stated that the people of Ad disregarded the resurrection of the flesh after it becomes dust and bones. They thought after death there would be no life, as many people of the old age believed that there is no life after death, for the womb brings forth life and the earth swallows it.

A similar passage is repeated in the following verses. Notice that there is more than one messenger when it says that they called the messengers liars although the story shows but one messenger, Houd.[17]

Qur'an 26:123-129 states: *¹²³Ad denied the messengers. ¹²⁴And when their brother Houd said to them, "Will you not fear? ¹²⁵Surely I am a faithful messenger to you. ¹²⁶So fear Allah, and obey me. ¹²⁷And I do not ask you any wage for it; my wage is but on the lord of the worlds. ¹²⁸Do you build in every high place a wasteful masterpiece? ¹²⁹And you take castles, perhaps you will live forever.* Ibn Kathir interpreted the last two verses by saying that Houd said to them, "Will you build in a very high place great buildings as castles? You have no need to build such buildings because they used to live in tents." Ibn Kathir gave another so-called proof by stating that some said that Aram was a city built of gold and silver and moved from one country to another country. He also stated that there was no need for this huge building because they were not going to live a long life.

Qur'an 26:130-138 states that Houd told the people of Ad: *¹³⁰and when you attack, you attacked powerfully.¹³¹So fear Allah, and obey me. ¹³²And fear who aided you in what you know. ¹³³He aided you with livestock and sons ¹³⁴and gardens and springs. ¹³⁵Surely I fear for you a torment of a great day." ¹³⁶They said, "It is the same to us if you preach or if you were not of the*

---

[17]Ibn Kathir, 144.

preachers. ¹³⁷*This is only the custom of the ancients,* ¹³⁸*and we will not be tormented."* Ibn Kathir interpreted the previous passage this way:

> Whatever message you preach is created by you, and you have taken it from the previous books. The religion we believe in is the religion of our fathers and grandfathers and our ancestors. We will not leave it or change it, and we will continue to believe in it, for we will not be tormented.

The story of Houd and the people of Ad is condensed into two verses in Qur'an 41:15-16. Notice that the punishment of Ad here is *unfortunate days* which Ibn Kathir explained was seven nights and eight days. Ibn Kathir stated that Ibn Abbas said it began on Friday, but others said it began on Wednesday.[18] We read in Qur'an 41:15-16: ¹⁵*So as for Ad, so they were proud on the earth, without the truth, and they said, "Who is stronger in power than us?" Have they not seen that Allah who created them was greater than they in power, and they were disbelieving our signs.* ¹⁶*So we sent on them a tempestuous wind for unfortunate days so that we might make them taste the shameful torment in the world's life. And the torment of the hereafter is more shameful, and they will not be helped.*

The punishment of the people of Ad is shown here as a storm which they obviously thought was rain. The story can be found in Qur'an 46:21-25: ²¹*And remember the brother of Ad, when he warned his people in the dunes, and indeed, the warners have passed from between his hands and from behind him: "That you do not serve any except Allah, surely I fear the torment of a great day for you."* ²²*They said, "Have you come to us to turn us away from our gods? So bring us what you promised us, if you were of the truthful."* ²³*He said, "Surely the knowledge is only with Allah, and I am delivering to you what I have been sent with. But I see you are an ignorant people."* ²⁴*So when they saw it coming straight for their valleys, they said, "It is a passing with rain." Yet, it is what you are hastening with, a storm, in it is a painful torment.* ²⁵*It will destroy everything with the command of its lord. So they became such that nothing could be seen except their dwellings. Likewise, we reward the criminal people.*

---

[18]Ibid., 148.

Also, in Qur'an 53:50-55: *⁵⁰And that he destroyed the first Ad, ⁵¹and Thcmoud, so he did not spare. ⁵²And the people of Noah before, surely they were more unjust and rebellious. ⁵³And he destroyed Al-Mu'tafikah.*[19] *⁵⁴So he covered it what he covered. ⁵⁵So which then of your lord's benefits will you dispute about?*

Then in Qur'an 69:6-8: *⁶And as for Ad, so they were destroyed with a roaring, violent wind. ⁷He made it subservient against them continuously for seven nights and eight days, so you see the people fallen in it as if they were the trunks of hollow palm trees. ⁸So did you see if any of them are left?*

Finally, in Qur'an 89:6-14: *⁶Have you not seen how your lord did with Ad? ⁷At Iram,*[20] *that with columns, ⁸which none like it was created in the countries? ⁹And Themoud who hewed out the rocks in the valley? ¹⁰And Pharaoh with the stakes? ¹¹Those who rebelled in the countries, ¹²so they increased the vandalism in them. ¹³So your lord poured on them a sawt*[21] *of torment. ¹⁴Surely your lord is ever watchful.*

Ibn Kathir stated that Aisha, Mohammed's child wife, said whenever a storm passed by, Mohammed used to say, "O Allah, I ask you its good. And the good of what is in it? And the good that came with it? And I seek refuge from you, its evil and from the evil that has been sent with it."[22] So when the clouds began to spread in the sky, Mohammed became anxious; but when the rain started, Mohammed relaxed. When Aisha noticed this, she asked him why he always said this prayer. He said, "Perhaps the storm would be like the one that destroyed Ad." Ibn Kathir ended the story by stating that Houd had performed the Hajj as was in the case of Noah. The Prince of the Believers, Ali Ibn Abu Talib, mentioned that the tomb of Houd is located in the country of Yemen. However, others disagree and believe that his tomb is in a mosque in Damascus. Ibn Kathir closed the story of Prophet Houd with the statement, *and Allah knows best.*

As I stated earlier, this story does not exist in the Bible. I trust that the significant disagreement among Muslim scholars as discussed above and the vagueness of the information is enough internal

---

[19] meaningless word. Scholars erroneously claimed this to be the name of the cities of Lot, which the Bible clearly teaches were called Sodom and Gomorrah

[20] non-Arabic word of undetermined origin

[21] scourge, non-Arabic word of Aramaic origin

[22] Ibn Kathir, 150.

evidence that the story was completely made up. There was no such person as Prophet Houd to the people of Ad because if it were true, the Bible and historical documents would have some mention of them.

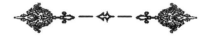

The Story of Saleh

Who was Saleh? Ibn Kathir stated that he was from the famous tribe of Themoud.[1] I wonder how Ibn Kathir can claim that Saleh came from a famous tribe if there are no historical or archaeological records of this prophet or tribe. Then Ibn Kathir gave us the genealogy of Saleh, that he was Saleh Ibn Abd, Ibn Mash, Ibn Abeed, Ibn Hager, Ibn Themoud, Ibn Aber, Ibn Aram, Ibn Shem, Ibn Noah. Saleh called his people to worship Allah alone and to leave their idols and not have any partner (another god) with Allah. A group of them believed him, but another group became infidels and plotted to kill him and his camel. Allah used this as an excuse to destroy them.

The story of Saleh, like the story of Houd, is repeated throughout the Qur'an in the following passages: 7:73-84; 11:61-68; 15:80-84; 17:59; 26:141-159; 27:45-53; 41:17-18; 54:23-32; and 91:11-15. The similarity between these two prophets is amazing. Since we do not have any details concerning the stories of these two prophets and considering the wording contained in both, it seems as if the stories were *copied and pasted* with just a change in the names. Ibn Kathir stated that the two prophets and their people are mentioned in Qur'an 14, 25, 38, 50, 53, and 89.[2] Ibn Kathir admitted that these two nations, Ad and Themoud, were not mentioned in the book of the People of the Book (Christians and Jews), neither the Bible nor the Torah.[3]

Ibn Kathir simply used the Qur'an to try to prove the existence of such two nations. I believe he struggled with this because there is no external evidence that these people or their prophets ever existed. Ibn Kathir used Qur'an 14:8-9: *[8]And Moses said, "If you and all who are on the earth be infidels, so surely Allah is rich, praised. [9]Have you not received the news of those who were before you, the people of Noah and Ad and Themoud, and of those who are after them, no one knows them but Allah? Their messengers came to them with proofs."* Ibn Kathir interpreted these verses by saying "what is clear from the words of Moses to his people concerning these two Arab nations was true." Since these two

---

[1]Ibn Kathir, *Stories of the Prophets*, vol. 1, Abo Al Fida Ishamail Ibn Kathir Al Kurashi Al Damashce (Beirut: Dar Al-Arab Heritage, 1408 AH, 1988), 152.
[2]Ibid.
[3]Ibid., 153.

Chapter 6

nations were Arab, however, Moses' people must not have kept their stories very well, even though according to Ibn Kathir they were "very famous in Moses' days."

Ibn Kathir stated they were Arabs and came after the people of Ad, but they did not learn a lesson from them and their history.[4] Ibn Kathir began by citing Qur'an 7:73-74: *[73]And to Themoud, their brother Saleh said, "O my people, serve Allah. You have no god other than him. Indeed, a proof came to you from your lord; this is a camel of Allah, a sign to you. So let her go at large to eat on Allah's earth, and do not touch her with evil so a painful torment will overtake you. [74]And remember when he made you viceroys after Ad and gave you dwellings on the earth, on its plains you take qasuran[5] and hew out of the mountains houses. So remember the favors of Allah, and do not act wickedly in the land, vandalizing."*

Ibn Kathir interpreted the previous verses by stating that "Allah makes the people of Themoud the successors that they may learn from their affairs."[6] Also, they would do the opposite of what the people of Ad did. Allah gave them permission to build castles on the plains and hew out houses in the mountains, so they should accept the grace of Allah with thanksgiving and the good deeds and serve him alone. If they disobeyed, the punishment would be great. Ibn Kathir wrote that this was why Saleh preached to them with his saying in Qur'an 26:146-148: *"...[146]Will you be left secure in what is here? [147]In gardens and springs [148]and plants and palm trees with tender shoots of flowers.* This was interpreted to mean *gathering a lot of mature plants and trees*.

Houd continued to speak to them in the following verses: *[149]And you carve skillful houses in the mountains. [150]So fear Allah, and obey me. [151]And do not obey the command of the extravagant, [152]those who vandalized on the earth and do not reform."*

He also said to them, in Qur'an 11:61: *[61]..."O my people, serve Allah. You have no god other than him. He brought you forth from the earth and has settled you in it. So ask forgiveness of him, then repent to him, surely my lord is near answering."*

---

[4]Ibid., 153.
[5]castles, non-Arabic word of Latin origin
[6]Ibn Kathir, 153.

The Revelation of Error

This meant that Allah was the one who created them and gave them all these plants and fruit because he is the provider. They should leave what they were doing and serve him alone because he is worthy to be served alone. He would accept from them and would ignore what they had done.

Qur'an 11:62-63 states: *[62]They said, "O Saleh, indeed, you were among us and hope was in you before that. Do you forbid us to serve that which our fathers serve? And surely we are in grave doubt of what you are calling us to." [63]He said, "O my people, have you seen that if I were with a proof from my lord, and he gave me from him mercy? So who will help me against Allah if I disobey him? So you will not increase me other than loss."* Ibn Kathir's interpretation was that the people of Themoud said they were hoping that Saleh was of sound mind.[7] They were astonished that he asked them to leave their service to their gods and the religion of their fathers and their grandfathers. There Saleh kindly and softly answered their question by calling them to what is good:

> What is your thought if my command to you and inviting you was the truth, then what will be your excuse with Allah? And you are asking me not to call you and be in disobedience to Allah? You cannot change me, and no one of you can change me. I will continue to call you to Allah without having any partner with him until Allah judges between me and you.

Their response to their Prophet Saleh is in Qur'an 26:153-154: *[153]They said, "Surely you are only from the bewitched! [154]You are only a human like us, so bring a sign if you were of the truthful."* Ibn Kathir said this meant that he was bewitched, that he did not know what he was saying. He was just a human like they were. They said he must show them a great miracle to prove the truth of his message.

I believe that was a reasonable request because, as we read in the Bible, whenever God sent a prophet there was always a miracle which was used to support the message of the prophet. Saleh's reply is in Qur'an 26:155-156: *[155]He said, "This is a camel. To her a drink, and to you a drink, a known day. [156]And do not touch her with evil so the torment of a great day will overtake you."* Also, in Qur'an 7:73: *[73]... Indeed, a proof came to you from your lord;*

---

[7] Ibn Kathir, 154.

this is a camel of Allah, a sign to you. So let her go at large to eat on Allah's earth, and do not touch her with evil so a painful torment will overtake you. Then in Qur'an 17:59: *⁵⁹And nothing prevented us from sending the signs except that the ancients denied them. And we gave the camel to Themoud, a visible,*[8] *so they treated her unjustly. And we do not send with the signs except to make fear.*

The people of Themoud requested a camel from Saleh as a sign to prove his message, and the scholar and the interpreter explained that the people of Themoud were gathered in their club and the messenger of Allah, Saleh, came calling them to Allah.[9] He reminded them, warned them, and preached to them. So they said, "If you bring to us a camel from this rock, pointing to a rock, with this description, she must be pregnant and tall and so forth." Their Prophet Saleh said, "If I answer your request, regarding what you asked, will you believe in what Allah said and accept my message?" They said, "Yes."

They made a covenant with Allah. Prophet Saleh stood up and prayed to Allah to answer their request. Allah commanded the rock to give out a great pregnant camel as they requested. When they saw it, many of them believed, but many of them became infidels and stubbornly were lost. I do not think Mohammed understood this request for neither Houd nor Saleh or even Mohammed himself performed any miracles. As we will see in the following verses, there was no miracle performed by Saleh for his people. Having a camel (and most likely, people had lots of camels) or asking the people of Themoud not to harm the camel is not a miracle. Then when they killed her, they were punished for killing her. This was a great excuse for Allah to punish them. *So where is the great miracle the people of Themoud asked for?*

I would like you to read once again the words from Qur'an 17:59: *⁵⁹And nothing prevented us from sending the signs except that the ancients denied them. And we gave the camel to Themoud, a visible,*[10] *so they treated her unjustly. And we do not send with the signs except to make fear.* The ancients considered the signs or the miracle a lie; but here, according to the interpretation of Ibn Kathir and others, many of the people became believers. *Who*

---

[8]miracle
[9]Ibn Kathir, 154.
[10]miracle

then was telling the truth, Allah or Muslim scholars? Did the camel really come out of the rock? Or is this a fabrication in the interpretation of these verses of the Qur'an? If this was the story, why did Allah and Gabreel not put it in the Qur'an exactly as it happened? The entire verses of the story concerning the camel were given three times, but neither Allah nor Gabreel or even Mohammed said from where the camel came. The true interpretation must be limited to the words of the verses in the Qur'an, without embellishment from the imagination of those who call themselves scholars.

The story of Themoud was repeated, but information about the rock was not given. The only place where Mohammed mentioned the rock is found in Qur'an 15:80-84: *[80]And indeed, the people of the rock denied the messengers. [81]And we brought to them our signs, so they were turned away from them. [82]And they were hewing houses from the mountains in security. [83]So a shout seized them in the morning. [84]So what they were earning did not profit them.* However, according to the interpretation of Muslim scholars, they were called The People of the Rock because they lived in houses which were hewn out of the mountain. Therefore, associating these verses with a camel-producing rock does not seem to me to be a reasonable interpretation. Neither the request for the camel to come out of the rock nor the miracle to be performed by Prophet Saleh happened. The story was inserted in the Qur'an without evidence, and the interpretation is fabrication without evidence.

Ibn Kathir ended his interpretation by quoting the statement, "They treated it unjustly."[11] He followed this statement with a listing of names of many people who believed in the miracle of the camel. Then he wrote a poem to tell the story of the camel. As for the statement, "This is a camel of Allah," it can be found in Qur'an 11:64: *[64]And, O my people, this is Allah's camel, a sign to you...* Also, Ibn Kathir said that he added the name *Allah* to it to bring honor to her.

Then he said, "So let her eat in Allah's earth, and do not touch her with evil so you will be overtaken with a near torment." This meant to leave the camel alone so that she may go, eat, and drink water day after day as she wished. Whenever she went to get water, they took

---

[11]Ibn Kathir, 154.

their water on the next day, meaning that they alternated their days to get water with the camel. It was also said they used to drink from her milk for all their needs. That was why Allah said in Qur'an 26:155: *[155]He said, "This is a camel. To her a drink, and to you a drink, a known day."*

Qur'an 54:27-28 states: *[27]Surely we will send the female camel [as] a sedition to them, so watch them and be patient. [28]And inform them that the water is shared between them, each drinks in turn.* Ibn Kathir interpreted these verses by stating that Allah sent this camel to them as a test to see if they believed in it or if they would become infidels in it, "*and Allah knows best what they are going to do.*" He told Saleh to be patient and wait to see the result of the test, but because it was so long, they met together and decided to kill the camel so that they might rest from it. They would save water and "the water would be completely to them. And Satan beautified their work for them."

We can read the result of the test in Qur'an 7:77: *[77]So they hamstrung the camel and rebelled against their lord's command and said, "O Saleh, bring on us that which you promise us, if you were of the messengers."* Ibn Kathir interpreted that the man who took the responsibility to kill the camel was their leader by the name of Kadar Ibn Salaf, the son of adultery.[12] Ibn Kathir wrote that Ibn Jarir and other scholars and interpreters said that there were two women, one beautiful and one rich, who lived in Themoud and whose husbands became Muslims.[13] One of the women by the name of Sadokah offered herself to her cousin if he would kill the camel. The other woman, who was old, by the name Anezah offered her four daughters to Kadar Ibn Salaf if he would kill the camel. Both of these men went to kill the camel. Seven of their people joined them, as written in Qur'an 27:48. *[48]And there was in the city nine persons who vandalized in the land and did not reform.*

So Kadar shot the camel with an arrow which stopped her; then he broke her feet. Then the women of the city came out playing the flute. Then Kadar Ibn Salaf rushed onto the camel with a sword and hamstrung the camel, and it fell to the ground and was killed. The camel's son went to the top of the mountain and called unto Allah

---
[12] Ibid., 155.
[13] Ibid., 156.

three times, "O my lord, where is my mother?" He entered inside the rock and disappeared. Others, however, said that they followed him and killed him also. The killing of the camel was the proof by Allah's word in Qur'an 54:29-30: *²⁹So they called their companion, so he took, so he hamstrung. ³⁰So how was my torment and my warning?* Also, in Qur'an 91:14-15: *¹⁴So they denied him, so they hamstrung her. So their lord got angry and destroyed them because of their sin, so he leveled them, ¹⁵and he did not fear its consequence.*

The Qur'an gives three different threats concerning the evil which would touch the people of Themoud if they disobeyed their Prophet Saleh. In Qur'an 7:73, Allah said: *⁷³...and do not touch her with evil so a painful torment will overtake you.* Then in Qur'an 11:64: *⁶⁴...and do not touch her with evil so you will be overtaken with a near torment.* Qur'an 26:156 states: *¹⁵⁶And do not touch her with evil so the torment of a great day will overtake you.* Which of the three words did Saleh really say? Did he say a painful torment will overtake you or a near torment or a torment of a great day?

I believe if Mohammed had repeated the story ten more times in the Qur'an, he would have used ten different words to describe ten different punishments. Ibn Kathir actually stated that the three different words are correct.[14] The second point Ibn Kathir made was that they were rushing to disbelieve the messenger of Allah, and "they insisted on refusing the truth and continued in their infidelity, so the torment fell on them."

In response to their evil act, Saleh told the people of Themoud to stay in their homes for three days. In Qur'an 27:49: *⁴⁹They said, "Swear one to another by Allah that we will surely fall on him and on his family by night. Then we will tell his guardian, 'We did not witness the destruction of his family, and surely we are truthful.'"* Ibn Kathir interpreted the previous verse to say that the "people of Saleh decided to kill Saleh and his immediate family, and they swear to lie, saying that they have no idea who killed him so that none of his extended family could require his blood from them (as revenge)."

The answer of Allah though is in Qur'an 27:50-53: *⁵⁰And they deceived a deception, and we deceived a deception. And they*

---

[14]Ibid., 157.

did not feel. ⁵¹So see how was the end of their deception. We destroyed them and all their people. ⁵²So these, their houses are ruins because of their injustice. Surely in this is a sign to a knowing people. ⁵³And we delivered those who believed, and they were fearing. Ibn Kathir interpreted these verses to mean that Allah sent rocks on those people who desired to kill Saleh by causing their heads to be crushed.[15] This was on Thursday, and their faces turned yellow as Saleh had warned them. As the evening came, they asked their people, "Has one day passed from the term of punishment yet?"

On the following day, which was Friday, their faces turned red. As the evening came, they asked their people, "Has one day passed from the term of punishment yet?" On the third day, which was Saturday, their faces turned black. As the evening came they asked their people, "Has one day passed from the term of punishment yet?" When it was Sunday morning, they were prepared to die, waiting for what torment of punishment would come on them. At sunrise, a loud shout came from heaven above and a shaking from below them. Their souls flowed out, and they lost their lives. They were paralyzed, their voices were hushed, and they became dead bodies in their homes without movement and without souls.

None of them were kept alive except one crippled woman named Kalbah, daughter of Al Salak. She was a complete infidel; and, while she was still alive, she went very quickly and told some Arabs what happened to her people. She asked them for water, and when she drank the water, she died.

I wonder where all this information came from. Few names are even mentioned in the Qur'an. *Where do Muslim scholars come up with all these names?* Ibn Kathir stated that Mohammed told his people not to ask for miracles.[16] The people of Saleh asked for a miracle (the camel). It came to them, but they killed her. "It drank their water one day, and they drank her milk the next day. The shout took them. All of them died except one man from the camp of Allah." The people asked him, "Who is this messenger of Allah?" Mohammed said he was Abu Rajal. When he came out of the camp of Allah, he died. The story is repeated in different words by various

---

[15] Ibid., 157-158.
[16] Ibid., 157.

Muslim theorists.[17] This proves to me that this story is a fairy tale with no truth in it. Ibn Kathir ended it with the statement, *Allah and his messenger know best.*

I believe the only reason Mohammed gave this hadith and claimed that he received the entire story of Saleh, the camel, and the people of Themoud, was to frighten Muslim followers so they would never ask Mohammed to perform a miracle. He knew that he could not perform any miracles.

Then Ibn Kathir quoted Qur'an 7:79: *[79]So he turned away from them, and said, "O my people, indeed, I delivered to you the message of my lord. And I gave you advice, but you do not love the advisers."* Ibn Kathir stated that Saleh addressed his people after their destruction, and he continued to go and speak from one place to another, saying the same thing.[18] He did everything he could to guide them to the right way with his words and his actions, but they refused to accept the truth. That is why what happened to them was happening. They would continue in this painful torment forever, and there was nothing that he could do for them, for Allah does what he wishes. It was said that Saleh moved to the camp of Allah until he died.

If you examine this story, I believe you will come to the same conclusion that I do. This is a fairy tale with one purpose and one purpose only. Mohammed made up this story to convince Muslims not to ever ask him to perform a miracle or the punishment of Allah would be on them. Reinforcing his point is the fact that it demonstrated that people would not believe, even if they saw a camel coming out of a rock. The many contradictions and huge exaggerations of all the nonsense of this story are internal evidence that this story is just a fairy tale. Also, an absence of details in the Qur'an verses left plenty of room for Muslim scholars to fabricate interpretations. We see this when we read the variety of interpretations by Muslims who call themselves scholars.

---

[17]Ibid., 158.
[18]Ibid., 159.

The Story of Abraham, Lot, Ishmael and Isaac

Abraham is considered by Muslims to be a great prophet. According to the Qur'an, Abraham was neither a Jew nor a Christian. He was *hanifan*, a meaningless word, but Muslim scholars claim it means *a Muslim* as written in Qur'an 3:67: *[67]Abraham was not a Jew nor a Nasranyan (Christian), but he was hanifan, a Muslim. And he was not of the polytheists.* In Qur'an 2:132, Abraham advised his sons and Jacob to die as Muslims: *[132]And Abraham advised by it[1] his sons and Jacob: "O my sons, surely Allah has chosen the religion for you, so do not die except you are Muslims."* He continued in Qur'an 2:133: *[133]Or were you witnesses when death came to Jacob when he said to his sons, "What will you serve after me?" They said, "We will serve your god and the god of your fathers, Abraham and Ishmael and Isaac.[2] One god and to him we are Muslims."* Ibn Kathir stated that Mohammed said, "We the group of prophets are paternally one religion."[3] He also stated, "Islam is the religion of the prophets as a whole." The belief that Abraham was neither Jew nor Christian but hanifan, a Muslim, was also repeated in the Qur'an in 2:135-136, 140; 3:65, 67-68, 84, 95, 97; 4:125; 6:161; 16:120; 22:26, 78; and 29:16.

In this section, we will be talking about the following four men whom Muslims call prophets: Abraham, Lot, Ishmael, and Isaac. Since their stories are intertwined, we will talk about them together.

Abraham and His Family

The story of Abraham, his family, and his people is repeated throughout the Qur'an, sometimes in exactly the same words and sometimes with a few words changed and a little extra information. *Is this just more filler?* Sometimes the action of one story contradicts another, so we have to wonder whether Abraham said this or that. The name Abraham or the family of Abraham is written throughout the Qur'an sixty-nine times in sixty-three verses, starting in Qur'an 2 and

---

[1] to become Muslims
[2] Hebrew name meaning *laughter*, non-Arabic word of Hebrew origin
[3] Ibn Kathir, *Stories of the Prophets*, vol. 1, Abo Al Fida Ishamail Ibn Kathir Al Kurashi Al Damashce (Beirut: Dar Al-Arab Heritage, 1408 AH, 1988), 161.

going through Qur'an 87. In verses 3:33; 4:54-55; 9:70; 12:6, 38; 19:58; 22:43; 33:7; 38:45; 42:13; 53:37; 57:26; 60:4; and 87:19, sometimes only his name is mentioned, while some of these verses tell just part of the story.

Who was Abraham? In his book, Ibn Kathir wrote that Abraham was Ibn Tasarh, Ibn Nahor, Ibn Sarok, Ibn Reu, Ibn Falak, Ibn Eber, Ibn Salah, Ibn Arfakshez, Ibn Shem.[4] *So, where did Ibn Kathir get these names?* The answer is very simple. They came from a book in the Bible called Genesis in chapter 11 and verses 10-27. Notice that half of the names he mentioned are wrong, for they are not spelled correctly in the Arabic language. It is sometimes difficult to grasp the significance of these spelling errors because of the challenge of translating some of the names into English, due to the English alphabet lacking some of the letters that are in the Arabic alphabet.

The genealogy of Abraham, along with more of his family history, is given in Genesis 11:24-32. Notice that the name of Abraham is listed here as Abram, which the Lord later changed to his covenant name of Abraham. The main verses that I would like to focus on are verses 24-27: **[24]*Nahor lived twenty-nine years, and begot Terah. [25]After he begot Terah, Nahor lived one hundred and nineteen years, and begot sons and daughters. [26]Now Terah lived seventy years, and begot Abram, Nahor, and Haran. [27]This is the genealogy of Terah: Terah begot Abram, Nahor, and Haran. Haran begot Lot.***

Who was Abraham's mother? Although the Bible does not mention the name of Abraham's mother, Muslims claim that they know her name because it is written in Ibn Kathir's book that Isaac Ibn Bashier Al Kahly said that the name of the mother of Abraham was Amelah.[5] Amazingly, in the following sentence of Ibn Kathir's book, he stated that Al Kelby said that her name was Bona, daughter of Krabana, Ibn Karsy, from the people of Arfakshez, Ibn Shem, Ibn Noah. *So who really was Abraham's mother?*

Who was Abraham's wife? Although the Qur'an does not mention the name of Abraham's wife, Muslims believe her name was Sarah. Obviously, they got this name from the Bible in Genesis 12:5 in which this verse describes how Abram took Sarai his wife along with

---

[4]Ibid.
[5]Ibid., 162.

his nephew Lot and all their possessions and servants and departed for the land of Canaan. Later, as God did with Abram in changing his name to Abraham, in Genesis 17:15 we read that God changed Sarai's name to Sarah: *¹⁵Then God said to Abraham, "As for Sarai your wife, you shall not call her name Sarai, but Sarah shall be her name."*

Qur'an 4:54-55 mentions the family of Abraham, as it is written: *⁵⁴Or they envy the people about what Allah has given them from his bounty. So indeed, we gave the family of Abraham the book and the wisdom, and we gave them a great kingdom. ⁵⁵So some of them believed in him. And some prevent [others] from him, and sufficient is the blaze of hell.* These verses are out of context with the surrounding verses.

The family of Abraham was envied by the people (the Muslim scholars did not tell us who these people were) because Allah favored them. In his interpretation, Ibn Kathir explained that the people were envious of Mohammed because he was a descendant of Abraham and had received the greatest prophecy.[6] The reason they did not believe in him was because he was an Arab and was not of the Children of Israel (Jacob). I believe this is a strange interpretation because the Qur'an clearly teaches that the prophethood and the book and the wisdom are given only to the children of Jacob (Israel), not to any Arab. We can read this in Qur'an 29:27: *²⁷And we granted him Isaac and Jacob, and we assigned the prophethood and the book to his descendants. And we gave him his wage in this world, and surely in the hereafter he is among the good.* This is also repeated in 45:16 which says: *¹⁶And indeed, we gave the book and the wisdom and the prophethood to the children of Israel, and we provided them with the good things. And we favored them above the worlds.* These verses will be explained in more detail when we talk about Jacob and again in the section about Mohammed.

An example of the verses that mention Abraham in a short story without any details is in Qur'an 2:258: *²⁵⁸Have you not seen him who disputed with Abraham about his lord, that Allah had given him the kingdom? When Abraham said, "My lord is he who*

---

[6] http://quran.Al-islam.com/Page.aspx?pageid= 221&BookID=11& Page=87, accessed March 12, 2011.

gives life and causes death." He said, "I give life and cause death." Abraham said, "So surely Allah brings the sun from the east, so bring it from the west." So the infidel was confounded. And Allah will not guide the unjust people. Ibn Kathir stated that this man who disputed with Abraham was the king of Babel, whom he named Nimrod.[7] Notice the ignorance of the Muslim scholar in that he said, "Nimrod, Ibn Canaan, Ibn Cush, Ibn Shem." *Where and how did Ibn Kathir get these names?* We will examine these names in a few moments.

At this point, we have to say that the student is no better than his teacher. Mohammed copied the stories of the Bible in the Qur'an without any details, with hardly any mention of names, and his scholars tried to make sense of Mohammed's writings by making up a cocktail of names. Because of Muslims' simple minds or the fact that they are ignorant of the biblical account or even their Qur'an, when they read Ibn Kathir's interpretation of these verses, they may think it is very enlightening. This is especially true when they hear all the names Ibn Kathir used to interpret verses like this one. Perhaps they think this adds credibility.

When we look at the previous verse, Qur'an 2:258, does this verse say who disputed with Abraham? Obviously, the answer is *no*. In Mohammed's Qur'an, there is hardly any mention of names. Most of the time he wrote "one of them said to the others," and when he mentioned names, he did exactly as Ibn Kathir did here; he mixed names and lineages that do not belong together.

That leads us to the second point. *Where did Ibn Kathir come up with these names?* I would like to explain the confusion of the names. He wrote that the name of the king was Nimrod, the son of Canaan, son of Cush, son of Shem. When we read the Bible in Genesis 10, we discover that Nimrod was the descendant of Ham, not the descendant of Shem. Genesis 10:6-10 says: **[6]The sons of Ham were Cush, Mizraim, Put, and Canaan. [7]The sons of Cush were Seba, Havilah, Sabtah, Raamah, and Sabtechah; and the sons of Raamah were Sheba and Dedan. [8]Cush begot Nimrod; he began to be a mighty one on the earth. [9]He was a mighty hunter before the LORD; therefore it is said, "Like Nimrod the mighty hunter before the**

---

[7]Ibn Kathir, 181-182.

LORD." ¹⁰And the beginning of his kingdom was Babel, Erech, Accad, and Calneh, in the land of Shinar.

This took place before the building of the Tower of Babel. Another important point is that Nimrod was the third generation after Ham, and there are ten generations between Abraham and Nimrod. There was no connection between the lifetime of Abraham and Nimrod. Cush, the father of Nimrod, had nothing to do with Shem, the ancestor of Abraham. Cush was not the son of Shem; Cush actually was the son of Ham. Shem was his uncle.

As for the rest of Mohammed's story in Qur'an 2:258, it is fabricated because Abraham did not dispute with anyone concerning his lord who gives life or causes death or concerning the rising of the sun from the east or the west. The interpretation of this story is in Ibn Kathir's book.[8] He wrote that this king was able to give life and cause death. When the king brought two people who were supposed to be put to death before him, he commanded one of them be put to death and the other to live. When Abraham spoke concerning the rising of the sun from the east and asked this king if he could raise it from the west, the king was astonished for he could not do such a thing.

Ibn Kathir continued by saying that people came to this king to receive food.[9] The dispute took place between Abraham and the king when Abraham went to him to receive food and the king did not give Abraham any food. Abraham filled two bags with dirt so he would not return to his family with empty bags. When he arrived at his home he slept, but his wife Sarah opened the bags while he was asleep and found them filled with good food. She cooked food from the bags. When Abraham woke up, he asked, "Where did you get this food to cook?" She answered, "It is from the bags you brought." Then Abraham knew it was from Allah.

Zayd Ibn Islam said that Allah sent a king to King Nimrod commanding him to believe in Allah, but King Nimrod refused. Then he called him the second time, and he refused again. He called him the third time, and he still refused; so the king said, "Gather your group, and I will gather my group." So King Nimrod gathered his military at the time of the sunrise.

---

[8]Ibid., 172-173.
[9]Ibid., 173.

Then Allah sent these flies against Nimrod and his army. There were so many flies that no one was able to see the sun. The flies ate flesh and blood and left them as bones in the valley. One of these flies entered the king's nostrils and stayed inside his nostrils for four hundred years. Allah tormented him with this fly. He used to beat his head all these years until Allah destroyed him with the fly. From my study, I believe that this king was probably a character patterned after Pharaoh rather than being Nimrod.

The true story, according to the account in Genesis 12:10-20, follows. We encourage the reader to read the entire account, but here is a summary.

Because there was a severe famine in the land, Abraham went to Egypt. Sarah, Abraham's wife, was very beautiful. For this reason, Abraham was afraid that he might be killed so Pharaoh could take Sarah for himself. Abraham asked Sarah to lie and say she was his sister. The princes of Pharaoh spoke very highly of her to Pharaoh, and Sarah was taken to Pharaoh's house. Abraham received cattle, herds, and slaves, but the Lord struck the house of Pharaoh with plagues because of Sarah. Then Pharaoh called Abraham and asked him: *[18]...""What is this you have done to me? Why did you not tell me that she was your wife? [19]Why did you say, 'She is my sister'? I might have taken her as my wife. Now therefore, here is your wife; take her and go your way."* Pharaoh told his men to let Abraham, his wife, and his possessions leave in peace.

As I mentioned before, there are many places in the Qur'an where just the name of Abraham is mentioned in one verse without any additional information as in 3:84; 4:125,163; 9:70; 12:6, 38; 19:58; 22:43, 78; 33:7; 38:45; 42:13; 53:37; 57:26; and 87:19. As you read these verses, you will discover that there is no story of Abraham or any mention about his life.

The following verses give a short portion about the life of Abraham as described by Mohammed. Qur'an 9:114 states: *[114]And the seeking of forgiveness of Abraham for his father was not but in [keeping of] a promise which he had promised to him. So when it was shown to him that he was an enemy to Allah, he declared himself innocent of him. Surely Abraham was very meek.* The same story is also mentioned in Qur'an 60:4: *[4]Indeed, there was a good example for you in Abraham and in those who were with him when they said to their people, "Surely we are innocent from you and of what you serve without Allah. We became infidels in you, and the enmity and the enduring hatred between us and you will appear forever until you believe in Allah alone." Except for the speech of Abraham to his father: "I will ask forgiveness for you, and I do not have control of anything to you from Allah." "Our lord, on you we depended and to you we turned and to you is the final return."*

In Ibn Kathir's interpretation of these two verses, he explained that when Mohammed stood by the tomb of his mother asking Allah if he could intercede on her behalf on the day of resurrection, Allah denied him because she was a polytheist.[10] Then some of Mohammed's followers saw him crying and cried with him. When they asked him the reason he was crying, he told them why. Since Abraham was an excellent example to be followed and sought forgiveness for his father, they asked Mohammed why he could not seek forgiveness for his mother. Mohammed explained that Abraham had promised his father to seek forgiveness for his sin. Since Allah showed Abraham and Mohammed that Abraham's father and Mohammed's mother had died as infidels, intercession on their behalf would not succeed. Therefore, Muslim believers do not intercede or seek forgiveness for those who die as polytheists.

Ibn Kathir told the story of the birth of Abraham.[11] He stated that this took place when Terah was seventy-five years old, which was the wrong age. We read in Genesis 11:26 that Abraham's father was seventy years old when he had his son. Notice that Ibn Kathir used the name Terah for Abraham's father, which is the true biblical name. He did not use the false qur'anical name of Azar as written in Qur'an 6:74. I believe the confusion about the age occurred because Muslim scholars did not read the Bible carefully. The Bible says Abraham was seventy-five years old when he left Haran. The rest of the interpretation on these two pages is literally copied from the Bible and pasted into Ibn Kathir's book by writing *they said.*

Believe me, my dear readers, the fact is, that without what is written in the Bible, as I said before, neither Ibn Kathir nor any other Muslim scholar nor Mohammed nor any angel had any idea who Abraham or any other biblical characters were. Remember, as I said before, Ibn Kathir stated that Abraham's wife was named Sarah. *How did he know that was her name, the place of their traveling, or how*

---

[10]Ibid., 164.
[11]Ibid., 162.

old they were? This information exists neither in the Qur'an nor in the hadith; it is only in the Bible.

The Qur'an states that Allah *revealed* to Abraham as he *revealed* to Noah and the prophets, including Mohammed. They all had a similar way of receiving revelations. We can see this in Qur'an 4:163: *[163]Surely we have revealed to you as we revealed to Noah and the prophets after him. And we revealed to Abraham and Ishmael and Isaac and Jacob and the tribes and 'Isā and Ayyūb[12] and Yunus[13] and Aaron and Solomon, and to David we gave Zabor.*[14]

Abraham and the Search for Allah

One of the stories written in the Qur'an concerning Abraham comes from Qur'an 6:74: *[74]And when Abraham said to his father Azar,[15] "Do you take asnam[16] for gods? Surely I see you and your people are in obvious error."* First, Abraham's father's name is an error; he was Terah not Azar. Second, his father and his people were idol worshipers. *So what was Abraham worshiping?* So far, nothing. The story continues in Qur'an 6:75-76: *[75]And likewise, we did show Abraham the kingdom of the heavens and the earth, and that he might be one of the certain. [76]So when the night covered him, he saw a planet. He said, "This is my lord." So when it set, he said, "I do not love the setting one."* Here Allah showed Abraham the heavens. *How old was Abraham at the time?* He was not a little boy; but even if he were a little boy, he must have been a very mature boy, or he would not have known that idols were nothing to be worshiped. In verse 74, he obviously showed that he rejected them.

Was this the first time Abraham looked up into the heavens to see the sun, moon, and stars? Obviously, the answer is *no*. Perhaps Allah opened his mind and his heart to see and meditate on it for the first time, so he saw a planet and said, "This is my lord." Since he did not worship idols, he would not have called a planet *lord*. Afterwards, the story continues by stating that the morning came and the star disappeared, and then Abraham realized this planet could not be his

---

[12] Job, non-Arabic word of Greek/Syriac origin
[13] name mistakenly used when Jonah was meant
[14] in singular form = Psalms, non-Arabic word of Hebrew/Syriac origin
[15] a name, non-Arabic word of Hebrew/Greek origin
[16] idols, non-Arabic word of Aramaic origin

lord. He chose not to love it or to worship it. Then in verse 77, it seemed as if it was the first time in his life that he had seen the moon. As written in Qur'an 6:77: *[77]So when he saw the moon rising, he said, "This is my lord." So when it set, he said, "If my lord does not guide me, I will surely be of the erring people."* According to the Qur'an, because he saw the bright moon, he said, "This is my lord." *Can we imagine Abraham sitting all night long looking at the moon and worshiping the moon and praising the moon saying, "You are my lord"?*

Suddenly, things changed dramatically, for the moon set and its brightness was gone. There Abraham cried, "Where are you, my lord? Lead me to you. I want to believe in you. I want to worship you. If you will not guide me, I will be of the erring people." So the lord came to lead Abraham to himself as if it was the first time in his life Abraham had seen the sun shining. It is a brand new day and a new beginning, as is written in verse 6:78: *[78]So when he saw the sun rising, he said, "This is my lord, this is bigger." So when it set, he said, "O my people, surely I am innocent of what you partner. Did Abraham really say to the sun that it was brighter, it was bigger, and that he missed it yesterday?* When the night came, the sun disappeared. *Did Abraham not realize that it would get dark later?* When it got dark and the sun disappeared, Abraham confessed to his people that he was innocent from all that they worship, or partner, with Allah. How amazing that Abraham quickly was able to stop worshiping the sun and turned his face to worship the creator of the heavens and the earth, and then he became a good Muslim!

We read in verse 6:79: *[79]Surely I turned my face to him who has created the heavens and the earth, hanifan, and I am not of the polytheists."* Immediately, Abraham began his mission as a prophet to his people to lead them to the true Allah, as he began to dispute with them in verses 6:80-82: *[80]And his people disputed with him. He said, "Do you dispute with me about Allah, and indeed, he guided me? And I do not fear what you partner with him, unless my lord wills anything. My lord embraces all things in knowledge. Do you not remember? [81]And how should I fear what you partner, and you do not fear what you partner with Allah, what he did not send down on you with authority? So which of the two groups are more worthy of security, if you*

The Revelation of Error

were knowing?" *⁸²Those who believed and do not mix their faith with injustice, those have security, and they are guided.*

Just three days earlier, Abraham had rejected his father and his people's gods and worshiped some star. On the following day, he worshiped the moon, thinking it was his lord. Then the day after that, he worshiped the sun. Then a few hours later, he was the prophet of Allah. Then in verse 6:83, Allah ended the story by saying: *⁸³And this is our argument we gave to Abraham against his people. We raise up in degrees whom we will. Surely your lord is wise, knowing.*

Ibn Kathir stated that the entire story was just an act, a lie created by Abraham and Allah to lead the people to worship the true god, Allah.[17] He continued to say the act of worshiping the stars was the practice of the people of Abraham in Haran. In Qur'an 21:52, though, we discover that the father of Abraham and his people did not worship stars. Instead they worshiped statues, as when he said to his father and to his people: *⁵²... "What are those statues which you are devoted to?"* If they were devoted to these statues, they would not also worship the stars. Notice in verse 53 that not only were they devoted to the statues, but their fathers were also. Qur'an 21:53 states: *⁵³They said, "We found our fathers serving them."* These statues were later broken by Abraham except for the biggest one, as written in Qur'an 21:58: *⁵⁸So he made them pieces except the biggest of them...*

The long story of Abraham can be found in Qur'an 19:41-48; 21:51-70; 26:69-83; 29:26-27; and 37:83-98. In Qur'an 19:41-48, we see the interaction of Abraham with his father and his people's gods. *⁴¹And remember in the book Abraham, surely he was a friend, a prophet. ⁴²When he said to his father, "O my father, why do you serve that which neither hears nor sees nor profits you anything? ⁴³O my father, surely indeed, some knowledge came to me which has not come to you. So follow me; I will guide you to a straight way. ⁴⁴O my father, do not serve Satan; surely Satan was a rebel against the merciful. ⁴⁵O my father, surely I fear lest a torment from the merciful touches you, so you will become a friend to Satan." ⁴⁶He said, "Are you forsaking my gods, O Abraham? If you do not stop that, I will stone you, and*

---

[17]Ibn Kathir, 176.

depart from me for a long time!" ⁴⁷He said, "Peace be on you. I will ask forgiveness for you from my lord, surely he was kind to me. ⁴⁸And I will separate from you and what you call on rather than Allah. And I will call to my lord. Perhaps I will not become miserable by calling to my lord."

According to the previous verses, this was a simple friendly conversation between Abraham and his father. Abraham tried to correct his father concerning his false worship of his gods by saying, "For they do not listen and they do not see and they do not benefit anything." Abraham explained to his father that he has more knowledge than his father and desired to lead his father to the straight way. Abraham advised his father that if he continued to worship Satan, he would be tormented by Allah the merciful. Abraham's father rebuked and threatened Abraham by stating if Abraham did not cease from forsaking his gods that he would stone Abraham and leave him. That is a strange statement because if he stoned Abraham, he would be dead. *How could Abraham's father then leave his son?* Then Abraham said to him, "Peace to you," and he added that he would seek forgiveness for him. Then Abraham left his father and his gods.

Is any of this story close to the true account in Genesis? Mohammed began his story by stating, "And remember in the book..." as if Mohammed is reminded by his Allah as to how the story is written in the Bible. One will discover that in reading Genesis 11:27-32 that no such conversation took place between Abraham and his father. They lived in Ur and then traveled together to go to the land of Canaan. During their travel, they stopped in Haran. While they were there, the father of Abraham, Terah, died at the age of 205 years. There was no worship of idols or anything like the words of the Qur'an.

Abraham and the Fire

Mohammed invented the story of the fire which occurs as a result of a misunderstanding of the word *Ur* (meaning *city*) because Genesis 15:7 was mistranslated by the Jewish interpreter Johnathan, son of Azreel. Johnathan translated the word as *light*, into the Chaldean language as "I am the Lord who got you out from the *light of the fire* of the Chaldeans," instead of saying "...the *city* of the Chaldeans" as written in the true translation of the verse. **⁷Then He said to him, "I am the Lord, who brought you out of Ur of the Chaldeans, to give**

The Revelation of Error

you this land to inherit it." Notice that Mohammed confused Abraham's story with Gideon's story from Judges 6:22-32. It was Gideon, not Abraham, who destroyed the altar of his father.

In Genesis 12, God called Abram to leave his country, his people, and his father's household that he might go to the Promised Land. There was no mention of the fabricated story of Abraham being thrown in the fire as written in Qur'an 21:51-73. It is also mentioned in Qur'an 37:97-99: *97 They said, "Build a building for him." So they threw him into the hell. 98 So they desired a scheme against him, so we made them the lowest. 99 And he said, "Surely I am going to my lord. He will guide me."* The portion concerning his burning can be found in Qur'an 21:68-70: *68 They said, "Burn him, and help your gods if you were doing." 69 We said, "O fire, be cold, and peace on Abraham." 70 And they sought to lay a plot against him, but we made them the losers.*

Obviously, a simple reading of such verses will not bring any understanding of what took place in Abraham's life concerning him being thrown into the fire, but enough information has been given in the interpretation of Ibn Kathir to make us wonder why Allah did not give this information in the Qur'an.[18]

This leads us to ask the question once again: *Where did Ibn Kathir get his information?* For example, he stated that they gathered many branches from many different places for a long time, to the point that, when some women got sick, they made a pledge to their gods that if they would be healed, they would carry branches to the fire of Abraham.[19] They gathered all these branches in a deep hole and burned them, and the fire became so large that it was unlike anything ever seen before. Then they put Abraham into a catapult which was made by a Kurdish man named Hazan, the creator of the catapult. Allah cursed Hazan for what he had done and sank him into the earth. In fact, Muslim scholars say he is still sinking down in the bottom of the seventh earth, continuing even to this day. Ibn Kathir continued by stating that as they were tying Abraham, he said, "To you the praise, and to you the kingdom. No partner with you." So they put him into a catapult and threw him into the fire as Abraham said, "Allah, you are our judge, and you are our counselor."

---

[18] Ibid., 179-181.
[19] Ibid.

Abu Horyrah said that Mohammed said, "When Abraham was thrown into the fire, he said, 'Our god, you are one in the heaven, and I am one on the earth serving you.'"[20] Some said that Angel Gabreel met Abraham in the air. Gabreel asked, "Do you have any needs?" Abraham replied, "To you, none."

Ibn Abbas said, "The angel of rain was made to say, 'When will I be commanded to send the rain?' And the command of Allah was, 'Hurry.'" As for the statement in Qur'an 21:69: [69]*"O fire, be cold, and peace on Abraham,"* Ibn Abbas stated, "If Allah did not say, 'and peace on Abraham,' the coldness of the fire would have harmed him."

Kaab Al Ahbar said, "No one of the people of the earth benefited from the fire on that day. And nothing was burned of him, except the ropes which bound him."[21] He also said that Al Dahak said that Angel Gabreel was there with him wiping off his sweat, which was the only consequence of the fire. Al Saddi said that the angel of shadow was with Abraham. Abu Horyrah said that the best word the father of Abraham said, when he saw his son in the fire in such a condition, was, "Blessed is the lord, your lord, O Abraham." *I wonder where all this information came from.*

Ibn Asakir stated that Akramah said that the mother of Abraham saw Abraham and called to him, "O my son, I desire to come to you, so call on your lord to spare me from the heat of the fire which is around you."[22] So he said, "Yes." So she came to him, and no harm came to her from the heat of the fire; and she hugged him, kissed him, and left. Scholars disagree on the length of time that the mother of Abraham spent with her son in the fire. Some say she stayed for forty days. Others say she stayed for fifty days.

Bukhari said that the apostle of Allah, Mohammed, commanded the Muslims to kill the salamanders because they were the only animals who were breathing on the fire to accelerate it.[23] Mohammed also stated that all the animals were putting the fire out except for the salamanders. Much has been written about Abraham's fire, but no Muslim scholar explained what took place after Abraham was put into the fire. Let's ask some questions. *How did Abraham get out of*

---

[20]Ibid.
[21]Ibid.
[22]Ibid.
[23]Ibid.

the fire? Did anybody believe him afterward? When did this take place? Why did his father not believe in Allah afterward? There are so many other questions we can ask, but for the sake of time I will leave the readers the responsibility of expanding upon what has been written above. *Is any of this fairy tale true?* Obviously, the answer is *no.*

The Emigration of Abraham

In the following two verses, the Qur'an states that Abraham and Lot emigrated to some land or to what was also called the blessed land. Qur'an 29:26-27 states: *[26]So Lot believed in him, and he said, "Surely I am emigrating to my lord; surely he is the dear, the wise." [27]And we granted him Isaac and Jacob, and we assigned the prophethood and the book to his descendants. And we gave him his wage in this world, and surely in the hereafter he is among the good.*

No one can come up with a reasonable interpretation as to where Abraham and Lot emigrated, for the passages do not indicate where they traveled, due to the nature and style of the writings of the Qur'an. However, Muslim scholars, as they usually do, are able to invent information about any passage in the Qur'an usually by taking the information from the Bible. There is always disagreement among Muslim scholars. Kaab Al Ahbar said that Abraham and Lot left the land of Babel to go to the land of Haran. He also stated that it was there that Terah, the father of Abraham, died, according to Ibn Kathir.[24]

However, Ibn Abbas stated that it was the land of Mecca to which they emigrated. Al Saddi stated also that Abraham and Lot left the land of Shem, and there Abraham met with Sarah. She was the daughter of the king of Haran. She rejected her people's religion, so Abraham married her with the condition that he would not change her. However, Ibn Kathir stated that it was common knowledge that she was the daughter of Abraham's uncle, Haran.[25] Ibn Kathir stated that some claimed she was the daughter of his brother Haran and the sister of Lot. They also claimed that it was customary at that time for a man to marry his brother's daughter, *and Allah knows best.* Ibn

---

[24]Ibid., 183.
[25]Ibid., 184.

Kathir also stated that it is common knowledge that Abraham emigrated from Babel and that Sarah was with him at the time.

They continued traveling, according to Ibn Kathir, and they arrived in Egypt during the famine.[26] That is when the king tried to take her after she and Abraham had lied concerning Sarah being Abraham's sister. That was how they got Hagar the slave and animals to take to the Promised Land. Much contradictory information and babbling has been given concerning the king of Egypt and the travelings of Abraham, but for the sake of time and space we will go no further than this. In conclusion, Ibn Kathir stated that some mighty people had invaded the land where Lot lived and took him captive. They took his money and his livestock. When Abraham found out about it, he took 380 men and saved Lot. He brought back all Lot's possessions and killed many of the enemies of Allah. He chased them and kept following them until they arrived at Damascus, *and Allah knows best.*

Where did Ibn Kathir get this information? He was following the pattern of his prophet, Mohammed, and copying from the Bible. Yet the story was still corrupted, and much information is missing, as it was with Mohammed's writing throughout the Qur'an.

What about the true account of Abraham's emigration as given in the Bible? Neither Mohammed nor his Muslim scholars read the story of Abraham directly from the Bible because if they had, they would not have made all the errors in the Qur'an and their ridiculous interpretations. We can read in Genesis 11:31-32 that Abraham's father was named Terah, not Azar, as Mohammed had written erroneously in the Qur'an. Terah took his son, Abram (Abraham), and his nephew, Lot, and Sarai (Sarah), his daughter-in-law (the wife of Abram), and together they left Ur (the *city*, not the *fire* of Chaldeans). During their travel they came to Haran and stayed there. There is no such story as that of Abram's father and the worshiping of idols; this was an entire conversation invented by Mohammed. Abram had never broken any idols, or statues, of his father and his people, nor had his father and his people thrown him into any fire. Therefore, Abram's mother would not have visited him in the fire. While they were in Haran, Abram's father, Terah, died at the age of 205 years.

---

[26]Ibid., 184-187.

In Genesis 12:5, the Bible states that Abram, his wife Sarai, and his nephew Lot continued to travel from Haran with all their possessions until they came to the land of Canaan. Not only does the Bible tell us the truth, but it also gives us the details. I advise the reader to read the account of Abram in Genesis, for there we find the names of the city and how Abram and Lot separated. Abram lived in the land of Canaan, and Lot lived in the land of Sodom and Gomorrah.

Abraham Lies

Ibn Kathir stated that Bukhari said Abu Horyrah said that Abraham lied only three lies.[27] He lied first concerning Allah when he said, "Surely I am sick." Second, he lied when confronted with the broken idols, and Abraham said, "Yet their biggest, this did it." The third time was when he said that Sarah was his sister when they met with a giant. It was said to the giant, "There is a man here who has a woman who is the most beautiful of the people." So the giant asked Abraham concerning her, "Who is she?" Abraham said, "She is my sister."

When the giant tried to take Sarah, his hands became paralyzed. So he said to Sarah, "Call on Allah, and I will not harm you." So she called on Allah, and the giant was healed. So the giant tried to take her again and became paralyzed even worse, so he asked her to call on Allah again. Then he said she was not a human; she was a devil. So he put Sarah out and gave her Hagar. So she came to Abraham while he was standing praying.[28] She said, "Allah is sufficient concerning the unjust, and he gave me Hagar as a servant." The story is repeated many times in different words. *I wonder where Muslim scholars came up with this myth.*

What does the Bible say about the lies of Abraham concerning his wife Sarah? He did not lie three times, only twice. Also, he did not lie about her being his sister because she was a half-sister from the same father but not the same mother. Instead, the lie here was he did not acknowledge that she was his wife. The first time took place when Abraham went to Egypt in the first famine. As it is written in Genesis 12:11-20, when Abraham went to Egypt with Sarah due to the severe famine, he was afraid that he might be killed because of the beauty of

---

[27]Ibid., 175.
[28]Ibid.

his wife, since this was a common occurrence at that time. If a husband had a beautiful wife, the people would kill the husband to take the wife for themselves. So Abraham lied and asked his wife Sarah to lie. He was given many gifts of animals and slaves because of Sarah, but the Lord protected Sarah and did not allow Pharaoh to touch her. That is the opposite of what happened in the stories from Muslim scholars. The Lord struck Pharaoh and his house with great plagues. Pharaoh rebuked Abraham when he found out that Sarah was Abraham's wife. Then Pharaoh asked his people to send Abraham and his wife away in peace. We encourage the reader to read the entire passage in Genesis 12:11-20.

According to Genesis 20:1-18, the second time that he lied was to Abimelech. This time Abraham was traveling south to Gerar and lied for the same reason. Abimelech, king of Gerar, took Sarah, but God spoke to him in a dream at night and said that he was dead because the woman he had was a married woman. Up to this point, Abimelech had not touched her. He asked God in a dream if He would destroy a righteous nation. Since Abraham and Sarah had both told him that they were brother and sister, the king told God that he was an innocent man. God told him that He knew that he had taken her with a sincere heart and that is why He had kept him from sinning against God. God told him to then return the woman to her husband, that Abraham was a prophet and would pray for Abimelech so that he would live. However, if Abimelech did not do that, then he and all his people would surely die. Once again, Abimelech rebuked Abraham for what he had done. Then Abimelech returned Sarah to Abraham along with livestock, slaves, and silver. Abraham prayed for Abimelech, and the king was healed. Then his wife and the servants who had been barren became fertile and able to have children.

The Birth of Ishmael

Ishmael would have to be the most important prophet because he was the firstborn son of Abraham, and Muslims claim he was the father of the Arab nation. Arabs believe that they are his descendants, and they claim Mohammed was the greatest prophet. Let's ask a reasonable question. *How much do they know about Prophet Ishmael?* The fact is, the name Ishmael appears a total of twelve times in twelve verses, as well as five times in Qur'an 2:125-141.

Ishmael is mentioned in Qur'an 2:125 where he is helping his father to purify the house for prayer: [125]*And when we made the*

The Revelation of Error

house[29] *as a resort for people and a haven: "And take from the place of Abraham a place of prayer." And we made a covenant with Abraham and Ishmael.*[30] *"That purify my house for those who march around it and the dwellers and the kneelers, the worshipers."*

In verse 2:127, Ishmael is mentioned as helping his father Abraham to build the house (Kaaba). *Shouldn't the house be built before it is purified as stated in verse 125?* What a strange order. [127]*And when Abraham was raising the foundations of the house and Ishmael: "Our lord, accept from us, surely you are the hearing, the knowing.* [128]*Our lord, and make us Muslims to you and among our offspring a Muslim umma*[31] *to you. And show us our ritual and relent on us. Surely you are the relenting, the merciful.* [129]*Our lord, and raise to them a messenger from among them who recites your verses to them and teaches them the book and the hikma*[32] *and purify them. Surely you are the dear, the wise."* In verses 127-129, Abraham and Ishmael are praying to Allah that he will send Mohammed. This is clear proof that Mohammed was interjecting himself as a prophet to come from a descendant of Ishmael.

In verse 2:133, Ishmael's name is mentioned as one of the forefathers of Jacob. This is an error. Actually, Ishmael was the half-brother of Isaac, and so he was Jacob's uncle. [133]*Or were you witnesses when death came to Jacob when he said to his sons, "What will you serve after me?" They said, "We will serve your god and the god of your fathers, Abraham and Ishmael and Isaac.*[33] *One god and to him we are Muslims."*

Verse 136 says that Ishmael had received a revelation. *What revelation?* Muslims believe in Prophet Ishmael and his book (his revelation) without knowing anything else about it. *Where does it exist?* [136]*Say, "We believed in Allah and what has been sent down to us, and what has been sent down to Abraham and Ishmael and Isaac and Jacob and the asbāt,*[34] *and what has*

---

[29] the Kaaba, the black stone building in Mecca
[30] Hebrew name meaning *God hears*, non-Arabic word of Greek/ Syriac/ Ethiopian/ Hebrew origin
[31] nation, non-Arabic word of Hebrew/Sumerian origin
[32] wisdom, non-Arabic word of Aramaic origin
[33] Hebrew name meaning *laughter*, non-Arabic word of Hebrew origin
[34] tribes, non-Arabic word of Hebrew/Syriac origin in its singular form

been given to Moses and 'Isā, and what has been given to the prophets from their lord. We do not differentiate between any of them, and to him we are Muslims."

In verse 2:140, the Qur'an states that neither Abraham, Ishmael, Isaac, Jacob, nor their descendants were Jews. *[140]Or do you say, "Surely Abraham and Ishmael and Isaac and Jacob and the tribes were Jews or Christians"? Say, "Do you know better, or Allah? And who is more unjust than he who hides the witness which he has from Allah? And Allah is not unaware of what you do."* It is hilarious that Allah stated in the Qur'an that some people considered Abraham, Ishmael, Isaac, Jacob, or any of the tribes to be Nasara, or Christian, for there is not one Jew or one Christian who has ever claimed that these people were Christians. It is even more hilarious that Allah and Mohammed did not know that these people were Jews, for not only was Abraham a Jew, but he was the father of all the Jewish people.

Ishmael was named as one of the prophets in Qur'an 3:84: *[84]Say, "We believed in Allah and in what has been sent down on us and what has been sent down on Abraham and Ishmael and Isaac and Jacob and the tribes and in what was given to Moses and 'Isā and the prophets from their lord. We do not differentiate between any one of them. And to him we are Muslims."*

Muslims and their scholars believe that Ishmael was a prophet, and they believe in the nonexistent Book of Ishmael for they believe that he, as a prophet, received a revelation as stated in the following verses.

In Qur'an 4:163-164, notice Mohammed's confusion of names and the incorrect order of historical events. *[163]Surely we have revealed to you as we revealed to Noah and the prophets after him. And we revealed to Abraham and Ishmael and Isaac and Jacob and the tribes and 'Isā and Ayyūb[35] and Yunus[36] and Aaron and Solomon, and to David we gave Zabor.[37] [164]And messengers, we have mentioned their story to you before, and messengers we have not mentioned their story to you. And Allah spoke to Moses, speaking.*

---

[35] Job, non-Arabic word of Greek/Syriac origin
[36] name mistakenly used when Jonah was meant
[37] in singular form = Psalms, non-Arabic word of Hebrew/Syriac origin

The Revelation of Error

A similar confusion of names can be also found in the following verses of Qur'an 6:86: *[86]And Ishmael and Alyas'a[38] and Yunus and Lūt,[39] and we preferred all those above the worlds.* How can Ishmael come before Elijah, before Jonah, and before Lot? What a strange order we find here. A similar passage can be found in Qur'an 21:85: *[85]And Ishmael and Idris[40] and Za Al Kafel,[41] all were among the patient.* Then Qur'an 38:48 states: *[48]And remember Ishmael and Alyas'a[42] and Za Al Kafel,[43] all from the chosen.*

As previously stated, many of the stories written in the Qur'an by Mohammed were not entire stories but bits and pieces here and there throughout the Qur'an. Sometimes, Mohammed would write in one portion of revelation about many stories in unrelated historical accounts. One has to use his imagination to tie together the story or any particular prophet from among the various snippets scattered throughout many portions of the Qur'an. I believe that the only story in the Qur'an which is mentioned in one passage is the story of Joseph as we can find in Qur'an 12. Unfortunately, it also contains many errors, contradictions, and fabrications, as you will see in the following sections of this book. To actually understand the story of Ishmael, one must read the account in the Bible, but as for the reading of the bits and pieces of information about Ishmael in the Qur'an, this will give us no understanding, only total confusion.

In the following verses we see small portions of writings in which we learn about Abraham and Ishmael. Typical of these snippets of information is Qur'an 14:39: *[39]The praise be to Allah who has granted me, in my old age, Ishmael and Isaac. Surely my lord is the hearer of the calling.* Abraham praised Allah who answered his prayer for his two sons, Ishmael and Isaac, whom Allah gave to him in his old age. No details were written concerning the births of the two sons. For the actual story to be known, one must go back to Genesis 16. Here is a summary, but we encourage the reader to read the entire account in the Bible.

This passage tells how Sarah took her slave Hagar, the Egyptian, and gave her to her husband Abraham to sleep with so that Sarah

---

[38] Elisha, non-Arabic word of Syriac/earlier Semitic origin
[39] Lot, non-Arabic word of Syriac origin
[40] wrong name, he meant Enoch
[41] wrong name, he meant Isaiah
[42] wrong name, he meant Elisha
[43] wrong name, some Muslim scholars say he meant Isaiah, others say Ezekiel

would receive children through her. Hagar became pregnant, Sarah became jealous, and Sarah treated Hagar harshly. This resulted in Hagar fleeing from her. After Hagar left, the angel of the Lord met with Hagar and told her that she would have many children and would have a son whom she would name Ishmael, which means "the Lord has heard her." The Lord described Ishmael saying that he would be a wild man and his hand would be against every man and everyone's hand would be against him. As for the place where he dwelled, the Bible states that he lived *"in the presence of all his brethren"* not where the Arabs lived. Abram was eighty-six years old when Ishmael was born.

As for the birth of Isaac and the change of Abram and Sarai's names, the Qur'an does not give any details of the information, but the entire information can be found in Genesis 17. Here is a brief summary. When Ishmael was thirteen years old, Abraham was ninety-nine, and the LORD appeared to him saying that *I am the Almighty God*. God changed his name from Abram to Abraham, a name meaning "father of many nations." He promised Abraham that the land of Canaan will be an everlasting possession. The establishment of circumcision was a mark of the covenant between God and the descendants of Abraham. As for the name of Sarai, God changed it to Sarah. God promised Abraham that she would have a son, but Abraham laughed in astonishment since he was almost a hundred years old and Sarah was ninety years old. Abraham asked God that Ishmael might live because he had given up on having children from Sarah.

However, God assured Abraham that Sarah would have a son, and he would be called Isaac. God said that He would establish His covenant with Isaac and his descendants forever. God promised Abraham that He would bless Ishmael, give him twelve princes, and make him a great nation. God stated that the covenant must be established with Isaac to whom Sarah will birth the following year. The rest of the account can be read in Genesis 21:1-5 which tells of Sarah being visited by the Lord and then conceiving a son. The boy was born and given the name Isaac. He was circumcised when he was eight days old and Abraham was one hundred years old. None of this information can be found in the pages of the Qur'an. All that we know from the Qur'an is that Abraham received two sons in his old age.

Mohammed provided one more thought about Ishmael in Qur'an 19:54-55: *[54]And remember in the book Ishmael, surely he was true to his promise and was a messenger, prophet. [55]And he was commanding his family with the prayer and the legal alms and was well-pleasing to his lord.* Mohammed claimed it to be a fact *in the book*, meaning the Bible, that Ishmael was true to his promise. Now, I would like to ask a question. *What promise?* The answer will be, *and Allah knows best.* For there is no information, neither in the Qur'an nor in the Bible, about Ishmael keeping any promises about anything. Then Mohammed stated that Ishmael was "a messenger, prophet." *A messenger to whom? What was his message? A prophet to whom? What was his prophecy?* It is amazing how Mohammed picked up names from the Bible, as well as other great historical figures, and made all of them prophets. Ishmael was a prophet, Lot was a prophet, and Alexander the Great was a prophet, among others. Then Mohammed ended his story with Ishmael commanding his family with prayer and legal alms.

Who was Ishmael's family? Did the Ishmaelites perform prayers and give alms as Muslims do today? Obviously, Mohammed did not know what he was talking about when he spoke of Ishmael, for neither Mohammed nor Allah nor Angel Gabreel must have had the opportunity to read the rest of the story of Ishmael as it is written in the Bible beginning in Genesis 21:8. When we ask the Muslim scholars to tell us the story of Ishmael with all the knowledge they can collect from the words of Allah in the Qur'an and the words of Mohammed in the hadith, they cannot tell much because their information is so limited. However, if they had actually read and accurately copied the account in the Bible, all the questions which we ask would be answered, from the birth of Ishmael until his death.

As we have already covered in the story, we know when Abraham had his son Ishmael. As we read in Genesis 21 through 25, we will discover the rest of the details about the life of Ishmael and know the names of the twelve sons of Ishmael and where they lived. Notably, there is no relationship between the sons of Ishmael and the Arabs, not by their names or by the location of where they lived, for the Bible clearly teaches that the Ishmaelites lived between Egypt and Assyria. The promise of God to Abraham concerning Ishmael was fulfilled for Ishmael and his children dwelled in the presence of his brethren. Then Ishmael died when he was 137 years old.

Chapter 7

Ibn Kathir stated that the two greatest prophets of the sons of Abraham were first Ishmael, for he was the firstborn, and then Isaac.[44] Ibn Kathir also insisted that Ishmael was the sacrificial son, not Isaac.[45] He claimed the proof was because Ishmael was the firstborn, but I would like to share the fact that there is no mention in the Qur'an that the sacrificed son was the firstborn. Moreover, Ishmael was the child of a slave woman rather than the wife of Abraham. Isaac was therefore the firstborn son of Abraham and his wife, Sarah.

Ibn Kathir also made many strange claims about Ishmael.[46] For example, he stated that Ishmael was the first person to ride a horse. His proof was that Mohammed said, "Take the horses for surely it is the inheritance of your father Ishmael." He claimed that Ishmael was the first person to speak the Arabic language in its pure dialect which he learned from the Bedouins, those who used to visit him and his mother in Mecca, and from the ancient people of Yemen. He spoke Arabic perfectly when he was fourteen years old. There are many errors in these statements. For example, Ishmael did not leave Abraham until he was seventeen years old. As we will see in the true story in the biblical account, Ishmael had never been with the Bedouins nor spoken the Arabic language. This raises a question. *How can Ishmael learn to speak Arabic from anyone if he was the first one to speak it?*

Ibn Kathir claimed that the Greeks and Romans were Ishmael's descendants, that he died and was buried at the age of 137 in a place called Hager, and that he used to complain to Allah concerning the heat of Mecca. *Where did these stories come from? There are many more stories, but what evidence do Muslim scholars have for their claims?*

The Kaaba

Mohammed and Muslims claim that the first house built for people to worship in was in Becca, as it is written in Qur'an 3:96: **[96]Surely the first house that was established for the people was that in Becca,[47] blessed and a guidance to the worlds.** Notice that the name Becca was written in error. The name should have been Mecca. This house is named the Kaaba. The second verse mentioned

---
[44]Ibn Kathir, 231.
[45]Ibid., 232.
[46]Ibid., 232-233.
[47]error, should be Mecca

concerning this house, which is also called the *ancient house*, comes from Qur'an 22:33: *[33]You have in them benefits until a fixed time, and then its place is the ancient house.* This house is also called the *forbidden house*. As it is written in Qur'an 5:97: *[97]Allah has made the Kaaba, the forbidden house...*

Here Allah explains that he showed Abraham the place where he would build the house and that Abraham should not have any partner (any other god) with Allah. He was showing him the ways of worship and telling Abraham that he must announce to the people that those who are able must come and perform the Hajj. Then according to Qur'an 2:124-129: *[124]And when Ibrahim[48] was tested by his lord with words, so he fulfilled them. He said, "I am making you an imam[49] to the people." He said, "And who is my offspring?" He said, "My covenant will not be received by the unjust." [125]And when we made the house[50] as a resort for people and a haven: "And take from the place of Abraham a place of prayer." And we made a covenant with Abraham and Ishmael.[51]*

"That purify my house for those who march around it and the dwellers and the kneelers, the worshipers." [126]And when Abraham said, "My lord, make this balad[52] secure and provide its people from the fruit to those who believe among them in Allah and in the last day." He said, "And whoever becomes an infidel, so I will give him a little enjoyment. Then I will force him into the fire of torment, and evil is the final place." [127]And when Abraham was raising the foundations of the house and Ishmael: "Our lord, accept from us, surely you are the hearing, the knowing. [128]Our lord, and make us Muslims to you and among our offspring a Muslim umma[53] to you. And show us our ritual and relent on us. Surely you are the relenting, the merciful. [129]Our lord, and raise to them a messenger from among them who recites your verses to them and teaches them the book and the hikma[54] and purify them. Surely you are the dear, the wise."

---

[48]Abraham, non-Arabic word which appears 69 times, of Hebrew/Syriac origin
[49]spiritual leader
[50]the Kaaba, the black stone building in Mecca
[51]Hebrew name meaning God *hears*, non-Arabic word of Greek/Syriac/Ethiopian/Hebrew origin
[52]country, non-Arabic word of Latin/Greek origin
[53]nation, non-Arabic word of Hebrew/Sumerian origin
[54]wisdom, non-Arabic word of Aramaic origin

Chapter 7

Ibn Kathir stated that the emigration of Abraham with his son Ishmael was to Paran Mountain which is in Mecca.[55] He also stated that Ibn Abbas said that Abraham took the mother of Ishmael, Hagar, and her son Ishmael while she was still breastfeeding him and put them near the house in Mecca. There was nobody living there at the time, and there was no water either. He left them with some dates and some water.

As he was leaving, Hagar called to him as she followed him, "O Abraham, where are you going, leaving us in this valley where there is no person or thing?" She repeated this to him, but he never looked back to her. Then she said to him, "Did Allah command you to do that?" He said, "Yes." She said, "Therefore he will not cause us to get lost." Then she went back. That is when Abraham said in Qur'an 14:37: **[37]Our lord, surely I have caused some of my offspring to dwell in a valley which has no plants, near to your forbidden house...**

One must ask several questions here. *Did Abraham leave Hagar and Ishmael near the forbidden house, the Kaaba? Then who built the Kaaba, and when was it built?* Muslims, the Qur'an, and the hadith claim that Abraham and Ishmael built the *forbidden house*; but in this verse, Abraham said that he left his baby Ishmael and Hagar his mother alone near the forbidden house.

The rest of the verse continues: **[37]... Our lord, so that they may perform the prayer, so make the hearts of the people therefore to yearn toward them, and provide them from the fruit.** Ibn Kathir stated that Hagar breastfed her son until the food and the water were gone.[56] She searched for water seven times as she traveled through the valley until she met the angel who showed her the water. The angel told her that she should not fear because the young man, Ishmael, and his father, Abraham, would build the house. People visited the land and asked the mother of Ishmael if she would let them visit her. She said, "Yes, you are welcome, but you have no right to the water." The young man, Ishmael, learned the Arabic language from them. *So, if Ishmael was the father of the Arab nation, why did he have to learn Arabic from others?*

---

[55]Ibn Kathir, 179-180.
[56]Ibid., 180.

Ibn Kathir wrote that when Ishmael grew up, he married one of the women of the people who taught him the Arabic language.[57] Abraham came to visit and to check on him, but he did not find Ishmael. So he asked his wife about him. She said he went out to find sustenance. So Abraham asked her about her life. She complained that life was hard. So he said to her that when her husband comes back, give him his (Abraham's) peace and greetings and tell him to change the threshold of the door. So when Ishmael came back, he asked, "Has anyone come to you?" She said, "Yes, an old man." Then she told him all that had happened. "Did he give you any advice?" She said, "Yes, he commanded me to give you his greeting, and he said for you to, 'Change the threshold of the door.'" So he said, "That was my father, and he commands me to leave you. So go to your family." So he divorced her and married another one from among them.

Ibn Kathir wrote that Abraham stayed away from them, Ishmael and his mother, for some time.[58] Then Abraham came to visit them a second time, but he didn't find Ishmael. So he visited with Ishmael's new wife. He asked her about Ishmael. She said, "He went to find sustenance." So he asked her, "How is life?" She said, "We are doing great, and we are blessed, praise be to Allah." So he said, "What is your food?" She said, "The meat." He said, "What is your drink?" She said, "Water." He said, "O Allah, bless for them the meat and water." The Prophet Mohammed said, "At this time they do not have seeds, for if they had seeds, Abraham would have asked a blessing on the seeds." So Abraham said to her, "When your husband comes, give him my greetings and ask him to tighten the threshold of his door." So when Ishmael came back to her, he asked her, "Has anyone come to you?" She said, "Yes, an old man with a beautiful appearance." Then she told him what happened. So Ishmael said, "Did he give you any advice?" "Yes, he gives you his greetings, and he commands you to tighten the threshold of your door." He said, "That was my father, and he commands me to hold on to you."

After Abraham waited for some time, he came back to visit Ishmael again, and they greeted each other.[59] Then Abraham said, "O Ishmael, surely Allah commands me to perform a duty." So he said,

---

[57]Ibid.
[58]Ibid.
[59]Ibid., 181.

"Do what your lord commands you." He said, "Will you help me?" He said, "I will help you." So he said, "Allah commands me to build the house here," and he pointed to a high place. There Abraham and Ishmael built the Kaaba. Some Muslims claim that the Kaaba was built by Adam; but obviously, this hadith and Qur'an 2:144-149 clearly teach that it was built by Abraham and Ishmael. Notice in the story we shared previously from the Qur'an, Abraham left Ishmael with his mother near the Kaaba.

Once again we must ask some questions. *Who built the Kaaba? Did Abraham leave Ishmael and his mother near the Kaaba when Ishmael was a baby? Did Abraham and Ishmael build the Kaaba together when Ishmael was a grown man?* It is too bad that Mohammed did not have a continuity editor, as they do in modern movie productions, when he was creating his stories in the Qur'an. Some may claim that Abraham was only remodeling the Kaaba which was built earlier by Adam, but the verses of the Qur'an above and the hadith clearly teach that it was built out from an empty place. There were no buildings there at all.

Notice that the Qur'an adds extraneous details about Abraham and Ishmael building the house, such as quoting the prayer, "Our lord, accept from us, surely you are the hearing, the knowing," which they were praying while building it, in an effort to convince Muslims to believe that this really happened. This would be a great fable to be told to little children before bedtime, but it is nonsense to older boys and girls. Note that Abraham's son, Ishmael, was now a mature, married man whom Abraham had not seen since he was a baby. *Does it make sense that a man with the wisdom of Abraham, in his maturity, would travel all the way from Jerusalem to Mecca several times and not wait for his son to return, so he can visit and spend time with him?*

Notice also that these are the only three times that Abraham visited with his son Ishmael in Mecca after he left Ishmael as a baby, according to Muslim scholars. First, Abraham left Ishmael in Mecca, as a baby with his mother as she was still breastfeeding him. Second, he visited Ishmael's two wives at different times but never saw Ishmael. Last, he and Ishmael built the Kaaba. One must ask a question. *When did Abraham, as Muslims claim, offer Ishmael as a sacrifice in Jerusalem?* We will answer this question in detail when we talk about Isaac, the son God called to be sacrificed.

The Revelation of Error

Although Muslim scholars fabricated much into the story of Ishmael, the story is still missing a great deal of information. That is why I decided to share some of the information from the Bible to prove my point that the story in the Qur'an is quite incomplete. I would like to ask some more questions. If Muslim scholars can answer any of them without using the Bible, that will prove me wrong, and they will have the right to believe that the Qur'an is the complete, perfect word of Allah.

Who was Ishmael's mother? Who introduced Abraham to Ishmael's mother? How many brothers and sisters did Ishmael have? How old was Abraham when he had his son Ishmael? Where was Ishmael born? How old was Ishmael when he left the house of Abraham and under what circumstances? What country did he go to after he left his father's household? Did he ever marry; and, if so, to whom? If he had children, what were their names? Was he involved in the burial of his father Abraham? When did Ishmael die? These are some examples of simple questions which I challenge Muslim scholars to answer. However, let me save them some time by giving you the answer they will come up with: *We do not know, and Allah knows best.* In a simple reading of the story of Ishmael as it is written in the Bible in Genesis 16 through 25, we can find the answers to these questions and many more. We encourage the reader to read the entire account in the book of Genesis.

As for the question of who Ishmael's mother was, she was Hagar. The Qur'an never mentions her name or her story. According to the Bible, in Genesis 16, we know she was an Egyptian slave who lived in Abraham's household for ten years after Abraham returned from his trip to Egypt.

Who introduced Abraham to Ishmael's mother? The answer can be found in Genesis 16:1-4. It was Sarah herself who chose Hagar to be Abraham's wife, for Sarah desired to have children through Hagar. After Hagar became pregnant by Abraham, Sarah became jealous and complained to Abraham. Abraham's response to Sarah was that she could do whatever she wanted with Hagar. Sarah mistreated Hagar to the point that Hagar ran away as seen in Genesis 16:5-6.

As for the question of how many brothers and sisters Ishmael had, there is not any reference in the Bible that Ishmael had any other brothers and sisters. According to Genesis 16:11, when the angel of the Lord met with Hagar, he commanded her to return to her mistress and declared that she would have many children through the child she was carrying and to call him Ishmael. As for the question of how old Abraham was when he had Ishmael, the answer is in Genesis 16:16 where we learn that Abraham was eighty-six years old.

As for the question of where Ishmael was born, he was born in the Promised Land in the tents of Abraham after his mother Hagar returned from having run away. As for the question of Ishmael's age when he left the household of Abraham and under what circumstances, the answer can only be found in the Bible in Genesis 21:9-19. Ishmael was around sixteen years old, for Abraham had his son Isaac when he was one hundred years old. His mother Sarah weaned Isaac when he was about two years old. That would make Abraham around 102 years old. When we subtract the age of Abraham when he had Ishmael at age eighty-six from Abraham's age when Isaac was weaned, 102, we get sixteen.

That would make Ishmael sixteen years old when he was mocking Isaac. Sarah became angry and asked Abraham to kick out the slave Hagar and her son, for she said that Ishmael, the son of a slave, would not share the inheritance with her son. This is a normal reaction toward a mistress who had a son in such circumstances. Abraham hated to do this because Ishmael was still his son, but God told him to listen to his wife and do as she said, for the promise of blessing was to be given through Isaac. However, God promised that Ishmael would also be blessed and be a father of nations.

Early in the morning, Abraham took bread and water, gave them to Hagar, and sent her and Ishmael away. Notice the circumstance was that Abraham did not take them to Mecca in Saudi Arabia as Muslims claim, but he sent them on their way. They became lost in the desert of Beersheba, around 50 km south of Hebron and Gaza in the land of Canaan as you travel towards Egypt. As to the question of which land Ishmael lived in after leaving Canaan, the answer is in the Desert of Paran which is in the Sinai Peninsula and has nothing to do with Saudi Arabia.

In Genesis 21:19-21, the Bible states that after Hagar and Ishmael ran out of water, she cried out, and the Lord heard her and the boy. The Lord opened her eyes, and she saw a well. She drew water for both herself and her son. The boy grew and became an archer. As for the question of whether or not Ishmael ever married, the answer can be found in Genesis 21:21 which states that while still living in the Desert of Paran, his mother found him a wife from Egypt.

In regard to Ishmael's children, how many he had and what their names were, the answers can be found in Genesis 25:12-16. Ishmael had twelve sons, and the Bible clearly states that they lived in the area between Havilah and Shur, close to the border of Egypt on the way to Asshur, which today is known as Iran. As to whether he was involved in the burial of his father, Abraham, the answer is *yes* and can be found in Genesis 25:9. The Scripture states that Isaac and Ishmael buried their father Abraham in the cave of Machpelah near Mamre in the field of Ephron where Sarah his wife was also buried. Abraham was 175 years old when he died, not 200 years old as Muslim scholars claimed. *When did Ishmael die?* The Bible gives us the answer which Muslim scholars do not know. Ishmael lived to be 137 years old, as is written in Genesis 25:17.

The Circumcision

There is much confusion and disagreement about the time of the circumcision of Abraham and his son Ishmael. Ibn Kathir stated that Abraham was circumcised at the age of ninety-nine.[60] He also circumcised Ishmael and all the slaves and others that were with him. That would have made Ishmael thirteen years old. One must ask a question here. *Where did Ibn Kathir come up with this information?*

As we discussed before, according to Muslim scholars, Ishmael had gone with his mother to Mecca when he was an infant. Ibn Kathir also stated that Abu Horyrah said that Mohammed said that Abraham was circumcised when he was eighty years old, *and Allah knows best*. Also, Abu Horyrah said that Mohammed said that Abraham was circumcised when he was one hundred twenty years old and lived eighty years after that, which makes Abraham a man who lived two hundred years. *Is that true?*

One must examine the Scripture to see the true account concerning the circumcision. In Genesis 17:23-25, the Scripture states that Abraham took his son Ishmael and all the men in his household and circumcised them as God commanded him. As we read in verses 24-26: **[24] *Abraham was ninety-nine years old when he was circumcised in the flesh of his foreskin. [25] And Ishmael his son was***

---

[60] Ibn Kathir, 181.

thirteen years old when he was circumcised in the flesh of his foreskin. ²⁶That very same day Abraham was circumcised, and his son Ishmael.

Obviously, Ibn Kathir was correct in his first interpretation concerning the age of Abraham, as he was ninety-nine years old and the son Ishmael was thirteen. At least on this one occasion, Ibn Kathir must have read and copied the Bible correctly, and he exposed the lies of Mohammed concerning the story of the infant Ishmael sent to Mecca with his mother Hagar.

The Birth of Isaac

The name Isaac is mentioned in the Qur'an sixteen times, in most places without details except for his name. The only portion of the story of Isaac with details is the good news of his birth which can be found in Qur'an 11:71-74: *⁷¹And his woman [wife] was standing by so she laughed. So we gave her the good news of Isaac and after Isaac, Jacob. ⁷²She said, "Oh, woe is to me! Will I bear a son when I am old and when my husband is old? Surely this is a wonderful thing." ⁷³They said, "Do you wonder at the command of Allah? The mercy of Allah and his blessings are on you, the people of the house. Surely he is praised, glorious." ⁷⁴So when Abraham's fear had gone and the good news had reached him, he disputed with us for the people of Lot.* Since there is information missing, Muslim scholars and Mohammed must not have known why Abraham sent his concubine Hagar and his son away. In the Bible, Isaac was the son of the free wife, and he was the important descendant on whom the promises of God had been given. That is why I believe it is important to cover the story of Isaac in more detail than Mohammed did.

We read about Isaac in the Bible in Genesis 17:19 where God assured Abraham that it would be his wife Sarah who would bring him a son whom he must call Isaac. God would establish his eternal covenant with him for his descendants. Abraham believed God. According to Genesis 17:1, Abraham was ninety-nine years old when God told him if he walked with Him and lived blameless, then God would make a covenant with him that He would multiply his descendants more than the stars. In Genesis 17:17, Abraham fell on his face and laughed when God told him that his wife Sarah, who was ninety years old at that time, would give him a son. Then Abraham said to God, "May Ishmael live before you," meaning Ishmael was enough for him, but God stated in Genesis 17:19 and assured Abraham that it would be Sarah his wife who would bring him a son and that he must call his name Isaac. God would establish His eternal covenant with him and his descendants.

Ishmael would be blessed, but the covenant must be established through Isaac. God assured Abraham that, at the same time of the following year, Sarah would have his son Isaac. In Genesis 21:3-13, we are told that Isaac was born and that Abraham circumcised his son Isaac when he was eight days old. Abraham himself was a hundred years old. Isaac was weaned, and Abraham made a great feast to celebrate the event. Then the problems began when Sarah saw that Ishmael, the son of the slave, was mocking her son Isaac. Then Sarah demanded that Abraham cast out Hagar the slave and Ishmael her son because she did not want Ishmael to inherit with her son Isaac. That was the reason why Abraham sent Ishmael away with Hagar, as we have mentioned earlier. At first, it grieved Abraham to do it, but God told Abraham to not let it grieve him for he would be blessed through Isaac and the son of the concubine as well.

Why did Abraham send Hagar and her son, Ishmael, far away? Where were they sent? Here is the answer for why Ishmael and his mother were sent away as we see in Genesis 21. It was a request of Sarah to Abraham because Ishmael was mocking her son, Isaac, and the jealousy of her heart that this slave child would inherit with her son. As mentioned above, it grieved Abraham's heart to do so, but God commanded him to listen to his wife and do what she asked. God also promised that he would bless Ishmael and would make him a great nation, for he was also a descendant of Abraham. Concerning what food Abraham gave Hagar, the Bible is very clear. It was bread and water, not dates and water as Muslims claim.[61] Concerning where they were sent, it was not Mecca, as Muslims claim, but the Wilderness of Beersheba as written in Genesis 21:14.

In Genesis 21:15-21, the beginning of the promise of God to Abraham was unfolding. When Hagar ran out of food and water, she cried out to God. The angel, who had appeared to her before, led her to the water, and the promise of God was given once again that this young lad would be a great nation. As he grew in the wilderness, he became a hunter. His mother, Hagar the Egyptian, took him and went

---

[61] Ibn Kathir, 179.

to Egypt. There she married him to an Egyptian wife, not Arab wives as Muslims claim.[62] He had twelve sons.

The names of Ishmael's sons are given in Genesis 25:13-16:
[13] And these were the names of the sons of Ishmael, by their names, according to their generations: The firstborn of Ishmael, Nebajoth; then Kedar, Adbeel, Mibsam, [14] Mishma, Dumah, Massa, [15] Hadar, Tema, Jetur, Naphish, and Kedemah. [16] These were the sons of Ishmael and these were their names, by their towns and their settlements, twelve princes according to their nations.

None of these names have any ties to Arab countries. We will discuss this further later in this chapter, but the obvious conclusion from the account of Genesis is that the wife was not an Arab as Muslims claim, Ishmael never spoke the Arabic language, and, as we explained, he did not dwell in the Arab land but lived 137 years between Egypt and Assyria, according to Genesis 25:17-18.

The Story of the Sacrifice

If you talk to any Muslim about the test which God gave to Abraham concerning the sacrifice of his son, Muslims immediately will state that the sacrificial son was their father, Prophet Ishmael. When you ask why they believe that the sacrificial son was Ishmael and not Isaac, their answer will be that it is because the Bible was corrupted and changed. They claim that the Bible originally stated that it was Ishmael who was sacrificed, but the Jews, because of their jealously of Mohammed, changed the sacrificial person to Isaac. Although all manuscripts, including the Dead Sea Scrolls which were written at least six hundred years before Mohammed was a gleam in his father's eye, these manuscripts said it was Isaac not Ishmael. This argument can be ended very easily. We know what the Bible says. *But who was the sacrificial son, even according to the Qur'an and the hadith?*

What we know from Muslim sources concerning the sacrificed one comes from the writing of Ibn Kathir, who stated that he knew for sure that the sacrifice was Ishmael.[63] In the same paragraph, he tells his Muslim students that Abraham met with Ishmael only three times after he left him as an infant with his mother. The first two were when he visited his son's wives and Ishmael was not home. The final visit

---

[62] Ibid., 180.
[63] Ibid., 182.

The Revelation of Error

was when he built the house, the Kaaba. In Ibn Kathir's writings, he stated that the earth used to fold in order to shorten the distance for Abraham, or he rode a magical, fast mule when he went to visit his son Ishmael. This way of traveling was similar to the mule which Mohammed used to ascend to the seventh heaven.

The only place in the Qur'an which mentions the sacrificial son comes from Qur'an 37:99-113: *[99]And he said, "Surely I am going to my lord. He will guide me." [100]"My lord, grant me from the good." [101]So we gave him the good news of a forbearing young man. [102]So when he came to the age of walking with him, he said, "My son, surely I see that I slaughtered you in my sleep, so see what you see." He said, "O my father, do what you are commanded. You will find me among the patient if Allah wills." [103]So when they surrendered and he had laid him down on his jabīn,[64] [104]and we called him, "O Abraham, [105]indeed, you have believed the vision." Likewise, we surely reward the doers of good. [106]Surely this is a clear trial. [107]And we redeemed him with a great sacrifice. [108]And we left for him among the others. [109]Peace be on Abraham. [110]Likewise, we reward the doers of good. [111]Surely he is of our believing servants. [112]And we gave him the good news of Isaac, a prophet among the good. [113]And we blessed on him and on Isaac, and from their offspring an obvious doer of good, and unjust to himself.*

When we read such a passage, even a cursory reading, we discover that there is no mention of the name Ishmael, but Isaac, in verses 112-113. From these verses concerning the sacrifice, we know that it was Abraham and his son, but we do not know which son. In verse 101, we learn this son was a forbearing young man. Compare this to Genesis 16:12, concerning the nature of Ishmael, ***[12]He shall be a wild man; His hand shall be against every man, and every man's hand against him. And he shall dwell in the presence of all his brethren.***

What was the nature of the character of Ishmael? Obviously, he was not a forbearing young man. Concerning the location of where Ishmael and his descendants would live, as it is stated in the Bible, it was not where Arabs live. In verse 102, the son was walking and talking with Abraham. As we have already established, according to the writing of Ibn Kathir and other Muslim scholars like Al Sohale,

---

[64]side of his forehead, non-Arabic word of Aramaic origin

the sacrificial son must have been Isaac because Ishmael was not with Abraham at the age of walking and talking according to Mohammed in the hadith.[65] He was living at that time in Mecca with his mother. Add to that in verse 112, the Qur'an stated: *[112]And we gave him the good news of Isaac, a prophet among the good.* This verse proves that the sacrificial son whom Abraham talked to in the previous verses was Isaac. One must ask the question. *Why would the Qur'an insert a new character (Isaac) in the end of the story of Ishmael without any introduction?*

What was the real reason for Muslims to claim and insist that the sacrificial son was Ishmael? It is simply because they claim they are the descendants of Ishmael and want to tie Mohammed to Abraham through Ishmael. Therefore, Mohammed would be the prophet from whom the blessing would come to the world. *Can any Muslim scholar prove such a theory by any document, historical or genealogical?* Muslims cannot even prove where Mohammed came from or who his father was. We will prove this, and we will record this proof at the end of this book, volume 2.

How can Mohammed be tied to Ishmael? What Muslims do not know, like most people do not know, is that Arabs are not the descendants of Hagar through Ishmael. They are the descendants of Keturah as it is written in Genesis 25:1-6. Neither the Qur'an nor the hadith mentions her existence in Abraham's life.

According to Genesis 25:1-6: *[1]Abraham again took a wife, and her name was Keturah. [2]And she bore him Zimran, Jokshan, Medan, Midian, Ishbak, and Shuah. [3]Jokshan begot Sheba and Dedan. And the sons of Dedan were Asshurim, Letushim, and Leummim. [4]And the sons of Midian were Ephah, Epher, Hanoch, Abidah, and Eldaah. All these were the children of Keturah. [5]And Abraham gave all that he had to Isaac. [6]But Abraham gave gifts to the sons of the concubines which Abraham had; and while he was still living he sent them eastward, away from Isaac his son, to the country of the east.*

Now where do the descendants of Keturah live, and can we tie them to Arab countries? Yes, we can. The Bible states in verse 6 that Keturah's descendants lived in the East country. *Where did Job live?* In Job 1:3, the Bible states that Job was living in the land of the East,

---

[65]Ibn Kathir, 185.

The Revelation of Error

as it says: *³...so that this man was the greatest of all the people of the East.* Many scholars believe that Job is the oldest book in the Bible, and we know that Job was an Arab man. *How about Job's friends?* One of them the Bible named was Bildad the Shuhite as written in Job 2:11: *¹¹Now when Job's three friends heard of all this adversity that had come upon him, each one came from his own place—Eliphaz the Temanite, Bildad the Shuhite, and Zophar the Naamathite. For they had made an appointment together to come and mourn with him, and to comfort him.* Bildad the Shuhite was one of Job's three friends and a descendant, or follower, of Shuah, son of Abraham and Keturah, whose family lived in the deserts of Arabia.[66] This can be read in Genesis 25:2.

How about the name Sheba in Genesis 25:3? That is another name that is tied to the Queen of Sheba whom we read about in 1 Kings 10:1-13. She was the queen of a country which includes modern day Yemen. One can continue to go through the names of the children and grandchildren of Keturah and tie them to Arab countries.

I remember when I was studying in New Orleans Baptist Theological Seminary in 2001 and was talking with my brother who lived in Egypt at the time. He asked me to do a research paper concerning the ancestors of the Arabs. I answered him that this would not require research; they are the descendants of Ishmael. He requested that I do the research anyway. In the beginning, I thought it would be a waste of time because *everyone knows* that Ishmael was the father of the Arabs. After the research topic was approved by one of my professors, I went to the seminary library. Amazingly, the first book I pulled off the shelf was a large, old book about people and ancestry; and when I looked under the name Keturah, it said that she was "the wife of Abraham after the death of Sarah, the mother of Arab ancestors." Wow! I could not believe my eyes!

Because many people believe in something for a long time, that does not make it true. For example, at one time the whole world believed that the earth was flat. Mohammed believed this, as it is written in the hadith and the Qur'an, but that does not make it flat. Muslims in Saudi Arabia and many places around the world believe that people in the West are lying when they say the earth is round. They insist the earth is flat! If those people would just read the Bible,

---

[66]"Bildad," Bibler.org., accessed December 11, 2012, http://www.bibler.org/glossary/bildad.html.

they would have discovered a long time ago that the earth is in the shape of a sphere which was written in the book of Isaiah 2,700 years ago. We can read in Isaiah 40:22: **[22]*It is He who sits above the circle of the earth, And its inhabitants are like grasshoppers, Who stretches out the heavens like a curtain, And spreads them out like a tent to dwell in.***

The Ishmaelites were the descendants of Ishmael who lived north between Havilah and Shur, which is between Egypt and Assyria. They had no ties to Mohammed or the Arabs, as we have seen in Genesis 25:12-18.

Now, I would like to examine the Genesis account concerning the test of Abraham and the true story of the son who was to be sacrificed. One can read the true account in its entirety in Genesis 22:1-14, but here is a summary of these verses. God tested Abraham by telling him to take his only son, Isaac, and go to Moriah and offer him as a sacrifice on one of the mountains. Even though Abraham loved Isaac very much, he obeyed God and took Isaac, along with two men, a donkey, and wood for the burnt offering. On the third day of traveling, Abraham saw the mountain in the distance and told the men to wait there with the donkey. Abraham and Isaac proceeded on with the wood on Isaac's back. When Isaac asked his father where the lamb was for the sacrifice, Abraham told him that ***God would provide Himself a lamb for the burnt offering.*** When they arrived at the place, Abraham built an altar and then tied Isaac and put him on the altar. As he raised the knife to slay Isaac, the angel of the Lord called to Abraham and told him not to sacrifice his son. Since Abraham did not withhold from God his own son whom he loved, God knew that Abraham feared, or reverenced, Him and placed a ram in a thicket for the sacrifice. Abraham released his son and sacrificed the ram instead. He then named the place "The Lord Will Provide."

I would like to share some thoughts concerning this passage. *Imagine: what if the sacrificed son was Ishmael and not Isaac? How difficult do you think this test would be for Abraham?* After all, God had promised Abraham he would have a son from his wife Sarah, as it is written in Genesis 17:16: **[16]*And I will bless her and also give you a son by her; then I will bless her, and she shall be a mother of nations; kings of peoples shall be from her.*** In my opinion, this test would not have been a big deal; after all, the promise of the inheritance had been given to Sarah and her son, not Hagar and Ishmael. Read carefully the specific request of God in Genesis 22:2, which very clearly states: *²Then He said, "Take now your son, your only son Isaac, whom you love, and go to the land of Moriah, and offer him there as a burnt offering on one of the mountains of which I shall tell you."* This verse does not require any interpretation or fabrication. Some Muslim scholars, in attempting to prove it was Ishmael, seize on the term *only son* to point out that Ishmael was firstborn, but Ishmael was born to a slave woman while Isaac was actually the firstborn to Abraham by his wife. Besides, the Bible did not stop with *only son*, but specifically named Isaac.

It is clearly Isaac, not as the story was written in the Qur'an saying *his* son and leaving us to ask *which* son. In the Qur'an it is written that Abraham was speaking to his son concerning a dream he saw. That is not true when compared to the account in the Bible. God spoke to Abraham and told him to take his only beloved son Isaac and offer him as a sacrifice.

The details of this account in Genesis help the reader understand what took place. The details are there to help us know *when, where, how, who,* and *why*. The Qur'an, the hadith, and Muslim scholars do not have answers for these questions. Their answer to such questions is simply *Allah knows best*. In other words, they don't know. Now, let's take these questions and briefly answer them.

First, let us answer the question of *when*. The Bible states in Genesis 22:1: *¹Now it came to pass after these things that God tested Abraham, and said to him, "Abraham!" And he said, "Here I am."* *What are these things?* This was the fulfillment of the promise of God concerning Isaac, sending Ishmael away with his mother, and now leaving Isaac alone to be sacrificed. That was the true test. Next, let us answer *where*. Abraham was to sacrifice his son Isaac in the land of Moriah and to offer him there for a burnt offering upon one of the mountains of which God would tell him.

Third, let us answer the question of *how*. It was through the audible voice of God to Abraham, not in a dream, when He said to him to take his only son to sacrifice him. Fourth, let us now answer the question *who*. It is his only son, whom he loved completely: Isaac. This is a clear answer, not a vague *his son* as it is written in the Qur'an. Fifth, let us answer *why*. It is a test wherein God proved to us today that Abraham feared and obeyed God. It is for us to fear and obey God. It is also a picture of what will take place within two thousand years when Jesus would be sacrificed, instead of the sinful human race. God provided the sacrificial ram in Genesis 22:13 to be sacrificed instead of Isaac. Then God provided His true Lamb, Jesus Christ, to be the sacrifice for our sin.

<u>Abraham and Lot</u>

There are strong ties between Abraham and Lot. When one reads the Qur'an in some passages, one may think that Lot himself was a prophet for his name is mentioned throughout the Qur'an twenty-seven times. We can read about this in Qur'an 6:86: *[86]And Ishmael and Alyas'a[67] and Yunus and Lūt,[68] and we preferred all those above the worlds.* In other verses of the Qur'an, it is written that Lot was sent to his people as a messenger. One can read about this in 37:133: *[133]And surely Lot was of the messengers.* More evidence that Lot was considered a prophet can be found when he was preaching to them, asking them to leave the indecency in Qur'an 7:80: *[80]And Lot, when he said to his people, "Do you enter into[69] the indecency which no one has committed before you of the worlds?..."* Similar passages concerning Lot's preaching are repeated in 26:161; 27:54; and 29:28. Also, they called the messengers who were sent to Lot liars, as it is written in 26:160: *[160]The people of Lot denied the messengers.*

Ibn Kathir then introduced a strange title which is called "The Sons of Abraham."[70] He explained that Ishmael was his firstborn son from Hagar, and Isaac was the second from Sarah.[71] He also mentioned that Kantorah (wrong name, he meant Keturah) had six sons, but only mentioned the names of five of which only one was the correct name and four were the wrong spellings in the Arabic language. Perhaps he did not know the names.

Then he mentioned that Abraham married another woman by the name of Jehon, and she had five more children for Abraham. Amazingly, he called the first son Lot. He explained that Lot lived in the city of Sodom in a land called Hor Zahr. He explained that these people were robbers and did evil that no one had done since Adam, referring to their homosexual lifestyle. Lot called them to serve the

---

[67]Elisha, non-Arabic word of Syriac/earlier Semitic origin
[68]Lot, non-Arabic word of Syriac origin
[69]commit
[70]Ibn Kathir, 203.
[71]Ibid., 214-223.

one true god, Allah, and to stop their evil ways. However, they did not listen because they did not believe in Lot or his message.

The family of Lot is also mentioned throughout the Qur'an in many places such as 15:59-61; 27:56; and 54:34. *So who was Lot, really? Was he a messenger, a prophet, or what? How was he related to Abraham? Where did they live? What was the true history of Lot and his relationship with Abraham? Who were his family and his people? How did Allah punish his people?* One can ask many more questions concerning Lot and Abraham. *Where can we find the answers?*

Let us first answer using the knowledge of the Qur'an and the hadith, and then we will respond with information from the Bible. Although the story is repeated many times in the Qur'an, the answers to all these questions still cannot be found. Since the story of Abraham and Lot intertwine, we must examine them together, as it is written in one of the lengthy passages concerning Abraham and Lot in Qur'an 11:69-70: **[69]And indeed, our messengers came to Abraham with good news. They said, "Peace." He said, "Peace." So he did not delay, but brought a haneez [a word without meaning] calf. [70]So when he saw that their hands did not reach out to it, he disliked them and grew fearful of them. They said, "Do not fear, surely we are sent to the people of Lot."**

When one reads the previous verses, one must ask the following question. *Who were the messengers that Allah sent to Abraham?* Some Muslim scholars say they were angels that looked like humans. *How do they know?* As a matter of fact, verse 70 proves that these Muslim scholars are not telling the truth. *If they were angels, why did Abraham not like them when they did not eat from the meal he offered them? Is this the true story? Did they not eat the meal?*

The true account in Genesis 18 informs us of the answers to all the above questions and more. We encourage the reader to read this passage in its entirety in Genesis 18:1-33. Here is a summary of the chapter. The Lord appeared to Abraham at the end of the day by the trees of Mamre while he was sitting at his tent's door. Abraham looked up and saw three men, and he ran to meet them and bowed down to the ground. He asked that if he had found favor in the Lord's sight for them to stay, rest under the tree, and allow him to wash their feet and feed them. When they agreed, Abraham fed them fine cakes which Sarah prepared along with butter, milk, and a tender calf from his herd.

While they were eating under the tree, they asked where Sarah was. Abraham answered that she was in the tent. Then the Lord told Abraham that he and Sarah would have a son. Sarah, who had been listening at the tent door, laughed to herself when she heard this. She laughed because both she and Abraham were very old. Then the Lord asked Abraham why Sarah had laughed. The Lord asked Abraham if there was anything too hard for the Lord to do and told him that she would have a son. Sarah denied that she had laughed because she was afraid, but the Lord told her that she had laughed.

Then the men rose to go to Sodom, and Abraham walked with them to send them on their way. The Lord told Abraham what He was going to do. The Lord told Abraham that because the outcry was so great against Sodom and Gomorrah and their sin was so serious, He was going down to see if they were doing what the outcry claimed. The men went toward Sodom, but Abraham still stood with the Lord. Then Abraham asked the Lord if he would destroy the righteous with the wicked or if He would spare the place if there were fifty righteous. The Lord said that He would spare them if fifty righteous could be found. Abraham continued by asking if the Lord would spare the place if only forty-five righteous could be found and continued the count on down to ten righteous. The Lord said that He would spare the place if there were only ten. Then the Lord left, and Abraham returned home.

Notice that the visitors whom Mohammed called messengers were three men, but the Bible actually clarified them to be the Lord and two angels who appeared before Abraham as men. Christian doctrine teaches that the Lord who met Abraham there was actually the incarnate Jesus Christ. Notice that they ate the meal which Abraham offered them, not as it is written in the Qur'an where Mohammed said they did not eat from the meal. As for the messengers who went to Lot, they were the two angels, and the story is clearly written in Genesis 19. However, at the end of the previous Qur'an passage, they told Abraham not to fear for they were going to the people of Lot.[72]

---

[72] Ibn Kathir, 206-207.

The Revelation of Error

Qur'an 11:71-73 states: *⁷¹And his woman [wife] was standing by so she laughed. So we gave her the good news of Isaac and after Isaac, Jacob. ⁷²She said, "Oh, woe is to me! Will I bear a son when I am old and when my husband is old? Surely this is a wonderful thing." ⁷³They said, "Do you wonder at the command of Allah? The mercy of Allah and his blessings are on you, the people of the house. Surely he is praised, glorious."*

In verse 71, we read that Sarah laughed.[73] One must ask *why*. It seemed to me the reason is when Mohammed heard the story he knew that Sarah laughed, but the order in which the verse was written is strange. *Shouldn't she laugh after they tell her she will have a baby? Will a person laugh before the joke is told? Did she cry, or did she shout and strike her face when she heard she would have a baby?* That is exactly what the Qur'an stated in 51:29 where it is written: **So his woman [wife] came in shouting and she struck her face and she said, "Old, barren."** One must wonder, when Muslims read these two different verses, how they can reconcile the contradiction in describing her reaction. *How can Muslim scholars explain the inconsistency in the Qur'an concerning the reaction of Sarah in these two passages above?*

Once again, we must return to the Genesis 18 account to see exactly what took place in this portion of the life of Abraham. When the Lord told Abraham that he and Sarah would have a son, Sarah was standing by the tent door. Both Abraham and Sarah were very old, and she was well past the age of childbearing. Upon hearing she would bear a son, she laughed to herself thinking how she at her age could bear a child. Then the Lord asked Abraham why Sarah laughed at having a child at her age. He then asked Abraham if there was anything too hard for the Lord and assured him that Sarah would have a son. Then Sarah denied that she had laughed because she was afraid, but the Lord told her that yes, she had laughed.

When we look closely at verse 12, we see that Sarah did not laugh out loud, but she actually laughed within her heart because the matter was laughable. *How can a woman in her nineties have a child?* That is not an unusual reaction because Abraham laughed outwardly, as he spoke in his heart, saying, as it is written in Genesis 17:17: *¹⁷Then Abraham fell upon his face, and laughed, and said in his heart, Shall a child be born unto him that is an hundred years old? And*

---

[73]Ibid., 187.

shall Sarah, that is ninety years old, bear? *Why did Sarah lie when the Lord told Abraham that she laughed?* The answer is very simple. In Genesis 18:15, we read that she lied because she was afraid.

Notice the difference between the writings of the Holy Bible and what is written in the Qur'an. Not only does the Bible not contain any inconsistency in telling the true account, as in the case of the Qur'an; but in the words of the Bible we can see clearly the details of the story, which leave no room for speculation or any fabrication by the interpreter. I can simply quote the Bible without any footnote or any interpretation, and the reader will come to a full understanding of what took place in the story of Abraham or in other stories that Mohammed copied in the Qur'an. Now we will go back to the story in the Qur'an.

Qur'an 11:74-76 states: *[74]So when Abraham's fear had gone and the good news had reached him, he disputed with us for the people of Lot. [75]Surely Abraham was meek, awah,[74] often turning. [76]"O Abraham, leave this. Surely indeed, the command of your lord came, and surely the torment will come to them. It will not be turned back."*

Abraham disputed with the messengers concerning the people of Lot. *What was the dispute about? What was the conversation?* Ibn Isaac said that Abraham disputed with the messengers by saying, "Will you destroy a village and therein three hundred believers?"[75] They said, "No." He said, "Two hundred believers?" They said, "No." He said, "Forty believers?" They said, "No." He said, "So fourteen believers?" They said, "No." Ibn Isaac said Abraham asked, "Even if there was in it one believer?" They said, "No." *Where did this great Muslim scholar, Ibn Isaac, come up with these numbers?* Then in Qur'an 29:32: *He said, "Surely Lot is in it." They said, "We know best who is in it..."* Muslim interpreters said the angels, whom they named Gabreel and Mika'il and Israfeel, went from Abraham to the land of Sodom with the appearance of beautiful young men as a temptation from Allah for the people of Lot because he wanted to prove the accusation against them. (Allah was the tempter in this situation.)

So they asked Lot if they could be his guests. This was about sunset, so he was afraid that if he did not host them that someone else

---

[74] a word without meaning
[75] Ibn Kathir, 217-218.

would host them (and presumedly assault them sexually), and he thought they were human. That is why it is written in Qur'an 11:77: **[77]*And when our messengers came to Lot, he was troubled because of them. And his arm was tight,*[76]** *and he said, "This is a dreadful day."* Qatadah stated these messengers came to Lot as he was working on his land and asked him to host them. He tried everything to get them to leave and go to another village. He said to them four times that the people of this city were schemers, and the messengers were ordered not to destroy them until their prophet witnessed against them.

On the other hand, a different interpretation was given by Al Saddi.[77] He said that the angels left Abraham and came in the middle of the day toward the people of Lot. So when they arrived at the Sodom River, they met with Lot's daughter. She was bringing water to her family. He used to have two daughters, the older named Retha and the younger named Zarata. So they said to her, "O young lady, is there a house (meaning a place to stay) here?" So she asked them to wait at the gate of the city.

She ran to her father to tell him about how beautiful they were and that she was concerned that Lot's people may take them, grab them, and assault them sexually. So Lot brought them to his home so that no one would know about them except his household, but his wife went out and told her people. She said, "In the house of Lot there are men who are so beautiful; I never saw such beautiful faces." So they came rushing to Lot's house.

I must ask from what sources do those who are called scholars come up with such strange interpretations? I thought Muslims have only one prophet, whose name is Mohammed. *Do Muslims not have enough common sense to investigate any claim by any of their scholars about what took place here and there? So which of the above interpretations is the true one, and who is lying? What is the original source of the interpretation? Were those men prophesying like Mohammed used to do? Did Angel Gabreel meet with them also? How did they know the names of Lot's daughters, even though the Bible does not give us their names?*

Continuing, because the people of Lot hastened to his house to have sex with his guests, Lot said, "These are my daughters. They are

---

[76]frustrated because he could not protect them
[77]Ibn Kathir, 218.

pure for you." Muslim scholars claim he meant by this that he was leading them to have sex with their own wives, not his daughters, for as a prophet to the nation he had the position like a father and all the girls are his daughters.[78] This cannot be true. First, this is a result of an assumption that Lot was a prophet so that Muslims can claim that the ladies of the city were his daughters. The Bible clearly teaches that this was not the case, for he was not thought to be a prophet, not by God or the people of the city. Second, it is an excellent fabrication, but it will not pass a simple test. Notice earlier, Muslim scholars interpreted that there was not one pure person in the city. *So how could Lot say "pure" daughters?* Third, the Qur'an said that there was not one person who was pure, but here Lot in the Qur'an said, "These are my daughters. They are pure for you." This indicates that Lot was speaking of his own daughters, not other women in the city, for there were no pure women according to the angels. Ibn Kathir stated that what is written in the Genesis account concerning the messengers, in that they were two angels and they ate dinner with Lot, is erroneous and confusing and is a great lie by the People of the Book.

The stories of Lot and the destruction of Sodom and Gomorrah are written throughout the Qur'an. Even if you read every one of these repeated stories, you cannot find an answer to these questions because the details of the story are not there. As we have seen in the Muslim scholars' interpretations, there are many inconsistencies and contradictions. *Again, how do we know the true story?* The answer is very simple. We must read the true account of Lot from the Bible as recorded in Genesis 19:1-38. I would like to point out that I do not have to add any comment because the story is written clearly and plainly. A simple reading of the 38 verses will tell us all we need to know about Lot and Sodom and Gomorrah. We encourage the reader to read the entire passage in the Genesis account, but I would like to highlight some of the important points. This will be repeated in more detail later.

First, there were two angels sent to Lot who appeared like men. Lot invited them to his house, and they ate with him. The men of the city asked Lot to give his visitors to them that they might have sex with them, but Lot refused and instead offered to give them his own

---

[78] Ibid., 219.

daughters. Then they threatened Lot, indicating that they would do worse to him than the visitors.

The two men forced Lot into his house and struck the wicked men of the city with blindness. Then the two men told Lot to leave the city. The angels commanded Lot, his wife, and his two daughters to escape the city and not to look back. However, Lot's wife looked back and became a pillar of salt.

In verse 24, we read that Sodom and Gomorrah were destroyed by a rain of brimstone and fire. Verse 32 is to Muslims one of the most controversial passages in the Bible. They literally use the passage to attack the Holy Bible by stating that the Bible teaches incest. That is why I would like to explain further.

When the Bible talks about the sins of men and women, it does not promote sin. It simply describes the history of what took place and points to the moral lessons which we can learn, so that we will not perform the same sin. For example, Peter denied Jesus three times and then repented. Jesus forgave and restored him. That does not teach us today to deny Jesus; it simply records the history of what took place in Peter's life.

When I read about the sin of many kings and leaders, as well as other men and women in the Bible, to me this is a great proof that the Bible is the Word of God and there is no change in it throughout all the years. If there were any change in the Bible, one may think the Jews would remove any mention of the sin of their kings or their leaders; Christians would do the same, if this practice were acceptable. *How many people today would write the history of his close family members and describe their wrongdoings and sins?* The more you love your people, the more you try to present them as godly, but that is not the case in the Bible. When David committed adultery with Bathsheba and killed her husband, Uriah, and when Peter denied Jesus three times, the Bible records what took place. The Jews and Christians did not change the story. We will talk about this in more detail when we get to that story.

Now we go back to Lot and his two daughters. *Did Lot sin with his two daughters?* The answer is *no*. For before the giving of the law, there is no sin. Imagine you lived alone in your city, you drove your car forty to fifty miles per hour, and you did not stop at the corners of the street. Then change took place, for people moved to the city and put stop signs on every street corner. When the city built a school, signs were also added to the streets to limit speed to 25 mph. As the city grew, they added red lights at big intersections. Now one can say, "If you drive your car again and do not obey the speed limit, the stop signs, and the red lights, you will be punished." Perhaps you will be fined and lose your driver's license or perhaps be imprisoned. *Why?* Simple, because the law was written, change took place in the city.

Whom did Adam's sons marry? They married their own sisters for that was the normal way of life. God did not create two Adams and two Eves but one man and one woman. I know that Muslim scholars lie and teach that every time Eve got pregnant, she had twins, a boy and a girl. The son of one pregnancy could marry the sister of another pregnancy. By such fabrication, Muslims claim that there was no incest, but that is foolishness, for they are still brothers and sisters, no matter from what pregnancy. Any person who has common sense can understand that.

Who did Abraham marry? He married Sarah, his half-sister, who was the daughter of his father but not of his own mother, as it is written in Genesis 20:12. This practice continued until Moses' time in Leviticus 18 where it clearly shows who a man can and cannot marry or even when he may marry. For example, in adherence to purification laws, a man cannot have sexual relations with his own wife during her menstruation or during a time of sickness. All this is written in the Law of Moses in detail.

Now back to Lot. *Did he have sexual relations with his two daughters?* It is written in Genesis 19:33 that he slept with his older daughter and in verse 35 that he slept with his younger daughter. It was not a lie. It was not for the purpose of his two daughters to enjoy a sexual relationship with their father, but it was for the purpose of having children to refill the earth, exactly as it was for Adam's sons and daughters. The Bible said the older daughter had a son whom she named Moab, the father of all the Moabites. The younger daughter had a son and named him Benammi, the father of all the Ammonites. This is the origin of the Moabites and the Ammonites, and it is proof that this account is true.

<u>The Delivery of Lot and His Family</u>

Ibn Kathir stated in his interpretation that, when Lot was trying hard to stop his people from entering his house as he spoke to them from behind his door, the angels said in Qur'an 11:81: *"...O Lot, surely we are messengers of your lord. They will not reach to you...*"[79] They said that Gabreel came out to him, and he struck their faces with the edge of his wing. Thus their eyes were blinded. It is also written in Qur'an 54:37: *So they hid their eyes.*

There are two different interpretations as to what happened to Lot's wife. First, she did not travel with them, as Qur'an 15:65 states: *"... ⁶⁵So walk with your family a part of the night, and follow their rear. And let none of you turn around, and go where you are commanded."* Second, she traveled with them, but she looked behind as it is written in Qur'an 11:81: *⁸¹They said, "O Lot, surely we are messengers of your lord. They will not reach to you, so depart with your family a part of the night, and no one of you turn around except your woman [wife]. Surely it will befall on her what will befall on them. Surely their appointed time is in the morning. Is not the morning near?"* When she looked back, according to Ibn Kathir, a rock fell and crushed her head, and then she *met* with her people, meaning she *spent eternity with them in hell*, because she was of their religion, for she was the one who told them about the two guests of Lot.[80]

Did she look behind, or was she left behind? The messenger asked Lot to leave with his family without his wife as it is written in Qur'an 15:60: *⁶⁰except his woman [wife]. We have decreed that she will be of those who will be left behind."* According to the interpretation of Ibn Kathir, the visitors who arrived at Lot's home were three angels, Gabreel, Mika'il, and Israfeel.[81] This contradicts the account of the Bible, for the Bible states that there were two angels. The Bible says that three angels appeared to Abraham in the form of men. Two of the angels went to Sodom, as it is written in Genesis 19:1. The third angel, according to the teaching of the Bible, was the Lord God himself. We can clearly see this in Genesis 18:13 and 18:17-33. The obvious conclusion was that whoever helped Mohammed to write the story in the Qur'an did not realize that only two angels went to visit Lot in Sodom. A simple reading of the Bible will resolve this conflict.

---

[79]Ibn Kathir, 209-210.
[80]Ibid., 210.
[81]Ibid., 208.

Chapter 7

Although the Bible does not mention the names of the wives of Lot or Noah, Muslim scholars fabricated names, for Al Sohale said that the name of Lot's wife was Wilhah and the name of the wife of Noah was Wiljah. The Qur'an states, although they were wives of honorable prophets, they burn in hell, as written in Qur'an 66:10:
[10] Allah set forth an example to those who became infidels: the woman [wife] of Noah and the woman [wife] of Lot. They were under two of our good servants, but they betrayed them. So they did not benefit them anything against Allah, and it was said, "Enter the fire with those who are entering."

As for the punishment for the people of Lot, the Qur'an states in Qur'an 11:82-83: *[82] So when our command came, we made on it its bottom.[82] And we rained down on them rocks of sijjīl,[83] one after another, [83] marked from your lord. And it is not far from the unjust.* Ibn Kathir stated that Gabreel pulled the cities out by the roots by the edge of his wings, and they were seven cities.[84] However, Muslim scholars disagree on the numbers of those who were killed for some Muslim scholars said there were four hundred souls, but other Muslim scholars said that there were four thousand souls, along with the animals in their land. They were all lifted up to the heavens until the angels of heaven heard the crowing of the roosters and the barking of the dogs. Then Gabreel turned it upside down.

Mujahid said, "The first who fell from heaven were the dignitaries of the city where Lot lived, and then Allah sent on it rain." There are contradictions concerning the rain which fell. (A.) Rain of hard, solid rock (sajiil). Qur'an 15:74: *[74] ... we rained on them rocks of baked clay.* (B.) Rocks which are rocks marked with the name of the person each rock will kill when it falls on them; it will crush their heads. Qur'an 11:82-83: *[82] ... And we rained down on them rocks of sijjīl,[85] one after another, [83] marked from your lord.* (C.) The third and final rain is found in Qur'an 26:173, which is just a simple rain: *[173] And we rained on them rain...*

Allah caused these cities to be a lake with a stench, and its water was of no use for the land around it. So it became a good example. I wonder where this lake is located. Ibn Abbas said that Mohammed

---

[82] turned upside down
[83] baked clay, non-Arabic word of Persian origin
[84] Ibn Kathir, 210-211.
[85] baked clay, non-Arabic word of Persian origin

said if you found any men who do what the men of Lot did (homosexual acts), then put both of them who committed this act to death.[86]

Here we find the end of the story as the messenger explained to Lot that they were from Allah and no harm would come to them. Notice that the messengers asked Lot to walk some of the night. That is funny, and what is even more amusing is that the messengers were telling Lot that no one should look behind except his wife! This is also repeated in Qur'an 7:83: *So we delivered him and his family, except his wife...* This poor quality of writing will become more evident as we examine the story from the Genesis account.

One must ask a question here. *Who are the members of Lot's family?* According to the Bible, he only had a wife and two daughters. *So why does the Qur'an not tell us who the family members were that were saved from the punishment on Lot's people?* Obviously, Mohammed, Gabreel, and Allah did not know how many people were in Lot's family. The loss of Lot's wife is repeated in Qur'an 15:60; 27:57; and 29:32.

Concerning the punishment of the people of Lot, the city was turned upside down in Qur'an 11:82: *[82]...we made on it its bottom.*[87] However, that was not the punishment in Qur'an 15:73-74: *[73]So the shout seized them at the time of sunrise. [74]So we made on it its bottom,*[88] *and we rained on them rocks of baked clay.* Notice that this is not consistent with Qur'an 26:173-174: *[173]And we rained on them rain, so evil is the rain of the warned. [174]Surely in this is a sign, and most of them were not believers.* It is amazing that Allah said that most of them were not believers. This is great evidence that Mohammed did not know how many there were. As we see throughout the Qur'an, there are no details, only general statements. Qur'an 54:33 records that the punishment was a violent wind: *[33]The people of Lot denied the warning. [34]Surely we sent a violent wind on them, except for the family of Lot.* This is an obvious inconsistency concerning the punishment.

Now let us go back to another portion of the story of Abraham. As mentioned before, the story of Abraham is written with many inconsistencies. Notice the differences of the writing in the following

---

[86]Ibn Kathir, 222.
[87]turned upside down
[88]turned upside down

Chapter 7

two passages in Qur'an 11 and Qur'an 15. First, as written in Qur'an 11:69-76: *⁶⁹And indeed, our messengers came to Abraham with good news. They said, "Peace." He said, "Peace." So he did not delay, but brought a haneez⁸⁹ calf. ⁷⁰So when he saw that their hands did not reach out to it, he disliked them and grew fearful of them. They said, "Do not fear, surely we are sent to the people of Lot." ⁷¹And his woman [wife] was standing by so she laughed. So we gave her the good news of Isaac and after Isaac, Jacob. ⁷²She said, "Oh, woe is to me! Will I bear a son when I am old and when my husband is old? Surely this is a wonderful thing." ⁷³They said, "Do you wonder at the command of Allah? The mercy of Allah and his blessings are on you, the people of the house. Surely he is praised, glorious." ⁷⁴So when Abraham's fear had gone and the good news had reached him, he disputed with us for the people of Lot. ⁷⁵Surely Abraham was meek, awah,⁹⁰ often turning. ⁷⁶"O Abraham, leave this. Surely indeed, the command of your lord came, and surely the torment will come to them. It will not be turned back."*

In the second passage in Qur'an 15:51-59, notice that the wording of the story is completely different: *⁵¹And inform them about Abraham's guest. ⁵²When they entered in to him, so they said, "Peace." He said, "Surely we are afraid of you." ⁵³They said, "Do not be afraid. We give you the good news of a boy full of knowledge." ⁵⁴He said, "Did you give me the good news when the old age has touched me? So by what good news do you bring?" ⁵⁵They said, "We gave you the good news with the truth; so do not be of the despairers." ⁵⁶He said, "And who despairs of the mercy of his lord except those who have gone astray?" ⁵⁷He said, "What did you come here for, O messengers?" ⁵⁸They said, "Surely we are sent to a criminal people, ⁵⁹except the family of Lot, of whom we will surely deliver them all..."* When we compare the above two passages, we must ask this question: *Are we talking about the same Abraham and the same messengers?*

Compare the previous passages with the following passage in Qur'an 51:24-37: *²⁴Has the saying of the honored guest of Abraham come to you? ²⁵When they entered unto him, so they*

---
⁸⁹a word without meaning, but Muslim scholars claim it means *roasted*
⁹⁰a word without meaning

The Revelation of Error

said, "Peace." He said, "Peace, unknown people." ²⁶So he went to his family, so he brought a fatted calf. ²⁷So he placed it near them. He said, "Will you not eat?" ²⁸So he began to be afraid of them. They said, "Do not fear." And they gave him the good news of a young, knowledgeable boy. ²⁹So his woman [wife] came in shouting and she struck her face and she said, "Old, barren." ³⁰They said, "Likewise, your lord said. Surely he is the wise, the knowing." ³¹He said, "What is your news, O you the messengers?" ³²They said, "Surely we have been sent to a criminal people ³³to send on them stones of mud ³⁴marked by your lord for the extravagant." ³⁵So we brought forth out of it who was among the believers. ³⁶So we did not find in it except one house of Muslims. ³⁷And we left in it a sign to those who fear the painful torment.*

One must ask another question. *When were the people of Lot destroyed? Was it before or after the messengers came to Abraham?* The Qur'an records in the first two passages that the people of Lot were destroyed after the messengers came to Abraham, but in the last passage, 51:24-37, the Qur'an clearly records that it had already taken place before the meeting of the messengers with Abraham.

Similarly to the story of Abraham, the story of Lot also contains many inconsistencies. We already covered much of this in discussing Qur'an 11:77-83 when it is compared with Qur'an 15:61-79. First, I would like the reader to read the following two passages, Qur'an 11:77-83 and Qur'an 15:61-79. Qur'an 11:77-83 states: *⁷⁷And when our messengers came to Lot, he was troubled because of them. And his arm was tight,[91] and he said, "This is a dreadful day." ⁷⁸And his people came hastily toward him, for before they were doing the evils." He said, "O my people, these are my daughters. They are pure for you, so fear Allah, and do not put me to shame to my guests. Is there not among you a man with a right mind?" ⁷⁹They said, "Indeed, you know we have no rights to your daughters, and surely you well know what we want." ⁸⁰He said, "Would that I had power to resist you or could seek a refuge with a strong supporter."*

⁸¹They said, "O Lot, surely we are messengers of your lord. They will not reach to you, so depart with your family a part of the night, and no one of you turn around except your woman

---

[91] frustrated because he could not protect them

Chapter 7

[wife]. Surely it will befall on her what will befall on them. Surely their appointed time is in the morning. Is not the morning near?" [82]So when our command came, we made on it its bottom.[92] And we rained down on them rocks of sijjīl,[93] one after another, [83]marked from your lord. And it is not far from the unjust.

In Qur'an 15:61-79: *[61]So when the messenger came to the family of Lot, [62]he said, "Surely you are an unknown people." [63]They said, "Yet, we bring to you in what they were doubting in. [64]And we bring to you with the truth, and surely we are truthful. [65]So walk with your family a part of the night, and follow their rear. And let none of you turn around, and go where you are commanded." [66]And this command we gave him because the last of those will be cut off in the morning. [67]And the inhabitants of the city came rejoicing. [68]He said, "Surely those are my guests, so do not disgrace me. [69]And fear Allah, and do not shame me." [70]They said, "Have we not forbidden you to any of the worlds?" [71]He said, "Those are my daughters, if you were doing.[94]" [72]By your life, surely they are blinded in their drunkenness. [73]So the shout seized them at the time of sunrise. [74]So we made on it its bottom,[95] and we rained on them rocks of baked clay. [75]Surely in this there are signs for those who ponder. [76]And surely it is an existing road. [77]Surely in this are signs to the believers, [78]and the unjust were companions of the thicket. [79]So we took vengeance on them, and surely they are on an obvious road.*

We discover a completely different wording and order of action in this preceding passage. First, let us look at the order of the conversation between Lot and the messengers in Qur'an 11. In verse 77, the messengers came to Lot. In verse 78, the people of the city came to Lot obviously seeking to have sex with these messengers. In verses 79-80, Lot continued to negotiate with the people. In verse 81, the messengers (the angels) commanded Lot to leave the city during part of the night, explaining that no one should look behind except for

---

[92]turned upside down
[93]baked clay, non-Arabic word of Persian origin
[94]having sex
[95]turned upside down

The Revelation of Error

his wife, for the punishment would be coming in the morning which was very near. That was the order of the story according to Qur'an 11.

Now in Qur'an 15 the order is completely different when compared to Qur'an 11, for here we see, in verse 61, the messengers came to the family of Lot. Verses 62-64 contain a strange conversation which is not mentioned in Qur'an 11. In verse 65, the messengers asked Lot to leave the city, stating that no one would look behind. It is not mentioned that Lot's wife would look behind. In verse 66, the messengers explained that the people of the city would be destroyed by morning. Surprise, surprise, the people of the city came to Lot's house, which was not the case as recorded in Qur'an 11, for there it is stated the people of the city came to his house before such a conversation took place. In verses 67-70, there was a negotiation between Lot and the people of the city. In verse 71, Lot offered his daughters to the people of the city. In verses 72-78, the punishment fell on the people of the city, but Mohammed forgot to mention that the wife of Lot was among those who died.

On the other hand, in the following verses in Qur'an 26:160-175, Mohammed rewrote the story of Lot with different wording and with many errors: *^{160}The people of Lot denied the messengers. ^{161}When their brother Lot said to them, "Will you not fear? ^{162}Surely I am a faithful messenger to you. ^{163}So fear Allah, and obey me. ^{164}And I do not ask you any wage for it; for my wage is but on the lord of the worlds. ^{165}Do you enter into^{96} the males from the worlds, ^{166}and forsaking what your lord created for you from your wives? Yet you are a transgressing people!" ^{167}They said, "O Lot, if you do not desist, you will become of the expelled." ^{168}He said, "Surely I am of those who detest what you are doing. ^{169}My lord, deliver me and my family from what they do." ^{170}So we delivered him and his whole family together, ^{171}except an elder among those who tarried. ^{172}Then we destroyed the others.^{173}And we rained on them rain, so evil is the rain of the warned. ^{174}Surely in this is a sign, and most of them were not believers. ^{175}And surely your lord, he is the dear, the merciful.*

In verse 160, Mohammed stated that the people of Lot considered the messengers liars. *What messengers?* For there were no messengers sent to the people of Lot according the account in

---

^{96}have sex within a homosexual lifestyle

Genesis. Amazingly, in verse 162, even according to the Qur'an there was only one messenger, Lot. *How can Allah call Lot "messengers"?* In verse 161, Allah called Lot a brother of the people of Lot (the people of Sodom). He was not their brother, as we will see in the true account in the Bible.

Verses 163-166 contain the preaching of Lot to the people of Lot. (Notice that Mohammad, Allah, and Gabreel did not know that there were no people called the people of Lot, but rather the people of Sodom, for Lot was a stranger in their land as we will see in the true account of the Bible.) In verse 167, the people of Lot threatened Lot by saying that they would cast him out of the city, which obviously never took place in the Bible. In verses 168-169, Lot called on Allah to save him. In verse 170, Allah saved him and all his family. In verse 171, an old person, and *only Allah knows*, from Lot's family was destroyed. In verses 172-173, the rain fell on them. In verse 174, the Qur'an declares that most of the people of Lot were not believers. When one reads such a verse, one can come to the conclusion that there were some believers among them. However, according to the Bible, there were not any believers among the *people of Lot*, not even one. Mohammed ended the story of Lot in this portion of revelation by stating that Allah is the dear, the merciful.

The story of Lot is repeated again in two short versions in Qur'an 29 and Qur'an 54. When we compare the following two passages, we discover that there is a major contradiction, for we see that Lot's wife was not delivered, as it is clearly written in Qur'an 29:33: *...Surely we will deliver you and your family except your woman [wife]...* The obvious conclusion from reading Qur'an 54:34 is that the family of Lot was delivered. Mohammed forgot to mention that Lot's wife was not delivered. *[34]Surely we sent a violent wind on them, except for the family of Lot. We delivered them at dawn.* Qur'an 54:34 contradicts what is written in these other verses throughout the Qur'an in which it is stated that Lot's wife was destroyed while Lot and the rest of his family were delivered.

Qur'an 29:33-35 states: *[33]And when our messengers came to Lot, he was troubled because of them, and his arm was tight.[97] And they said, "Do not fear, and do not grieve. Surely we will deliver you and your family except your woman [wife]; she was of those who stayed behind." [34]Surely we will bring down wrath*

---

[97] frustrated because he could not protect them

The Revelation of Error

from the heaven on the people in this village because they were transgressors. ³⁵And indeed, we left from it a clear sign to people who understand.

According to Qur'an 54:33-40: ³³The people of Lot denied the warning. ³⁴Surely we sent a violent wind on them, except for the family of Lot. We delivered them at dawn. ³⁵A grace from us. Likewise, we rewarded those who gave thanks. ³⁶And indeed, he warned them of our severity, so they doubted the warning. ³⁷And indeed, they negotiated with him about his guests, so we hid their eyes. So taste my torment and my warning! ³⁸And indeed, in the early morning a torment rested on them. ³⁹So taste my torment and my warning. ⁴⁰And indeed, we made the Qur'an easy to remember. So is there any who remember?

So it is, in the following verses in Qur'an 26:160-175: ¹⁶⁰The people of Lot denied the messengers. ¹⁶¹When their brother Lot said to them, "Will you not fear? ¹⁶²Surely I am a faithful messenger to you. ¹⁶³So fear Allah, and obey me. ¹⁶⁴And I do not ask you any wage for it; for my wage is but on the lord of the worlds. ¹⁶⁵Do you enter into[98] the males from the worlds, ¹⁶⁶and forsaking what your lord created for you from your wives? Yet you are a transgressing people!" ¹⁶⁷They said, "O Lot, if you do not desist, you will become of the expelled." ¹⁶⁸He said, "Surely I am of those who detest what you are doing. ¹⁶⁹My lord, deliver me and my family from what they do." ¹⁷⁰So we delivered him and his whole family together, ¹⁷¹except an elder among those who tarried. ¹⁷²Then we destroyed the others.¹⁷³And we rained on them rain, so evil is the rain of the warned. ¹⁷⁴Surely in this is a sign, and most of them were not believers. ¹⁷⁵And surely your lord, he is the dear, the merciful.

A Summary of the Story of Lot According to the Bible

When we read the account of Genesis, as we stated before, Lot's story is intertwined with the story of Abraham. It begins in Genesis 12. In verse 1, God called Abram to leave his homeland to go to the Promised Land. In verse 4, Abram departed when he was seventy-five years old, and Lot traveled with him to the Promised Land. They took all of their possessions with them, and they came to the land of

---

[98]have sex within a homosexual lifestyle

Canaan. Abram traveled to the south because there was a great famine in the land, as it is written in verse 10. That is why Abram, Sarai, and Lot went to Egypt. That is where Abram told Sarai to say that she was his sister because he was afraid that they might kill him to take her for a wife, in verse 13. That is when Abram lied, by saying that Sarai was his sister. Abram received livestock, slaves, and possessions when they were asked to leave Egypt.

In Genesis 13:1-13, we read that Abram left Egypt with his wife and all his possessions along with Lot until they arrived at Bethel. Lot was also rich with many possessions. The land was not able to support them, for they had an abundance of livestock, slaves, and possessions. Strife and conflict took place between the herdsmen of Abram and the herdsmen of Lot. Abram asked Lot to separate himself and his possessions from those of Abram, so that there would not be any contention between them. Lot lifted up his eyes and saw Sodom and Gomorrah, noticing that it was a good land. Therefore, he chose for himself the Plain of Jordan and traveled toward the east, and he pitched his tents in Sodom. The people of Sodom, however, were sinners and very wicked. So far, we cannot discover from the account of the Bible any indication that Lot was ever sent to Sodom as a prophet as Mohammed claimed in the Qur'an.

In Genesis 14, we discover a very important event in Lot's life which Mohammed disregarded completely. It was one of the early wars in the history of men. Four kings engaged in war against five kings. As it is written in verses 1-2: *[1] And it came to pass in the days of Amraphel king of Shinar, Arioch king of Ellasar, Chedorlaomer king of Elam, and Tidal king of nations, [2] that they made war with Bera king of Sodom, Birsha king of Gomorrah, Shinab king of Admah, Shemeber king of Zeboiim, and the king of Bela (that is, Zoar).* This war lasted fourteen years as clearly stated in verses 3-5. When the war was over, the king of Sodom and the king of Gomorrah fled because they had lost the war. The winning kings took the spoils of Sodom and Gomorrah. Since Lot was living in Sodom, he was taken with all of his possessions as spoils of war, as it is written in verse 12. When Abram heard of what happened to Lot, as it is written in verse 14, he took 318 of his servants and followed them to Dan. There he divided himself against them with his servants at night. He had a great victory over them, and he brought back Lot and all his goods. Abram refused to take any of the spoils from the king of

Sodom. He only took food for the young men and a portion, a wage, for the men who fought for him.

In Genesis 18:20, we read that the Lord stated that the outcry against Sodom and Gomorrah was great because of their sin. That's when the two angels of the Lord, who appeared like men to Abram, left Abram with the Lord and traveled toward Sodom. After finding out that the Lord was going to destroy Sodom, Abram negotiated with the Lord (verse 24), when he said to the Lord that perhaps there were fifty righteous in the city. The Lord's response was that if there are fifty righteous, He would not destroy the city. The number went down to forty-five, then forty, then thirty, then twenty, then ten, and the conclusion was that there were not even ten righteous in the city.

The story of the destruction of Sodom and the new beginning for the daughters of Lot can be found in Genesis 19:1-38, as we mentioned earlier. The two angels came to Sodom in the evening. Lot welcomed them and asked them to spend the night at his house, but they refused by stating that they would abide in the streets all night, which is exactly the opposite of the story as it is fabricated by Muslim scholars. Lot pressed upon them to come and to stay in his house. He made them a feast. Before they lay down, all of the men of the city of Sodom surrounded the house of Lot and asked Lot to bring the two men out so they may *know* (have sex with) them.

Lot spoke to the men of the city and asked them not to do evil and offered them his two virgin daughters. The men asked Lot to move aside, as he was a stranger in the land. They rejected his judging of them, and they threatened Lot by saying they would deal worse with him than with the two visitors. As the men of the city were about to break down the door, the two men reached out with their hands, took Lot inside the house, and closed the door. As for all the men who were outside the house, they were stricken with blindness and could not find the door.

The two men asked Lot to bring his relatives and his household outside of the city as they explained to Lot that the city would be destroyed. Lot spoke to his sons-in-law, but they considered him to be joking. Early in the morning, the angels hastened Lot to take his wife and his two daughters out of the city. Notice that the angels asked Lot to take his wife, not as Mohammed stated throughout the Qur'an that she was *left* behind. Nor did the angels tell Lot that his wife would die. Because Lot lingered, the angels laid hands upon him, his wife, and his daughters. They put them outside of the city because the Lord was merciful unto Lot, and they asked Lot's family to run for their lives and not to look behind.

Lot asked the angels if he could stay at a nearby city, instead of going to the mountains, for he feared they may die in the mountains. The angels accepted his proposition and saved this city. When the sun rose, Lot entered the city, and the Lord rained brimstone and fire on the plains of Sodom and Gomorrah. It was not rock nor storm nor a shout nor regular rain, as Mohammed claimed throughout the Qur'an. The city, the plain, the inhabitants of the city, and all the plants were destroyed. Notice that Angel Gabriel was not involved at all, and he did not use his wing to do such a thing as Mohammed and Muslim scholars claimed.

Lot's wife looked behind, so she became a pillar of salt. Notice that no rock fell on her, and she did not die like the people of the city, as erroneously written in the Qur'an and in Muslim scholars' interpretations. Then Lot left the city with his two daughters to live in the mountains, for he feared to live in the city. He dwelled in a cave with his two daughters. The older daughter spoke to the younger daughter saying that their father was getting old and there were no men in the earth to be with them in order to have children. They gave their father a drink of wine, and during the first night, the older daughter lay with her father. He did not know what happened. They gave their father a drink of wine once again. The younger daughter lay with her father, and he again did not know what happened. They both became pregnant from their father. The older daughter had a son, and she called him Moab. He was the father of the Moabites. The younger daughter had a son. She named him Benammi, and he was the father of the children of Ammon.

Abraham and His Concern about the Resurrection

Qur'an 2:260 states: *^{260}And when Abraham said, "My lord, show me how you give life to the dead." He said, "Have you not believed?" He said, "Yes, but so that my heart be assured." He said, "So take four of the birds and cut them and mix them; then place a part of them on every mountain. Then call them, and they will come swiftly to you. And know that Allah is dear, wise."*

Did this really happen? Was Abraham concerned about proof of the resurrection? If these verses came before verse 258, it would be more acceptable regarding the order of these verses. For verse 258 states: *²⁵⁸Have you not seen him who disputed with Abraham about his lord, that Allah had given him the kingdom? When Abraham said, "My lord is he who gives life and causes death." He said, "I give life and cause death." Abraham said, "So surely Allah brings the sun from the east, so bring it from the west." So the infidel was confounded. And Allah will not guide the unjust people.* Abraham was speaking to the king, and he knew for sure that Allah, his lord, gives life and causes death. However here, two verses later, he was questioning Allah. Amazingly, Muslim scholars will go in circles trying to say that he was not doubting Allah by saying that Abraham surely knew Allah's ability to raise the dead, but he wanted to see for himself so he would know for sure. Therefore, Allah answered his question and gave him his desire. According to Ibn Kathir, Abraham answered, "So my heart be assured," which means his heart before seeing the resurrection of his sacrifice was not assured.[99]

The Qur'an does not mention any specific type of birds which Abraham sacrificed; as usual, Muslim scholars disagree on what they were. However, they know for sure that the miracle happened when Abraham called these birds by the permission of Allah, after he ripped their flesh to pieces, tore off their feathers, and mixed them together; behold, every piece of flesh and every feather came back together as they flew back to him. *So where did Mohammed come up with this story? Were there really four different kinds of birds?*

Perhaps it is time for Muslims to know the source of another story found in the Qur'an. The source of this story comes from Genesis 15:7-11. This was not a question from Abraham to God concerning the resurrection, but it was a sacrifice of the first covenant between God and Abraham concerning the Promised Land. Abraham asked the question, "Whereby shall I know that I shall inherit it?" Notice also there were not four birds as Mohammed described.

The following passage is from Genesis 15:7-11: *⁷Then He said to him, "I am the Lord, who brought you out of Ur of the Chaldeans, to give you this land to inherit it." ⁸And he said, "Lord God, how shall I know that I will inherit it?" ⁹So He said to him, "Bring Me a three-year-old heifer, a three-year-old female goat, a three-year-old ram, a turtledove, and a young pigeon." ¹⁰Then he brought all these to Him and cut them in two, down the middle, and placed each piece*

---

[99]Ibn Kathir, 204.

opposite the other; but he did not cut the birds in two. ¹¹And when the vultures came down on the carcasses, Abram drove them away.

In Matthew Henry's Commentary on this passage he states:
> Assurance was given to Abram of the land of Canaan for an inheritance. God never promises more than He is able to perform, as men often do. Abram did as God commanded him. He divided the beasts in the midst, according to the ceremony used in confirming covenants, described in Jeremiah 34:18-19. Having prepared according to God's appointment, he set himself to wait for the sign God might give him. A watch must be kept upon our spiritual sacrifices. When vain thoughts, like these fowls, come down upon our sacrifices, we must drive them away, and seek to attend on God without distraction.[100]

Notice that the Bible explains the details of Abram's life, even the change of his name from Abram to Abraham and the change of his wife's name from Sarai to Sarah. The rest of Abraham's story is written for us to read and to know exactly what happened in the account of Genesis. There is no place for speculation, suggestion, conjecture, or any other interpretation. All was written as it took place 3,900 years ago in the account of Genesis. For we know where, when, how, why, who, and what took place in the life of Abraham. If the reader spends a few hours reading the account of Genesis, he or she will find the great differences between the corrupt story of the Qur'an and the true account of Genesis concerning the life and the death of Abraham.

Was Abraham a Muslim? When we read the verses in Qur'an 2:130-132 which state: *¹³⁰And who forsakes the religion of Abraham except him who fools himself? And we indeed choose him in this world, and surely in the hereafter he is among the good. ¹³¹When his lord said to him, "Be Muslim." He said, "I became a Muslim to the lord of the worlds." ¹³²And Abraham advised by it[101] his sons and Jacob: "O my sons, surely Allah has chosen the religion for you, so do not die except you are Muslims."*

---

[100]"Genesis 15," *The Bible in Arabic,* accessed December 20, 2012, http://injeel.com/Read.aspx?vn=1,3&t=1&b=1&svn=3&btp=1&stp=1&tx=Jesus+ Christ&cmnt= 1&c=15.
[101]to become Muslims

Also in Qur'an 2:133-136: *¹³³Or were you witnesses when death came to Jacob when he said to his sons, "What will you serve after me?" They said, "We will serve your god and the god of your fathers, Abraham and Ishmael and Isaac.*[102] *One god and to him we are Muslims." ¹³⁴This nation indeed passed away. To them what they earned and to you what you earned. And do not ask about what they were doing. ¹³⁵And they said, "Become Jews or Christians; you will be guided." Say, "Yet the religion of Abraham is hanifan,*[103] *and he was not of the polytheists. ¹³⁶Say, "We believed in Allah and what has been sent down to us, and what has been sent down to Abraham and Ishmael and Isaac and Jacob and the asbāt,*[104] *and what has been given to Moses and 'Isā, and what has been given to the prophets from their lord. We do not differentiate between any of them, and to him we are Muslims."*

Obviously, these verses clearly teach, as many Muslim scholars teach, that Abraham was a Muslim and every baby is born Muslim. The reason some children grow up to be believers in any other religion is because children are indoctrinated into the religion that their fathers follow. That is why the Muslims use the term *revert to Islam* when someone converts from another religion to Islam.

On the other hand, there are Muslims who claim that the real meaning of the writings of the Qur'an, concerning Abraham or any other prophet, is that they *submitted* or *surrendered* to Allah. It does not mean that they were Muslim believers who believed in Mohammed and the religion of Islam. This interpretation is not true because the hadith states that, since the great sign that Adam saw in the heaven, which was written in lights saying, "There is no god but Allah, and Mohammed is his messenger," Adam believed in Mohammed and became a Muslim.[105] In Islam, children follow the religion of the father; therefore, the entire world is Muslim. Those who do not believe in Islam must revert to Islam. That is what Muslims truly believe. Do not forget that Muslims believe that Abraham and his son Ishmael built the Kaaba, and they began the pilgrimage of Hajj which is still practiced today. No Christian or Jew believes in such a practice.

---

[102]Hebrew name meaning *laughter*, non-Arabic word of Hebrew origin
[103]a word without meaning
[104]tribes, non-Arabic word of Hebrew/Syriac origin in its singular form
[105]Ibn Kathir, 91.

Some may say the Qur'an teaches that there are three religions: Judaism, Christianity, and Islam. They may quote some of the early verses of the Qur'an such as 2:62: *⁶²Surely those who believed¹⁰⁶ and those who are Jews and the Nasara¹⁰⁷ and the Sābeen,¹⁰⁸ whoever believed in Allah and the last day and did good deed, so they will have their ajoor¹⁰⁹ with their lord and no fear on them, and they will not grieve.* We must remind them that these verses have been abrogated by Qur'an 3:85. *⁸⁵And whoever desires any other religion except Islam, so it¹¹⁰ will not be accepted from him, and in the hereafter he will be of the losers.* Therefore, Islam is the final religion which is the accepted religion by Allah, according to the final word of Allah.

The Castle of Abraham in the Garden

Ibn Kathir stated that Abu Horyrah said that Mohammed said, "In the garden there is a castle, and it is made out of pearl that Allah prepared for his friend Abraham."¹¹¹ When we compare such a teaching with the Bible, we discover that Mohammed has not told the truth. He lied, for the heaven of the Bible where Abraham will be does not have a garden as Mohammed imagined it with a castle made out of pearls. We will be talking in more detail about Mohammed's garden later.

The Death of Abraham and What Was Said about His Age

Ibn Kathir said that Ibn Jarir said that Abraham was born at the time of Nimrod, son of Canaan who was a famous king known by the name of Dahak, who reigned for a thousand years.¹¹² Some said that a bright star showed up, whose light was brighter than the sun and the moon. Then Nimrod was so frightened that he brought the priest and the astrologers and asked them about this bright star. They told him that a boy will be born from his people, and Nimrod would lose his kingdom by the boy's hand. Therefore, the king gave an order that

---

[106] Muslims
[107] word made up to mean Christians
[108] Sabians, idol worshipers, uncertain what specific people this represents; may have been a word play on the name of the Sabaean Christians of S. Arabia, non-Arabic word of unknown origin
[109] wage, non-Arabic word of possible Syriac origin
[110] any other religion
[111] Ibn Kathir, 200.
[112] Ibid., 201.

The Revelation of Error

men must separate from women (he meant sexually), and everyone born from that day on would be put to death. That's when Abraham was born, but Allah protected him.

Muslim scholars disagree about where Abraham was born. Some said he was born in Soeth, some said he was born in Babel, and others said he was born in Soad. However, Ibn Abbas said that Abraham was born in Barzah, east of Damascus. Ibn Kathir continued by stating that Sarah died before Abraham in the village of Hebron when she was 127 years old.[113] Abraham was sorrowful, and he buried her in a cave that he bought from a man named Ephron. He bought the cave for 400 weights. 400 weights! *Where did Ibn Kathir come up with this information concerning the place of Sarah's death, her age at death, Abraham's sorrow, and the price of the cave?*

Ibn Kathir reminds me of Mohammed once again. As Mohammed used to copy from the Bible, so it is with Ibn Kathir. We encourage the reader to read the entire account in Genesis 23. Ibn Kathir continued to tell the story of the engagement of Isaac to Rebecca. He summarized Genesis 24, which includes sixty-seven verses, into one sentence. We encourage the reader to once again read the account in the Bible. All Ibn Kathir said was that Abraham engaged Isaac to Rifka, the daughter of Bethuel. He sent his servant who brought her from her country and brought with her nurses and her slaves on camels. Ibn Kathir continued to state that Abraham married Quentora. He meant Keturah. Then he mentioned her children's names. *Once again, where did Ibn Kathir come up with this information?* The answer is found in Genesis 25.

As for the death of Abraham, Ibn Kathir stated that it was said that Abraham died suddenly as it was in the case of David and Solomon. As usual, Muslim scholars disagree on the age of Abraham when he died. Ibn Kathir also wrote that Abraham was sick, and he was 175 years old when he died. It was also said that he was 190 years old and was buried in the same tomb as his wife. His sons, Ishmael and Isaac, buried him, but Ibn Al Kelby said that he died when he was two hundred years old. Abu Hatem said that Abu Horyrah said that Mohammed said that Abraham was circumcised when he was 120 years old, and then he lived eighty more years. *Is this number correct?*

---

[113]Ibid., 202.

First, I am surprised. *Why did Ibn Kathir not look at the Bible as he usually did to get his information?* Second, if he or Mohammed had done a quick search in the Bible, they would have saved themselves from so many contradictions and errors. For example, if they had just read Genesis 17:24, they would have discovered that Abraham was ninety-nine years old when he was circumcised. If they had read Genesis 25:7, they would have discovered that Abraham died when he was 175 years old.

I believe that Ibn Kathir, like all Muslim scholars, only used the Bible to fill in some of the important information if they did not have it. They would use Mohammed's teaching, even if it was false and disagreed with the Bible. For example, as we just wrote above, Ibn Kathir stated that Isaac and Ishmael buried their father Abraham in the cave in which Abraham buried his wife Sarah. *Where did Ibn Kathir come up with this information?*

The answer is in Genesis 25:9-10. *Why did Ibn Kathir copy this information from the Bible?* Also, notice in 25:7 the age of Abraham when he died. Ibn Kathir used verses 9-10 but not verse 7. The reason is that *Mohammed* stated that Abraham was circumcised when he was 120 and died eighty years later, which means that Abraham lived 200 years which is a great error. The conclusion is that Ibn Kathir used the Bible when the information was missing in the Qur'an and the hadith; but if it was mentioned in the Qur'an, he would use it, even if it was false information.

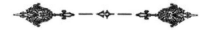

8 The Story of Midian and Shoaib

Ibn Kathir told the story of Midian by stating there were Arabs living in their city of Midian which was near the land of Maan on the edge of the land of Sham which followed the Hijaz area, near the lake of the people of Lot.[1] They were the children of Midian, Ibn Midiana, Ibn Abraham. Their prophet's name was Shoaib Ibn Mikel, Ibn Yshjan. Ibn Kathir, however, said it was also said their prophet was Shoaib Ibn Yashkhar, Ibn Levi, Ibn Jacob. Then he contradicted himself by saying Shoaib was again Shoaib Ibn Naoyeb, Ibn Ayfa, Ibn Thabet, Ibn Midian, Ibn Abraham. Ibn Kathir said he could also be *somebody else*.

If he was the son of Isaac or the son of Levi, then he was not an Arab, which means the story is a complete fairy tale. Since Shoaib could be anyone else, I would like to say the famous statement that Ibn Kathir forgot to say this time: *and Allah knows best*. It is amazing that Muslim scholars could go into detail about a prophet without knowing who the prophet was.

Ibn Kathir stated that Ibn Asakir said his grandmother, or perhaps his mother, was the daughter of Lot.[2] *Was she the mother or the grandmother?* From the Bible, Genesis 19:37-38, we know that the two daughters of Lot had two sons; the older had a son by the name of Moab who was the father of the Moabites, and the younger had a son by the name of Benammi who was the father of the children of Ammon. If this was the case, then Shoaib could not have been an Arab for he was not a descendant of Keturah. To this day, Muslim scholars do not know who Shoaib was.

The Bible states in Genesis 12:4-5 that Abraham, Lot, and Sarah are the ones who came to the land of Canaan with all they owned, including their slaves. Since Shoaib was not a slave, he could not have been one of those who emigrated. According to the genealogy given by Ibn Kathir and other scholars, Shoaib was the great-grandson of Isaac or the great-grandson of Jacob or the great-grandson of Abraham or the sixth generation of Abraham. In any

---

[1] Ibn Kathir, *Stories of the Prophets*, vol. 1, Abo Al Fida Ishamail Ibn Kathir Al Kurashi Al Damashce (Beirut: Dar Al-Arab Heritage, 1408 AH, 1988), 214.
[2] Ibid., 214.

case, there is no way he existed in Abraham's time because, before Shoaib was *a gleam in his father's eye*, Abraham was dead; therefore, he could neither *believe* nor *emigrate* with Abraham.

Wahab Ibn Monabah said Shoaib and Molagam believed in Abraham when he was thrown into the fire, and they emigrated with Abraham to Sham.[3] Abraham married them to the daughters of Lot, *and Allah knows best*. This was another error because Lot's daughters were never married to anyone. They only had children by their father, a fact which we mentioned previously.

Ibn Kathir stated that the people of Shoaib and two sisters of Moses were relatives.[4] Then he corrected himself, stating that the time between them was too great.

Ibn Kathir stated that there were four prophets from the Arabs: Houd, Saleh, Shoaib, and Mohammed.[5] Mohammed said that Shoaib was the orator, the people of Midian were infidels and highway robbers who brought fear to travelers, and they worshiped the trees. He also said that they were the worst people to do business with, especially when they weighed or measured, because they took more and gave less.

Allah sent to them a man from among them, and he was the messenger from Allah: Shoaib.[6] He called them to worship Allah alone without partners and advised them to stop all that they were doing which was displeasing. As Allah said in Qur'an 7:85: *[85]And to Midian, their brother Shoaib said, "O my people, serve Allah. You have no god other than him. Indeed, a proof came to you from your lord, so fulfill the measure and the weight. And do not defraud the people their things, and do not vandalize on the earth after its reform. This will be better for you, if you were believers.*

Ibn Kathir said that Allah performed miracles by the hand of Shoaib.[7] In Qur'an 7:86: *[86]And do not sit down in every way, threatening and preventing [others] from Allah's way, those who believed in him, nor seek to make it crooked. And remember when you were few, so he multiplied you. And see*

---

[3] Ibid.
[4] Ibid., 214-215.
[5] Ibid., 215.
[6] Ibid.
[7] Ibn Kathir, 215-216.

how was the end of the vandals." Ibn Kathir interpreted this verse by saying that Shoaib commanded them to do justice and forbade them to do injustice. As for the statement, *"do not sit down in every way,"* Al Saddi said that they used to take tithes of the people who traveled. He reminded them of the grace of Allah on them for they used to be a small number and had become a large number, and he asked them to be fair in their dealings with others, as written in Qur'an 11:84: *⁸⁴And to Midian, their brother Shoaib said, "O my people, serve Allah. You have no god other than him, do not lessen the measure and the weights. Surely I see you are fine, and surely I fear for you the torment of an encompassing day.* He meant they must not continue in their sin or Allah would make them poor, and he would add the torment of the hereafter to them. So he gently forbade them from doing what was wrong and threatened to take his grace from them and torment them in the hereafter.

After this, he warned them harshly when he said in Qur'an 11:85-86: *⁸⁵And, O my people, give full in the measure and the weights with fairness, and do not defraud the people their things. And do not act wickedly in the land, vandalizing. ⁸⁶What abides with Allah is better for you if you were believers, and I am not a keeper over you."*⁸ Ibn Abbas interpreted that portion of verse 11:86 reading, *what abides with Allah is better for you,* to mean the provision of Allah is *better than the taking of money or stealing from the people.* Ibn Kathir quoted Mohammed in a hadith, stating that "the interest, even if it got large, will end up being small. Also, the lawful profit was blessed even if it was not much, and the unlawful shall not last even if it was much." As for the saying, "I am not a guardian over you," this was interpreted to mean they should do it for the sake of Allah, rather than for Shoaib or others to see.

According to Qur'an 11:87: *⁸⁷They said, "O Shoaib, does your prayer command you that we should leave what our fathers served or that we do with our money as pleases us? Surely you are the forbearing, the right mind."* Ibn Kathir said they said this in a way that mocked Shoaib; in other words, "Should we leave our god and do what you say?"⁹

---

[8] Ibid., 216.
[9] Ibid.

It is written in Qur'an 11:88: *⁸⁸He said, "O my people, have you seen that if I were with a proof from my lord and he provides for me an excellent provision from him? And I do not want to disagree with you about what he has forbidden you of. That I desire except the reform of which I am able, and my success is not except by Allah, on him I depend and to him I turn.* Ibn Kathir interpreted this verse by stating that he spoke with them gently and guided them to the truth. Shoaib was saying, in effect, that Allah had provided him with the prophethood and the message which they could not know. Ibn Kathir said this same statement was given by Noah. Ibn Kathir interpreted this by writing that Shoaib meant, "I only order you with what I am doing and forbid you from the things I forbid from myself."

Then Ibn Kathir quoted a hadith from Mohammed who said, "When a man will be taken to the fire and his guts will be out of his abdomen so he will travel with it as a donkey does."[10] So the people of the fire will gather around, and they will say to him, "O, so and so, did you not command what is good and forbid what is evil?" So he will say, "Yes, I did command what is good, but I did not do it. And I forbade the evil, but I did it." Ibn Kathir summarized that this was a description of the difference between the prophets and the wicked.

He also stated that this meant Shoaib desired only what was good and depended on Allah in all circumstances, for it was to Allah he would return. Here, he was encouraging them. Then he moved into threatening them when he said in Qur'an 11:89: *⁸⁹And, O my people, let not my disagreement with you cause you to be stricken as what struck Noah's people or Houd's people or Saleh's people. And the people of Lot are not far from you.* Ibn Kathir said that Shoaib meant by this that they should not let the disagreement endure because their anger would cause them to continue in their error and foolishness in disobeying Allah. The torment would fall on them as it had with all these other people. He reminded them that the people of Lot were not far away from them in time or location. Then Shoaib mixed the threat with encouragement by saying, in Qur'an 11:90, *⁹⁰And ask forgiveness of your lord, then repent to him. Surely my lord is merciful, friendly."*

In Qur'an 11:91a: *⁹¹They said, "O Shoaib, we do not understand much of what you say, and we surely see that you*

---

[10]Ibid., 217.

are weak among us... Ibn Abbas said that it was said that Shoaib cried for the love of Allah until he lost his eyesight.[11] That was the weakness in his body. Allah then returned his sight to him and said, "O Shoaib, do you cry for fear of the fire or for your longing for the garden?" He answered, "No, it is for my love for you. So when I look at you, I do not know what will happen to me." So Allah revealed to Shoaib, "Congratulations to you for meeting with me. Therefore I will make Moses, son of Amran, to be your servant."

As for their saying in Qur'an 11:91: [91]*... And were it not for your family, we surely would have stoned you, and you are not dear to us."* Because of their level of infidelity and disobedience, they said, "We do not understand and we do not love and we do not want what you say. It has no value to us. If it was not for your family, we would surely stone you."

That is when Shoaib said in Qur'an 11:92: [92]*..."O my people, is my family dearer to you than Allah? And you cast him behind your back. Surely my lord surrounds what you do."* As interpreted by Ibn Kathir, this means, "Do you fear my family and my people, and you do not fear Allah? And you do not have any respect for me as a messenger of Allah?" As for the statement, *And you cast him behind your back*, this means, "Are you casting Allah behind your back?" Then the statement, *Surely my lord surrounds what you do*, means "Allah knows what you are doing, and he will reward you on the day you return to him." Qur'an 11:93 states: [93]*And, O my people, do what you are able, surely I will do. You will know who will receive torment which will disgrace him and who is the liar. And watch, surely I am a watcher with you."* This was a strong threat and a promise that, if they continued in their way, they would be punished with utter destruction.

Ibn Kathir stated that this same saying is in Qur'an 7:87-88: [87]*And if it was an assembly of you who believed in what I am sent with and an assembly who did not believe, so be patient until Allah judges between us. And he is the best of judges."* [88]*The leaders of his people who were proud said, "Surely we will get you out, O Shoaib, and those who believed with you, from our village, or you will come back to our religion."* He said,

---

[11]Ibid., 217-218.

Chapter 8

"*Even though we were hating it?*"[12] Ibn Kathir interpreted this by saying that the non-believers of Shoaib asked those who believed in Shoaib to revert from their belief back to their original religion. Shoaib answered them "…even though we were hating it?" Ibn Kathir maintained that meant "those will not return to you by their choice, but they will return to you if you force them because when the belief enters the man's heart, he will not return from it."

That's why Shoaib said in 7:89a: *[89]Indeed, we have forged a lie against Allah if we return to your religion after Allah has delivered us from it, and it will not be for us to return to it, except if Allah our lord wills. Our lord's knowledge encompasses everything. On Allah we depend….* He meant that Allah is our provider and our protector, and from him we will seek refuge in all our affairs. Then he gives the good news to his people as he seeks the help of his lord to hasten on them what they deserve when he said in Qur'an 7:89b: *[89]…'Our lord, open (judge) between us and between our people with the truth. And you are the best opener (judge).'* This meant he called out against them, and Allah will not avoid the call of his messenger if they seek his help against the infidels and those who disobey his messenger, even though they insist on continuing in their way. That was when they said in Qur'an 7:90: [90]*And the leaders of his people who became infidels said, "If you follow Shoaib, surely you will be losers."*[13]

Allah said in Qur'an 7:91: *[91]So the quake seized them, so they became motionless in their homes.* Ibn Kathir interpreted the punishment to be the earth shaking with a strong earthquake which caused their souls to be lost from their flesh. Additionally, the animals of their land became hard and lifeless.[14] They could not move nor have any feeling. Allah sent on them sparks of fire from every direction. Then Ibn Kathir said that Allah told about the people of Shoaib's punishment in every portion of revelation that is suitable to the context and in agreement with the nature of the portion of the story in the Qur'an.

This was a very slick way to cover a contradiction in the Qur'an, for Mohammed repeated the story in the Qur'an three times, and

---

[12] Ibid., 218-219.
[13] Ibn Kathir, 219.
[14] Ibid.

The Revelation of Error

every time he described a different punishment. Instead of Muslims realizing the contradiction, Ibn Kathir fabricated an interpretation.

For an example of what Ibn Kathir tried to do, imagine with me some wicked person whom I tell about in three different stories. First, we say a certain man made fun of Thomas Edison, especially about his invention of the light bulb. Then he mocked Michael Phelps who had won a large number of medals as a great swimmer in a recent Olympics, and he also made a video on YouTube accusing Ford Motor Company of not doing a good job of making cars. So because of his sin, God punished him by taking his life. So far the story makes sense.

Would you believe me though if I tell you he died three different ways? I will write the story in three different chapters in a book. In one chapter, I will say he died when he was electrocuted while changing a light bulb because he made fun of Thomas Edison. In the next chapter, I will write that he drowned in the ocean because he made fun of Michael Phelps. In the last chapter, I will say he was hit by a 2010 Ford Ranger pickup truck because he falsely accused the Ford factory of fraud. *Would you still believe my story, or will you recognize that the story is a lie? Further, if you ask me who this person is, his name, where he lived, and his age; and I give you several different answers to the same questions in each chapter and then end every chapter with the statement, and Allah knows best, would I be credible and worthy of your trust?* To make it even more interesting, what if the facts are that he died before Thomas Edison was born and that he was the son of a very famous woman who never had any children. This would be analogous to the story of Shoaib as it is written in the Qur'an.

Let us read about the ending of the people of Midian, and you can judge for yourself whether or not the Qur'an is the word of God or just some rambling, jumbled, and repeated stories without facts and full of error. In the following three passages we read three different punishments.

Qur'an 7:91 states: *[91]So the quake seized them, so they became motionless in their homes.* Also, in Qur'an 11: 94-95: *[94]And when our command came, we delivered Shoaib and those who believed with him, with mercy from us. And a shout seized the unjust, so they became motionless in their homes. [95]As if they had never dwelt in it in riches, is it not away with the Midian, as away with Themoud.* However, in Qur'an 26:189, Allah said: *189So they denied him, so the torment seized them on the covering day. Surely it was a day of great torment.*

Ibn Kathir attempted to fix these contradictions by trying to equate the Midianites' sin to their punishment.[15] He attempted to explain the punishment in Qur'an 7:91 by saying that they tried to scare the prophet of Allah and his companion to cast them out of the village or revert back to their religion. That is why Allah scared them with the quake. According to Qur'an 11:94, because they were speaking against Shoaib, the prophet of Allah, with mockery, the punishment was that the shout took them in their homes. According to Qur'an 26:189, the punishment was that the torment took them on the day of covering simply because they asked Shoaib to drop on them a part of heaven. As it is written in Qur'an 26:187: *187So drop on us a part of the heaven if you were of the truthful.*

Another attempt to remove this contradiction was made by Al Hafaz Ibn Asakir.[16] He claimed that the people of Midian and the dwellers of the woods were two different nations and that Prophet Shoaib was sent to both of them.

Ibn Kathir himself considered this to be a strange hadith for the Qur'an clearly teaches they were the same people, as we read in the verses of the story in Qur'an 26:176-191: *176The dwellers of the woods denied the messengers. 177When Shoaib said to them, "Will you not fear? 178Surely I am a faithful messenger to you. 179So fear Allah, and obey me. 180 And I do not ask you any wage for it; my wage is but on the lord of the worlds. 181Fulfill the measure, and do not be of those who give less. 182Weigh with the straight balance. 183And do not defraud people their things, and do not act wickedly in the land, vandalizing. 184And fear who created you and the ancient generations." 185They said, "Surely you are only of the bewitched. 186And you are only a human like us, and we think that you are surely among the liars. 187So drop on us a part of the heaven if you were of the truthful." 188He said, "My lord knows best what you do." 189So they denied him, so the torment seized them on the covering day. Surely it was a day of great torment. 190Surely in this is a sign, and most of them were not believers. 191And surely your lord, he is the dear, the merciful.*

---

[15]Ibid., 219-220.
[16]Ibid., 220.

The Revelation of Error

We can conclude that either all of the Muslim scholars were ignorant and did not know what they were talking about or that the scholars were desperately trying to construct a framework for the few verses in the Qur'an in a desperate attempt to try and make sense of them for the followers of Islam.

Was there ever a prophet named Shoaib? Had he been sent to the people of Midian who were sinners whose sin was that they were unjust by cheating the people when using the measure or the weight?

There are so many stories like this repeated throughout the Qur'an which I totally believe are made up by Mohammed or those who helped him make up the Qur'an. Mohammed himself stated in Qur'an 7:101: *[101] Those the villages, we narrate to you some of their news. And indeed, their messengers came to them with the proofs, so they were not to believe in what they denied before. Likewise, Allah seals the hearts of the infidels.* The evidence that these stories are made up is not only do they not exist in the account of the Bible, as some may say that God chose to reveal it in the Qur'an but not the Bible, but that the greatest evidence is in the supposed revelations of Allah or Mohammed in the Qur'an, which are repeated so often that he could not remember what he had said before. This caused the stories to contradict each other and thus provide further evidence that the stories are fabricated.

There are facts we must have in a true story. First, a character of the story must be known at least to the writer of the story. In the case of Shoaib, neither Allah nor Mohammed or any other Muslim scholars knew exactly who Shoaib or his people were.

Second is the location of the story. The existence of the city of Midian is well documented in the biblical account, with reference to the people throughout the writing of the Bible, including the sale of Joseph by his brothers to the Midianites (Genesis 37:28); Moses' forty years in Midian after he killed the Egyptian and escaped from Egypt (Exodus 2:11-15); Moses' marriage to Zipporah, the daughter of Jethro who was the priest of Midian (Exodus 2:21); God's instruction to Moses to collect an army to destroy Midian (Exodus 31:1); the Jewish people oppressed by Midianites during the time of Judges; and God's delivery of them by a judge named Gideon (Judges 6).

Throughout the biblical references there is no mention of the man whom Mohammed claimed to be a prophet named Shoaib. *If he lived, how did he live, and how did he die? Who are the new believers of*

Shoaib? There are many other questions one can ask. The answers will be created by Muslim scholars. In the end, their answer is *and Allah knows best.* So Muslims do not know the answers, but they believe in a story repeated in the Qur'an with incomplete details and full of contradictions.

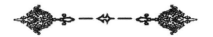

9. The Story of Joseph

When we want to find what is written in Ibn Kathir's interpretation about the life of Joseph, we must go to his book on Jacob/Israel titled *The Mention of What Happened of Wonderful Things in the Life of Israel: The Life of Joseph* which we see is not about Jacob but is rather about the life of Jacob as it took place in the life of Joseph.[1] It seems very strange to me that the life of the father can only be known through the life of his son, unless, of course, you know little or nothing about the father. This apparently resulted from Mohammed's ignorance about Jacob and many other biblical characters including Jacob's brother, Esau, and their father, Isaac.

How much do we know about the life of Jacob/Israel through the writings in The Generous Qur'an, the hadith (Mohammed's sayings), and all the Muslim scholars' interpretations? If we search for the name *Jacob* throughout the Qur'an, we discover it is only mentioned in the Qur'an fourteen times in fourteen verses without any details. The family of Jacob is mentioned twice, also without any details. The term *Children of Israel* is mentioned forty-one times in the Qur'an as Mohammed included the Jewish nation that descended from Israel. The name Israel is mentioned in the Qur'an only twice. Since Ibn Kathir did not have any information from the Qur'an to write about Jacob, he moved on to the story of Joseph to cover the story of Jacob. Some of the information about Jacob that he did mention in his book was taken from the Bible's account.

Therefore, we must ask this question: *What does the Qur'an state about Jacob and his life?* From reading the Qur'an and studying the hadith, we know almost nothing. *Can we find the answers to the following simple questions of who, how, where, when, what, and why throughout the story of Jacob? For example, who changed Jacob's name; how, where, when, and why was it changed from Jacob to Israel; and what do the names Jacob and Israel mean?* We know that the Qur'an uses the name *Israel* for Jacob twice. Obviously, there are no answers for these questions in the Qur'an.

---

[1] Ibn Kathir, *Stories of the Prophets*, vol. 1, Abo Al Fida Ishamail Ibn Kathir Al Kurashi Al Damashce (Beirut: Dar Al-Arab Heritage, 1408 AH, 1988), 228-255.

The answers can be found when we read the account in Genesis 32:22-32 about how Jacob took his two wives, his two female servants, his eleven sons, and all his possessions across a brook called Jabbok. Then Jacob was alone and wrestled with a Man until morning was breaking. When the Man saw that He could not prevail, He touched Jacob's hip socket which caused his hip to become out of joint. As they wrestled, the Man and Jacob had this conversation in verses 26-29: *[26]And He said, "Let Me go, for the day breaks." But he said, "I will not let You go unless You bless me!" [27]So He said to him, "What is your name?" He said, "Jacob." [28]And He said, "Your name shall no longer be called Jacob, but Israel; for you have struggled with God and with men, and have prevailed." [29]Then Jacob asked, saying, "Tell me Your name, I pray." And He said, "Why is it that you ask about My name?"* Then the Man blessed him; therefore, Jacob named the place Peniel (meaning *face of God*) because as he stated in verse 30: *"…For I have seen God face to face, and my life is preserved."*

The sun rose just as Jacob crossed over Peniel. He limped because of his hip, and that is the reason why the Children of Israel do not eat the muscle portion of the shank. When uneducated Muslims read these verses, they make fun of the Bible, especially when they hear the interpretation of these verses from Christian scholars that the Man (Angel of the Lord) was actually the incarnation of Jesus Christ when He appeared to Jacob. The truth is that this is exactly what took place in Jacob's life for he wrestled with God as it is written above. That is how he was blessed by God and his name was changed from Jacob, meaning *the supplanter,* to Israel which means *he will rule as God.*

Did Jacob have any brothers or sisters? If so, what were their occupations? Where did they live? Was Jacob married? If so, what was/were the name/s of his wife/wives? How many children did he have? How old was Jacob when he died? We could ask many other questions. The short and only answer from Muslim scholars is *Allah knows best,* for they do not know what the answers are. They have no answer for who Jacob or Israel was.

All Muslims believe Jacob was a prophet, and they even believe in his book, *The Book of Jacob.* They also believe in the tribe of

The Revelation of Error

Israel. Ibn Kathir said that Jacob had twelve sons, and he called them the tribes of Israel.[2] Ibn Kathir also said that the noblest and greatest son was Joseph.

How did Ibn Kathir know that Jacob had twelve sons? Some Muslim scholars stated that Joseph was the only prophet among them and that none of his brothers received any revelation. That contradicts Qur'an 2:136: *[136]Say, "We believed in Allah and what has been sent down to us, and what has been sent down to Abraham and Ishmael and Isaac and Jacob and the asbāt[3]...*

To understand the life of Jacob, perhaps we must know the life of his father Isaac. Sadly, though, the Qur'an does not say much concerning Isaac either. To be fair, however, Ibn Kathir copied enough from the Genesis account to help the reader understand the Qur'an.[4] As mentioned before, without the Bible, neither Muslims nor Mohammed nor his scholars could understand or explain any of the stories of the Qur'an.

When Muslims read the interpretation of Ibn Kathir, do they even think to ask where he got his information? How did he know that the name of Isaac's wife was Rebekah? How did he know that Isaac was forty years old when he married her? How did he or any other Muslim scholar know that Rebekah was barren? It is amazing how Ibn Kathir knew their sons' names but that he wrote the first son's name in error since it is misspelled in the Arabic language.

How did Ibn Kathir know the story of how Esau sold his birthright to his brother Jacob for food and how Jacob stole the blessing from his father Isaac? Did he know that Esau decided to kill his brother Jacob but that Jacob escaped and went to his Uncle Laban's home? How did he know about the story of Jacob and the angels going up and down the stairs in Jacob's dream? How did he know about the anointing of the rock with oil? How did he know Laban's daughters' names, Leah and Rachel, or that Jacob was deceived into marrying the older daughter and not the younger, after working for her for seven years?

Strangely enough, Ibn Kathir said that Jacob's father-in-law gave the younger sister as a wife to Jacob and that this was lawful in their religion and was abrogated in the law of the Torah (for Jacob took

---

[2] Ibn Kathir, 229.
[3] tribes, non-Arabic word of Hebrew/Syriac origin in its singular form
[4] Ibn Kathir, 228-255.

two sisters as wives at the same time). He stated that this was enough evidence that abrogation happened (obviously he was attempting to defend abrogation in the Qur'an), and this was why Jacob could marry two sisters, even though this was forbidden in the laws of the Torah. What Ibn Kathir did not understand was that before Moses, there was no law; therefore, Jacob did not sin by marrying two sisters. There was actually no abrogation of law, for the law did not yet exist.

How did he know that Laban gave two maidservants to his two daughters? How did he know the names of the sons of Jacob (although some of their names were written with the wrong spelling in the Arabic language)? Concerning the work of Jacob with his uncle, how did Ibn Kathir know how Jacob was able to gain large flocks of sheep and goats? How did he know that Jacob met with angels and who these angels were? How did he know the story of the Angel who appeared as a human and wrestled with Jacob all morning, even though he did not know why Jacob was wrestling with this Man, and amazingly why the Angel (our Incarnated Lord Jesus Christ) changed his name from Jacob to Israel as we have seen earlier?

We could ask more questions about the rest of the story of Jacob, but the answers to these questions can be given in one simple sentence. The information which Ibn Kathir wrote in his book was plagiarized. He did exactly what his prophet Mohammed did in the past because Mohammed also copied many of his stories from the Bible. The difference between Mohammed and Ibn Kathir was that Mohammed did not give very many details, while Ibn Kathir gave many details. This cannot be considered interpretation of the Qur'an, but rather fabrication and filling in missing information by taking it from the Bible.

Now I would like to look at the story of Joseph in the Qur'an as we compare it to what is written in the Genesis account in the Bible. In the Qur'an, Joseph's name is mentioned in three different locations.

In Qur'an 6:84, Mohammed first mentioned the name of Joseph. In this verse through verse 87, Mohammed confused the names of some well-known men in the Bible with Arabic men's names and their relationships to one another. The false names have the correct names in the footnotes. According to Qur'an 6:84-87: *[84]And we granted to him[5] Isaac and Jacob, both we guided, and Noah we*

---

[5] Abraham

The Revelation of Error

guided before and among his descendants, David and Solomon and Job and Joseph and Moses and Aaron. And likewise, we reward the doers of good. [85]And Zacharias and Yahya[6] and 'Isā and Iliyas,[7] all were from the good. [86]And Ishmael and Alyas'a[8] and Yunus and Lūt,[9] and we preferred all those above the worlds. [87]And among their fathers and their descendants and their brethren, and we chose them and guided them into a straight way.

The final place that Mohammed mentioned Joseph's name is in Qur'an 40:34: *[34]And indeed, Joseph brought to you the proofs before. So you are still in doubt from what he brought you until, when he perished, you said, 'Allah will not send a messenger after him.' Likewise, Allah leads astray who is extravagant, a doubter.* According to the Qur'an, this statement was told (was given) by a secret believer from the family of Pharaoh in his defense of the Prophet Moses when Pharaoh decided to kill him. We will explain this in more detail in the story of Prophet Moses. We can understand from this verse that Joseph was a prophet whom Allah sent to the Egyptians, but they did not believe in him. This not only contradicts the story of Joseph in the Bible, but it also contradicts the Qur'an itself, as we will investigate it in Qur'an 12 where we see that Joseph was never sent as a prophet to the Egyptians.

Most of what was written about Joseph is in Qur'an 12, so let us look at the story of Joseph as it is written there. This portion of the revelation is named after Joseph. It begins with verse 1, stating: *[1]Alr.[10] These are verses of the clear book. Alr* is a word without any meaning. Some Muslims, like Al Jalalyn said that Abu Jafar said that this word was made of three letters which means in the Arabic language *I am Allah see*, but Ibn Abbas said this word contains three letters from the name of Allah.[11] Others said this word is one of the names of the Qur'an and that it is a miracle or secret word, and no one understands its meaning except Allah. Of course, the end of the verse states: *These are verses of the clear book.* I believe this is a

---

[6]John the Baptist
[7]name mistakenly used, Elijah was meant
[8]Elisha, non-Arabic word of Syriac/earlier Semitic origin
[9]Lot, non-Arabic word of Syriac origin
[10]a word containing three Arabic letters without meaning
[11]http://quran.al-islam.com/Page.aspx?pageid=221&BookID=12&Page=235, accessed February 3, 2013.

major contradiction. *How can the Qur'an claim in this verse that it is clear Arabic when this verse begins with a word of which no one knows the meaning?*

Continuing with verse 2, which says: **²Surely we have sent it down, an Arabic Qur'an, perhaps you might understand.** Ibn Kathir stated in his book that "the Qur'an is the noblest book which has descended from heaven from the noblest angel to the noblest prophet in the noblest place and time."[12] It also stated that it had descended in the pure Arabic language. Actually, the Qur'an contains over 270 words that are not from the Arabic language but rather are words from many other languages. Some of these words are mentioned once and others are mentioned over a hundred times throughout the Qur'an.[13] One of the strange words Mohammed repeated throughout the Qur'an is the word *perhaps*, especially when it was said by Allah. *Did Allah know that the followers of Islam would understand the Qur'an when he revealed it in Arabic?* Obviously, the answer is *no*.

How can Allah send his religion of Islam as mercy to the whole world, as Muslims claim, but at the same time hardly any people of the world can read or understand the Qur'an, especially when we know that 87 percent of Muslims in the world today cannot read or understand the Qur'an, such as Muslims in Afghanistan, Pakistan, Iran, Turkey, Indonesia, and China? What is so sad is that now large numbers, over 30 percent of Arabs, are uneducated and cannot read or write the Arabic language. Add to this a large number, including those very educated who have college degrees, who can read the Arabic language but cannot understand what is written in the Qur'an. Verse 12:3 states: **³We narrate to you the best of the stories by which we reveal to you this Qur'an, and before it you were among the unaware.** *The best of the stories?*

When we read these verses, we immediately assume that this portion of the revelation contains the best stories ever told, for Allah does not lie. Joseph is one of my favorite stories in the Bible. I remember the first time I read this story in the Bible was when I was in my early teens. Some parts of the account made me laugh while other parts made me cry. It touched me and moved me. It was a very easy story to understand, and then I remembered when I read it for the

---

[12] Ibn Kathir, 239.
[13] *The Generous Qur'an*, trans. by Usama K. Dakdok.

The Revelation of Error

first time in the Qur'an. My reaction was completely different, for I did not know what I should do. Should I laugh, or should I cry? There was a huge difference and a large number of errors and contradictions because there was so much missing information and added fabrications within these verses in Qur'an 12. Years later, as I now write about this story, I realize why Muslims cannot understand the Qur'an. It was not I who said that the story of Joseph, in the Qur'an, is the best of the Qur'an; these are the words of Allah himself as we just read in verse 3: *We narrate to you the best of the stories. If the story of Joseph in the Qur'an is the best of the Qur'an, I wonder, what is the condition of the rest of the Qur'an?*

The Dreams of Joseph

Let us move on to verses 4-6 which state: *⁴When Joseph said to his father, "O my father, surely I saw eleven stars and the sun and the moon. I saw them worshiping me." ⁵He said, "O my son, do not relate your dream to your brothers, so they plot a plot against you. Surely Satan is an obvious enemy to the human." ⁶And likewise, your lord will choose you and will teach you the interpretation of the sayings and will fulfill his grace on you and on the family of Jacob as he fulfilled it before on your fathers Abraham and Isaac. Surely your lord is knowing, wise.*
Ibn Kathir stated that when Joseph was young, before the age of puberty, he saw in a dream eleven stars, which represented his brothers, and the sun and the moon, which represented his father and his mother, worshiping him.[14] This scared him, so when he awoke from his sleep, he told the dream to his father. His father told him that he would have a great position. His father commanded Joseph not to tell his dreams to his brothers so that they would not envy, resent, or treat him with deception.

Ibn Kathir made fun of and accused the People of the Book (Jews and Christians) of corrupting their Bible when they said that Joseph told the dream to his father and his brothers.[15] We encourage the reader to read the entire account in the book of Genesis. As we look at chapter 37 in Genesis, many of the verses we will be using will be paraphrased. Genesis 37:5-11 describes how Joseph had a dream which he revealed to his brothers. This caused them to hate him even

---

[14] Ibn Kathir, 229.
[15] Ibid., 230.

more. In the dream, they were in a field binding sheaves, and Joseph's sheaf stood upright. The brothers' sheaves bowed down to his sheaf. Then his brothers asked Joseph if he were going to reign or have dominion over them. They hated him even more because of his dreams and his words. Joseph had yet another dream. This time he told his brothers and their father that he had had another dream in which the sun, moon, and eleven stars had bowed down to him. The father rebuked Joseph and asked if Joseph's father, mother, and brothers would all bow before him. Then his brothers envied him, but his father kept this in his mind.

Notice in the Qur'an that Joseph dreamed one dream, but in the Bible he had two dreams. Then, in the interpretations of the Qur'an story, Joseph was at the age prior to puberty when he had the dream, even as young as three or four years of age.[16] According to Qur'an 12:11-14: *[11]They said, "O our father, why do you not trust us with Joseph? And surely we will be advisers to him. [12]Send him with us tomorrow so that he may enjoy and play, and surely we will be keepers to him." [13]He said, "Surely it will grieve me if you take him, and I fear that the wolf will eat him while you are not watching him." [14]They said, "If the wolf eats him, and we are many, surely then we are losers."* The Bible gives his age as seventeen years old. *So how did scholars determine Joseph's age from verses 4-6 or from any other verses?* Nowhere does the Qur'an give any information from which one can suggest that Joseph, at the time of his dream, was younger than this.

Ibn Kathir stated that Jacob advised Joseph to keep the dream a secret because Allah would give him kindness and mercy and teach him the interpretation of the dream.[17] Allah would "fulfill his grace upon Joseph by giving him the revelation, and Allah would be good to him as he had been to Joseph's ancestors: Jacob, Isaac, and Abraham." This leads us to ask the following questions. *What is the relationship between having a dream and interpreting a dream? Because someone dreams a dream, does that mean that this person can automatically interpret dreams? Why would Joseph's brothers hate him to the point that they wanted to kill him if he was just a little boy and they knew nothing of his dream?*

---

[16]Ibid.
[17]Ibid.

The Revelation of Error

In order to see the consistency of the original account in the Bible, one must read Genesis 37:18-20 which states that when the brothers saw Joseph in the distance, they conspired to kill him. Then they said to one another as it is written in verse 18: *[18]Look, this dreamer is coming!* This verse shows that Joseph's brothers called him *the dreamer,* which is evidence that they knew about his dream.

When Mohammed was asked who was the most noble among the people, Ibn Kathir stated that he answered, "Joseph, the prophet of Allah, the son of the prophet of Allah (Jacob), the son of the prophet of Allah (Isaac), the son of the friend of Allah (Abraham)."[18]

Although the Qur'an does not give details of any of the important stories, the hadith of Mohammed sometimes gives such odd information that we wonder why we need it. A great example of this is when Ibn Kathir said, "A man by the name of Jaber said, 'A Jewish man by the name of Bostanet Al Yahody came to Mohammed.' He said, 'O Mohammed, inform me about the stars which worshiped Joseph. What were their names?' Jaber said, 'The prophet did not answer him with anything, and Angel Gabreel descended to him with their names.' He said, 'The prophet of Allah descended to him. Will you believe if I told you their names?' He said, 'Yes.' So he said, 'They are Geryan, Al Tark, Al Dyal, Zo Al Ktfan, Kabs, Wosab, Amrdan, Al Fylk, Al Msbh, Al Droh, Zo Al Fra, Al Dyaa, and Al Nor.' The Jewish man said, 'By Allah, surely it is their names.'"[19]

Where did Mohammed come up with these names, and how did Jaber know that these were the correct names if neither Joseph himself nor any other Jewish or Christian scholar knew the names of any stars? How did Mohammed know this Jewish man? If we asked Mohammed the names of Joseph's eleven brothers, would he know the answer? I doubt it, as will be shown in the rest of the story. In many hadith, just as in this case, Mohammed or perhaps his followers made up a story, implying that we must conclude with them that Mohammed was a prophet.

This is a great example, I believe, of Mohammed copying what took place in Joseph's life. Throughout His life as recorded in the Scriptures, the Jewish leaders, as well as the priests and Pharisees, tested Jesus by asking Him questions; thus, Mohammed and his followers used the same course of action. Mohammed came up with

---

[18]Ibid.
[19]Ibid.

the answers to the questions (about the stars' names) which he may have made up himself; and even though the answers were false, he still received credit for answering correctly, providing proof to the ignorant reader or hearer that he was a prophet.

Let us continue with the story of Joseph in Qur'an 12:7-8: *⁷Indeed, it was in Joseph and his brothers, signs for the inquirers. ⁸When they said, "Surely Joseph and his brother are more loved by our father than us, and we are a large group. Surely our father is in obvious error.* Ibn Kathir stated that Joseph and his brother Benjamin, who had the same mother, were loved more by their father than were the rest of his brothers.

One must stop here and ask the following questions. *How did Ibn Kathir know that the name of the blood brother was Benjamin? Were they not blood brothers? Did they have a different mother?* For most Jews and Christians, this story from Genesis 29-30 is very well known, but Muslims have no knowledge of this information simply because this information was never written in the Qur'an. One must also ask why Jacob loved Joseph and his brother Benjamin more than his other sons. Without the account in Genesis in these two portions of revelation, one cannot give an answer. The Bible tells us the story of Jacob, his relationship with his uncle Laban, the growth of his family, and how God increased his livestock and possessions.

A Missing Story of the Qur'an

The story we are about to share is found in the book of Genesis in chapters 25-30. I know that my Muslim friends do not know anything about this portion of the story because Mohammed did not include this information in his stories in the Qur'an. To understand the story of Joseph, we must understand the story of his father Jacob. However, to understand the story of Jacob, we must first know about the story of his father Isaac.

Isaac married Rebekah. Because she was barren, Isaac prayed for her, and she became pregnant with twins. The firstborn son was hairy and was named Esau. The second son was born holding on to the heel of Esau. That is why he was named Jacob, meaning *he who follows upon the heels of one* or *supplanter*.[20] Isaac loved Esau, who was a hunter, but Rebekah loved Jacob, who stayed closer to home. One day

---

[20] "Jacob," *Wikipedia*, last modified January 12, 2012, accessed January 22, 2012, http://en.wikipedia.org/wiki/Jacob#cite_note-7.

The Revelation of Error

Esau came from the fields and had been unsuccessful while hunting. Jacob was cooking red pottage and said that he would sell it to Esau for his birthright. Esau swore to him and gave Jacob his birthright because Esau despised it. When Isaac was old and his vision dim, he asked Esau to go out in the wilderness and hunt and then prepare a meal for him so that he could eat it and bless Esau before he died.

Rebekah heard the conversation and asked Jacob to go to the flock and bring her two kids, so she could prepare a meal of them and feed this meal to his father Isaac. Then Isaac would eat it and bless Jacob before he died. Jacob reminded his mother that he was a smooth man, but his brother was very hairy. Jacob was afraid that he would receive a curse instead of a blessing. However, Rebekah assured Jacob that the curse would be upon her; therefore, he did what his mother asked him to do. He put on Esau's clothing, Rebekah covered his hands and his neck with animal skins, and Jacob took the food to his father.

Jacob lied and said that he was Esau, the firstborn son, and asked his father to eat so that Isaac would bless him. Isaac was surprised that he was able to hunt so quickly, but Jacob explained that the Lord his God had made it easy for him. Isaac asked his son to come close, so he would know that this was Esau. Isaac said that the voice was the voice of Jacob but the hands were the hands of Esau. Isaac asked again if he was Esau, his son. Jacob lied again and said that he was Esau. As Jacob drew near to Isaac to give him the food and the wine, Isaac smelled his clothes and then blessed him.

After Jacob received the blessing and left his father's presence, Esau returned from hunting. Esau cooked the meat and brought it to his father and said, "May my father eat and bless me." Isaac asked who this was. Esau replied that he was his firstborn, Esau. That is when Isaac told Esau about what had just taken place. When Esau found out about what had happened, he cried out with a great shout and a very bitter cry. He asked Isaac to bless him also, but Isaac said that there was no blessing for him because the blessing had been given to his brother Jacob. Esau asked if there was any blessing for him. Isaac explained that now Jacob was his master and all his brothers were now servants to him, and then Isaac asked what he could do for him. Esau asked his father if he even had only one blessing, to bless him also. Esau lifted his voice and wept. Isaac said that Esau would live in a land without fatness and without dew, and living by his sword, he would be a slave to his brother. That is why Esau hated Jacob his brother and decided to kill Jacob after the death of their father, Isaac.

When Jacob's mother Rebekah heard about Esau's plan to kill Jacob, she told Jacob to escape to her brother Laban in Haran. She told Isaac that she hated the daughters of Heth and did not want her son Jacob the marry any of these daughters. That is why Isaac called Jacob, blessed him, and asked him to not marry any of the daughters of Canaan but instead to go to the house of Bethuel, his mother's father, to marry a daughter of his Uncle Laban.

Jacob escaped from his brother Esau and journeyed to his Uncle Laban's home. After he arrived, he asked some shepherds about his uncle, and they pointed to a young lady who was taking her father's sheep to be watered. When Jacob saw her, he kissed her as he lifted up his voice and cried and introduced himself to her. He went home with her to meet his Uncle Laban. After Jacob lived and served his uncle for one month, his uncle asked, if he was just a relative, why he should serve him for nothing. Laban then asked Jacob what he wanted to be paid in wages for his work. Jacob replied that he would serve Laban seven more years for Rachel to become his wife.

Laban had two daughters. Rachel, the young lady with the sheep, was the younger sister. She was a beautiful young woman while the older sister, Leah, had a problem with her eyes. Jacob asked his Uncle Laban for Rachel to be his wife because he truly loved her. After seven long years of work, he married the daughter of Laban, but in the morning he discovered that the woman he married the night before was not Rachel but instead her sister Leah. It was the custom of the culture in those days that the older sister must marry first. A new deal was made between Jacob and Laban in which Jacob could have Rachel as his wife after seven more years of labor.

Because Leah was not loved, the Lord blessed her, and she bore four sons: Reuben, Simeon, Levi, and Judah. Because Rachel could not have any children, she asked Jacob to know her servant Bilhah. So Bilhah bore him two sons, Dan and Naphtali. During this time Leah stopped having children, and she gave her servant Zilpah to Jacob. Zilpah bore him two sons, Gad and Asher. Then Leah became fruitful again and bore two more sons, Issachar and Zebulun, and his only daughter, Dinah.

During these long years, the beautiful and beloved wife Rachel could not have any children of her own. Finally, she became pregnant and bore a son, Joseph. Later, Rachel had another child by the name of Benjamin.

If Mohammed had read the account in the Bible before he made up his Qur'an, perhaps he would have told a more accurate story. In addition, neither Muslim scholars nor Mohammed could have given the true answer to my question of why Jacob loved Joseph and his brother Benjamin more than the rest of his other sons, unless they had read the Bible. Their answer to any contradictory information is, as always, *Allah knows best*.

Now a simple reading of the Genesis account will give us the answer. Joseph and Benjamin were the children of his beloved wife Rachel. Genesis 35:17-19 gives the account of Rachel's death just after giving birth to Benjamin. Genesis 37:3-4 describes that Jacob loved Joseph because he was born when Jacob was an old man. Jacob made Joseph a beautiful tunic of many colors. However, his brothers became jealous and hated Joseph when they saw the beautiful tunic that Jacob had made for him. Another reason Joseph's brothers hated him was because he reported their evil behavior to their father Jacob as we read in Genesis 37:2: *"...²and Joseph brought a bad report of them to his father."*

The Plot to Kill Joseph

Qur'an 12:9-10 says: *⁹Kill Joseph or throw him to a land, and to you your father's face will be set, and after this, you will become a good people." ¹⁰A speaker among them said, "Do not kill Joseph, and cast him down to the bottom of the jubb.*[21] *Some travelers will pick him up if you were doing."* In Ibn Kathir's interpretation, Mujahid said that *this person* (a speaker among them) was Simeon.[22] Al Saddi said he was Judah. Qatadah and Mohammed Ibn Isaac said he was the older, Reubel (they meant Reuben).

How did they know these three names? Obviously, they are confused for the true answer comes from Genesis 37:21-24. Verses 21-22 state: *²¹But Reuben heard it, and he delivered him out of their*

---

[21] well, non-Arabic word of Aramaic origin
[22] Ibn Kathir, 231.

hands, and said, "Let us not kill him." ²²And Reuben said to them, "Shed no blood, but cast him into this pit which is in the wilderness, and do not lay a hand on him"- that he might deliver him out of their hands, and bring him back to his father. Verses 23-24 go on to say that when Joseph came to his brothers, they took his colorful tunic off of him and then threw him into a dry well.

A simple reading of these verses in Genesis, without any interpretation, shows that the brother who saved Joseph's life and asked to have him thrown into the well was Reuben. The reason he did that was simply to return Joseph to his father. As for the confusion of the scholars concerning Judah, perhaps it is because of what is written in Genesis 37:26-27 where we can read it was Judah who came up with the idea to sell Joseph to the Ishmaelites.

When we read Qur'an 12:10, we discover that the speaker is the one who asked that Joseph not be killed. Mohammed, in his Qur'an, made this person a genius prophet because all this took place even before Joseph was sent to them. *Did the person speaking here know exactly what was going to happen, as if the story had already been told to him? Did he know that this was not the true account of Genesis, where the idea of putting Joseph in a well was given by Reuben, as written in Genesis 37:22, for the purpose of saving Joseph and so that he would not to be sold to any travelers?* Also, the idea of selling him to the Ishmaelites was Judah's idea, according to verses 26-27. When Reuben came back to check on Joseph, he did not find Joseph in the well; so he ripped his own clothes, and his heart was sorrowful as we see in Genesis 37:29-30.

The Fulfilling of the Plot to Kill Joseph

Qur'an 12:11-14 states: *¹¹They said, "O our father, why do you not trust us with Joseph? And surely we will be advisers to him. ¹²Send him with us tomorrow so that he may enjoy and play, and surely we will be keepers to him." ¹³He said, "Surely it will grieve me if you take him, and I fear that the wolf will eat him while you are not watching him." ¹⁴They said, "If the wolf eats him, and we are many, surely then we are losers."* What a strange request from Joseph's brothers. By reading such verses one can come to the conclusion that Joseph might have been a toddler or a very young child.

As it is stated in Ibn Kathir's interpretation, if a wolf comes to attack Joseph, he would not be able to defend himself at such a young

The Revelation of Error

age, and the wolf could then devour him.[23] Ibn Kathir made fun of the Bible, showing the ignorance of these Muslim scholars, when he stated that Joseph was sent by Jacob himself to his brothers, while the Qur'an clearly states that Jacob was very afraid to send Joseph with them. *How can Jacob send Joseph alone to his brothers?* The obvious answer to this question is that Joseph was seventeen years old, not a baby as Ibn Kathir thought.

Now let us return to the real account in Genesis 37:1-2: **[1]*Now Jacob dwelt in the land where his father was a stranger, in the land of Canaan. [2]This is the history of Jacob. Joseph, being seventeen years old, was feeding the flock with his brothers. And the lad was with the sons of Bilhah and the sons of Zilpah, his father's wives; and Joseph brought a bad report of them to his father.*** Again, Joseph was seventeen when he was shepherding with his brothers. He was not a young boy. The brothers did not ask Jacob for Joseph to come out and play with them.

As a matter of fact, Joseph was sent by Jacob to his brothers who were tending the flock in Shechem as written in Genesis 37:12-17. Jacob asked Joseph to go to Shechem to see if everything was well with the flock and to bring back word to him. When Joseph arrived in Shechem, he wandered around in a field. A man saw him and asked Joseph what he was looking for. Joseph told the man that he was looking for his brothers and his father's flock. The man then told Joseph that they had left for Dothan. Then Joseph left Shechem and found his brothers in Dothan. Notice the details, such as the names of the cities, mentioned in this story. In Mohammed's story, there are no details, not a mention of the names of the cities or the names of people. We can see this not only in the story of Joseph but in the entire Qur'an.

<u>Joseph in the Well and the Blood on the Shirt</u>

Now let us continue reading the story by Mohammed in Qur'an 12:15-18: *[15]So when they had gone with him and they agreed to place him at the bottom of the well, and we revealed to him: "You will inform them of this, their affair." And they did not feel. [16]And they came at evening to their father weeping. [17]They said, "O our father, surely we went away racing, and we left*

---

[23]Ibn Kathir, 231.

Joseph with our goods. So the wolf ate him, and you will not believe us even if we were truthful." ¹⁸And they put on his qamīs²⁴ with a lie [false] blood. He said, "Yet, your soul lightens the affair. So patience is beautiful, and Allah is the one who is asked for assistance about what you describe."

According to Ibn Kathir's interpretation, from the moment the brothers had gone out of sight from Jacob, they began to curse and mock Joseph with their words and actions.[25] They all agreed to throw him on the top of a rock which was in the bottom of the well. Normally, this rock was where a man would stand to fill the buckets when the water level was low. When they threw him in it, Allah revealed to Joseph that, out of this hardship, his brothers would come to know that he was *the dear*, that they would have need of him, and that they would be afraid of him.

We must ask a question. *How could a person have interpreted the verses this way?* In the interpretation of the words "**And they did not feel**." Mujahid and Qatadah said that the brothers were unaware of the revelation of Allah to Joseph. Ibn Abbas interpreted this as that Joseph would inform them of their condition, but they would not recognize him. As for the brothers returning to Jacob, Ibn Kathir stated, "They came by night in the darkness." They explained to their father that a wolf ate him. They assured Jacob that they were truthful, even if he did not believe them. They told their father that he was excused for not accepting their story, especially since Jacob had told them that "this would happen." As for the blood which was put on Joseph's shirt, it "was the blood of some animal" that they had killed in order to deceive their father and claim that a wolf had eaten Joseph. It was said that they forgot to rip the shirt, for "the liar is forgetful."

Ibn Kathir also stated that the father knew how much they hated Joseph, how much they envied him, and how Jacob had loved Joseph since his childhood, for Allah chose him to be a prophet.[26] Notice the reaction of the father in Qur'an 12:18: *¹⁸And they put on his qamīs²⁷ with a lie [false] blood. He said, "Yet, your soul lightens the affair. So patience is beautiful, and Allah is the one who is asked for assistance about what you describe."* Is this not a

---

[24]shirt, non-Arabic word of Greek/Syriac origin
[25]Ibn Kathir, 231.
[26]Ibid., 230.
[27]shirt, non-Arabic word of Greek/Syriac origin

The Revelation of Error

strange reaction for a father who has just lost his beloved son? We realize the complete nonsense of the story in the Qur'an, for no one, when he loses his little son, especially if the child were devoured by a wolf, would fail to show any sorrow whatsoever. Someone may say that because Jacob was a prophet, he knew from Allah that his son Joseph was alive, so that is why he did not cry or show any sorrow. However, this theory is refuted by the later action of Jacob in verse 84: **[84]And he turned away from them and said, "Oh, my sorrow for Joseph," and his eyes became white from the grief so he was full of anger.** *Why did Jacob cry to the point of losing his eyesight if he knew from Allah that Joseph was alive?* The truth is, according to the biblical account, even after many years, Jacob would cry to the point of losing his sight.

The true account is found in the Bible in Genesis 37:31-35. The brothers took Joseph's tunic and dipped it in the blood of a goat's kid that they had killed. Then they took the colorful tunic to their father and told him that they had found this tunic. They asked Jacob if he knew if it was Joseph's. He recognized it as Joseph's and said that a wild beast had devoured Joseph and that Joseph, without a doubt, had been torn to pieces. Jacob then tore his own clothes, put on sackcloth, and mourned his son for many days. All his sons and daughters tried to comfort him, but he refused to be comforted. Jacob told them that he would go down into the grave to Joseph in mourning. Jacob then wept.

Notice in the Qur'an that there was no specific animal's blood mentioned that was found on the coat, but according to the Bible, it was goat's blood. Also, it was the colored shirt or coat of Joseph, but Mohammed did not describe Joseph's coat as a colorful shirt but only said that it was *his* shirt. The second very important difference is that, in the Genesis account, Jacob examined the shirt and said that an evil beast had devoured him. The story in the Qur'an is in error; Jacob declared the beast to be a wolf. It would be very unlikely for a single wolf to kill and devour a healthy strong seventeen-year-old man. In reading the Bible, we see that the reaction was appropriate to the action for Jacob tore his clothes, put on sackcloth, wept for many days, and refused to be comforted. This is a much more believable account of the story.

Chapter 9

Joseph Sold to the Travelers

According to Qur'an 12:19: *¹⁹And a traveler came there, and so they sent a drawer of water, so he let down his bucket. He said, "Good news, here is a young man!" And they hid him merchandise.*[28] *And Allah knew in what they are doing.* Ibn Kathir interpreted this passage in the Qur'an in the following way. Joseph sat in the well, waiting for the deliverance of Allah, when the travelers came.[29] The People of the Book said that their goods were pistachios, pine nuts, and some green seeds, and that they were traveling to Egypt after coming from the Levant, the old Syrian border. So they sent one of their party to draw water from the well. Joseph hung onto the bucket. When this man saw Joseph, he said, "O good news," and they added him to their goods. I find this to be a pattern that Ibn Kathir used in his writing. He always wrote that the People of the Book said *this* or the People of the Book said *that*. However, when I examined the account in the Bible, I found that Ibn Kathir lied, for as we read in the Genesis 37:25-28 account, the travelers, the Ishmaelites, did not have pistachio, pine nuts, and green seeds as he stated. What they had were spices, balm, and myrrh. There was no mention whatsoever of a bucket or the statement of the good news of finding the merchandise (Joseph).

A simple reading of Genesis 37:25-28 shows this: *²⁵"And they sat down to eat a meal. Then they lifted their eyes and looked, and there was a company of Ishmaelites, coming from Gilead with their camels, bearing spices, balm, and myrrh, on their way to carry them down to Egypt. ²⁶So Judah said to his brothers, "What profit is there if we kill our brother and conceal his blood? ²⁷Come and let us sell him to the Ishmaelites, and let not our hand be upon him, for he is our brother and our flesh." And his brothers listened. ²⁸Then Midianite traders passed by; so the brothers pulled Joseph up and lifted him out of the pit, and sold him to the Ishmaelites for twenty shekels of silver. And they took Joseph to Egypt."*

Also, from reading the passage above, we discover that the true story is that the Ishmaelites did not come from the Levant but from Gilead on their way to Egypt. The Bible clearly states that Judah is the one who came up with the idea to sell Joseph to the Ishmaelites. The Midianites were passing through the land. They pulled Joseph out

---
[28] meaning as an article of merchandise
[29] Ibn Kathir, 232.

of the well and sold him to the Ishmaelites for twenty pieces of silver. The Ishmaelites then sold Joseph in Egypt to Potiphar.

The Qur'an account of the price for which Joseph was sold is found in Qur'an 12:20: *²⁰And they bought him for a lesser price of a numbered dirham,³⁰ and they were not interested in him.* Ibn Kathir's interpretation was that when Joseph's brothers found out that the travelers had taken Joseph, they followed the travelers and told them that the young man was theirs. They then sold Joseph to the travelers for a numbered dirham (a coin). *How did Ibn Kathir come up with this interpretation?* Although the Qur'an does not say how many dirhams, Muslim scholars tell us what they believe. For example, Ibn Abbas, Qatadah, and many others said they sold Joseph for twenty dirham, and each brother took two dirham.³¹ Mujahid said that Joseph was sold for twenty-two dirham, but Akramah and Mohammed Ibn Isaac said that Joseph was sold for forty dirham. Finally, Ibn Kathir entered his suggestion concerning the price with the words, *and Allah knows best*. The Bible, however, is very clear. Joseph was sold to the Ishmaelites for twenty pieces of silver.

<u>Joseph's New Home in Egypt</u>

In Qur'an 12:21, Allah stated: *²¹And he who bought him in Egypt said to his woman [wife], "Treat him generously, perhaps he may be useful to us, or maybe we can take him a son." And likewise, we did settle Joseph in the land, and we will teach him the interpretation of the sayings. And Allah has victory over his affair, but most people do not know.* Ibn Kathir's interpretation was, "They said the Egyptian who bought him was the prince, and he was in charge of the entire treasury."³² Ibn Isaac said his name was Atfeer Ibn Roheeb, and that the king of Egypt on that day was Al Ryen. Ibn Al Waled said that the wife of the prince, Al 'Aziz, was Raael, daughter of Raaeel. Others said that her name was Zleka, and it also has been said that her name was Feka, daughter of Unos. Ibn Abbas said that the person who bought Joseph in Egypt was Malk, Ibn Zar, Ibn Noeb, Ibn Aska, Ibn Mzean, Ibn Abraham (Father Abraham). Ibn Kathir ends this long list of Arabic names with the words, *and Allah knows best*.

---

[30] a coin, non-Arabic word of Greek origin
[31] Ibn Kathir, 233.
[32] Ibid., 230.

None of the scholars we quote claimed to be a prophet, but they implied they were more knowledgeable than Angel Gabreel. Neither Mohammed nor his Angel Gabreel knew the names of all the characters in the Qur'an. Also, all of these names existed in Mohammed's day among his Arab people, but not in Egypt because none of these names are Coptic, or ancient Egyptian.

What does the Bible say concerning the name of the man who bought Joseph? In Genesis 39:1: *¹Now Joseph had been taken down to Egypt. And Potiphar, an officer of Pharaoh, captain of the guard, an Egyptian, bought him from the Ishmaelites who had taken him down there.*

This man was Potiphar, a Coptic name meaning *a gift from the sun god*. There is much more, but I will not waste our time with these unimportant details. I will translate the most important aspects of the story.

As for the saying, *"we take him as a son,"* I do not find any proof or evidence of this act either in the biblical account or historically, for Egyptians did not adopt slaves. I believe this fabrication by Mohammed is the result of him believing that Joseph at the time was still a little boy.

In Ibn Kathir's interpretation of *"we did settle Joseph in the land,"* he stated that Al 'Aziz and his wife were forced to *do good* to Joseph and take care of him.[33] *Where did Ibn Kathir come up with this information?* The Qur'an does not mention any of this information.

Let us look at the true account in Genesis 39:3-6: *³And his master saw that the LORD was with him and that the LORD made all he did to prosper in his hand. ⁴So Joseph found favor in his sight, and served him. Then he made him overseer of his house, and all that he had he put under his authority. ⁵So it was, from the time that he had made him overseer of his house and all that he had, that the LORD blessed the Egyptian's house for Joseph's sake; and the blessing of the LORD was on all that he had in the house and in the field. ⁶Thus he left all that he had in Joseph's hand, and he did not know what he had except for the bread which he ate. Now Joseph was handsome in form and appearance."*

The reason that Joseph was put in charge of all the household of the Egyptian master was because he found grace in his master's eyes.

---

[33]Ibid., 234.

The Revelation of Error

Joseph was the reason for all the blessings his master received. None of this information is mentioned in the Qur'an.

In Qur'an 12:22, Allah said: *²²And when he had reached his age of strength, we gave him judgment and knowledge, and likewise, we reward the doers of good.* *What was the age of Joseph at this time?* Muslim scholars disagree. Without mentioning hardly any scholars' names, Ibn Kathir gave different ages.[34] One scholar said that Joseph was at the age of puberty, another said he was eighteen years old, another said twenty, another said twenty-five, another said thirty, another said thirty-three, and Al Hasan said he was forty years old.

We do not know where Ibn Kathir got these ages because he did not name his sources. The Qur'an does not contain any information about Joseph's age during this time, but there is a reference to the "age of strength" later in Qur'an 46:15: *¹⁵...when he attains his strength and attains to forty years...* The Bible does not mention any ages, but simply stated that Joseph was handsome and favored.

The Seduction of Joseph

Next we come to the part about the attempted seduction of Joseph which begins in Qur'an 12:23: *²³The one whom he stayed with in her house sought to seduce him. And she closed the doors, and she said, "I am prepared for you." He said, "Allah's refuge! Surely he is my lord who treats me good, surely the unjust will not prosper."* Ibn Kathir went into great detail of how the wife of Al 'Aziz tried to seduce Joseph by explaining what took place in the house. He described her and what she did. He wrote that she was very beautiful, had lots of money, held a high position, and was full of youth (young, beautiful, and desirable). *How did Ibn Kathir know this information which was not mentioned in the Qur'an?* He described how she closed the doors and prepared herself for Joseph by the way she was dressed in her most elegant and best clothes.

She called him to herself as she asked Joseph to *be with her* (have sexual relations with her). She was very demanding and desirous of him, but Joseph responded by asking how he could do this thing since her husband was his lord and had done much good to him. Notice though in the following verse, Qur'an 12:24: *²⁴And indeed, she*

---

[34]Ibid.

moved to him, and he moved to her,[35] *were it not that he saw his lord's*[36] *proof. Likewise, we averted him from committing the evil and indecency, surely he is of our sincere servants.* When Muslim scholars meet a difficulty in the passages of the Qur'an, I believe they decide to omit it or fail to illuminate it in any way, just as the ancient scholars did with this verse and the modern Muslims do today. I believe they choose to formulate stories and details, as we see in the English translation of the preceding verse. For example, Khan said, "And indeed she did desire him and he would have inclined to her desire, had he not seen the evidence of his Lord."[37] As for Maulana, his translation says, "And certainly she desired him, and he would have desired her, were it not he had seen the manifest evidence of his Lord."

Pickthal translated it as, "She verily desired him, and he would have desired her if it had not been that he saw the argument of his Lord." Rashad said, "She almost succumbed to him, and he almost succumbed to her if it were not that he saw a proof from his Lord." Sawar translated it to be, "She was determined to have him and were it not for his faith in God, he would certainly have yielded to her."

In Shakir's translation, he said, "And certainly she made for him, and he would have made for her, were it not that he had seen the manifest evidence of his Lord." Sherali, on the other hand, said, "And she made up her mind with regard to him, to seduce him, and he made up his mind with regard to her, to resist her. If he had not seen the manifest Sign of his Lord." Yusufali translated it as, "And (with passion) did she desire him, and he would have desired her, but he saw the evidence of his Lord."

As we have seen above, none of these translations are faithful to the actual words of the Qur'an when it states that Joseph lusted after her sexually; however, some, like Sherali, added words: "He made his mind to resist her." This is not an accurate translation. All that they have tried to do in the above translations is manipulate the words to influence the reader to assume that Joseph was about to do this act, but he actually was not. That is not what the Qur'an contains about

---

[35] with lust
[36] her husband's
[37] *Parallel English Qur'an,* ed. Clay C. Smith, accessed December 28, 2011, http://www.claychipsmith.com.

this event, in the original Arabic, as we will see in my accurate English translation. Abu Horyrah said:
> Mohammed said that Allah said, 'If one of my servants moved (thought about it) to do a good deed, then write it as one good deed; but if he performed it (did the action), then write it to him as ten good deeds. If he thought of an evil thing but did not do it, then write it to him as one good deed; but if he performs the evil deed, then write it to him as one evil deed.'

This was also repeated in the hadith according to Sahih Muslim and Sahih Bukhari. Muslim scholars also tried to say that he sinned with her in his heart by wanting to have sex with her but that he only desired her as a wife. The hadith above is one of the more bizarre hadith. In it Mohammed assured the Muslims that sinful thoughts are not counted as sin, but actually can be counted as good deeds as long as the believers of Allah do not act upon them. In other words, if a man thought of an evil sin, for example, killing someone or lusting after women, but he did not act upon such evil thoughts, this man would receive a blessing of doing good deeds. This is the opposite of the teaching of our Lord Jesus, for the Bible clearly teaches that we will be judged for every thought and every word that comes out of our lips according to Matthew 12:36: ***But I say to you that for every idle word men may speak, they will give account of it in the day of judgment.*** Looking after someone with a lustful eye is equal to committing adultery in the eyes of the Lord.

We see further evidence of this wide gap between the morality of the Qur'an and the morality of the Bible in Qur'an 53:32: *[32]Those who avoid big sins and sexual immorality except al-lemam.[38] Surely your lord is broad in the forgiveness...* Here the Qur'an teaches that fornication is not complete without penetration. So, as long as there is no copulation, such an act is only a small sin. This is contrary to the teachings of the Bible in Matthew 5:28: ***[28]But I say to you that whoever looks at a woman to lust for her has already committed adultery with her in his heart.***

Although the Qur'an does not tell us who *the lord* is and what the *evidence* of the lord is, Al Qurtobi and Al Tabari gave us interpretations to this verse, while Ibn Kathir in his book, *The Story of*

---

[38] that is, everything that men can do with women without actual penetration—see interpretation of Al Qurtobi

the Prophets, chose not to go into detail. For example, Al Qurtobi stated that she, the master's wife, covered a statue or idol with clothes.[39] Joseph asked her, "What are you doing?" She said, "I am ashamed that my god sees me having sex with you." That is when Allah brought shame to Joseph for what he was about to do. Others said that he saw writing on the ceiling of the house which was the writing of Qur'an 17:32: *[32]And do not get near the fornication, surely it was indecent and an evil way.* The interpretation of Muslim scholars as to the evidence of his lord is "(O son of Jacob) or (O you Joseph), will you commit adultery like the birds? We will remove the feathers of him (of the bird) as it is written that the birds who commit adultery that Allah will remove their feathers." *Do birds really commit adultery?*

Others said the evidence of his lord was that Joseph saw Jacob in the ceiling of the house biting his hand and "asking his son not to do that." I conclude, according to the Qur'an, that Joseph had desired and moved toward his master's wife, but the scholars rewrote Mohammed's story to say that Joseph did not do these things.

What really took place, according to Muslim scholars, between Joseph and the master's wife? In Al Tabari's interpretation, he described the conversation which took place between Joseph and the wife of Al 'Aziz as she spoke nicely about his hair, face, and body.[40] Then he stated that "she moved to him, and he moved to her with lust. Both entered the house, and the doors were closed. Joseph began to loosen his underwear, and that is when he saw his father Jacob biting his hand and advising him not to do such a thing." Al Tabari repeated this interpretation in similar words as to how they both sat with each other, how he sat between her legs, and how he took her clothes or his clothes off. Another said that she "dropped herself and threw herself at him, and he took his clothes off."

Scholars disagree with each other as to how Joseph could have been a prophet of Allah and have done such a thing. Al Qurtobi stated that Joseph moved toward her with lust. He also stated that she threw herself on her back as he sat between her legs, removing his clothes, and he sat with her as a man sits with his wife. In his interpretation,

---

[39]http://quran.Al-islam.com/Page.aspx?pageid=221&BookID=14&Page=238, accessed September 10, 2011.

[40]http://quran.Al-islam.com/Page.aspx?pageid=221&BookID=13&Page=238, accessed September 10, 2011.

The Revelation of Error

Al Qurtobi went in circles. In one place he said that Joseph had committed the sin while in another place he stated that Joseph could not have committed this sin because he was a prophet. I believe that this struggle was a result of the ambiguity and fabrication of verse 24 by Allah, for when we read the account in Genesis, we do not face such a problem as you will see below.

When we read the interpretations of other Muslim scholars, we can almost feel their pain, as they struggled to prove Joseph's innocence. Because Muslim scholars believe all prophets were sinless, they reject all the stories of the Bible which point to many prophets who sinned openly at some time or another.

Muslims also believe that Mohammed was the final and greatest prophet. However, the Qur'an states in five different locations (4:106; 23:118; 40:55; 47:19; and 48:2) that Mohammed was a sinful man and that Allah forgave his sins. Allah not only forgave his past sins, but he asked Mohammed to seek forgiveness of his future sins. Mohammed had not only sinned before his prophethood, but Allah would also forgive his sins in the future. Mohammed's sins are covered in detail in the section bearing his name in our book.

<u>Joseph Escaping the Temptation and the Reaction of the Husband</u>

Qur'an 12:25 states: *[25]And they ran for the door, and she tore his shirt behind. And at the door they met her master. She said, "What is the penalty for one who would desire to do evil to your people, except to be put in prison or a painful torment?"* Al Qurtobi interpreted these verses in the following way: as Joseph ran away from the wife of the master, she ran after him.[41] He ran toward the door to escape the temptation of having sexual relations with her, but she ran so that she might catch him and fulfill her sexual desire with him. That is why she held onto his shirt, and the shirt was torn from top to bottom.

Then they met her master and husband at the door, but when she saw her husband's face, she began talking with deceptive speech. When she asked, "What is the punishment to those that desire to do evil (commit adultery) to your people?" that she meant by this, what the punishment would be for Joseph who tried to rape her. She

---

[41] http://quran.Al-islam.com/Page.aspx?pageid=221&Book ID=14&Page=238, accessed September 13, 2011.

offered her husband two options: to be put in prison or to be punished severely.

Is this what really took place between the wife and Potiphar? Did Joseph really lust after her and desire her sexually? Was his shirt ever ripped? Did they really meet the husband at the door? We can ask many questions, but again the answers are in the original and true Genesis account.

What about the response of Joseph, the conclusion of the witness in her household, and the reaction of her husband? To answer these three questions, we must have a quick look at Qur'an 12:26-29: **²⁶He said, "She sought to seduce me." And a witness from her family testified, "If his shirt was torn in the front, so she is truthful, and he is of the liars. ²⁷And if his shirt was torn from behind, so she lied, and he is of the truthful." ²⁸So when his lord saw his shirt torn behind, he said, "Surely this is one of your devices, surely your devices are great." ²⁹"Joseph, turn away from this, and⁴² ask forgiveness for your sins, surely you were among the sinners."** In verse 26, Joseph simply stated that she was the one to be blamed. Ibn Kathir said that Ibn Abbas interpreted the witness of her household in which he wrote that it was an infant who miraculously spoke, as written in verses 26 and 27.⁴³ Another scholar said it was a male relative of her husband, but another said it was a relative of hers. In other words, as usual, the answer is *Allah knows best*. The wisdom given in the statement was that if the shirt was ripped from the front, she must have told the truth and that he must be the liar.

What does this mean? The answer is very simple. If a man is forcing himself on a woman to rape her, the normal reaction of the woman is to push him away from her. In doing so, using both hands to force him away from her will cause his clothes to be ripped in the front. If the shirt is ripped from the back, this would prove the opposite to be true since the man had tried to get away from the woman; but if she had pulled him toward her by holding onto his clothes, this would cause the shirt to be ripped from the back.

Where was the shirt ripped? The husband saw that the rip was on the back. *What does that mean?* This means that Joseph was innocent and that she was forcing him to have sex with her. *What was her husband's reaction?* Surely he killed his wife after stoning her for

---
⁴²addressing the wife
⁴³Ibn Kathir, 235.

some time. He surely punished Joseph as well. He could have put Joseph in prison for life; this was the normal reaction of an Egyptian man, especially if he was rich or held a high position in the government. However, this is not what the Qur'an states.

He knew that his wife was trying to cheat on him, but he did not get upset. He gave a simple statement and some advice. He said to his wife, "Surely this is of your devices, surely your devices are great," as if he did not desire to hurt his wife's feelings. Then he advised Joseph to "turn away from this." Ibn Kathir wrote that he asked Joseph not to mention this to anyone but to keep this situation secret which would be the most respectable thing to do.[44] *How did Ibn Kathir know this? Was the matter kept secret?* He advised his wife to seek forgiveness for her sins, meaning by this that she must repent to her lord, for surely if she repented to Allah, Allah would forgive her. *Did Al 'Aziz really advise his wife to seek forgiveness from Allah? Was he a Muslim believer?* Al 'Aziz was an Egyptian. *How did he know Allah?*

Ibn Kathir obviously knew that he created a problem with his fabrication, so he tried to fix it by stating, "Although the people of Egypt were worshiping idols, surely they knew the one who forgives sin is Allah alone for he has no partner. That is why her husband excused her because she had no patience with Joseph for he was innocent, gentle, and excellent."[45] That is why her husband said to her to seek forgiveness for she was the sinner.

Remember that Joseph lived four hundred years before Moses, and at this time the Egyptians worshiped all kinds of pharaohs and gods. Judaism did not yet exist, nor did the laws of Moses. No Egyptian knew anything about Allah. If what Mohammed claimed in the life of Joseph was true, surely his master would have killed him and the master's wife without a thought, especially after he had proof that she desired his slave sexually over himself.

I would now like to take the reader to the true account in Genesis 39:7-20. First, as we will see in these verses, the master's wife desired the single young slave sexually, as she tempted Joseph many times. You will notice that the Bible does not mention that Joseph desired her. As we read in the following passages, the great response he gave was in verses 7-10: *⁷And it came to pass after these things that his*

---

[44]Ibid., 235-236.
[45]Ibid., 236.

master's wife cast longing eyes on Joseph, and she said, "Lie with me." ⁸But he refused and said to his master's wife, "Look, my master does not know what is with me in the house, and he has committed all that he has to my hand. ⁹There is no one greater in this house than I, nor has he kept back anything from me but you, because you are his wife. How then can I do this great wickedness, and sin against God?" ¹⁰So it was, as she spoke to Joseph day by day, that he did not heed her, to lie with her or to be with her.

Second, the account of the seduction is found in Genesis 39:11-15: *¹¹But it happened about this time, when Joseph went into the house to do his work, and none of the men of the house was inside, ¹²that she caught him by his garment, saying, "Lie with me." But he left his garment in her hand, and fled and ran outside. ¹³And so it was, when she saw that he had left his garment in her hand and fled outside, ¹⁴that she called to the men of her house and spoke to them, saying, "See, he has brought in to us a Hebrew to mock us. He came in to me to lie with me, and I cried out with a loud voice. ¹⁵And it happened, when he heard that I lifted my voice and cried out, that he left his garment with me, and fled and went outside."*

When she tried to force Joseph to lay with her by holding onto his shirt, he left the shirt in her hands and ran outside. Notice that verse 11 states that there was no one in the house. Because Joseph rejected her, her pride was hurt. She became mad and told the household that he tried to mock (rape) her.

Third, she complained to her husband, Joseph's master; and he reacted as we read in verses 16-20: *¹⁶So she kept his garment with her until his master came home. ¹⁷Then she spoke to him with words like these, saying, "The Hebrew servant whom you brought to us came in to me to mock me; ¹⁸so it happened, as I lifted my voice and cried out, that he left his garment with me and fled outside." ¹⁹So it was, when his master heard the words which his wife spoke to him, saying, "Your servant did to me after this manner," that his anger was aroused. ²⁰Then Joseph's master took him and put him into the prison, a place where the king's prisoners were confined. And he was there in the prison.*

In verse 16, we discover that Potiphar was not in the house, and he never saw them by the door as written in the Qur'an. She lied to her husband once again, repeating the lie that she had told her household because she was really angry that she had been rejected

The Revelation of Error

sexually. The shirt was not cut, not from the front or from the back, but was completely in good condition, not on his body but in her hands.

There was no witness, neither an infant nor an old man. Her words and her words alone gave the testimony, for a slave was not allowed to speak against his master's accusation. Potiphar's wrath was kindled by his wife's accusation. That would be a normal reaction for such an accusation given by a wife. In the end, Joseph was put into prison because his master believed he had sinned against him. It did not matter what good Joseph had done earlier. This was the normal reaction, and he was put into prison.

The Banquet and the Women of the City

Now we will continue with the story of Joseph as Mohammed wove it by adding ridiculous and unnecessary information to the story as we see in Qur'an 12:30-33: *[30]And the women of the city said, "The woman [wife] of Al-'Aziz has sought to seduce her young man. He has infatuated her with love, surely we see her in obvious error." [31]So when she heard of their deceit, she sent for them and prepared a banquet for them and gave each one of them a sikkin.[46] And she said, "Joseph, come out to them." So when they saw him, they were amazed at him and cut their hands and said, "Allah forbid. This is not a human. This is but a generous angel." [32]She said, "This is he about whom you blamed me. And indeed, I sought to seduce him, so he refused. But if he does not do what I command him, he surely will be imprisoned and be of the disgraced." [33]He said, "My lord, the prison is more loved by me than that which they call me to. And if you do not turn away their devices from me, I will lean toward them, and I will become of the foolish."*

In Ibn Kathir's interpretation, he emphasized that the elite and important women of the city shamed the wife of Al 'Aziz and spread rumors around about how she sought to seduce the young man, of her great love for him, and how they disrespected Joseph for he was only a servant.[47] When she heard of their gossip and how they had shamed her for what she had done, she decided to give her reasons for loving this young man. *How did the women of the city know of her lust for*

---

[46]knife, non-Arabic word of Aramaic/Syriac origin
[47]Ibn Kathir, 236.

Joseph? She desired to prove to them that he was not as they thought, so she sent them an invitation and gathered them in her house since she was hospitable. She offered them food that required to be eaten with a knife, so she gave each one of the women a knife. She had prepared Joseph and dressed him in the best clothes since he was in the prime of his youth, and she commanded him to come out for them in his best condition.

When he came out, he was in "his best condition like the moon (meaning that he was beautiful, bright, shining, and handsome). So when they saw him, they honored him, magnified him, and glorified him."[48] They did not think any of the sons of Adam were like him. Because of their admiration of him, they began to cut their hands with these knives but did not feel the cuts. Muslim scholars write many descriptions of Joseph's physical appearance since he was as beautiful as Adam in that his face was like the lightning and that he used to cover his head with a veil so people could not see him.

Then the wife of Al 'Aziz began praising him highly because of his infallibility (perfect, no sin), and she confessed that she was the one who sought to seduce him. Then she made a surprisingly incongruent statement in Qur'an 12:32, in which she said, **But if he does not do what I command him, he surely will be imprisoned and be of the disgraced.**

In summary, according to Mohammed's story, she sought to seduce Joseph, she closed the doors, he sat between her legs, he took his clothes off, and she covered the statue (her god's statue) because she did not want her god to see her fall into sin with Joseph. Allah spoke to him and conviction took place in his heart, so he changed his mind. He ran away from her. She ran after him, desiring to fulfill her sexual desire. She held onto his shirt, and the shirt was cut from the back which proved to her husband, along with a witness in her household, that she was the one who tried to have an affair with him which took place at the door where they met her husband. The husband did not get upset, nor did he have any jealousy toward Joseph; rather, the husband left her in the house alone with Joseph.

The people in the city had begun gossiping, so the master's wife gave this party. After all of the women of the city had cut their hands after admiring his beauty, she asked him arrogantly and boldly to have sex with her in front of all the women of the city, as if there

---

[48]Ibid., 237.

The Revelation of Error

were nothing wrong with such an act. She blackmailed him, saying that if he did not do so, she would imprison him and disgrace him.

Of course, the husband did not mind because he knew that she wanted Joseph sexually and had left them alone together. *And what was the final word of Joseph in verse 33?* He chose prison over having sexual relations with her.

Let me remind the reader once again of what had taken place in the Bible in Genesis 39:19-20. When the master heard what his wife told him regarding what his servant had done to her, he became angry. Joseph's master took him and put him in prison. This also was the prison where the king's prisoners were confined. The Bible states that the Lord was with Joseph even in prison and blessed his work for he had favor with the keeper of the prison, and whatever he did prospered, as it is written in Genesis 39:21-23.

Mohammed stated that Allah answered Joseph's prayer, and he removed his sin from heaven as it is written in verses 34-35: *³⁴So his lord answered him, so he took away their devices from him. Surely he is the hearing, the knowing. ³⁵Then it occurred to them, after they saw the signs, to imprison him for a time.* Muslim scholars said that the master and his wife had decided to put Joseph in prison because they thought that this would make others believe that he was guilty.[49] They put him in prison unjustly as a way to cover up their bad behavior and as the scapegoat for the sake of the reputation of the master's wife. *What reputation?* She asked him in front of all the women of the city to have sex with her, and now Muslim scholars are worried about her reputation! The interpretation of verse 35 by all Muslim scholars does not make sense because in verses 31-32, we saw the boldness and immorality of the master's wife and how she blackmailed Joseph in front of all the exalted women of the city, after she confessed that he was innocent.

The Dreams of the Prisoners and Joseph's Interpretation

When we read the story in the Qur'an in verse 36, the preaching message in verses 37-40, and the interpretation of verses 41-42, we discover several errors. Look first at Qur'an 12:36: *³⁶And entered into the prison with him two young men. One of them said, "Surely I saw myself pressing wine." And the other said, "Surely

---

[49]Ibid.

Chapter 9

I saw myself carrying khubz[50] above my head, the birds eat from it. Inform us of its interpretation, surely we see that you are of the doers of good." Immediately after these two young men entered the prison with Joseph, they shared their dreams with him. The Qur'an does not say who these two young men were. They did not know Joseph, but they saw him to be of the "doers of the good."

The Bible describes the two young men in Genesis 40:1-5. After Joseph was put into prison, the king of Egypt was offended by his butler and his baker. Because the king was angry with them, he put them both in the prison where Joseph was. Joseph at this time was assigned to attend to them, and that is why Joseph served them for many days. Both the butler and the baker had a dream the same night, and it was God's will for them to be in the same prison with Joseph.

However, this is not the Qur'an's story. From the account in the Bible, we can realize that there was a relationship between Joseph and the two men which suggests that they built a friendship. The Qur'an uses the word *fata*, which means *early teens*. It is the age that comes before youth, but this is not clarified in this story in the Qur'an.

How does the Bible describe the dreams, and how did Joseph know about their dreams? To answer these questions, we must read the following verses in Genesis 40:6-8 which describe how Joseph went to the butler and the baker in the morning, saw them in sorrow, and asked them why they were sad. Obviously, that is how he knew about their dreams. Notice that he did not preach to them, as we will see in the Qur'an's verses, but he simply asked them, "Don't interpretations belong to God?" Then Joseph asked them to tell him their dreams.

As it is written in the preaching sermon of Joseph in the Qur'an, although Mohammed cut the introduction of the story of the dreamers too short, he went into a very lengthy speech by Joseph (which I call preaching) before he gave the short interpretation of the dreams. For example, in verse 37: *[37]He said, "You will not be provided with food, but I will inform you of its interpretation before it will come to you. This is a part of that which my lord has taught me; surely I have left the religion of people who do not believe in Allah and in the hereafter. They are infidels.*

Although Mohammed did not give us any information as to who these two young men were, Muslim scholars fabricated an answer as

---

[50] bread, non-Arabic word of Ethiopian origin

if they themselves were prophets as well. So Ibn Kathir interpreted that one of these young men was the cupbearer, and his name was Bno.[51] The other young man was a baker, and his name was Mogls. The king had accused them of some matters, so he imprisoned them. When they saw Joseph in the prison, they liked him and his guidance, his ways, his sayings, his speech, his deeds, his frequent worship of his lord, and his good character. So each one had his dream, and Muslim interpreters said that both saw their dreams in one night as written in Ibn Kathir's book.[52] *How did Ibn Kathir know all of the above information?*

Then Ibn Kathir continued his story, seeming to quote the Bible exactly as it is written in Genesis. He explained the statement, *"surely we see that you are of the doers of good,"* to mean that Joseph had informed them that he knew how to interpret their dreams. He wrote quite a lot of information about the incident by using information from the Bible, claiming it came from this simple, singular verse: Qur'an 12:37. As we have seen, that verse gives us no information as to who these two men were.

All we do know is that they were two young men, which does not make sense since the positions in Pharaoh's court required mature men. They fed and gave drink to the king. It is a great job with great responsibilities, and the king would not choose young men (in their early teens) to do so. These persons must be mature enough to make sure that the king's food and drink were not poisoned.

As for how Joseph could give them the interpretations of their dreams before they received their food, there are two different opinions by Ibn Kathir.[53] First, Joseph meant whatever dream they received, so surely he would give them its interpretation before the dream came to pass so that it would be fulfilled exactly as he had told them. Second, Joseph meant that he would tell them what food would come to them before it came to them and if it would be sweet or sour. Joseph said that it was because "Allah informed him of that." Earlier we read the last part of Qur'an 12:37: *[37]... This is a part of that which my lord has taught me; surely I have left the religion of people who do not believe in Allah and in the hereafter. They*

---

[51] Ibn Kathir, 238.
[52] Ibid., 239.
[53] Ibid.

are infidels. Joseph stated to them that he came from a religion of people who did not believe in Allah.

According to the writings of Mohammed, Joseph then contradicted himself in the following verses in which he stated that his people are believers in one god (Allah). *[38]And I follow the religion of my fathers, Abraham and Isaac and Jacob, and it was not for us to partner with Allah anything. This is a favor from Allah on us and on the people, but most people do not give thanks. [39]O my two companions of the prison, are disunited lords better, or Allah, the one, the dominant? [40]You do not serve other than him, except names you have named them, you and your fathers; Allah has not sent down with them any authority. That the judgment but to Allah. [He] orders to serve no one but him. This is the right religion, but most people do not know.* Then Joseph asked them whether it is better to serve one god or more than one god, and he advised them to come and worship the one true Allah. None of these verses exist in the Bible, and Ibn Kathir did not add any information concerning the true story of Joseph. It is the style of Mohammed's writing because it has, as in many cases, neglected the important information from the biblical story and then added some illogical information which does not help the reader in any case.

Then in verse 41, Joseph gave an interpretation which did not make sense unless the dreams had been told to him, as it is written in the Genesis account. In other words, they told the dreams to Joseph, and as seen in verse 36, the dreams could not be interpreted by verse 41, for the details in the story did not exist in the Qur'an. *How can Joseph interpret the dreams unless they had been told to him?* We do not read in the Qur'an that Allah gave Joseph the dreams and their interpretations. All that we read in Qur'an 12:41 is: *[41]O my two companions of the prison, as for one of you, so he will give a drink of wine to his lord; but as to the other, so he will be crucified, so the birds will eat from his head. This affair is decreed concerning in which you were consulting me."* I would like to point out some errors in this verse.

First, crucifixion did not exist in Joseph's time. Britannica reports that the first historical record of crucifixion was about 519 BC when Darius I, king of Persia, crucified three thousand political opponents

The Revelation of Error

in Babylon.[54] This was long after the time of Joseph's imprisonment in Egypt. Also, when Mohammed said, "So the birds will eat from his head," the Bible said that the birds will eat his body because his head will be gone, as we read in Genesis 40:19: *[19]Within three days Pharaoh will lift off your head from you and hang you on a tree; and the birds will eat your flesh from you.* Cutting the head off and hanging up the body is nothing like crucifixion. The point of crucifixion is that the person be alive and suffer for a long time, not only as punishment to the criminal but as a warning to put fear into others.

When we read the account in Genesis 40:9-13, we discover that this dream and the detailed information, along with the interpretation of the three branches, which Joseph interpreted to represent three days, revealed the time in which Pharaoh would return the cupbearer to his previous job. As for the baker, although his dream was different, he had a dream that same night. The cupbearer had three branches in his dream. The baker had three baskets over his head. It is written in Genesis 40:16-19: *[16]When the chief baker saw that the interpretation was good, he said to Joseph, 'I also was in my dream, and there were three white baskets on my head. [17]In the uppermost basket were all kinds of baked goods for Pharaoh, and the birds ate them out of the basket on my head." [18]So Joseph answered and said, "This is the interpretation of it: The three baskets are three days. [19]Within three days Pharaoh will lift off your head from you and hang you on a tree; and the birds will eat your flesh from you."*

Joseph said to the chief of the bakers (notice that this is a mature man not a young man as stated by Mohammed in the Qur'an) that the interpretation of such a dream was that he would be beheaded and the birds would eat his flesh. Also, notice that Pharaoh did not kill the baker by crucifixion, as Mohammed erroneously stated in the Qur'an, but simply said he would be beheaded and his body would be hung on a tree. To hang a corpse on a tree is not crucifixion. Crucifixion was done to a living person with the intent of prolonged suffering with death from suffocation or loss of blood. A crucified person could live for days before dying.

---

[54]*Encyclopaedia Britannica*, s.v. "crucifixion," accessed January 22, 2012, http://www.britannica.com/EBchecked/topic/14583/crucifixion.

Mohammed ended this portion of the story in Qur'an 12:42 by stating that he asked the one whom Joseph thought would be saved to remember him to his lord, but Satan caused him to forget: *⁴²And he said to the one whom he thought would be delivered, "Remember me to your lord." So Satan caused him to forget the remembrance to his lord, so he abided some years in prison.* There are three important errors I would like to share with the reader in this verse. The first is that Joseph *thought* he would be saved, but according to the Bible he spoke with confidence that the cupbearer would be saved. In Genesis 40:14, we read: **¹⁴*But remember me when it is well with you, and please show kindness to me; make mention of me to Pharaoh, and get me out of this house.***

The second error is that Mohammed claimed that Satan caused the cupbearer to forget to remember Joseph to his lord, but that is not the truth as it is written in the Genesis account. In verse 23, we read: **²³*Yet the chief butler did not remember Joseph, but forgot him.*** He forgot, and that was in the wisdom and plan of God. Perhaps if the cupbearer remembered Joseph, he may have helped Joseph leave the prison to be a slave for another owner or a poor man who lived in the land of Egypt, but God's will was for Joseph to stay longer so that he would become the prince of Egypt, as we will see in the rest of the story.

As for the third error, it is the term *some years* in the original language of the Qur'an. Muslim scholars state that it was a period between three and nine years.[55] That is not correct according to Genesis 41:1: **¹*Then it came to pass, at the end of two full years, that Pharaoh had a dream; and behold, he stood by the river.*** The Bible is clear; it was only two years.

Pharaoh's Dream and Joseph's Interpretation

Verse 43 of the Qur'an describes the dream of Pharaoh. *⁴³And the king said, "Surely I see seven fat cows consumed by seven lean cows and seven green heads of grain and others dried. O you the leaders, consult with me of my dream, if you were interpreters of dreams."* Ibn Kathir explained that this dream was the reason that Joseph left the prison with honor and respect.[56] Ibn Kathir stated that the king of Egypt's name was Al Ryan, Ibn

---

[55]Ibn Kathir, 239.
[56]Ibid., 240.

Alwalyd, Ibn Srwan, Ibn Arshah, Ibn Faran, Ibn Amron, Ibn Anlq, Ibn Lawz, Ibn Shem, and Ibn Noah.

How can Muslims consider such a man a scholar? Where did they get these names? It is truly funny for me, as an Egyptian, to read so many Arabic names as people of my ancestry. As I mentioned above, there were no such names in the heritage of my people. When one studies Egyptian history, he will never find any Arabic names among them. Imagine studying the history of the United States of America and reading about the early fathers' names written in a document with Arabic names. For example, President George Washington was followed by a new President with the name of Mohammed, and after President Mohammed, a new President was elected by the name of Ali, then President Mostasa, then President Shib, and so on.

The people of the United States would know this document was a fraud, for even a ten-year-old child in America knows there are no Presidents by these names. The names in it are obviously Arab Muslim men's names. These are not American or European names, and there was no Muslim President in the history of the United States of America until Barack Hussein Obama. Before him there has never been a Muslim President of the United States, and I pray that he will be the last Muslim President of the United States of America.

Notice the last name Ibn Kathir gave for the genealogy of the king of Egypt. He said, "Son of Shem, son of Noah." This is a profound error; anyone who reads the Bible knows Egyptians are the descendants of Ham, not Shem. In Genesis 10:6: **[6]*The sons of Ham were Cush, <u>Mizraim</u>, Put, and Canaan. [emphasis mine]*** Mizraim is the father of all Egyptians, and the country of Egypt in the Arabic language is called Masar. Masar was named after Mizraim. As for the rest of the descendants of Ham, you can read about them in verses 7-20. As for the descendants of Shem, you can read about them in Genesis 10:21-31. Then in Genesis 10:2-5, the descendants of Jephath are listed. Such genealogies cannot be found in any writings of the Qur'an or hadith, and when these genealogies *are* found in Muslim scholars' writings, they are simply copied from the Bible.

In regard to Pharaoh's dream found in his book, Ibn Kathir stated, without any hesitation, that he used the writings of the People of the Book (Jews and Christians).[57] Ibn Kathir wrote in his introduction

---

[57]Ibid., 241.

Chapter 9

that he had no need to use the Bible for any reason, but he would use it only to shed some light on the story of the Qur'an, not from necessity, but as a complement.

That was really a bold statement as we have shown already. As we will continue to prove, Ibn Kathir routinely used the Bible to interpret the stories of the Qur'an. Believe me, as I have said before, no Muslim, not Mohammed nor Gabreel nor even Allah could explain the stories of the Qur'an without the Bible. Here is another example. In verse 43, the king saw seven fat cows consumed by seven lean cows. A question needs to be asked here: *Where did this take place? Was it (A.) by the pyramids, (B.) by the Valley of the Kings, or (C.) in the backyard of the king's castle?* Obviously, the truth is *none of the above*, for the true answer comes from the Bible.

The answer is very clear, from reading Genesis 41:1, that Pharaoh had a dream as he stood by the river. Other questions I would like to ask are these. *Did Pharaoh have one dream or two separate dreams? In other words, was Pharaoh's dream, of the grain ears and the seven cows, two separate dreams or just one dream?* From reading Qur'an 12:43, as given above, they were one dream, but the Bible account is completely different. According to Genesis 41:2-4, in Pharaoh's dream, there were seven fine-looking, fat cows that rose up out of the river; but then seven other ugly, gaunt cows stood on the bank of the river. The gaunt cows ate up the fat cows. Pharaoh woke up from his dream, but then he went to sleep again and had a second separate dream. In it, he saw seven good, healthy heads of grain coming out of one stalk; but then the east wind blew, and Pharaoh saw seven withered heads of grain which ate up the healthy heads of grain. This shows that there were two separate dreams with many details.

Let's ask another question. *Who are the people that Pharaoh asked to interpret his dreams?* The Qur'an says that Pharaoh asked his leaders to interpret his dream. Other people translated this word to be *notables*, others translated it to be *chiefs*, others translated it as *elders*, others translated it as *nobles*, and still others translated it as *dignitaries*. Although English translators came up with these names, they did not give the real names in Arabic nor the real words as written in the Genesis account. The Bible stated that Pharaoh's magicians and the wise men of all Egypt were troubled, as written in Genesis 41:8: *[8]Now it came to pass in the morning that his spirit was troubled, and he sent and called for all the magicians of Egypt and*

The Revelation of Error

all its wise men. And Pharaoh told them his dreams, but there was no one who could interpret them for Pharaoh.

One may ask, "Why am I picking on the verses of the Qur'an?" I am not picking on the Qur'an. This is just a simple critique. If I were to do so in an expository, a word-for-word analysis of the writings of the Qur'an, this book, *Exposing the Truth about the Qur'an: The Revelation of Error,* would be many volumes in length. However, my point here is to simply show that the Qur'an is a counterfeit copy of the Bible, missing much information, and that it cannot be understood without the true account of the Bible. To help the Muslim and non-Muslim readers to see a glimpse of the truth, perhaps they may return to the Bible and see that it is not a book of corruption, as Muslims claim, but the excellent Word of God with every truth which can literally be understood by simply reading it without any need of interpretation, especially in the portions describing the stories.

According to Qur'an 12:44-46: *[44]They said, "Confused dream. And we do not know the interpretation of dreams." [45]And the one who was delivered of them and remembered after a while said, "I will inform you its interpretation, so send me." [46]"Joseph, O the truthful, consult with us of the seven fat cows which the seven lean consumed and of the seven green heads of grain and others dried; perhaps I may return to the people, perhaps they may know."* Notice that none were able to interpret the dream for the king. Not surprisingly, the Qur'an makes another erroneous statement, which is that the one who remembered asked to be sent (to Joseph) so he could bring the interpretation of the dream to the king. So the king and the people sent him. *Is this really what happened?*

The account of the Bible is completely different. As it is written in Genesis 41:9-16, we see that the people whom Pharaoh sent to get Joseph hurried to bring him before Pharaoh. Joseph shaved himself, changed his clothes, and stood before Pharaoh. Pharaoh said to Joseph directly, "I heard that you can interpret dreams." Then Joseph gave honor to God by stating that it is God who gives the interpretation, not Joseph himself.

Once again, Pharaoh described his dream this time to Joseph in Genesis 41:17-24. Pharaoh said that he dreamed he stood at the bank of the river and saw seven fat, beautiful cows and seven skinny, ugly cows. These skinny, ugly cows ate the seven fat cows. Then Pharaoh woke up from his dream, but then he went back to sleep and had another dream. Seven ears of corn on one stalk were full and good. Then he saw seven withered ears which grew up the good stalks. He saw the thin ears devour the good ears. Pharaoh asked his sorcerers to interpret his dream, but there was no one who could do so.

In Qur'an 12:46, it is written that the one who was saved was able to go and meet with Joseph, and he told the dream to Joseph. He asked Joseph to give him the interpretation that he may return to the people so they may know the interpretation of the dream.

Wow! I am amazed as I continue to read the interpretation of Ibn Kathir when he made fun of the People of the Book. He wrote that they said that the king brought Joseph to him and the king told the dream to Joseph. Then Joseph interpreted the dream to the king directly. Ibn Kathir stated that this was false, and he emphasized that the true answer is what Allah said in his book, the Qur'an.[58]

As Ibn Kathir stated in his own book, and I quote, "Note what the foolish and animals (here Ibn Kathir meant Christians and Jews) wrote in the Arabic from the readers and the teachers." Pharaoh told the dream to Joseph, and the interpretation of the dream took place before Pharaoh, not by the cupbearer as Mohammed erroneously stated in the Qur'an.

Let us look at the true interpretation in Genesis 41:25-36. Joseph interpreted the dream to Pharaoh by explaining that these two dreams of Pharaoh were one dream. The seven fat cows were the same as the seven good ears. The fat cows and good ears are seven years of plenty. After the seven years of plenty, there would be seven years of famine which was represented in the dream by seven skinny cows and seven withered ears. God had revealed this to Pharaoh to show him what He would do.

Then Joseph asked Pharaoh to find a wise person and put him in charge. This person would save grain during the years of plenty in preparation for the years of famine because the famine would be so severe.

Ibn Kathir continued by saying that Joseph did not delay or require any deals, nor did he ask to come out of prison.[59] He just answered the questions and interpreted the dream of the king concerning the plentiful seven years, which would be followed by a famine. In Qur'an 12:47-48: *[47]He said, "You will sow seven years*

---

[58]Ibn Kathir, 241.
[59]Ibid.

The Revelation of Error

continually. So whatever you hasada,[60] *so leave in its heads of grain except a little of what you eat.* ⁴⁸*Then after that will come seven hard years, will consume what you have stored for them except a little of what you will have stored.* Notice in verse 47 Joseph said that they would eat only a little of what they had harvested.

That is not true as we will see in Genesis 41:33-36. Joseph asked Pharaoh to search for a wise man and put him in charge of all the land of Egypt, so they could collect the produce during the plentiful years and store up grain under the authority of Pharaoh. This grain would then be used during the famine years so that the land would not perish. The Bible states that the amount of grain which Joseph recommended to be put aside was one fifth of the harvest, not the majority of the harvest as stated in the Qur'an.

In verse 49 of the Qur'an, Mohammed made another huge error simply because Mohammed had never been in Egypt and did not understand the agriculture and meteorology of Egypt. For Qur'an 12:49 states: ⁴⁹*Then will come after this a year in which people will have rain and in it they will press."* Rain in Egypt? This is an absolute 100 percent false statement. I was born and raised in Egypt. It rarely rains in Egypt and then for only a few minutes. The rain in Egypt is not sufficient at all to grow plants. Egyptians depend on the water from the Nile River, not from the rain.

Perhaps if Mohammed or those who helped him by telling him the account of Joseph in the Bible had read it carefully, they would not have made such an error. Since Mohammed did not know the dream of Pharaoh with its details, Mohammed thought that it rained in Egypt. Once again, the Bible said that Pharaoh saw the cows coming up out of the river. The river had a great role in Pharaoh's dream because from the river came the seven fat cows and from the river came the seven skinny cows. The interpretation was for seven years of plenty and seven years of famine.

As it is repeated in the second dream with the seven full ears of grain and the seven thin, blighted ears of grain, Joseph said that both dreams were one dream about the water of the Nile and the harvest of the field. It is not about rain as Mohammed thought. In Ibn Kathir's

---

[60]reap, non-Arabic word of Aramaic origin

interpretation, referring to the word *press,* he stated that he meant the pressing of sugar cane, grapes, olives, sesame seeds, and other produce.[61]

In verse 50 in Qur'an 12, the king asked for Joseph to come to him: *[50]And the king said, "Bring him to me." So when the messenger came to him, he said, "Return to your lord, so ask him what the women meant who cut their hands, surely my lord knows well their devices."* However, Joseph declined to go to the king, for he was imprisoned unjustly, according to Ibn Kathir's interpretation.[62]

Back to the Women of the City

Then Joseph asked those who were sent to bring him out of the prison to return to the king and command the king to investigate his unjust imprisonment by asking the women, who cut their hands, about how he very strongly rejected them when they tried to seduce him. Joseph also wanted the king to inquire of them about how they had asked him to do what was not right (have sex with them).

Then Ibn Kathir continued by stating that when the women were asked about their actions to which they had confessed, they commended Joseph for doing only what was right. When the wife of Al 'Aziz stated that the truth had come, she confessed that she sought to seduce Joseph and that he was innocent and had not tried to have sex with her. She said that he was imprisoned unjustly and unfairly. In Qur'an 12:51: *[51]He said, "What was your purpose when you sought to seduce Joseph?" They said, "Allah forbid. We do not know any evil of him. The woman [wife] of Al-'Aziz said, 'Now the truth hashas.[63] I sought to seduce him, and he is surely of the truthful.'"*

Then Mohammed continued in verse 52: *[52]"That he might know that I have not cheated him in secret, and surely Allah does not guide the device of the betrayers.* Ibn Kathir stated that these words were from Joseph and that he said them in order for Al 'Aziz to know that Joseph had not betrayed him.[64] That's why Joseph required the investigation; but amazingly, in the following paragraph on the

---

[61] Ibn Kathir, 241.
[62] Ibid., 241-242.
[63] a word without meaning
[64] Ibn Kathir, 242.

The Revelation of Error

same page, Ibn Kathir stated that perhaps it was not the words of Joseph but of Al 'Aziz's wife and that she meant Joseph did not commit indecent acts with her. Perhaps Muslim scholars do not know who said this statement in verse 52.

The exact problem is found in Qur'an 12:53: *⁵³And I do not declare myself innocent, surely the self commands with the evil, except for those on whom my lord has mercy. Surely my lord is forgiving, merciful."* Muslim scholars do not know who said this verse. Some say Joseph said it. Others said it was Al 'Aziz's wife. The two things Muslim scholars agree on are the following: that the truth is in the Qur'an, not the Bible, for the Bible is corrupted, and *Allah knows best*!

As we continue with the story in the Qur'an, we will discover many more errors. Qur'an 12:54 states: *⁵⁴And the king said, "Bring him to me. I will take him for myself." So when he had spoken with him, he said, "Surely today you are with us in a prominent position, secure."* In his interpretation, Ibn Kathir stated that when the king discovered the innocence and integrity of Joseph concerning what he had been accused of by the women, he said, "Bring him to me. I will give him a very special position, so he will be one of the dignitaries of my country." And he said to Joseph, "You are in a position of safety."[65] According to verse 54, once again the king required Joseph to come to him which means the interpretation of the king's dream took place while Joseph was in prison which is an error.

That is not what is written in the Genesis account. In addition, a strange aspect of the writing in the Qur'an is that there are huge gaps in the stories, such as Joseph being in prison in verse 54 and then in verse 55 being right in front of the king. Also, the characters in these verses, from 53-56, change from verse to verse; for example, going from someone unknown, to the king, then Joseph, and then Allah speaking. There is no continuity in these verses as the details change from verse to verse.

Another error is in Qur'an 12:55, which states that Joseph was the one who was asked to be put in charge of the land, as he bragged about himself saying that he was a knowledgeable guardian. *⁵⁵He said, "Set me over the treasuries of the land, surely I am a keeper, knowledgeable."* That is not what the Bible says.

---

[65] Ibid.

Chapter 9

    In his interpretation, Ibn Kathir literally quoted the Bible, as found in Genesis 41:41-46, and Ibn Kathir said *this was what was written* by the People of the Book.[66] Pharaoh honored Joseph very much and gave him authority over the land of Egypt and had him wear Pharaoh's ring and silk and even some gold around his neck. He had Joseph ride in the second chariot, and they announced before him to the people that he was lord with all the authority. Pharaoh said to Joseph that no one would be greater than Joseph except for Pharaoh. Ibn Kathir said the People of the Book said Joseph was thirty years old. Pharaoh married Joseph to a very important woman. You can find the exact information in Genesis 41:41-46.

    I wonder if, when Muslims read the interpretation of Ibn Kathir, they credit him as a scholar with his knowledge about Joseph. Also, I wonder if Muslims credit Mohammed for Qur'an 12, the story of Joseph, with the knowledge he mentioned in the Qur'an, as if Mohammed was a prophet. The fact is, Mohammed copied the story of Joseph from the Bible and missed much of the information. He added ridiculous and erroneous information throughout his copying of the story of Joseph by adding information from the Bible to the Qur'an. This does not make the newer book, the Qur'an, a book of prophecy, nor does it make the person who copied the information a prophet. Actually, this is called *plagiarism*.

    If Moses, Mohammed, and Ibn Kathir were alive today, Moses could file many lawsuits against Mohammed and Ibn Kathir because they plagiarized his writings as they took many of his verses and added to, misconstrued, or elaborated on them. They also took away verses from Moses' writings. Here we must mention the true account of how Joseph became the prince of Egypt, as recorded in Genesis 41:33-36, in which Joseph, after telling Pharaoh about the seven years of plenty followed by the seven years of famine, recommended that Pharaoh get someone wise to collect one fifth of the produce of the land during the years of plenty to be stored for the seven years of famine to come. Upon hearing the words of Joseph, Pharaoh appointed him to be ruler over the land, with only Pharaoh being greater than he.

    Because Joseph interpreted the dream to Pharaoh, the wisdom of God was shown in his interpretation. Moreover, he gave advice in verses 33-36 which showed the answer to the problem to come.

---

[66]Ibid.

Wisdom is not only identifying the problem; it is also having a solution for the problem. Saving a portion of the harvest of the plentiful years for the years of famine proved to Pharaoh and his servants that Joseph was the wise man whom they needed in the following years to save their country.

Joseph and His New Position in the Land of Egypt

Another major difference between the account of Genesis and the story of Mohammed in the Qur'an is how Joseph attained his position in the land. In Genesis 41:33, Joseph said that Pharaoh should search for a discreet and wise man. He did not say to *put me over the land* as Mohammed stated in Qur'an 12:55. The truth is that Joseph did not ask for this position, but Pharaoh offered this position to Joseph, as written in Genesis 41:37-44. Because Joseph's advice was wise, Pharaoh asked his servants in verse 38, *"...Can we find such a one as this, a man in whom is the Spirit of God?"* In verses 39-41:
[39] Then Pharaoh said to Joseph, "Inasmuch as God has shown you all this, there is no one as discerning and wise as you. [40] You shall be over my house, and all my people shall be ruled according to your word; only in regard to the throne will I be greater than you." [41] And Pharaoh said to Joseph, "See, I have set you over all the land of Egypt. Then Pharaoh put his own signet ring on Joseph's hand, clothed him in fine linen, put a gold chain around his neck, and had him ride in the second chariot before the people. **[44] Pharaoh also said to Joseph, "I am Pharaoh, and without your consent no man may lift his hand or foot in all the land of Egypt."**

One of the exaggerated statements written by Ibn Kathir was that Joseph was thirty years old when he met with the king, the king spoke to him in seventy different languages, and Joseph was able to respond in all these languages which caused the king to like Joseph, especially since Joseph was so young.[67] As usual, Ibn Kathir ended this statement by saying, *and Allah knows best.*

To put Joseph at thirty years of age will contradict the earlier statement in which Muslim scholars mentioned that he was at the *age of strength,* meaning forty years of age, as stated in Ibn Kathir's interpretation of Qur'an 22:5. We all know people get older as years go by, not younger.

---

[67] Ibid.

Chapter 9

In conclusion of this session, Allah said in Qur'an 12:56-57: *⁵⁶And likewise, we established for Joseph in the land that he may choose from it whatever he wills. We give our mercy to whom we will, and we do not waste the wage of the doers of good. ⁵⁷And the wage of the hereafter is better to those who believed and were fearers.* Ibn Kathir said that this was the reward of Allah to the believers, which is another astonishing interpretation he gave.[68] Ibn Kathir also stated that when the king of Egypt had fired Al 'Aziz (which Al Salabe named Katfer), the husband of Zleka, the king gave that position to Joseph. (These were the two Egyptians who had bought Joseph as a slave, and Zleka was the woman who tried to seduce Joseph.)

Joseph's Marriage

Another interpretation is that after Pharaoh fired her husband, Al 'Aziz, Joseph got his job; and after Al 'Aziz died, the king married Joseph to Al 'Aziz's wife. After Joseph married her, he found her to be a virgin, for her husband did not have any desire to be with women. Then she bore two sons to Joseph, Ephraim and Manasseh. Ibn Kathir stated that Joseph led the king of Egypt to accept Islam, *and Allah knows best!*[69] Then Joseph became the king of Egypt. He ruled with justice in the land, and the men and women loved him. *Where did Ibn Kathir get all this information?* The answer is that he copied it from the Bible, and he added lies and fairy tales to the biblical account.

Did that really take place in Genesis? In Genesis 41:45-46, we read that Pharaoh changed the name of Joseph to Zaphenathpaneah, and he married him to Asenath, the daughter of Poti-Pherah, the priest of On. This is the true account concerning Joseph's marriage. As for his two sons, Manasseh[70] and Ephraim,[71] one can read about them in Genesis 41:50-52.

Joseph was never the Pharaoh of Egypt as we see in Exodus 1:8. When Joseph died at the age of 110 years, as Genesis 50:25 shows, he had never been a king. The Bible stated that there was a new king, who knew neither Joseph nor his people, and he took over the kingdom of Egypt. If Joseph had become the king, one of his sons

---

[68] Ibid., 243.
[69] Ibid.
[70] name means *for God has made me forget all my toil and all my father's house*
[71] name means *for God has caused me to be fruitful in the land of my affliction*

The Revelation of Error

would have become the heir to be the new king. So many errors are found throughout the stories of the Qur'an.

<u>The First Trip of Joseph's Brothers to Egypt</u>

In Qur'an 12:58-62, we discover the first visit of Joseph's brothers to Egypt: *^{58}And Joseph's brothers came, so they entered to him. So he knew them, and they were unaware of him. ^{59}And when he had provided them with their provision, he said, "Bring me a brother of you from your father. Do you not see that I fill the measure and I am the best of hosts? ^{60}So if you do not bring him to me, so no measure will there be for you from me, nor will you come near me." ^{61}They said, "We will persuade his father of him, and we will surely do that." ^{62}And he said to his young men, "Put their merchandise into their bags. Perhaps they may know it when they return to their family; perhaps they will come back."* This long account with its details as written in the Bible is condensed in just five verses. *How can Muslims understand the big gap in the Qur'an's verses without knowing the Bible verses?* In verse 58, the brothers came to Egypt. In verse 59, he gave them their provision, and he immediately asked them to bring a brother to him from their father. In verse 60, he threatened them that if they did not bring their brother, then they could not come near him. Then the brothers told Joseph they would persuade their father to let them bring his son with them.

According to Ibn Kathir as stated, this took place when Joseph was in control of the Egyptians' homes, religion, and worldly affairs.[72] When Joseph's brothers came to him, he knew them, but they did not know him, for it never entered their thoughts that he would hold such a high position. Finally in verse 60, Joseph asked that their money be put in their sacks, so that perhaps they would come back.

We must ask some questions. For those of us who are Jewish or Christians and familiar with the account from the Bible, we can always insert the missing pieces of the big puzzle of Joseph's story. *But how can Muslims understand the story without the information from the Bible?* When Joseph said, "Bring me a brother of you from your father," this was a strange request.

---
[72]Ibn Kathir, 243.

Chapter 9

Why did Joseph say for them to "bring me a brother of you from your father"? How can a person have a brother who is not from their own mother? Do they have another brother from a different mother? Did the father have an affair with another woman? These are simple questions which cannot be answered without returning to the Genesis account.

Without the account of Genesis, as we have shown previously, how can a Muslim explain such a strange request of Joseph? Why did he not say, "Bring me your little brother"? What led Joseph in the conversation to ask his brothers to bring their brother? One must wonder how Joseph came up with a request for them to bring his brother without any introductory questions as the story was told in the Bible. *Why did Joseph threaten them and insist that they must bring their brother? For what reason and by what right did Joseph make such a demand?*

Finally, in verse 62, Joseph requested that their merchandise be put in their bags, and he said, "Perhaps they will come back." That is a very strange statement because Joseph knew that they would come back since this was the first of seven years of famine. By giving the merchandise back to them, they would come back for sure. In Ibn Kathir's interpretation, he stated that the reason that Joseph put their merchandise back in their bags was perhaps this would be an excuse for them to come back to Egypt so they could return the merchandise, or maybe they would not have enough money to come back to buy more food.[73] This was ridiculous because the brothers were not poor but rich. The problem that they were facing at the time was not money or riches but the lack of food. Ibn Kathir also stated that Muslim scholars disagreed on what kind of merchandise they had.

Mohammed forgot to mention the famine years in Egypt and all over the face of the earth, the account of which is found in Genesis 41:55-57. When the land of Egypt was suffering during the famine, the people cried to Pharaoh for bread. Pharaoh told them to do whatever Joseph said for them to do and sent the people to him. Not only was there famine in Egypt, but it was also over the face of the earth. Joseph opened up the storehouses and sold to the Egyptians. As the famine became more severe, all countries came to Egypt to buy grain.

---

[73]Ibid., 244.

Here are some very important pieces of information omitted by Mohammed. He forgot to mention that the number of Joseph's brothers who came to Egypt was ten because Jacob refused to send the youngest, Benjamin. As it is written in Genesis 42:1-5: *¹When Jacob saw that there was grain in Egypt, Jacob said to his sons, "Why do you look at one another?" ²And he said, "Indeed I have heard that there is grain in Egypt; go down to that place and buy for us there, that we may live and not die." ³So Joseph's ten brothers went down to buy grain in Egypt. ⁴But Jacob did not send Joseph's brother Benjamin with his brothers, for he said, "Lest some calamity befall him." ⁵And the sons of Israel went to buy grain among those who journeyed, for the famine was in the land of Canaan.*

Mohammed also forgot to mention the rest of the story as it is written in Genesis 42:7-9. These verses show that Joseph recognized his brothers, but they did not know him, and that he spoke roughly with them by accusing them of being spies in the land. Joseph interrogated them, and they told him that they were not spies but twelve brothers from one man from the land of Canaan. They told Joseph that they had a young brother who had stayed with their father and another brother who had been lost. As it is written in Genesis 42:10-13: *¹⁰And they said to him, "No, my lord, but your servants have come to buy food. ¹¹We are all one man's sons; we are honest men; your servants are not spies." ¹²But he said to them, "No, but you have come to see the nakedness of the land." ¹³And they said, "Your servants are twelve brothers, the sons of one man in the land of Canaan; and in fact, the youngest is with our father today, and one is no more."*

Continuing with his interrogation, as he insisted they were spies, Joseph commanded them to stay until their youngest brother came. Since he said that they must prove to him they were not spies, Joseph imprisoned them for three days, as written in Genesis 42:14-17.

Mohammed also forgot to mention that on the third day Joseph released the brothers, except for one, so that they could go home with the food. They then would bring their youngest brother back in order to prove they were not spies and that they might live. See Genesis 42:18-20.

Mohammed also forgot to record the conversation they had with one another and how they confessed to one another their guilt over their brother Joseph when he, distressed at their lack of mercy towards him, begged them not to harm him or sell him as a slave. Reuben spoke to them about their young brother and that now his blood was required from them. One can see this in Genesis 42:21-22.

You can read the original story in Genesis 37:21-22. *²¹But Reuben heard it, and he delivered him out of their hands, and said, "Let us not kill him." ²²And Reuben said to them, "Shed no blood, but cast him into this pit which is in the wilderness, and do not lay a hand on him"- that he might deliver him out of their hands, and bring him back to his father.*

One of the most important things that Mohammed forgot was the language which Joseph spoke with his brothers in the Qur'an. Joseph spoke directly to his brothers without an interpreter. The Bible says that he was speaking to them through an interpreter, for he had heard them confessing their guilt about their little brother Joseph, and he saw their distress. They did not know that he understood what they were saying, as written in Genesis 42:23: *²³But they did not know that Joseph understood them, for he spoke to them through an interpreter.*

Mohammed forgot to mention the broken heart of Joseph and how he turned away and cried after hearing their struggle and seeing their distress. Then he took Simeon and bound him before their eyes, as written in Genesis 42:24. Instead of holding Simeon in Egypt, Mohammed erred by saying that Joseph allowed all of his brothers to go back home together.

Although Muslim scholars disagree on what kind of merchandise Joseph's brothers used to buy grain, Ibn Kathir stated that, according to the Bible, it was money made out of paper or something that looked like paper.[74] We will go into this in more detail later in this chapter. If Ibn Kathir had read the Bible carefully, he would have discovered that it was not paper but silver. The Bible clearly teaches that it was silver because Joseph commanded that their silver be put back into their sacks. When one of the brothers opened his bag, he found the silver in the mouth of the sack. Also, Mohammed neglected to mention how fearful they were when they found that their silver had been returned to them.

We can read this in Genesis 42:25-28. Joseph instructed that their sacks be filled with grain, their money be returned back to their sacks, and provisions be given to them for the trip. After they had departed

---
[74]Ibn Kathir, 244.

for home, one of the brothers opened his sack to feed his donkey and saw his money. He told his brothers that his money had been restored and was in his sack. Then the brothers became afraid and said one to another in verse 28: *²⁸...**What is this that God has done to us?***

The Return of the Sons of Israel Back Home

Now let us go back to Qur'an 12:63: *⁶³So when they returned to their father, they said, "O our father, we have been denied our measure, so send our brother with us. And we will have our measure, and surely we will be keepers to him."* A simple reading of this verse will show that the brothers of Joseph lied to their father Jacob by stating that they were denied any measure of food from their first trip to Egypt. Muslim scholars fabricated an interpretation of this verse by stating that they meant that the brothers would not receive any measure of food the following year if Jacob did not send his son Benjamin with them. This can be proven in verse 65: *⁶⁵And when they opened their bags, they found their merchandise had been returned to them. They said, "O our father, we did not desire that our merchandise would be returned to us. We will bring food to our families, and we will keep our brother and will increase a ba'ir⁷⁵ measure. This is an easy measure."* Another fabrication of Al Qurtobi and Al Tabari is their statement that the sons of Jacob really told their father all that had taken place on their trip to Egypt, how they had been treated, and how Simeon had been taken as a ransom so that the ruler would know that they were truthful.[76] It is amazing how Muslim scholars such as these are greatly influenced by the true account of Genesis.

The Bible had such a great influence on Muslim scholars that they quote the account from the Bible, not only to interpret the Qur'an when the information does not exist in the Qur'an, but even when it teaches something completely different from the Qur'an. *For example, how did Muslim scholars, Al Qurtobi and Al Tabari, know about Simeon and that he was taken as a ransom because the Qur'an did not mention such a thing?* It is interesting that they used the name of Simeon, even though it was never mentioned in the Qur'an.

---

[75] camel, non-Arabic word of Syriac origin
[76] http://quran.Al-islam.com/Page.aspx?pageid=221&BookID=14&Page=243, accessed February 3, 2013.

On the other hand, the account in the Bible is very clear about what took place between Jacob and his sons. Jacob's sons told him what had taken place in Egypt and how the master of the land had spoken to them with harshness and thought they were spies, even though they assured this ruler that they were not spies but twelve sons of one man. They described to Jacob how the master had given them some grain and told them to bring their youngest brother back with them, so that he would know they were not spies. They told Jacob they had found their silver in their sacks. They and their father were afraid when they saw that the money had been returned to them.

The Bible clearly stated that Jacob was very saddened as he said that ***Joseph is missed and Simeon is taken away,*** in Genesis 42:36. Jacob refused to allow them to take Benjamin with them. Reuben tried to persuade his father to let Benjamin go with them to Egypt by saying that if he did not bring Benjamin back with him, Jacob could kill Reuben's own son. However, Jacob refused to send Benjamin with them because he was afraid that something would happen to him, which would bring Jacob to the grave in sorrow, as we read in Genesis 42:29-38.

That is not what took place in the Qur'an version. Jacob simply asked a question about the sending of his son to Egypt, when he said in verse 64 of the Qur'an: *[64]He said, "Will I entrust you with him except as I entrusted you before with his brother? So Allah is the best keeper, and he is the most merciful of the merciful."*

However, Mohammed said in the Qur'an that Jacob said that he would not send his son with them to Egypt until they brought to him a solemn oath from Allah. This is a strange statement without any meaning. *What does it mean? What was this oath? Did Allah send him permission by mail or fax or some other method? How could they receive such an oath from Allah?* Muslim scholars fabricated an answer when interpreting this verse; they said Jacob meant that if they swore by Allah, then they would bring his son back. Mohammed stated that they brought their oath as it is written in Qur'an 12:66: *[66]He said, "I will not send him with you until you bring to me a firm oath from Allah that you will return him back to me unless you are constrained." So when they brought him their pledge, he said, "Allah is the guardian above what we say."* The following verses of the Qur'an contain another strange statement which lacks any facts, as Mohammed said Jacob stated the following

The Revelation of Error

in verses 67-68: *⁶⁷And he said, "O my sons, do not enter by one door. And enter by different doors, and yet I cannot profit you against anything decreed by Allah, for the judgment to Allah alone. On him I depend, and on him, so let the depender depend." ⁶⁸And when they entered as their father had commanded them, it was not averted from them anything against Allah, but it only served to satisfy a need in the soul of Jacob. And surely he was possessed of knowledge we had taught him, but most people do not know.*

In his interpretation, Ibn Kathir stated that Jacob commanded his sons to enter the city from different doors.[77] Ibn Kathir stated that Jacob desired to protect them from being *envied*,[78] for they were a beautiful looking group. Another reason that Ibn Kathir's statement is particularly erroneous is that Jacob asked them to enter from separate doors, so they could search for Joseph from different places. *If true, shouldn't this advice have been given to Jacob's sons on their first trip instead of their second trip to Egypt?* However, had Mohammed been to Egypt even once, he would have known that Egypt is not a city but a large country, much bigger than Mecca or Medina. It does not have a fence or gate, and there is no way for Jacob's sons to enter from different doors as written in verse 68. *Did you notice they were searching for Joseph? Did Jacob send his sons to search for Joseph?*

What really took place according to the Bible? As I read in Genesis 43, I found that there is no need for any commentary or any interpretation because the account speaks for itself. I will summarize it in a few words.

The hunger was severe in the land. Jacob asked his sons to buy more grain from Egypt. Judah said that they must take their brother Benjamin with them. Israel (Jacob) asked, "Why did you do evil to me? Why did you tell the man (the ruler in Egypt) that you have a brother?" Then they explained to Jacob what took place in Egypt. Judah begged his father to send Benjamin with them. Israel (Jacob), after a long struggle, sent Benjamin and a gift of the best fruit of the land with them, and they took double the silver with them. Jacob prayed to the Mighty God that He would give them mercy and that

---

[77] Ibn Kathir, 245.
[78] an Arabic belief that if someone gives a person(s) the evil eye; that is, if someone looked at Jacob's sons, who were beautiful and powerful, then the sons would get sick or die

the man of Egypt might release Simeon and Benjamin. Then they went down to Egypt as written in Genesis 43:1-15.

The Second Trip of Joseph's Brothers to Egypt

Now let us return to Qur'an 12:69 which states: *[69]And when they entered unto Joseph, he took his brother to him. He said, "Surely I am your brother. So do not grieve for what they were doing."* In their interpretation, Al Tabari and Al Qurtobi said that Joseph brought his brothers into his house and put every two of the brothers in one bed. This took place after he fed them at night. Since there were eleven brothers, ten of them took five beds. This left Benjamin without a bed, and he was alone. Then Joseph said, "This (Benjamin) sleep with me on my bed." So he slept with him.

During the night, Joseph began to smell Benjamin and hold him tight to himself; he continued to do this until morning. That is when he told Benjamin that he was his brother and for him not to tell the other brothers. Reuben said, "We have never seen anything like that before."

When I was ten or eleven years old, I remember reading the account of Joseph for the first time. It felt just like yesterday as I came to this part once again and read the account of Joseph meeting with his brothers the second time and revealing his identity. How emotional this meeting was, we see once again, as we read the biblical account. When I read it years ago, I cried because it was a very moving moment.

However, when I read the same portion in the Qur'an, I literally do not know if I should cry for the ignorance of Mohammed and his scholars, concerning the true account in the Bible, or if I should laugh because it is so ridiculous how the Qur'an destroys the true account of the Bible. *What did Allah mean when he stated in the Qur'an, "When they entered unto Joseph."? Was Joseph sitting in his living room or maybe in his dining room? What does Mohammed mean by that? How can Muslims understand Ibn Kathir's statement about when the brothers met with Joseph, and he talked with Benjamin in secret and told Benjamin that he was his brother?*[79]

Joseph then commanded Benjamin not to tell his brothers about this. *Where did Ibn Kathir come up with this information because the Qur'an never mentions this?* Then Ibn Kathir stated that Joseph

---
[79]Ibn Kathir, 245.

The Revelation of Error

deceived them and did this by hiding the cup. Ibn Kathir stated that this was the cup Joseph used to drink from and used to measure the people's food.[80] *Was Joseph a worker who measured the people's food with his own cup? Why? Didn't he own another cup, or did he just have only one cup to use? Was he really measuring the people's food with his own cup? Does this sound as foolish to you as it does to me?*

Then Joseph told them that they had stolen the king's cup. He promised them that if they would return it, he would give them a camel's load[81] as a reward. This also sounds like another foolish statement, not by a Muslim scholar but by Mohammed himself. *Would a man like Joseph in his position reward a thief with a camel's load of grain for stealing his own cup?* The brothers responded that he accused them of something they did not do.

Ibn Kathir stated that, according to the culture of the day, the person who stole would be made a slave as a punishment for the theft.[82] Ibn Kathir stated that Allah had said that the Egyptians began searching the brothers' bags. Benjamin's bag was the last to be searched, so that their deception would be discovered. Ibn Kathir continued by saying, that because of their confession, whoever had the cup in his bag would be the punished person (who would become a slave). Joseph would then be able to take his brother from them, according to Egyptian (law) political practice.

This was Ibn Kathir's interpretation of the following verses 70-76 of the Qur'an: *[70]So when he had provided them with their supplies, he placed his drinking vessel in his brother's pack. Then a caller called, "O travelers, surely you are thieves!" [71]They said, and they turned back to them, "What did you miss?" [72]They said, "We miss the king's suwā.[83] And to him who will restore it a camel's load, and I guarantee it." [73]They said, "[We swear] by Allah, indeed, you know we did not come to vandalize in the land. And we were not thieves." [74]They said, "So what is the penalty if you were liars?" [75]They said, "His penalty for the one in whose pack you find it, so he is the penalty. Likewise, we reward the unjust." [76]So he began with*

---

[80]Ibid., 246.
[81]grain, most likely
[82]Ibn Kathir, 246.
[83]drinking cup, non-Arabic word of Ethiopian origin-same word as from the story of Joseph in the Ethiopian Bible

their bags before his brother's bag. And then he drew it out from his brother's bag. Likewise, we schemed for Joseph that he was not to take his brother into the judgment of the king, except if Allah wills. We raise degrees of whom we will, and above everyone with knowledge more knowledgeable. In verse 77, Mohammed fabricated a lie, and then Muslim scholars fabricated an interpretation to Mohammed's lie. For the verse said, *[77]They said, "If he has stolen, so indeed, his brother has stolen before." So Joseph kept it secret in his soul and did not disclose it to them. He said, "You are in an evil position, and Allah knows what you describe."* Concerning the brother who stole in the past, Ibn Kathir said that they meant Joseph.[84] Ibn Kathir also said that Joseph had stolen an idol from his grandfather, the father of his mother, and he had broken it. *Where did this information come from? Was Ibn Kathir a prophet too?*

It also has been said that Joseph's aunt had put something like a sash belonging to Isaac on him between his clothes (two shirts) when he was a child. He removed it from under his clothes, and he did not feel it. His aunt did that because she desired for him to have it because of her love for him. It is also said that he used to take the food from the house and feed it to the poor. These are some examples of the fabrications of some of the things that Joseph supposedly had stolen. As for the statement, *"You are in an evil position, and Allah knows what you describe,"* Ibn Kathir stated that Joseph said it in secret (in his thoughts), not in the open, so as a way to show his generosity, calmness, kindness, and forgiveness.[85] *How did Ibn Kathir know that Joseph said this statement in secret? How did the man in charge of Egypt (Joseph) know Allah?*

What happened in the true account of the Bible? In the following summary of Genesis 43, the Bible states that when Joseph saw Benjamin with them when they returned to Egypt the second time, he told the ruler of his house to bring the men to his house and prepare a meal for them. (That is possibly what Mohammed meant in verse 69 by "they entered unto Joseph.") There Joseph's brothers were full of fear, and they thought it was because of the silver which had been returned to their sacks from the first trip. That is why they tried to explain to the man in charge of Joseph's house what took place on

---

[84]Ibn Kathir, 246.
[85]Ibid.

The Revelation of Error

their first trip and how they found their silver in their sacks. They also explained to him that they had brought the silver back with them, along with extra silver to buy grain for their second trip.

Mohammed did not mention that the man had received their silver in the previous trip, and then he brought out to them their brother Simeon. Then they entered Joseph's house and gave him the gift. Joseph asked them about their old father, and they said that he was in good health. Then Joseph lifted up his eyes and saw his brother Benjamin. Because Joseph's heart ached for Benjamin, he quickly left the room, for his bowels yearned for his brother, and he wept. Joseph washed his face, returned to the room, composed himself, and directed that the meal be served. The account goes on to say that the Egyptians ate separately from the Hebrews, that Joseph set his brothers at the table according to their birth order, from oldest to youngest, and that Benjamin received five portions of food compared to the rest of his brothers. All this occurred, and Joseph never told any of his brothers who he was. This can be read in Genesis 43:15-34.

I'll continue the summary by paraphrasing Genesis 44. We can read there that Joseph commanded the steward of his house to give his brothers plenty of food and to put the silver cup in the mouth of Benjamin's sack. After the brothers had left in the morning, Joseph asked the steward of his house to follow them and stop them from leaving the country. When the brothers said that they had not stolen from the master, they said that whoever took the cup must die. As the steward searched, he began with the bags of the oldest brother and continued in order down to the youngest brother's. The steward found the cup in Benjamin's sack. *So what happened then? Did the Egyptian offer them the camel's load, as written in the erroneous story of the Qur'an?* No. *Did Joseph's brothers say that Benjamin's brother had stolen before as Mohammed made up this story in the Qur'an?* No. The normal reaction was that they ripped their clothes.

When they returned to the city, they stood before Joseph, and Joseph angrily spoke to them saying, "How dare you steal my cup!" There Judah spoke before Joseph, and Judah condemned himself and his brothers so that they would all be slaves to the master. However, Joseph refused and said, "No. Only the man in whose sack the cup was found will be my slave, and the rest of you may go back to your father in peace." There Judah spoke again before Joseph and told him the story once again about their old father and how the loss of Benjamin would take the life of their father if they did not return with

Benjamin. They explained to the ruler, Joseph, that Benjamin's brother Joseph had died and that Benjamin was the only one the father had, and he loved his youngest son so very much. Judah explained to Joseph that if he were to take Benjamin, their father would die. Judah offered himself as a slave in place of Benjamin.

Now let us continue with the summary of Genesis 45. Joseph could not contain himself, and he shouted, asking everyone to leave except for his brothers. He cried so loudly that all the Egyptians in the house of Pharaoh heard him. Joseph revealed to his brothers that he was their brother and asked if his father was still alive. Then Joseph asked his brothers to come near him. He revealed that he was Joseph whom they had sold into slavery and that God had sent him before them to Egypt. Joseph explained to them that the famine had been going on for two years and that five more years were then to come. Then Joseph told them to bring their father and all of their possessions to Egypt.

After that, Joseph fell upon his brother Benjamin's neck, and they both wept. Joseph kissed his brothers and wept upon them also. Notice the great difference between the true account of Genesis and the counterfeit story of the Qur'an, especially when you add the foolish interpretation of Muslim scholars. Joseph did not sleep all night with his brother Benjamin, holding him and smelling his clothes. Joseph did not tell Benjamin in private that he was his brother. The true story is just as we have stated from the Genesis account.

The news of Joseph being reunited with his brothers was told to Pharaoh's household, and Pharaoh invited them to come to Egypt. Joseph asked his brothers to go and bring their father to him. He gave them carts to bring Jacob and their possessions back to Egypt. When they arrived back at their father's home and told Jacob what had occurred, Jacob rejoiced and his spirit revived as he said, "It is enough. My son Joseph is alive. I will go and see him before I die."

What a moving story. Every time I read it, I can't stop the tears as they flow from my eyes, and my heart fills with compassion for Joseph and his life's story.

O how Mohammed destroyed this wonderful account as he wrote it in the Qur'an! It is like taking the color out of a flower and removing the smell out of a rose. When we read the story in the Qur'an, it is like watching a movie without sound or in black and white. Notice how Mohammed continued the story of Joseph in the

The Revelation of Error

Qur'an, as in 12:78-79: *[78]They said, "O you the dear, surely he has a very aged father. So take one of us instead of him, surely we see that you are of the doers of good." [79]He said, "Allah's refuge! That we should take anyone but him with whom our property was found, for then we should act unjustly."* When Joseph's brothers tried to ask the mighty one, Joseph, according to Ibn Kathir's interpretation, to take an innocent person instead of the guilty one, Benjamin, Joseph refused this suggestion because it was not allowed. They only took the person with whom they found their property.[86] Then Ibn Kathir made fun of the People of the Book as he said that Joseph had told them at this point who he was and that this is just one of the errors that reveal the corruption of their books (the Genesis account). Ibn Kathir stated that the People of the Book did not understand at all.

When I look at the interpretation of Ibn Kathir and his opinion concerning the record of the account of Joseph in the Bible, I see that he always looked at the Bible as a corrupt story, simply because it did not agree with story in the Qur'an. In simple words, if the story in the Bible did not match what was in the Qur'an, then his conclusion was that the Bible was wrong, even if the story in the Qur'an was incoherent.

The account in the Bible is not only true but complete, with all the details we need to understand the history of Joseph's life. Ibn Kathir himself used this account from the Bible, as we have seen at length, as he knew he could not interpret or explain the Qur'an without the written account of Genesis.

Now I would like to continue to reveal more errors in the story as Mohammed recorded it in Qur'an 12:80-82: *[80]So when they had lost hope of him, they went and spoke privately. The oldest of them said, "Did you not know that your father, indeed, has taken a firm oath from you before Allah and how formerly you failed in your duty with regard to Joseph? So I will not depart the land until my father gives me permission, or may Allah judge for me, and he is the best of the judges. [81]Return to your father, so say, 'O our father, surely your son has stolen. We bear witness only of what we knew; and we were not a keeper to the unseen. [82]And ask the village which we were in and of the caravan with which we have arrived, and surely we are*

---

[86]Ibn Kathir, 246.

truthful.'" Ibn Kathir's interpretation of these verses was almost a word-for-word copy of the Genesis account with some alteration, such as mistakenly indicating that it was Reuben instead of Simeon who was held by Joseph, and by adding a few other words.[87] He said this bad news had spread all over Egypt to the point that the travelers knew about it. Once again, I ask these questions: *How did Ibn Kathir know that the oldest son's name was Reuben, for the Qur'an never mentions any of these names? Since this information does not exist in the Qur'an, how was the news spread all over Egypt?*

Let us summarize what we have so far in the story from the Qur'an. Benjamin had been taken by Joseph. Joseph told Benjamin that he was his brother. All the brothers left and returned to their father, except Reuben (rather than Simeon as the Bible states). Jacob was about to receive the bad news about losing his son Benjamin.

Let us see the reaction of Jacob to the sad news. I would like to remind the reader of what took place when Jacob received the first sad news that his son Joseph had been devoured by a wolf. As it is written in verse 18: *[18]And they put on his qamīs[88] with a lie [false] blood. He said, "Yet, your soul lightens the affair. So patience is beautiful, and Allah is the one who is asked for assistance about what you describe."* That was it, according to the Qur'an! That was how much Jacob reacted to the terrible news of losing his son Joseph. What a pathetic reaction!

Perhaps some Muslims will say that Jacob did not weep or react, as it was written in the Bible, because the account of the Bible is not true. They would say that he knew Joseph was okay and was not eaten by the wolf because Jacob was a prophet, and Allah had told Jacob the truth about his son Joseph.

Let us look at the response to such fabrication. Now we will see if this interpretation is true or not. Verse 83 in the Qur'an states, *[83]He said, "Yet, you have arranged all this affair among yourselves. So patience is beautiful, perhaps Allah will bring all of them to me. Surely he is the knowing, the wise."* Ibn Kathir said that Jacob meant that the matter was not what you (his sons) described it as, for he (Benjamin) did not steal but was only the sons' arrangement of this matter among themselves.[89]

---

[87]Ibid., 247.
[88]shirt, non-Arabic word of Greek/Syriac origin
[89]Ibn Kathir, 247.

Ibn Kathir stated that Ibn Isaac mentioned that the brothers' neglect of Benjamin was expected, since they had done that before with Joseph.[90] As for the interpretation of the phrase, *"perhaps Allah will bring all of them to me,"* Ibn Isaac said what Jacob meant by *all* was Joseph, Benjamin, and Reuben. However, then in verse 84, *[84]And he turned away from them and said, "Oh, my sorrow for Joseph," and his eyes became white from the grief so he was full of anger.* Here is the proof of the amazing contradiction between the verses of the Qur'an and the scholars' interpretation. Perhaps because Mohammed knew the end of the story, he mixed truth with lies to manipulate the story's ending.

If Jacob actually knew that his son Joseph was alive, then that was why he did not weep for him or show any sorrow in verse 18 of the Qur'an when his sons informed him that Joseph was devoured by a wolf. Similarly in verse 83, he would be justified in hoping that he would have Joseph back. If this were true, then one must ask a question. *Why did Jacob turn away from his sons? Why did Jacob show his sorrow and grieve for Joseph to the point that his eyes turned white?* Ibn Kathir stated that Jacob cried so much that he lost his sight.[91] This proved that he did not know that Joseph was alive. It is simply a huge error in Mohammed's earlier description of the story.

In Qur'an 12:85: *[85]They said, "[We swear] by Allah, you will continue to remember Joseph until you are very sick or you be among the perished."* The sons of Jacob were so surprised that Jacob still remembered Joseph and wondered if he would continue to be sorrowful and cry until he died. Then, in verse 86, *[86]He said, "Surely I only complain about my sorrow and grief to Allah, and I know from Allah what you do not know.* This verse shows a contradiction because Jacob was complaining to Allah, but at the same time, he told his sons that he knew from Allah something they themselves did not know. The greatest contradiction of the entire story comes in verse 87 which leads us to the next subheading.

Joseph's Brothers' Third Trip to Egypt

According to the Bible, the third trip to Egypt never took place, and we know it is just another error in the Qur'an. We see in Qur'an 12:87 where Jacob said: *[87]O my sons, go and inquire of Joseph*

---

[90]Ibid.
[91]Ibid., 247-248.

and his brother and do not give up hope from the spirit of Allah. Surely no one will give up hope from the spirit of Allah except the infidel people."

Have you ever met a drunken person who, as he is telling you a story, you know that he is under the influence of alcohol because the story is just as confused as the person telling the story? He may tell you that he has lost a thousand dollars. He will cry for a little bit, shed some tears, but then tell you how happy he is because he bought a new car. Then he slaps his face hard and hits his head on the floor because the color of the interior of the car is not the color he wanted. Now we know he is lying, or he is under the influence of alcohol or drugs.

When I read the story of the Qur'an or the interpretation of Muslim scholars, I feel like I am reading a drunk's writings. Perhaps Mohammed or his Angel Gabreel was drunk when he made up the story, or perhaps it is because the so-called scholars were so blinded or deceived that they completely agreed with him. That must be why Mohammed stated in verse 87 that Jacob had his sons go back to Egypt to search for Joseph. Jacob said to not give up, for after the hardship, an easy time would be coming. **"Do not give up hope from the spirit of Allah."** *Now, did this really happen? Did Joseph's brothers leave Benjamin in Egypt and go back to their father Jacob?*

Let me remind the reader once again by giving a summary of what really took place in the life of Joseph as it is written in the Bible. In Genesis 42, Jacob sent his ten sons to Egypt to buy grain because the famine had just begun. Joseph knew them, but they did not know him. Joseph accused them of being spies. He started a conversation with them so that he might discover the wellbeing of his father and his younger brother. He held their brother Simeon as a prisoner until they proved that they were not spies by returning with their brother Benjamin. Jacob heard this news when they returned to their own land, and he was very upset.

The hunger was so severe, as written in Genesis 43, that Jacob asked his sons to go back to Egypt. After a long struggle, Jacob allowed them to take Benjamin and return, which was their second trip to Egypt. In Genesis 44, they took their purchased grain in the early morning when they left Joseph's house. They were stopped not far away by Joseph's steward as he accused them of being thieves, and they were brought back. While staying in Joseph's house, repentance took place in the brothers' hearts for they knew that God was punishing them for what they had done to their brother Joseph many years ago. In Genesis 45, Joseph broke down before his brothers and told them that he was Joseph, their brother. He cried over them and kissed them. He explained to his brothers that the famine would continue for five more years, and he asked them to bring their father and all their possessions and come back to Egypt. It was Simeon who was held as a hostage, not Reuben; and this took place during the first trip for Benjamin was not with them until the second trip. Obviously, Mohammed heard the story from some Jew or Christian because he barely knew any of the details.

Let us continue with the rest of the story from Qur'an 12:88: *[88]So when they entered into him, they said, "O you the dear, distress has touched us and our family, and we brought deficient merchandise. So fulfill to us the measure, and be charitable to us. Surely Allah will reward the charitable."* Ibn Kathir stated that the condition of the sons of Jacob was not good because of their hardship, in that they had so many children that they did not have enough money or that their money was bad money, and it was said that it was just some nuts.[92] Ibn Kathir continued by stating that Ibn Abbas said that it (their money) was some ropes or other materials.

Once again, I personally believe Mohammed and his scholars were totally confused concerning the financial status of Jacob and his sons. When we read this interpretation concerning the merchandise which the sons of Jacob took with them to Egypt to purchase the grain, it literally gives a picture that Jacob and his children were very poor. Obviously, that is false for they were not poor financially, but to the contrary, they were rich. They were only in need of grain.

According to Genesis 43:11-12, they took with them the best fruit of the land as a gift to the man: a little balm, a little honey, spices, myrrh, nuts, and almonds. That is what is written in verse 11, and the Bible did not stop there, for in verse 12 they took with them double the amount of silver required to pay for the old grain, in case it was an oversight, and more silver to buy new grain.

Mohammed continued in the Qur'an by stating that they asked Joseph to fulfill the measure and to be charitable to them. In his interpretation, Ibn Kathir said that sadly Joseph accepted their merchandise.[93] Ibn Kathir continued by saying that because Joseph

---
[92]Ibn Kathir, 248.
[93]Ibid., 249.

saw their condition and knew that they had no money, he told them who he was and showed compassion for them. Then Joseph said to them, [89]*He said, "Do you know what you have done to Joseph and his brother when you were ignorant?"* Ibn Kathir said that they were so surprised although they had met with him many times before but did not recognize him. [90]*They said, "Are you surely Joseph?" He said, "I am Joseph, and this is my brother. Indeed, Allah has been gracious to us. Surely who fears and is patient, so surely Allah will not lose the wage of the doers of good."*

Can you see how ridiculous the story is as it has been written here? Any person with common sense can figure out that this could never be the true story, especially when this is compared to the true account of Genesis 45:1-7. That is when Joseph could not restrain himself and told his brothers that he was Joseph. He cried so loudly that the Egyptians heard his cries. He asked his brothers about his father, if he was still alive. His brothers were afraid of him, but he came near to them and explained to them all that had happened in his life had been God's plan, for God had chosen him to preserve life because there were still five more years of famine yet to come.

In verses 91-92, the Qur'an states, [91]*They said, "[We swear] by Allah indeed. Allah exalted you above us, and that we were surely sinners." [92]He said, "No sin will be on you today. Allah will forgive you, and he is the most merciful of the merciful.* Ibn Kathir stated that the brothers said to Joseph that Allah had favored him above them and had given Joseph what he did not give them because they had sinned against him.[94] Therefore, they were now at his mercy. In response, Joseph said that he would not punish them for what they had done on that day. Then he added to that by saying, "Allah is forgiving, most merciful."

The Magic Shirt

Mohammed added a fictional magic shirt to the story of Joseph, beginning in Qur'an 12:93: [93]*Go with this my shirt, so throw it on my father's face, and he will recover his sight. And bring me all your family."* *What about this magic shirt?* In his interpretation, Al Qurtobi said that the shirt was made out of silk from the garden which

---
[94]Ibid.

The Revelation of Error

Allah put on Abraham when he was put into the fire.[95] It was the same shirt which Isaac wore, and Isaac also gave it to Jacob to wear. Jacob had put this same shirt in a silver tube which he hung around the neck of Joseph.

Angel Gabreel informed Joseph that this shirt was from the garden and had the breeze of the garden,[96] and if this shirt touched anyone who was sick or had any physical problem, he would be healed. Al Hasan said that if Allah had not told Abraham the secret of this shirt, Joseph would not have known that his father's sight would return. Al Hasan also said that the person who carried the shirt was Judah because Judah told Joseph, "I am the one who carried your shirt with the false blood, and I saddened him (Jacob). And I will carry this silk shirt to please him that his sight might come back to him." Then Joseph asked them to bring all their family to him in Egypt. *How did Al Hasan know this information? Did Allah make him a prophet too?*

Another amazing thing was the smell of Joseph. As it is written in Qur'an 12:94: [94]*And when the caravan departed, their father said, "I surely found the smell of Joseph, were it not that you refute it."* In his book, Ibn Kathir said that Ibn Abbas stated that when the caravan traveled to Jacob, a wind storm with the smell of his shirt (Joseph's silk shirt) took eight days to travel and carry the smell of Joseph to Jacob.[97] Ibn Kathir stated that Al Hasan said that it had been eighty years since Joseph last saw Jacob.[98] *If Jacob had not seen Joseph for eighty years, how could Jacob still remember Joseph's smell?*

Jacob said that the rest of the family was with him in verse 95. [95]*They said, "[We swear] by Allah, you are surely in your old error."* A miracle took place when the shirt was cast on Jacob's face as it is written in verse 96: [96]*So when the bearer of good news came, he cast it on his face, so he regained his sight. He said, "Did I not say to you that surely I knew from Allah what you do not know?"* In his interpretation, Ibn Kathir said the knowledge which Jacob knew from Allah, which his sons did not know, was that

---

[95] http://quran.al-islam.com/Page.aspx?pageid=221&BookID=14&Page=246, accessed February 3, 2013.
[96] the smell of the Garden of Eden/heaven
[97] Ibn Kathir, 249.
[98] Ibid., 250.

Jacob would be gathered with his son Joseph.[99] Allah would allow Jacob to see Joseph again, and Jacob would see in Joseph what would please him.

The brothers of Joseph asked Jacob to ask forgiveness from Allah for them for their sins, and Jacob promised to do so. In verses 97-98, *[97]They said, "O our father, ask forgiveness for our sins, surely we were sinners." [98]He said, "I will ask my lord to forgive you. Surely he is the forgiving, the merciful."* Ibn Kathir stated that some Muslim scholars such as Ibn Jarir said they asked for Jacob to seek their forgiveness from Allah at daybreak, but Ibn Abbas said that Jacob sought forgiveness for them on Friday night.[100] As usual, Muslim scholars disagree on the ridiculous information, disregarding the important facts about almost every story. Here we have seen disagreement about when Jacob asked forgiveness for his sons.

What about the true account of the Bible? Is there any truth in the story we read in the Qur'an, which originates in the Bible? Let us examine the Scripture. The Bible does not mention any magic shirt or the smell of Joseph in the wind.

I would like to summarize what really happened in the true account in Genesis 45:17-28 in a few words. Pharaoh found out about Joseph's family, and he asked Joseph to ask his brothers to go and bring their household. Joseph gave them wagons to carry the children and women, along with Jacob, back to Egypt according to Pharaoh's orders. Joseph gave them many gifts. Then Joseph's brothers left Egypt and went to Canaan. Upon arriving back in Canaan, Joseph's brothers told Jacob that Joseph was alive and was the ruler over the land of Egypt, but Jacob did not believe them. However, when he saw the Egyptian wagons which Joseph had sent to carry him, not only did he believe but his spirit revived. *Did Jacob see the wagons?* **Yes, indeed!**

In Genesis 46:2-4, God spoke to Jacob through a vision in the night: *[2]Then God spoke to Israel in the visions of the night, and said, "Jacob, Jacob!" And he said, "Here I am." [3]So He said, "I am God, the God of your father; do not fear to go down to Egypt, for I will make of you a great nation there. [4]I will go down with you to Egypt, and I will also surely bring you up again; and Joseph will*

---

[99]Ibid.
[100]Ibid.

put his hand on your eyes." Notice that God said to Jacob that Joseph will put his hands on his eyes, not on his blind eyes.

Another proof that Israel did not lose his sight is written clearly in Genesis 46:29-30 when Joseph met with his father in the land of Goshen. *²⁹So Joseph made ready his chariot and went up to Goshen to meet his father Israel; and he presented himself to him, and fell on his neck and wept on his neck a good while. ³⁰And Israel said to Joseph, "Now let me die, since I have seen your face, because you are still alive."* Notice in verse 30 that Israel said to Joseph, "I have *seen* thy face." Yes, Jacob had his eyesight and was able to *see* Joseph's face.

More details are given in Genesis 47. Jacob's age was 130 years when he came to Egypt, but he lived in Egypt an additional seventeen years before he died at the age of 147 as written in Genesis 47:28. Even though he was an old man, Genesis 48 revealed that Israel (Jacob) saw the sons of Joseph, and he asked who they were. The Bible clearly states that Jacob's eyes were dim from age, as written in Genesis 48:10. On the other hand, Israel was thankful to God for he was able not only to see Joseph, but also see Joseph's descendants during his lifetime as we see in Genesis 48:11. These short simple words prove that Mohammed's fabrication or fairy tale concerning the magic shirt and the loss of the sight of Israel (Jacob) was nothing but errors and lies.

<u>The Third and Final Trip from Canaan to Egypt</u>

Mohammed could not describe the number and names of the Children of Israel who came to Egypt. However, these can be found in Genesis 46:8-26. *How many members of Jacob's family came to Egypt?* Although the Qur'an does not mention how many there were, Muslim scholars, as usual, disagree. Ibn Kathir gave us many choices for the numbers of people in Jacob's family that came to Egypt.[101] One can choose from the following numbers: 63, 83, and 390. (Ibn Kathir mentioned that when the Hebrews left Egypt with Moses, there were more than six hundred thousand fighters.) It is written, according to the People of the Book (Bible), that there were **seventy** souls since they are named in the biblical account. Although Muslim scholars had access to the true knowledge of the numbers in the account of the Bible, they chose to ignore it. There were sixty-six

---

[101]Ibid., 252.

souls of men, not including the females. Add to this number Joseph, Joseph's two sons, and Jacob himself, and this adds up to seventy souls, as written in Genesis 46:27.

More errors are revealed in Qur'an 12:99-100: *[99]And when they entered to Joseph, he lodged his parents with him, and said, "Enter Egypt, if Allah is willing, in security." [100]And he raised his parents to the throne, and they fell down worshiping him. And he said, "O my father, this is the interpretation of my previous dream. Indeed, my lord has now made it true, and he has indeed been good to me, since he took me out of the prison and has brought you from the Bedouins. After that, Satan had stirred up strife between me and my brothers. Surely my lord is kind to whom he wills. Surely he is the knowing, the wise.*

When I read the story of Joseph in the Qur'an for the first time, I was perhaps twelve years old. I said to myself, *"What? What did Joseph do?* He lodged his parents as it was written in verse 99! I said to myself, "Perhaps I misunderstood the reading of the word." Then I read verse 100 where he raised his parents to the throne. *Joseph did that?* There is nothing wrong with the story. *I mean, who would not welcome his mom and dad to his country, especially after not seeing them after many long years, and who would not raise his mom and dad to the throne for that is the most honorable thing a man should do for his parents?*

The error of these two verses can be exposed, if we simply read Genesis 35:16-20. Here is a summary: When they were traveling (Jacob and his family) from Bethel and were only a little way from Ephrath, Rachel (Joseph's mother) had a difficult labor during childbirth. As she was dying, she named her son Ben-Oni, but Jacob called him Benjamin. Rachel died and was buried on the way to Ephrath (Bethlehem). Jacob placed a pillar on her grave.

The problem here is very simple. Mohammed or whoever helped him write the story of Joseph did not read Genesis 35; for obviously, the story of Joseph began in Genesis 37. If Mohammed or whoever helped him to write the Qur'an had read Genesis 35, they would never have made such a huge error because Rachel, the mother of Joseph and Benjamin, had died a long time before Jacob arrived in Egypt. *How did Ibn Kathir solve this problem*? As usual, Muslim scholars disagree on the length of time that had passed since Jacob had seen Joseph.

According to Ibn Kathir, Muslim scholars said that the number of years Jacob and Joseph had been apart was eighteen, some said eighty-three, others said fifty-five, and yet another said eighty.[102] Ibn Kathir mocked the People of the Book and claimed that it was forty years, but the Bible never mentions forty years. Ibn Kathir maintained that the scholars of the Torah were wrong because the Qur'an cannot be wrong. He also said that some Muslim scholars said that Allah had raised her (Rachel) back to life. *If the Qur'an emphasized in detail concerning the eyes of Jacob with the magic shirt, does the reader not think that raising Joseph's mother from the dead even more important and worthy of discussion?*

Then other Muslim scholars said that it was not his mother who was raised from the dead but his Aunt Laya (they meant Leah). Then they said that the status of the aunt was equal to the status of the mother. Here we must reread the Qur'an once again. *Did the Qur'an say Joseph's parents or his father and his aunt in both verses 99 and 100?* "The important thing is," as Ibn Kathir said that Ibn Jarir stated, "that the Qur'an is very clear that his mother was alive on that day. Therefore, there is no need to read from the book (Bible), and this is a very strong belief."[103] *And Allah knows best.*

Another interpretation is found in the following sentence when the Qur'an said that Joseph raised his parents to the throne. Ibn Kathir stated that he (Joseph) meant that he raised them (his parents) with him on his bed (the three of them lay on his bed), and Ibn Kathir also stated that they (his father, mother, and little brother) worshiped (prostrated themselves to) Joseph as to give honor and respect.[104] This was allowed or accepted by them as it is in many religions, but it is unlawful in the religion of Islam.

Mohammed forgot to mention in Qur'an 12:58, 69, 76 (when Joseph took the cup out of Benjamin's bag), 88, and 99, that when Joseph's brothers met with him, they fell prostrate before him. However, when we read the biblical account in Genesis 42:6 and 43:26, 28, we see that they fell prostrate before him, which fulfilled the dream that Joseph had as a young man in the land of Canaan.

Much important information about the life of Joseph is missing from the Qur'an. On the other hand, a lot of fabrication has been

---

[102]Ibid., 251.
[103]Ibid., 251-252.
[104]Ibid., 252.

added, as we have already seen, to the story in the Qur'an. For the sake of time and space, we strongly recommend that Muslims and others read the story of Joseph, as it is written in Genesis, and compare it to what is written in Qur'an 12.

More questions can be asked, but you can find the answers only in the Bible. *Where did Joseph's family live in Egypt? What happened during the years of famine to Joseph's family and the Egyptians? Where did the Egyptians live afterwards? Were there any special taxes on the Egyptians? If so, how much? What happened to the body of Jacob? Where was Jacob buried? What about the advice, blessings, farewells, and prophecies of Jacob to his sons? What about Jacob's blindness? How did Israel bless the sons of Joseph and why? What was the relationship between Joseph and the other brothers after the death of Jacob? How many years did Joseph live? Who took the body of Joseph and where?* I hope these questions will challenge you to open the Genesis account and seek the answers for yourself.

Qur'an 12:101 states that Joseph said, *[101]"My lord, indeed, you have given to me from the kingdom and have taught me the interpretation of the sayings. Creator of the heavens and the earth, you are my friend in this world and the hereafter. Cause me to die a Muslim, and gather me with the good."*

Another error by Muslim scholars and Mohammed is that Joseph was a king. Amazingly, Joseph's last wish, according to the Qur'an, was to die as a Muslim. Ibn Kathir stated that before Joseph, there had never been a prophet who wished to die.[105] In Islamic law, it is not allowed except in the case of temptation. As it is written in the hadith, it is better for the *son of Adam* (any human being) to die than to be tempted.

One of the amusing things which Ibn Kathir stated throughout his writings was that he always rejected the dates or ages of the characters in the Bible, simply because they did not agree with the dates and ages given by Muslim scholars which vary greatly and conflict with one another. For example, Ibn Kathir stated, "With the People of the Book, the age of Jacob when he entered Egypt was 130 years, and he lived in Egypt seventeen years, which indicates that his age was a total of 147 years; and this is false."[106]

---

[105]Ibid., 254.
[106]Ibid.

The Revelation of Error

Ibn Kathir disagreed about how long Jacob lived, since he believed it was wrong. *How then can he or any other Muslim scholar or Gabreel or Mohammed or Allah himself tell us definitively how many years Jacob lived? What is their proof that the ages in the Bible are wrong?*

As for the rest of the information given by Ibn Kathir, we used direct quotations from the Bible to answer most of the questions we have listed above. Amazingly, the last sentence with which Ibn Kathir closed the story, as it is also written by Mobark, Ibn Sbalah, and Al Hasan, said that Joseph was put into the well when he was seventeen years old, he was far away from his father for eighty years, he lived after that twenty-three years, and he died when he was 120 years old. This sentence not only contradicts the Bible but also contradicts the Qur'an. The Bible states that Joseph lived 110 years (Genesis 50:22). The Qur'an states that when Joseph was put into the well he was a little boy, not seventeen years as stated above, which is the true number according to the Bible. Once again, here we see the Bible's great influence on Muslim scholars.

10. The Story of Job

The name Job is mentioned in the Qur'an four times in four different locations. His name is mentioned without any detail in Qur'an 4:163: *¹⁶³Surely we have revealed to you as we revealed to Noah and the prophets after him. And we revealed to Abraham and Ishmael and Isaac and Jacob and the tribes and 'Isā and Ayyūb[1] and Yunus[2] and Aaron and Solomon, and to David we gave Zabor.[3]* Then in Qur'an 6:84: *⁸⁴And we granted to him[4] Isaac and Jacob, both we guided, and Noah we guided before and among his descendants, David and Solomon and Job and Joseph and Moses and Aaron. And likewise, we reward the doers of good.*

Notice the first error is that the names are in a jumbled and confused order which makes no sense, and note how the name of Job sits in the middle of these names. For example, in the first case, Job is listed after Jesus, although Job preceded Jesus by nearly two thousand years. In the second case, Job comes after David and Solomon, when, in fact, he came many centuries before David. The frequent occurrence of such errors indicates that neither Mohammed nor Muslim scholars had any understanding of the historical timelines pertaining to the names they used.

The second error is found in Qur'an 4:163 where we see the claim that Allah revealed directly to Mohammed, just as he revealed to Noah and to the rest of the prophets. However, when we read the story in the Qur'an, we discover the reality that Allah never revealed any revelation to the prophets through angels, except in the case of Mohammed, where Allah revealed to Mohammed through Angel Gabreel.

The story of Job is actually written in the Bible in the forty-two chapters in the book of Job. The true historical account of Job is known by many Jewish and Christian scholars to be the oldest book in the Bible. I am very surprised that Muslims, scholars or not, can understand the long story of Job by simply reading the very brief

---

[1] Job, non-Arabic word of Greek/Syriac origin
[2] name mistakenly used when Jonah was meant
[3] in singular form = Psalms, non-Arabic word of Hebrew/Syriac origin
[4] Abraham

information which Mohammed put in Qur'an 21:83 and Qur'an 38:41-44. *In other words, how can Muslims understand forty-two chapters when they are condensed into six verses?* It makes no sense whatsoever.

Who was Job? Ibn Kathir gave us the answer by stating that Ibn Isaac said that Job was a man from Byzantium.[5] That is foolishness because Job was an Arab, but Arab Muslims do not know that. The Bible in Job 1:1 and the last portion of verse 3 stated that he was from the land of Uz and that he was the (greatest) man who lived in the land of the East.[6]

Uz is sometimes identified with the kingdom of Edom, roughly in the area of modern-day southwestern Jordan and southern Israel.[7] Lamentations 4:21 reads: **[21]Rejoice and be glad, O daughter of Edom, You who dwell in the land of Uz! ...** Other locations proposed for Uz include more southern Arabia, especially Dhofar, said to be the home of the original Arabs[8]; Bashan in modern-day southern Syria/western Jordan; Arabia east of Petra, Jordan[9]; and even modern-day Uzbekistan.[10] According to the Dead Sea document "The War Scroll," the land of Uz is mentioned as existing somewhere beyond the Euphrates River, possibly in relation to Aram.[11] Whichever the case, it is clear that the reference is to someone from an Arab land to the East, not a Byzantine.

We gain additional evidence that Job was an Arab from the Bible in Job 2:11: *[1]Now when Job's three friends heard of all this adversity that had come upon him, each one came from his own place—Eliphaz the Temanite, Bildad the Shuhite, and Zophar the*

---

[5]Ibn Kathir, *Stories of the Prophets*, vol. 1, Abo Al Fida Ishamail Ibn Kathir Al Kurashi Al Damashce (Beirut: Dar Al-Arab Heritage, 1408 AH, 1988), 255.

[6]"Land of Uz," *Wikipedia*, last modified January 19, 2012, accessed January 25, 2012, http://en.wikipedia.org/wiki/Land_of_Uz,.

[7]Paul S. Taylor, "The Land of Uz," *WebBible Encyclopedia*, accessed January 25, 2012, http://christiananswers.net/dictionary/uzthelandof.html

[8]G. Wyman Bury, *The Land of Uz* (London: Macmillan, 1911, reprinted in 1998), accessed January 25, 2012.

[9]Wayne Blank, "Where Was Uz?" *Daily Bible Study*, accessed January 25, 2012, http://www.keyway.ca/htm2001/20010806.htm

[10]James I. Nienhuis, "Uzbekistan Is Book of Job Land of Uz Where Ice Age Climate Explains the Environment Described, *The Dancing from Genesis Blog*, September 15, 2007, accessed 01/25/2012, https://dancingfromgenesis.wordpress.com/2007/09/15/uzbekistan-is-book-of-job-land-of-uz-where-ice-age-climate-explains-the-environment-described/

[11]"Land of Uz," *Wikipedia*, last modified December 19, 2012, accessed January 25, 2012, http://en.wikipedia.org/wiki/Land_of_Uz.

Naamathite. For they had made an appointment together to come and mourn with him, and to comfort him. We note that his three friends have Arab locations or backgrounds (from Teman, an Arab town; a descendant of Shuah, an Arab; and from Naameh, on the Arabian border of Syria).

Ibn Kathir stated that Job was Ibn Mos, Ibn Zarah, Ibn Alays, Ibn Isaac, Ibn Abraham. Then Ibn Kathir also stated that others referred to Job as Ibn Mos, Ibn Raoel, Ibn Alays, Ibn Isaac, Ibn Jacob.[12] *Which of the two genealogies is correct? Who was the father of Mos? Was it Zarah or Raoel? Who was the father of Isaac? Was it Abraham or Jacob?*

Ibn Kathir continued, telling us that Ibn Asakir said that Job's mother was the daughter of Lot and his father was one of those who believed in Abraham when he was thrown into the fire that did not burn him. Ibn Kathir said that what is known is that he was a descendant of Abraham as written in Qur'an 6:84 and that he was one of the prophets Allah revealed to them, as it is written in Qur'an 4:163. Ibn Kathir continued by stating that Job was a descendant of Alays, Ibn Isaac, and his wife's name was Lyah, daughter of Jacob; and it was also said that his wife was Rahmah, daughter of Afraeem. It was also said that his wife was Mansha, daughter of Joseph, Ibn Jacob.

Where did Ibn Kathir get these names? There is not one verse in the Qur'an or the hadith that mentions these names. The only way for a Muslim to certify the actual names is to go to the source: Job's account in the Bible. Ibn Kathir cited two passages. The first was Qur'an 21:83-84: *[83]And Job, when he called his lord: "Surely harm has touched me, and you are the most merciful of the merciful!" [84]So we answered him. So we removed what is in him from harm, and we gave him his family and like them with them, a mercy from us and a reminder to the servants.* He then cited Qur'an 38:41-44: *[41]And remember our servant Job when he called his lord: "Surely Satan has touched me with distress and torment!" [42]"Strike with your foot; this is a cold wash-place and a drink." [43]And we granted to him his family, and like them, with them, a mercy from us and a reminder to those who have understanding. [44]"And take a bundle in your hand, so strike with it. Do not break your oath." Surely we found him patient,*

---

[12]Ibn Kathir, 255.

blessed is the servant, surely he is repentant. Ibn Kathir interpreted these two verses in five pages of his book.

I maintain that these are not interpretations but fabrications, for an interpretation cannot exist without some basis of information in the text. Ibn Kathir said that Ibn Asakir said that the first prophet was Idris, then Noah, then Abraham, then Ishmael, then Isaac, then Jacob, then Joseph, then Lot, then Houd, then Saleh, then Shaeeb, then Moses, then Aaron, then Alyas, then Alysa, then Orfe Ibn Soylkh, Ibn Afraeem, Ibn Joseph, Ibn Jacob, Ibn Yunes, Ibn Matthew, Ibn Jacob, then Job, Ibn Zarah, Ibn Amos, Ibn Lbfrz, Ibn Alysa, Ibn Isaac, Ibn Abraham.[13] Then Ibn Kathir said that there was a consideration about this order for Houd and Saleh; it was known that they were after Noah and before Abraham, *and Allah knows best.*

Ibn Kathir stated that the scholars of interpretation and history and other people said that Job was a man with a lot of money from different sources, cattle, slaves, livestock, and land.[14] Ibn Asakir said that all this land was Job's, he had many sons, and all his riches were stolen from him. He continued by writing that Job had many scourges to the point that there was not any one part of his body that was sound except his heart and his tongue, that Job mentioned Allah by the heart and the tongue, and that he was patient. He remembered Allah night and day, morning and evening. His sickness lasted a long time. Then he lost all of his friends, was kicked out of his city, and was thrown on top of the dump outside of the city. *What is the source of this information?*

There was no one who showed compassion to him except his wife who showed respect and compassion toward him. She used to come and visit with him, help him use the toilet, and take care of him. She became weak and lost all financial resources to the point that she was serving people to receive a salary in order for her to be able to feed him, but she was patient with him due to the loss of the money and their children. Job and his wife used to have happiness and grace and riches and servants, but because of the calamity, they lost everything. Ibn Kathir concluded, "So surely to Allah we belong and to him we return. Even with all of these bad things that happened to Job, he continued to have patience and thanks to the point that a parable was used as an example of his patience." Once again I would love to ask

---

[13] Ibid.
[14] Ibid., 256.

Chapter 10

this same question: *Where did the above information come from, for none of this information is found in the Qur'an?*

Ibn Kathir also stated that Mujahid said that Job was the first man to be sick with smallpox, and the scholars disagree how long he was sick with this disease.[15] Wahab said that it was exactly three years, but Anas said that it was seven years and a few months. Ibn Kathir stated that Hamid said it was eighteen years.[16] Al Saddi said that his flesh fell off of him to the point that only bones and nerves were left. His wife used to come to him with ashes and spread them under him because his sickness lasted a long time. His wife said, "O Job, if you call on your lord, he will remove this from you." So he said to her, "I lived seventy years healthy. Can't I be patient with Allah seventy years?"

So she became sorrowful from his words, and she used to serve people for wages so that she could feed Job. Ibn Kathir continued by saying that people would not use her service because they knew that she was the wife of Job and were afraid that they might get sick by touching her. She then sold one of her hair braids to some of the rich girls to get some good food, so Job asked her where she got the good food.

Ibn Kathir continued to write that she did not answer the question; she lied to him. She said that she served some people, and they gave her food. She denied the truth of what she had done. On the following day, she sold the other hair braid for more food, but Job refused to eat it and swore that he would not eat it until she would tell him where she got the food. Then she removed the cover from her head, and he saw her hair shaved. That is when he called to Allah and said in Qur'an 21:83: *[83]Surely harm has touched me, and you are the most merciful of the merciful! Where is the source of this information?*

This is a strange way to interpret verses in the Qur'an, a long fabricated story with many words which have no truth in them. It is amazing that, with the entire struggle and hardship Job went through, the Qur'an recorded no reaction from Job. However, when his wife sold her hair, which did not happen in the actual story, Job was so

---
[15]Ibid.
[16]Ibid.

moved that he began to call on Allah. *Is the loss of children and riches not comparable to the loss of his wife's hair which will grow back again?*

Ibn Kathir recorded another fabricated story when he wrote that Ibn Abu Hatem said that Job used to have brethren.[17] They came to him one day, but they could not get close to him because of his smell. One of them told his friend that if Allah had known of something good in Job, he would not have struck him with this sickness.

Job became panicked from their sayings, and he said, "O Allah, if you know that I did not go to bed full when I knew that there was someone who was hungry, prove me." So Allah proved him from heaven, and they heard it. Then he said one more thing, "O Allah, if you know that I had two shirts and I knew of a person who was naked, so prove what I am saying is true." So Allah proved him, and his friends heard Allah. Then he said, "O Allah, I swear by your honor." Then he fell down worshiping Allah and said, "O Allah, with your honor I will not lift up my head forever until you remove the sickness from me." So he did not lift up his head until Allah removed the sickness from him.[18]

What was written about Job's friends was copied from the Bible in Job, for the Qur'an does not mention anything about any friends. We could ask many simple questions concerning these brethren, and Muslim scholars would not be able to answer them. *For example, how many friends were there, what were their names, and what was the real conversation between them and Job?* A simple reading of the book of Job will give full answers to all these questions.

Ibn Kathir quoted a hadith given by Anas Ibn Malik who said that Mohammed said that Job was ill for eighteen years.[19] Everyone rejected him except two of his brethren. They visited Job every day. One of them said to the other that Allah knew that Job had committed a sin that no one in the world had ever committed. His friend asked what the sin was. The other friend answered that his lord had not forgiven Job in eighteen years, so he told him what the sin was. So when they went back to Job, this man mentioned this idea to Job. Job said, "I do not know what you say, but Allah knows that one time I was walking by two men who were fighting with each other. They

---

[17] Ibid., 257.
[18] Ibid.
[19] Ibid.

mentioned Allah so when I returned home, I offered a sacrifice on their behalf that the name of Allah had not been mentioned during their fight except in truth."

It was said that Job used to go out to relieve himself and that his wife used to hold his hand until he returned. One day she was slow to get to him, so Allah revealed to Job at the place that he was located, as stated in Qur'an 38:42: [42]*"Strike with your foot; this is a cold wash-place and a drink."* So she looked at him, and he came to her for Allah had taken away from him his sickness; and he was in the best condition so when she saw him she said, "Allah bless you. Did you see the prophet of Allah, the sick one? I swear by Allah that you look a lot like him if he were not sick." He said, "I am he."

Job had two silos, one for wheat and one for barley.[20] Allah sent two clouds so that one of these clouds stopped over the silo of wheat and filled it with gold until it overflowed. The other cloud stopped over the other silo of barley and filled it with paper (money) until it overflowed. Apparently, Muslim scholars thought that there was paper money during the time of Job; but, of course, neither they nor Mohammed knew the time period of Job's life.

Ibn Abu Hatem said that Ibn Abbas said that Allah dressed Job with a suit from the garden (heaven).[21] He sat on one side, and his wife did not know him. She said, "O servant of Allah, the man who was sick here, what happened to him?" Then she talked to him for an hour. He said, "Perhaps I am Job." She said, "Are you making fun of me, O servant of Allah?" He said, "Woe to you, I am Job. Allah has restored my flesh." This was a different telling of the same event. *Who is telling the truth, Mohammed or Ibn Abu Hatem?*

Ibn Abbas said that "Allah restored his money and his children and more like them with them (double)."[22] Wahab Ibn Monabah said that Allah revealed to Job, "I restored to you your family and your money and double of what you had, so wash yourself with this water. Surely in it is your healing and offer sacrifice for your companions and seek forgiveness for them, for surely they have disobeyed me concerning you." Ibn Abu Hatem said that Mohammed said, "When Allah healed Job that he rained on him locusts made of gold." So Job

---

[20]Ibid., 242.
[21]Ibid.
[22]Ibid.

The Revelation of Error

took it by his hands and put it in his clothes. So Allah said to Job, "Aren't you satisfied?" He said, "And who will satisfy from your mercy, O lord?"

Ibn Kathir quoted another hadith written by Imam Ahmed which said that Mohammed said that while Prophet Job washed naked, a locust excreted gold above him. Then Job took the gold feces and put it in his clothes. So Allah called him, "O Job, haven't I made you rich?" He said, "Yes, lord, but I am not rich from your blessings (meaning he wanted more gold)." As for the interpretation for the saying *"strike your foot,"* Ibn Kathir meant to strike the earth with his feet.[23] When Job did that, Allah caused a spring of cold water to gush from the earth to him, and then Allah commanded him to wash and drink from it. Allah took all the sickness and pain from Job's flesh and replaced it with health and beauty and lots of money - money was coming down as great rain of gold locusts.

As for Qur'an 21:84: *[84]So we answered him. So we removed what is in him from harm, and we gave him his family and like them with them, a mercy from us and a reminder to the servants.* Ibn Kathir interpreted this statement by stating that it was said that Allah raised Job's own children back to life and this was restitution for Job, giving him another set of children. Allah then gathered them all for Job in the hereafter. Allah did this as a mercy from him when he said, "A mercy and compassion and good deed from Allah to Job."

As for the statement *"a reminder to the servants,"* Ibn Kathir said that he meant by that for anyone in the future who would be harmed in the flesh or money or children, he may remember Job and that Job may be a good example for him, so that he may be patient until Allah relieves him. Al Dahak said that Ibn Abbas said that Allah restored the youth of his wife and increased her until she begat twenty-six male children. Job lived after that seventy years in the land of the Romans, and he was of the religion of Abraham (hanifan). Then the religion of Abraham changed after Job.

Ibn Kathir interpreted Qur'an 38:44: *[44]"And take a bundle in your hand, so strike with it. Do not break your oath." Surely we found him patient, blessed is the servant, surely he is repentant,* by stating that Allah gave a special license to his servant

---
[23]Ibid., 259.

Chapter 10

and messenger Job that he could strike his wife a hundred times for he had sworn to scourge her when she sold her hair braids.[24] It was said that he swore to scourge her because Satan appeared to her as a doctor and gave her medicine to give to Job. When she gave this medicine to Job, she told him, so he knew it was Satan. That is why he swore to scourge her a hundred times. So Allah healed him, and Allah gave Job permission to take a whip made out of a group of strands and hit her only once. Allah did this to remove the obligation from scourging his wife, especially because she was patient and was good to Job. That is why Allah followed this license and gave excuse by stating, **"Surely we found him patient."**

Ibn Kathir stated that Ibn Jarir said that Job died when he was ninety-three years old, but others said that Job lived even longer.[25] On the day of resurrection, Allah will use Solomon against the rich that do not believe in him, Joseph against the slaves, and Job against those who have sickness. Job recommended to his son Homel and his son Bishr to fulfill the matters after him. Many people believed that Bishr was Za Al Kafel, *and Allah knows best.* Bishr died when he was seventy-five years old, and he was a prophet.

As we finish covering the story of Job as constructed by Muslim scholars, I would like to share with you a quick summary of the true account of Job as it is written in the Bible. Once again, I encourage the reader to read the entire story in the forty-two chapters of Job.

In Job 1, many important details are given about Job. Job was from the land of Uz. He was a blameless man who feared God and shunned evil. He had so many possessions that he was called the greatest of all the people of the East. Among the possessions that he owned were thousands of sheep and cattle along with hundreds of oxen and donkeys. He was the father of seven sons and three daughters. The sons took turns giving feasts at their homes and would invite their sisters to join them. Because Job was concerned that his children might have sinned against God, he offered a burnt sacrifice for each of them as was his habit.

One day Satan, along with some other angels, appeared before the throne of God. During the conversation that took place, God asked Satan if he had observed Job during Satan's roaming to and fro over

---
[24]Ibid.
[25]Ibid., 260.

The Revelation of Error

the earth. God Himself called Job a blameless man who feared God and shunned evil. Satan accused God of making it too easy for Job to follow God because He blessed everything that Job did. Satan declared that Job worshiped God only because He had protected Job and richly blessed him with many possessions and family. Satan challenged God by saying that if Job lost everything, he would then surely curse God. God told Satan that he could test Job in any way, with the exception that Satan could not harm Job physically. Satan left God's presence and then proceeded to test Job.

One day, while Job's children were feasting at the oldest brother's home, a messenger came to Job and told him that the Sabeans had attacked and carried off the donkeys and oxen and had killed all the servants except for himself. While this servant was yet speaking, another messenger came and told Job that a fire had just consumed the sheep and that he was the only person to escape. Again, while this servant was still speaking, another messenger arrived to tell Job that the Chaldeans had raided the camels and carried them off and then killed all the servants except for him. Finally, another messenger appeared and told Job that while his children were feasting, a huge wind caused the house to fall, killing everyone except for himself. Thus, in one day Job lost all his possessions and all of his children.

When Job heard this news, he got up, tore his clothes, and shaved his head, as was the custom in those days. He fell to his knees and worshiped God. Job did not sin by charging God for what had just happened.

In Job 2, Satan then went before God again. God asked Satan where he had been traveling. His answer and God's reply were the same as before. Job still remained faithful and worshiped God. Satan told God that Job would surely curse God if he were allowed to attack Job physically. God gave permission for Satan to attack Job physically with the exception that he could not take Job's life. Satan then afflicted Job's body with terrible boils to the point that Job scraped his skin with broken pottery. At this point, Job's wife told Job to curse God and die. Job responded to her by saying that she was foolish talking like that. Were they only to take the good from God and not any troubles? Again, Job did not sin.

At this point, three sympathetic friends arrived to comfort him. Their names were Eliphaz the Temanite, Bildad the Shuhite, and Zophar the Naamathite. They barely recognized Job and began to weep. They tore their clothes and sprinkled dust or ashes on their

Chapter 10

heads just as Job had done and sat with him on the ground. They sat with him like this for seven days and nights with no one speaking during this entire time because they saw how great Job's suffering was. You can read about the conversations between these three friends and Job in Job 3 through 31.

In Job 3, Job finally spoke and cursed the day of his birth but did not curse or blame God. Job questioned why this terrible tragedy had happened to him when he had done nothing wrong. His friends endeavored to have Job understand that he must have done something wrong–some sin, but Job maintained that he had been righteous. In Job 32 through 37, another younger friend joined them with his discourse. His name was Elihu. Because he was younger, he remained respectfully quiet until after the three older friends had stopped answering Job. Because Job maintained that he was righteous, Elihu became angry with Job because Job was justifying himself rather than God. Elihu was also angry with the three older friends because they had found no way to refute Job while still condemning him.

Finally, in Job 38 through 41, God spoke to Job out of a storm. God asked Job many questions such as where was Job when God formed the earth, had the gates of death been shown to Job, where does darkness and light abide, who controls the aspects of the weather (who forms the lightning, rain, winds, thunderstorms, ice), who controls nature, who gives the heart wisdom or the mind understanding, and who formed and gave the animals, birds, and the rest of creatures their characteristics.

Even though Job is the oldest book in the Bible according to many scholars, written about thirty-six hundred years ago, it has many wonderful facts about dinosaurs and the moon. Dinosaurs such as the land dinosaur called the behemoth can be found in Job 40:15: *[15]Behold now behemoth, which I made with thee; he eateth grass as an ox (KJV)*. The sea dinosaur called the leviathan can be found in Job 41:1: *[1]Canst thou draw out leviathan with an hook? or his tongue with a cord which thou lettest down (KJV)?* The moon is also described as being dark which we today know that it just reflects the sun's light. This can be found in 25:5: *[5]Behold even to the moon, and it shineth not; yea, the stars are not pure in his sight (KJV).*

Job responded in Job 42 by stating that he had spoken of things that he did not understand or were too wonderful for him to know. He despised himself and repented in the dust and ashes. God also spoke to Eliphaz the Temanite and said that He was angry with him and his two friends because they had not spoken the truth about God as Job had done. God instructed Eliphaz to have Job offer up a sacrifice that they would bring to him on their behalf, and God would not deal with them as they actually deserved. God then instructed Job to pray for his friends, and God accepted Job's prayer.

The result of Job praying for his friends, as God instructed him to do, was that God made Job prosperous again and blessed the last part of Job's life more than the first part. The number of livestock that were lost was restored to him by twice the amount that was lost. He had another seven sons and three beautiful daughters and lived a long, full life. Notice that this was not a fabrication of the story as Muslim scholars wrote concerning Job, but a summary of the true account found in the Bible. We encourage the reader to read the entire account in the forty-two chapters of Job.

The Story of Za Al Kafel

Muslim scholars do not know the identity of Za Al Kafel. The name is mentioned in the Qur'an twice, but it is only his name. In Qur'an 21:85-86: *[85]And Ishmael and Idris[1] and Za Al Kafel,[2] all were among the patient. [86]And we admitted them in our mercy, surely they were of the good.* Then in Qur'an 38:45-48: *[45]And remember our servants Abraham and Isaac and Jacob, who have substantial hands and visions. [46]Surely we favored them with pure remembering of the home. [47]And surely they are with us from the best of the chosen. [48]And remember Ishmael and Alyas'a[3] and Za Al Kafel,[4] all from the chosen.*

Ibn Kathir stated that Ibn Jarir said that it appeared in the Qur'an that Za Al Kafel was one of Allah's prophets, and Allah's prayers and peace be on him.[5] Others claimed that he was not a prophet but that he was righteous and good, *and Allah knows best*. Ibn Jarir stated that Mujahid said that he was not a prophet but a just judge among his people. That is why he was named Za Al Kafel.

Ibn Kathir stated that Ibn Jarir said that Mujahid said that when Elisha became old, he asked a question, "Who will take my place to lead the people? I want to see him in my life, to see how he leads while I'm alive."[6] When the people gathered, he asked that whoever would take his place should be able to fast all day, stay up all night, and not get angry. One man stood up and said, "I will do that." So he sent all the people away. Another day he gathered the people again and asked the same question. The same man said, "I will do that." So Satan met with his demons and asked them to give this man a hard time. The demons became tired, but the man did not. Satan said, "Let me handle this." So he came to the man at night in the appearance of an old man and knocked on the door.

---

[1] wrong name, he meant Enoch
[2] wrong name, he meant Isaiah
[3] wrong name, he meant Elisha
[4] wrong name, some Muslim scholars say he meant Isaiah, others say Ezekiel
[5] Ibn Kathir, *Stories of the Prophets*, vol. 1, Abo Al Fida Ishamail Ibn Kathir Al Kurashi Al Damashce (Beirut: Dar Al-Arab Heritage, 1408 AH, 1988), 260.
[6] Ibid., 261.

The old man (Satan) told the man a story of how that man's people did not treat him (Satan) justly. The man asked the old man to come back so he could give him justice. However, the old man never came the second day, but he knocked at the man's door the following night once again. He told the old man, "Why did you not come to me when I was sitting to judge in the middle of the day?" He said, "Because my people are deceitful. When they knew you were set to judge, they said they would treat me justly. After you left your judging, they changed their minds."

The following night Satan, as an old man, came to him again, but he had already told his people that he was so tired that he needed to sleep. "If the old man comes, do not let him come near the door so I can sleep." They refused to let the old man come to the door, but the old man looked and saw a window. He entered the house from the window and knocked on the door from the inside of the house. The man woke up and told his people, "Did I not tell you to not let this old man come near my door?" They said, "Yes, we did not let him. Look! The door is locked. We do not know where he came from." So he rose and looked at the door, and it was closed. Behold, the old man was with him inside, and he recognized him and asked him, "Are you the enemy of Allah?" The old man said, "Yes, you have won over me in everything. I tried everything to make you angry, but Allah saved you from me." Allah named him Za Al Kafel.

Ibn Abu Hatem said that Za Al Kafel was not a prophet but a righteous man who used to pray a hundred times every day. Ibn Kathir stated that Imam Ahmed said that Mohammed said Za Al Kafel was one of the Children of Israel who did not shy from sin, and he did fall in sin.[7] A woman came to him, so he gave her sixty denarii so that he could have sex with her. He lay down with her as a man lies with a woman. She was shaking and crying. He asked her, "Why are you crying? Did I force you to do this?" She said, "No, but this work I have never done before and because of my need, I am doing this." He said, "So you are going to do this because you want some money?" He rose up away from her and said, "Go and take the money with you."

Then Mohammed said, "Za Al Kafel never sinned against Allah. Then he died on that night, and it was written on his door, 'Allah

---

[7]Ibid., 262.

forgives Za Al Kafel.'" Here is another fairy tale story made up just because his name is mentioned in the Qur'an. There is hardly any information about the man, and the Bible never mentions him; therefore, he was not a prophet.

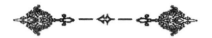

12. The Story of When All People Perished Together

Ibn Kathir stated that this type of perishing, when an entire people died together collectively, took place before the descending of the Torah, the book of Moses, and then he proved his point with the following verse in Qur'an 28:43: *[43]And indeed, we gave Moses the book after we had destroyed the first generations to become to the people a guidance and a mercy, perhaps they may remember.*[1]

Ibn Kathir continued by stating that Ibn Jarir and other scholars said that Allah did not destroy a people with a torment from the heaven or earth until after he sent the Torah, except to the people of the village whom Allah transformed into monkeys, *and Allah knows best.*[2]

You may be surprised to learn that this chapter is only two paragraphs in length. *Also, you may ask, what is the message of this chapter?* The answer is that there is no message in this chapter, but we can learn something of the level of ignorance of the Muslim scholars. I believe that Ibn Kathir had never studied the Torah, for if he had read the Torah carefully, he would have learned that the Torah contains all of the information beginning with the Creation through the Exodus of the Children of Israel from Egypt and their entry into the Promised Land.

Another important fact is that there were only two times, according to the Bible, when all people perished together. The first one was in Noah's day when people perished by The Flood as we read about in Genesis in chapters 6-8. The second time was in Lot's day as we read about in Genesis in chapter 19. As for the statement that Allah tormented the people of the village by causing them to be monkeys, this was just an invention of Mohammed's imagination as fabricated in the Qur'an.

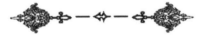

---

[1] Ibn Kathir, *Stories of the Prophets*, vol. 1, Abo Al Fida Ishamail Ibn Kathir Al Kurashi Al Damashce (Beirut: Dar Al-Arab Heritage, 1408 AH, 1988) 262.
[2] Ibid.

13. The Story of the Companions of the Rass

In Qur'an 25:38-39, Allah said: *³⁸And Ad and Themoud and the companion of the Rass and many generations between them. ³⁹And we gave parables to each of them, and each we destroyed with utter destruction.* Then in Qur'an 50:12-14, Allah said: *¹²Before them, the people of Noah and the companions of Rass and Themoud denied. ¹³And Ad and Pharaoh and the brethren of Lot, ¹⁴and the companions of the woods and the people of Tubba', they all denied the messengers, so my threat becomes established.*

These are the only two verses in which the Rass are mentioned. Although there is not any other information about them in the Qur'an, Ibn Kathir wrote two pages about them in his book.[1] He interpreted from the reading of the verses that they were utterly destroyed. Ibn Jarir said that they were the companions of the moat, as it is written in Qur'an 85:4: *⁴Killed are the companions of the moat.* However, Ibn Isaac disagreed by saying that they were a people after the days of the Christ. Ibn Jarir stated that Ibn Abbas said that the companions of the Rass were a people of one of the villages of Themoud.

Ibn Kathir stated that Muslim scholars said that the companions of the Rass used to live in Hodor, a city in Yemen.[2] Allah sent to them a prophet named Hanzalah Ibn Safwan. They called him a liar and killed him. So Ad Ibn Aos took his son and left Rass and went to Ahqaf, a valley between Aman and land of Mhrah. Allah destroyed all the companions of the Rass. Although Ibn Kathir said they were all destroyed, in the next statement, he wrote that they were spread all over Yemen and infected the whole earth until Geeron Ibn Saad came down and built the city which he named Iram of the Pillars. Then Allah sent Houd to the people of Ad, but they called him a liar. Then Allah destroyed them. From that, Ibn Kathir said he knew that the companions of the Rass were living many years before Ad, *and Allah knows best.*

---

[1] Ibn Kathir, *Stories of the Prophets*, vol. 1, Abo Al Fida Ishamail Ibn Kathir Al Kurashi Al Damashce (Beirut: Dar Al-Arab Heritage, 1408 AH, 1988), 263-264.
[2] Ibid., 263.

There are many opinions given as to what the Rass was. Ibn Abu Hatem said that the Rass was a well in Azerbaijan, but Al Thory said that it was a well where they buried their prophets. Ibn Jarir said that the companions of the Rass are in Flag and were companions of Yaseen. Qatadah said they were a village in Yamamah and were completely destroyed as Allah said in Qur'an 36:29: *²⁹It was only a single shout, so they were extinguished.*

Ibn Kathir said that Abu Bukhari Mohammed said that the companions of the Rass used to have a well from which all of them drank and that it was enough for their land. They had a just king, so when the king died, the people were sad for him. Days later, Satan appeared to them in the image of the king and said, "I did not die. I just left you to see how you would act in my absence." So they were rejoicing greatly, and he gave the order to build a veil between him and them. He told them he would never die. So people were deceived by him and believed him. They worshiped him. So Allah sent to them a prophet from among them who told them, "This is Satan." The prophet forbade them from serving him. He ordered them to serve Allah alone without any partner.

Ibn Kathir stated that Al Sohale said Hanzalah Ibn Safwan used to receive revelation in his sleep, so the people killed him.[3] The water in the well went dry, and they became thirsty. Their trees died and the fruit ceased and their homes were destroyed. It became a harsh life after living a comfortable life, and they were destroyed to the last one of them. The jinn dwelt in their houses, and so did the wild animals. Nothing could be heard in their places but the voices of the jinn, the roars of the lions, and the voices of the hyenas. Mohammed said that the first one to enter the garden (Mohammed's paradise) would be a black slave because Allah sent a prophet to the people of the village, but no one believed him except this black (he meant *the slave*).

Although previously Al Sohale did not give more information about the well that the prophet was thrown into, Ibn Kathir stated that the people of the village dug a well and threw the prophet in it. Then they threw a rock on top of the well. This slave used to go and sell firewood. Then he would buy food and drink and then go back to the well. Allah used to help him remove the stone so he could feed the prophet and put the stone back after he fed the prophet and gave him

---

[3] Ibid., 264.

drink. One day he went and got his wood, but he took a nap. Allah caused him to sleep on one side for seven years. Then he turned over to the other side, and Allah caused him to sleep another seven years. When he woke up from his sleep, he thought that he had only slept for an hour. He went back to the village, sold his wood, and bought food and drink as he used to do in the past. He went to feed the prophet in the well, but he could not find the well, for his people had taken the prophet out because they believed in him. It was said that their prophet used to ask them about this black man. They said, "We do not know," until their prophet died. That was why Mohammed said the first one to enter the garden would be that black.

Ibn Kathir stated that Ibn Jarir disagreed with this hadith because the Qur'an clearly taught that the companions of the Rass were completely destroyed.[4] However, since these people believed, Ibn Jarir stated that perhaps these were the children of the Rass who believed after the destruction of their parents, *and Allah knows best*.

How can the children come to exist if the entire population of the Rass was destroyed? Once again, we have another made-up story with solid contradictions between what is written in the Qur'an and what is written in the hadith. I personally believe no such people ever existed. If there had been a true prophet to a true people, I believe there would be a true message written with more information in the Scripture, not just a name in the Qur'an without any details.

---

[4]Ibid., 265.

14 The Story of Yassin

Ibn Kathir began this story simply by stating Qur'an 36:13-29.[1] Notice that the name of this portion of revelation in the Qur'an is YS, pronounced in Arabic as *Yassin*. Although the name Yassin is not written in these verses, Ibn Kathir stated that these verses are about the people of Yassin: *[13]And give them a parable of the companion of the village when the messenger came to them. [14]When we sent to them two, so they denied them, so we strengthened them with a third. So they said, "Surely we are sent to you." [15]They said, "You are not except humans like us, and the merciful did not send down anything, but you are only liars."*

[16]They said, "Our lord knows that surely we are sent to you. [17]And our duty is nothing except the clear delivering." [18]They said, "Surely our bird[2] is in you if you do not cease, we will surely stone you. And surely you will be touched with a painful torment from us." [19]They said, "Your bird[3] is with you. What if you are reminded? Yet you are an extravagant people." [20]And a man came from the far part of the city striving. He said, "O my people, follow the messengers. [21]Follow those who do not ask a wage from you, and they are guided. [22]And why should I not serve him who created me and to whom you will be returned? [23]Will I take gods without him? Should the merciful desire to afflict me, their intercession will not avert anything from me, nor will they deliver me. [24]Surely then I am in an obvious error. [25]Surely I believed in your lord, so hear me."

[26]It was said, "Enter the garden." He said, "I wish my people knew [27]about what my lord has forgiven me, and he made me of the honorable." [28]And we did not send down troops from the heavens on his people after him, nor were we the sender. [29]It was only a single shout, so they were extinguished. Ibn Kathir stated that it is well known that this village is the village of Antioch.[4]

---

[1] Ibn Kathir, *Stories of the Prophets*, vol. 1, Abo Al Fida Ishamail Ibn Kathir Al Kurashi Al Damashce (Beirut: Dar Al-Arab Heritage, 1408 AH, 1988), 265.
[2] evil omen
[3] evil omen
[4] Ibn Kathir, 265.

Ibn Isaac said that Ibn Abbas and others said that it used to have a king by the name of Aentikhos Ibn Aentikhos and that he used to worship idols. So Allah sent to him three messengers: Sadq, Masdoq, and Shalom. He called them liars, and that is why it is clear they were messengers from Allah. Qatadah, on the other hand, said they were messengers of the Christ (Jesus). Many other Muslim scholars agreed with him. They stated that the names of these messengers were Simon, John, and Paul, and the name of the village was Antioch.

However, Ibn Kathir said that this saying was very weak (most likely it was not true).[5] It was said that Jesus had sent three of his disciples to the people of Antioch, and it became the first city to believe in Christ at that time. That is why it is one of the four largest cities for the Christian church: Antioch, Jerusalem, Alexandria, and Rome. After them was the church of Constantine. The people of Antioch were never destroyed, but the people of this village, according the Qur'an, were destroyed after they killed the messengers.

As written in Qur'an 36:29: *[29]It was only a single shout, so they were extinguished.* Ibn Kathir said that perhaps the three messengers who were sent, according to the Qur'an, were different than the three messengers the Christ (Jesus) sent, and the descendants of the early people were the ones whom the Christ (Jesus) sent. Ibn Kathir rejected that these could be the same messengers for the Qur'an clearly teaches that it was Allah who sent them, not the Christ (Jesus).

As for the interpretation of verses 13-29, Ibn Kathir stated that it was a parable given by Allah to Mohammed so that he could give it to his people concerning the city to which he sent three messengers. The people found out that the messengers were human just like them, but they responded that they knew that they were human. They continued by saying that "if we have lied, so surely Allah would punish and get revenge on us. We are only telling you the message; but Allah will guide whom he wills, and he will lead astray whom he wills." The people said that "your coming to us brings us bad luck." So the people threatened them that they would kill them and humiliate them. The messengers responded that their bad luck was against them. The messengers wanted to know why the people accused them of bringing

---

[5]Ibid., 266.

bad luck and why the people threatened to kill and humiliate them. They continued to ask if the people were doing all of this because they had called the people to guidance! Then Ibn Kathir stated that the messengers said that their people were not believers in the truth.

As for the saying: *[20]And a man came from the far part of the city striving. He said, "O my people, follow the messengers."* Ibn Kathir interpreted by stating this man came to support the messengers and showed his belief in them.[6] He assured his people that the three messengers were calling them to the truth without asking for wages, for they called them to worship Allah alone, that the man was in error by worshiping others and leaving Allah. Then he spoke to the messengers, "Surely I believe in your lord, so hear me." It was also said he was speaking to his people to tell about his faith in the messengers of Allah. Then they killed him. It was said that they killed him by stoning him; or, it was said, they killed him by rods. It was also said they jumped on him all at once and killed him.

Ibn Kathir stated that Ibn Isaac said that they jumped on him with their legs until his bowels came out of his anus.[7] Abu Mojlez said that the name of this man was Habeeb Ibn Marie. It was said that he was a carpenter and a rope maker and had many other jobs, but it was also said that he was worshiping in a cave, *and Allah knows best.*

Ibn Abbas said that he was a great giver of good deeds in a hurry.[8] That's why Allah said he would admit him into the garden. When he saw what was in the garden of joy and happiness, he prayed, "May Allah forgive him and make him of the noble ones and may his people know that," meaning that he wished his people would believe so they could have what he had received. Ibn Abbas said this man advised his people in his life when he said, "O my people, follow the messengers." He also advised them after his death when he said in Qur'an 36:26-27: *"...I wish my people knew [27]about what my lord has forgiven me, and he made me of the honorable."* He meant that he wished that Allah would let his people know what good things had happened to him.

Qur'an 36:28 states: *[28]And we did not send down troops from the heavens on his people after him, nor were we the sender.* Ibn Kathir said that means that Allah said, "We did not need to take

---

[6]Ibid.
[7]Ibid., 267.
[8]Ibid.

revenge upon them, until the troops came down from heaven on them." However, Mujahid and Qatadah said that he meant *message* not *troops*. Ibn Jarir said Allah did not need to take revenge upon them until they called the messengers liars and killed their friend. Then Qur'an 36:29 states: *²⁹It was only a single shout, so they were extinguished.* Ibn Kathir said that interpreters said that Allah sent Angel Gabreel on them and shouted over them a great shout, and they were extinguished, meaning their voices were silent and their movements were so still that their eyelids did not move. That was the proof that this was not the village of Antioch because these people did not believe in Jesus, and they called their messengers liars. Antioch was the first city to believe in the Christ (Jesus) when he sent his messengers to Antioch.

This is an error which has been repeated many times in the writings of Ibn Kathir. Jesus did not send messengers to Antioch, but it was Paul who sent them after Jesus' ascension. As we stated before, this portion of revelation is named Yassin. One could think that if the portion is specifically named after a person, readers would know a little bit more than what is written; but sadly, the paragraph which was written in Qur'an 36:13-29 is very vague. It could fit any group of people at any time. Not one specific bit of information was given to point to what Allah or Mohammed was talking about.

No one knows who these people were, when they lived, who their messengers were, or what their message was about. It was just a vague statement that could mean anything. Perhaps this story is a twisted version of the parable of the vineyard in the Bible which is found in Luke 20:9-18. We encourage the reader to read the passage. Here is a summary of these verses.

There was a man who planted a vineyard and put workers in it. When the time came, he sent a servant to bring him some of the fruit, but the vineyard workers beat the servant and sent him away empty-handed. The owner sent another servant, and the workers scourged and dishonored him and sent him away empty-handed. Then the owner sent a third servant, and the same thing happened to him.

Then the owner of the vineyard said, "What should I do? I will send my beloved son. Perhaps if they see and receive him, they will revere him." Instead when they saw him, they said among themselves, "He is the heir, so let's kill him and the inheritance will be ours." So they took him outside the vineyard and killed him. What should be done to such people? The father must come and destroy all those people and give the vineyard to others. At the end of the parable, those who heard Jesus say this said, "God forbid."

This is a very important parable because it tells the entire story of what God is trying to do with man. God sent many prophets, but people refused to believe and turn from their wicked ways. Instead they killed His prophets. Then God sent His Son, and He was killed. That is the message of the story. Jesus said that the stone which the builders rejected is the cornerstone, Jesus Christ himself.

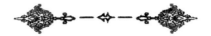

The Story of Jonah

Who was Yunus? Where did he live? When did he live? To whom was he sent? What was his message? How was his message received? How many people lived in the city to which he was sent? When was he swallowed by the whale? Was it before or after he was sent to the people? All these questions and more can be answered from the Bible, but none can be correctly answered from the Qur'an or by Muslim scholars. Ibn Kathir tried to answer these questions in his book, *Stories of the Prophets*, but his answers were all wrong.[1] As has been mentioned before, the problem is that the data is unavailable in any other source except the Bible, the original source.

Ibn Kathir actually inserted the story of Yunus (Jonah, according to the Bible) just before the book of Moses, as if Jonah came before Moses.[2] This shortcoming was not a fault of Ibn Kathir himself because he had no way of knowing that Mohammed simply did not know. Neither Gabreel nor Allah knew who came first: Moses or Jonah. Muslim scholars disagree about everything concerning Yunus, as we will see, except for one thing; they agree that the Bible has been corrupted concerning the story of Jonah (Yunus).

The story of Yunus is written in six locations throughout the Qur'an. Ibn Kathir interpreted the verses of the Qur'an by simply copying answers from the Bible, as will be demonstrated by the following interpretation. However, I would first like to emphasize that the name Yunus is a wrong name in the Arabic language. Obviously, Mohammed was not familiar with the name Jonah in the Arabic language for it is Yunan, not Yunus. This may suggest that Mohammed obtained some of his biblical information verbally, perhaps verbally translated from Hebrew, and he made his best guess as to the spelling of names in Arabic. We know he was talking about Jonah because the few details he provides match the story of Jonah in the Bible.

The name Yunus was mentioned in the Qur'an four times. His name is mentioned among some of the men whom Mohammed

---

[1] Ibn Kathir, *Stories of the Prophets*, vol. 1, Abo Al Fida Ishamail Ibn Kathir Al Kurashi Al Damashce (Beirut: Dar Al-Arab Heritage, 1408 AH, 1988), 268.
[2] Ibid.

claimed to be prophets. No details are mentioned in two passages. These two passages can be found as follows: first in Qur'an 4:163: *[163]Surely we have revealed to you as we revealed to Noah and the prophets after him. And we revealed to Abraham and Ishmael and Isaac and Jacob and the tribes and 'Isā and Ayyūb[3] and Yunus[4] and Aaron and Solomon, and to David we gave Zabor.*[5] The second location where the name of Yunus is only mentioned can be found in Qur'an 6:86: *[86]And Ishmael and Alyas'a*[6] *and Yunus and Lūt,*[7] *and we preferred all those above the worlds.* Notice how Mohammed in the previous two verses listed the names incorrectly in historical order, and he listed them all as prophets, which they were not.

In Qur'an 10, Yunus is mentioned with his own people. Mohammed indicated that when his people believed in him and their faith, it benefited them, for Allah gave them enjoyment in this world's life for a while as we see in Qur'an 10:98: *[98]So were it not that a village had believed so its faith profited, except the people of Yunus? When they believed, we removed from them the torment of disgrace in the world's life, and we gave them enjoyment for a while.*

As for the entire story, it is found in Qur'an 37. The story of Jonah as written in the Bible is written in four chapters and has a total of forty-eight verses, while Mohammed condensed it to a small number of verses of less than fifty Arabic words in the Qur'an. Qur'an 37:139-148 states: *[139]And surely Yunus[8] was among those sent. [140]When he fled in the loaded ship. [141]So he shared, so he was of the losers. [142]So the whale swallowed him, and he was blamed. [143]So were it not that he was of those who praised, [144]then he would have stayed in its belly until a day they are raised. [145]So we cast him on the barren shore, and he was sick. [146]And we caused a gourd tree to grow up over him. [147]And we sent him to one hundred thousand or more. [148]So they believed, so we gave them enjoyment for a time.*

---

[3] Job, non-Arabic word of Greek/Syriac origin
[4] name mistakenly used when Jonah was meant
[5] in singular form = Psalms, non-Arabic word of Hebrew/Syriac origin
[6] Elisha, non-Arabic word of Syriac/earlier Semitic origin
[7] Lot, non-Arabic word of Syriac origin
[8] wrong name, he meant Jonah

Chapter 15

Ibn Kathir stated that Allah sent Yunus to the people of Nineveh, but they called him a liar and rebelled with infidelity.[9] Because they did this for a long time, he left them and promised them that the torment would befall on them in three days. *How did Ibn Kathir know about the city of Nineveh? How did he know about the three days? Did the people of Nineveh become infidels after hearing Jonah's message? Did the people of Nineveh respond to his invitation by calling him a liar? How long did he speak or preach to them?* No answers could be found.

Surprisingly, Ibn Kathir continued by citing some other Muslim scholars' stories. He said that Ibn Masood and Mujahid and Saeed and Ibn Jaber and Qatadah said that when Jonah left the people, they realized that "Yunus was telling them the truth for they knew for sure that the torment was coming to them. And Allah put repentance in their hearts, and they regretted what they did to their prophet. So they dressed in sackcloth, and they separated between every animal and the animals' children."

Then they hurried to Allah, crying and pleading with him, and the men and women and the boys and the girls cried. They said all the animals were crying and groaning and mooing and bleating, so Allah spared them from the punishment, and he showed his compassion and mercy to all of them. As we have seen above and repeated in the following verse, Ibn Kathir stated that this was why Allah said in Qur'an 10:98: *[98]So were it not that a village had believed so its faith profited, except the people of Yunus? When they believed, we removed from them the torment of disgrace in the world's life, and we gave them enjoyment for a while.*[10]

The Qur'an does not mention the people of Nineveh, but simply said that Yunus was sent to his (own) people. Amazingly, when we compare this to the true account of the Bible, we discover that Jonah was a Hebrew man (Jonah 1:9). As for the people of Nineveh, they were Gentiles and not from Jonah's people, meaning that they were not Hebrews. Even though Nineveh was a very sinful city, it was from the love of God and His mercy that He called Jonah to go and preach to these sinful people (Jonah 1:1-2). They did not become infidels when Jonah went to them. In God's loving mercy, He reached out to save and forgive them. As for the three days' warning, this was

---

[9]Ibn Kathir, 268.
[10]Ibid.

another error, for the Bible clearly teaches that Jonah preached and said to the people of Nineveh that in forty days the city would be destroyed. The three days confusion could be a result concerning the size of the city of Nineveh for Jonah spent three days walking through the city to preach his message. See Jonah 3:3-4.

There were many disagreements among Muslim scholars concerning the story of Jonah.[11] One of these disagreements was concerning *when* Yunus was sent to his people. Some said it was before he was swallowed by the whale, others said it was after he was swallowed by the whale, but erroneously the majority agreed that he was swallowed by the whale after he preached to the people of Nineveh.

This can be proven also by Mohammed's teachings, as written in Ibn Kathir's interpretation. In Qur'an 68:48-50: *[48]So be patient to the judgment of your lord, and do not be like the companion of the whale[12] when he called and he was distressed. [49]Were it not that a grace from his lord reached him, he would be cast on the naked ground while he is blamed. [50]So his lord chose him, so he made him of the good.* Ibn Kathir interpreted these three verses to mean that Allah called on Mohammed to have patience with his people. Because they called him a liar, Allah would judge them and would reward Mohammed and his followers in this world and the hereafter. Allah advised Mohammed "not to be like the companion of the whale (Jonah) who angrily left his people. That is why he sailed on the ship and the whale swallowed him. He traveled with him (inside the whale) through the seas and the darkness."

Here Ibn Kathir misunderstood the story of Jonah. The story from Mohammed's teachings is that Jonah was upset and left his people when they rejected him. Then he was swallowed by the whale.

Ibn Kathir stated that when the waves were so powerful and the ship was rocked and so heavy because of all the people on it, the people of the ship decided to cast lots.[13] So whoever was picked by the lots, he would be thrown off of the ship. So when they did so, the choice fell on Yunus, the prophet of Allah. They refused to cast him off of the ship, so they cast lots a second time. It fell on him again, so he began to take his clothes off so that he could throw himself

---

[11]Ibid.
[12]Jonah
[13]Ibn Kathir, 269.

overboard, but they refused to let him do so. So they cast lots a third time, and it fell on him again, for that is what Allah desired from the great matter.

That is why Allah said in Qur'an 37:139-142: *¹³⁹And surely Yunus[14] was among those sent. ¹⁴⁰When he fled in the loaded ship. ¹⁴¹So he shared, so he was of the losers. ¹⁴²So the whale swallowed him, and he was blamed.* Ibn Kathir continued in his interpretation by stating that when the lot fell on Yunus, he was cast into the sea.[15] So Allah sent a great whale from the Green Sea, and he swallowed Yunus.

How can we find the true answers concerning this disagreement? Did the people of the ship cast the lots three times as mentioned above? Was Jonah swallowed by the whale after he was sent to his people, the people of Nineveh, as the majority of Muslim scholars agree? The answers are found in the true account in the Bible. When we compare this interpretation and the story in the Qur'an with the simple account of Jonah as it is written in the Bible, we will see the error of the Qur'an.

Jonah refused to go to Nineveh as God asked him. Instead, he went to another city which was called Tarshish, for the Scripture stated that he went to Joppa and from there he took a ship to go to Tarshish. (Notice that Joppa was a city on the big sea which is known as the Mediterranean Sea, not the Green Sea as Muslim scholars say.) So Jonah decided to run away from God by taking this ship to Tarshish, and because of this, the sea became a tempest. In the meantime, Jonah went down in the bottom of the ship and slept, but all the people on the ship cried out to their gods. Then they started throwing their goods off of the ship, but it did not help for the wind was so strong. Notice that they cast lots only one time, not three times. (Jonah 1:1-7). All of this took place **before** Jonah met with the people of Nineveh.

When the people on the ship found out the truth about Jonah and how he had disobeyed God's command, they were full of fear. Then the people of the ship asked Jonah what they should do so that they would be safe. Jonah said to take him and throw him in the water so the sea would calm (Jonah 1:8-12). Instead in the next verses (13-17), the men tried to return to the shore, but they were not able to do so

---

[14] wrong name, he meant Jonah
[15] Ibn Kathir, 270.

The Revelation of Error

because the tempest of the sea was increasing. So they cried out to God that He would not hold them responsible for the innocent blood of Jonah whom they then threw into the water. Suddenly, the sea became calm, and then the men were exceedingly fearful. They offered sacrifices to the Lord and made vows.

Muslim scholars say that it was said that when Yunus was inside the belly of the whale cruising through the seas and as he moved through the waves of the waters, he heard the fish praising the Merciful and the rocks on the bottom of the seas glorifying Allah. That was when Yunus called to Allah in Qur'an 21:87-88, *[87]And Za Al Nōn,[16] when he went in wrath, so he thought that we had no power over him. So he called from the darkness, "There is no god except you; praise be to you, surely I was of the unjust!" [88]So we answered to him and delivered him from the grief, and likewise, we deliver the believers.* Mohammed introduced a new name for Jonah which was Za Al Nōn. It seems to me that there is a great deal of emphasis on the anger of Jonah. If asked why Jonah was angry and with whom he was angry, the answer of Muslim scholars like Ibn Kathir was that he was angry against his people simply because they did not believe in him. Therefore, they became infidels. Obviously, that is a wrong answer when compared to the biblical account.

Another question we can ask is how the writing of the Qur'an could skip important parts of the story of Jonah, and in the same verse (87) go from being angry, to calling on Allah from the darkness. How quickly the Qur'an in the next verse (88) showed that Allah removed the sorrow from him and how Allah saved him as he saved all the believers.

Another disagreement among Muslim scholars is concerning the three *darkness*. Some Muslim scholars claim there are three *darknesses* in the phrase *"so he called from the darkness,"* but they disagree about what they are. In Ibn Kathir's interpretation for the phrase, he questioned other Muslim scholars like Ibn Masood, Ibn Abbas, and others who stated that the three darknesses were in the darkness of the whale, the darkness of the sea, and the darkness of the night.[17] Salm Ibn Abu Al Jad disagreed, writing that the three darknesses are the darkness of the first whale, the darkness of the

---

[16] wrong name, he meant Jonah
[17] Ibn Kathir, 270.

second larger whale which swallowed the first whale, and the third darkness is the darkness of the sea.

Another disagreement among Muslim scholars is the length of time Jonah stayed in the belly of the whale. Ibn Kathir wrote that scholars disagree about the time. Mojalid said it was between afternoon and evening.[18] Qatadah said Yunus was inside the belly of the whale for three days. Jaafer said it was seven days. Saeed and Abu Malik said that it was forty days, a*nd Allah knows best.*

To respond to the previous disagreements among Muslim scholars, we can simply read of the account in the Bible which will show that there was no such thing as three darknesses. Jonah spent three days and three nights in the belly of the great fish (Jonah 1:17), which the Lord in His mercy prepared to swallowed Jonah; he was not there three hours, not one week, not one month, nor forty days as Muslim scholars claim. The Bible, however, is very clear as even Jesus quoted the story that it was three days and three nights. Notice that it was one fish, not a fish swallowed by a larger fish.

Another disagreement is when Jonah praised Allah. *Was it before, after, or during the swallowing by the whale?* One can find this disagreement in Qur'an 37:143-144 which says: **[143]So were it not that he was of those who praised, [144]then he would have stayed in its belly until a day they are raised.** Even in these two statements, Muslim scholars disagree.

When did he praise Allah? Was it before or after being inside the whale? Ibn Kathir said that Mohammed stated when Yunus praised Allah, the angels heard his praises.[19] Then they said, "O lord, we hear a weak voice in a strange land." Allah said, "This is my servant Yunus. He disobeyed me, so I imprisoned him in the belly of the whale in the sea." They said, "Is this Yunus the good servant who used to send up to you every day and every night good deeds?" Allah said, "Yes." Mohammed said that the angels interceded on his behalf, so Allah ordered the whale to spew Yunus out onto the shore. As for his cry in the depths of the darkness, Yunus said, "There is no god except you; praise be to you, surely I was of the unjust!" However, Saeed Ibn Jaber said, and Ibn Abbas along with others were in agreement, that Jonah was among those who praised in the years

---
[18]Ibid.
[19]Ibid., 271.

preceding his being swallowed by the whale, so the praises heard by the angels were prior to his being swallowed.

Mohammed and his scholars made a big deal about Jonah's prayer. Mohammed emphasized the particular words of his prayer as Mohammed said that if people repeated Jonah's prayer, Allah would answer their prayers.

The fact is that Jonah never prayed any such words. In Jonah 2, there are nine wonderful verses of the prayer of Jonah, and finally in verse 10, God answered his prayer. Mohammed shortened Jonah's prayer into some ridiculous words when Mohammed said that Jonah's prayer was: "There is no god except you; praise be to you, surely I was of the unjust!"

Compare this claim to the actual prayer of Jonah when he said in Jonah 2: *¹Then Jonah prayed to the Lord his God from the fish's belly. ²And he said: "I cried out to the Lord because of my affliction, and He answered me. "Out of the belly of Sheol I cried, and You heard my voice. ³For You cast me into the deep, into the heart of the seas, and the floods surrounded me; all Your billows and Your waves passed over me. ⁴Then I said, 'I have been cast out of Your sight; yet I will look again toward Your holy temple.' ⁵The waters surrounded me, even to my soul; the deep closed around me; weeds were wrapped around my head. ⁶I went down to the moorings of the mountains; the earth with its bars closed behind me forever; yet You have brought up my life from the pit, O Lord, my God. ⁷"When my soul fainted within me, I remembered the Lord; and my prayer went up to You, into Your holy temple. ⁸"Those who regard worthless idols forsake their own Mercy. ⁹But I will sacrifice to You with the voice of thanksgiving; I will pay what I have vowed. Salvation is of the Lord."*

What a prayer! Perhaps if Mohammed had read the biblical account, he would have figured out that he was wrong about Jonah's prayer in the Qur'an. There were no angels involved to intercede on behalf of Jonah. As Mohammed and his scholars claim, those angels who allegedly heard the weak voice of Jonah, reminded Allah of how good Jonah was and how many good deeds he had performed in his life.

Ibn Kathir stated that Allah commanded the whale not to eat his (Yunus's) meat or crush his bones, so he took him through all the seas.[20] It was also said that this whale was swallowed by another larger whale, and it was said that when Yunus was inside the whale, he thought he was dead. Then he began to move his body, and he discovered that he was still alive. So he bowed down to Allah, and said, "O lord, I took to you a place of worship. No one worshiped you before."

Jonah 1:17 teaches: *[17]Now the Lord had prepared a great fish to swallow Jonah. And Jonah was in the belly of the fish three days and three nights.* Notice that God commanded the fish and that there was not a conversation between God and the whale. In Qur'an 37:145: *[145]So we cast him out on the barren shore and he was sick.* Ibn Kathir said that Ibn Masood said, "He (Yunus) was like a chicken without feathers."[21] Ibn Abbas and others said that he was like a baby when he was born, naked without any clothes.

Muslim scholars gave us very significant details about unimportant information concerning Jonah, yet they dismissed the important information. The Bible, in simple words without any fabrication, stated in Jonah 2:10: *[10]So the Lord spoke to the fish, and it vomited Jonah onto dry land.* Because the God of Jonah is Almighty God, He had the power to prepare the great fish to swallow Jonah. He also had the power to command such a fish to keep Jonah inside it three days and three nights, without any harm, and then to cast Jonah unharmed on the shore.

Muslim scholars who interpreted the verses as written in the Qur'an made some great errors when they claim that the anger of Jonah was against the people of Nineveh, for the true story is the anger of Jonah was not in the beginning of his mission trip but after he finished his ministry to the people of Nineveh. Jonah's anger was not against the people of Nineveh because they had turned away and repented to God. His anger was against God himself, because God relented and turned His anger away from the people of Nineveh by choosing not to punish the people for their sin. We can see this in Jonah 3:10, and it also is repeated in Jonah 4:3. Then God answered Jonah in 4:4 by asking him if he was angry because the people of Nineveh did what was right. It is amazing that Jonah chose death over life, not only for the people of Nineveh but for himself as well.

---

[20]Ibid., 270.
[21]Ibid., 272.

The God of Jonah is a God of second chances. We can see this clearly in Jonah 3:1-2. God saved Jonah's life when he prepared a great fish for him. After his rebellion and rejecting the mission trip to Nineveh, God called Jonah once again to go to the large city of Nineveh. In verses 3-4 we can find that Nineveh was not a small city for it required three days to walk through it. Jonah called on the people of the city with the message of God that, if they didn't repent, their city would be destroyed in forty days.

What a great revival! Not only did the people believe Jonah, but they called everyone to fast and wear sackcloth. The people cried out to God, not the animals as Muslim scholars interpreted, and everyone turned from his wicked ways so that perhaps God would change His mind concerning the destruction of the city. Notice that not only did Mohammed not understand the story, but he fabricated a lie.

In the Muslim scholars' interpretations of the story, they claim that Jonah was angry at the people of Nineveh because the people did not believe in him and insisted on their infidelity. Muslim scholars claim that there was a long period of rebellion, but that is not the true account of the Bible. Muslim scholars claim that when Jonah left them, they investigated the descending of the torment on them, so Allah cast repentance and sorrow in their hearts. The Muslim scholars said that all the animals were crying and groaning and mooing and bleating, so Allah spared them from the punishment, and he showed his compassion and mercy to all of them.

That was a huge error. I believe it is a result of misunderstanding the biblical account which states that all the animals fasted. They did not fast by their choice, but it was the command of the king and because their owners did not feed them or give them any drink. As a result of such an act, the merciful God poured His love and grace on them, and the city was saved.

Ibn Kathir continued to interpret the following verses in Qur'an 37:145-146: *[145]So we cast him on the barren shore, and he was sick. [146]And we caused a gourd tree to grow up over him.*[22] When Allah tested Yunus, he cast him into a barren land which had no trees in it. Yunus was sick and weak. Allah caused a gourd plant to grow above him. Ibn Kathir continued by stating that some scholars said that the gourd plant had several good attributes. Its leaves were

---

[22]Ibid.

soft, and it gave lots of shade. No fly could get near him. Because the fruit of the tree was edible, raw or cooked, with the skins and seeds, it had many benefits.

This explanation does not give us the real reason why God caused the tree to grow over Jonah. We can ask some questions of Muslim scholars just to prove that they are speaking of something about which they are not knowledgeable. *How long did it take this tree to grow? How long did it live? Did Jonah eat from its fruit? What was the real purpose for the growth of the tree?* This was a great object lesson; and sadly, Mohammed and his scholars missed it.

First, I would like to set the stage. We see that Jonah was no longer in the city, for his mission was completed. Outside the city he sat, specifically, on the east side of the city. It was a hot day, and Jonah knew how to make a booth for himself so that the sun's heat would not harm his head. He was sitting and waiting for what would happen to the city. *Would it be destroyed or saved?*

God, in His compassion and mercy, miraculously prepared a gourd plant to cover Jonah that he might have comfort as he sat under the shade. Suddenly, the sun rose, and the hot wind blew from the east. Quickly the plant withered and blew away. Once again Jonah grumbled, wishing death for himself. Then God visited him again in 4:9, and God repeated the same question: **⁹*Then God said to Jonah, "Is it right for you to be angry about the plant?" And he said, "It is right for me to be angry, even to death!"***

Notice that the tree here was not for Jonah to eat its fruit or to enjoy its shade; it was simply to be used as an object lesson. God spoke through it, not only to Jonah, but also to you and me even today. Everything we have around us is temporary; the only eternal things are people's souls. We must not be concerned about things we may or may not have, but we must be concerned about people who may die without knowing Christ and spend eternity in hell.

Then Ibn Kathir said Allah caused some animal to come to him, in the early morning and late at night, which he used to breastfeed him.[23] *Where did Ibn Kathir come up with this information?*

Although the verses clearly teach that the people of Yunus repented and their faith benefited them, Muslim scholars disagree that their belief or faith would benefit them in the hereafter. *Will their belief save them from the eternal torment and save them from the*

---

[23]Ibid.

The Revelation of Error

earthly torment? Some Muslim scholars said *yes*, but others said *no*; and, as usual, Ibn Kathir said that *only Allah knows best*.[24] For Ibn Kathir said Allah himself said that in Qur'an 37:147-148: *[147]And we sent him to one hundred thousand or more. [148]So they believed, so we gave them enjoyment for a time.*

Another disagreement among Muslim scholars is how many people lived in the city of Nineveh. Ibn Kathir assured his Muslim readers that there were more than one hundred thousand, but he did not know how many more.[25] Ibn Kaab said that Mohammed said there were twenty thousand more than one hundred thousand, but Ibn Abbas said one hundred thirty thousand or one hundred forty thousand. Saeed Ibn Jaber said that there were one hundred and seventy thousand. The answer to this disagreement can be very easily resolved when one reads Jonah 4:11: *[11]And should I not pity Nineveh, that great city, in which are more than one hundred and twenty thousand persons who cannot discern between their right hand and their left—and much livestock?*

Mohammed stated, "No servant should say that I am better than Yunus, Ibn Matthew."[26] Ibn Kathir said that Mohammed said this because Mohammed was very humble. Notice that in this hadith Mohammed not only gave the wrong name for Jonah but also made another error by stating that Jonah's father's name was Matthew. However, the Bible gives his name as Amittai as we read in Jonah 1:1: *[1]Now the word of the Lord came unto Jonah the son of Amittai, saying...*

Once again, we see a very simple account in the Bible, in four chapters with clear facts, which can be read with ease. Mohammed erroneously confused and changed the story, removing many facts, summarizing it in less than fifty words. His scholars tried their best to fill in the missing information in the revelation of the Qur'an to fix the many errors, and in doing so, they added more errors.

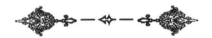

---

[24]Ibid.
[25]Ibid., 269.
[26]Ibid., 274.

16 The Story of Moses

Muslims all over the world claim that they believe in the Prophet Moses and in the book of Moses, the Torah. Therefore, they believe in Judaism, the religion of Prophet Moses. *But is that true? How can Muslims claim to believe in Judaism, the religion of Moses, if their religion, Islam, commands them not only to hate the Jews but to kill the last Jew as Allah declared in Qur'an 1:5-6 because Allah is angry with the Jews simply because they are Jews? Do Muslims really believe in Moses? How can they reconcile the doctrine of their cult, Islam, with the teaching of the Jewish faith when they compare the teaching of the Qur'an with the teaching of Judaism?* I believe that if Muslims knew the Jewish faith, not only would they leave the cult of Islam, but they would believe in the Christian faith. I believe Muslims do not know the Moses of the Torah, but simply the false Muslim Moses of the Qur'an. To prove my point, let us begin our study of Moses' life in the Qur'an by simply asking this question: *Who was Moses?*

According to Ibn Kathir, "Moses is Ibn Amran, Ibn Kah'es, Ibn Azer, Ibn Levi, Ibn Jacob, Ibn Isaac, Ibn Abraham."[1] *Once again, though, where did Ibn Kathir come up with these names and genealogy?* Not a single verse in the Qur'an or hadith indicates such a lineage.

According to the Bible, the name of Moses' father was not Amran; it was Amram, as written in Exodus 6:20: **[20]Now Amram took for himself Jochebed, his father's sister, as wife; and she bore him Aaron and Moses. And the years of the life of Amram were one hundred and thirty-seven.**

The name Amran is also mentioned in Qur'an 3:33 and 66:12. Muslim scholars disagree on the identity of the Amran mentioned in Qur'an 3:33: [33]*Surely Allah chose Adam and Noah and the family of Abraham and the family of 'Imrān,[2] above the worlds,* in which some say that he was the father of Moses; however, others

---

[1] Ibn Kathir, *Stories of the Prophets*, vol. 1, Abo Al Fida Ishamail Ibn Kathir Al Kurashi Al Damashce (Beirut: Dar Al-Arab Heritage, 1408 AH, 1988), 274.

[2] Amran, non-Arabic word of Syriac origin

say that he was the father of Mary, the mother of Jesus, as stated by Al Qurtobi in his interpretation of Qur'an 3:33.[3]

As for Qur'an 66:12: *[12]And Mary, the daughter of Amran, who guarded her sexual parts, so we breathed into it[4] from our spirit, and she believed in the words of her lord and his books, and she was among the obedient.* All Muslim scholars agree that Amran was the father of Mary, the mother of Jesus. I believe that Mohammed was clearly in error in all his writings concerning Mary, the mother of Jesus. Obviously, he thought that she was the sister of Moses and Aaron, as proven by his reference to Mary, Jesus' mother, in Qur'an 19:28: *[28]O sister of Aaron, your father was not an evil man, and your mother was not unchaste!"*

The Qur'an mentions Moses in 131 verses in 47 locations. Sometimes only the name is mentioned as in Qur'an 2:108: *[108]Or do you wish to ask your messenger as Moses was asked before?* Also, in Qur'an 2:136: *[136]Say, "We believed in Allah and what has been sent down to us, and what has been sent down to Abraham and Ishmael and Isaac and Jacob and the asbāt,[5] and what has been given to Moses and 'Isā, and what has been given to the prophets from their lord. We do not differentiate between any of them, and to him we are Muslims."* Moses is mentioned in the following verses of the Qur'an: 3:84, 164; 6:84, 91, 154; 11:17, 110; 21:48; 22:44; 29:39; 32:23; 33:7, 69; 41:45; 42:13; 46:12, 30; 53:36; and 87:19. The verses add nothing to the information given for the story of Moses' life; they simply take up space. Sometimes the name is inserted into a listing of names, with no apparent purpose. For example, in Qur'an 6:84: *[84]And we granted to him[6] Isaac and Jacob, both we guided, and Noah we guided before and among his descendants, David and Solomon and Job and Joseph and Moses and Aaron. And likewise, we reward the doers of good.*

This pattern of inserting names is repeated in 2:136; 3:84; 29:39; 33:7; 42:13; and 87:19. The names given along with Moses are in no particular order, causing us to wonder if Mohammed really knew who

---

[3] http://quran.al-islam.com/Page.aspx?pageid=221&BookID=14&Page=54, accessed November 1, 2011.
[4] her sexual parts
[5] tribes, non-Arabic word of Hebrew/Syriac origin in its singular form
[6] Abraham

came first. These names are not in correct historical order, and they are often not related to each other.

The story of Moses in the Qur'an is written in two different styles which we will call the short and the long versions. The short version ranges from one verse, as in Qur'an 61:5: *⁵And when Moses said to his people, "O my people, why do you harm me? And indeed, you know that I am a messenger of Allah to you." So when they deviate, Allah deviates their hearts. And Allah will not guide the transgressing people;* to twelve short verses as in Qur'an 79:15-26: *¹⁵Have the sayings of Moses come to you? ¹⁶When his lord called him in the holy valley of Tuwa. ¹⁷"Go to Pharaoh, surely he has rebelled." ¹⁸So say, "Would you become purified, ¹⁹and I guide you to your lord so that you may fear?" ²⁰So he showed him the big sign. ²¹So he denied and disobeyed. ²²Then he turned back, striving. ²³So he gathered, so he called. ²⁴So he said, "I am your lord, the highest." ²⁵So Allah seized him with the punishment of the hereafter and of the first. ²⁶Surely in this is a lesson to him who fears.*

This short style is repeated in 2:87-96, 246-248; 3:153-155; 5:20-26; 11:96-99; 14:5-8; 17:2-6, 101-104; 19:51-53; 23:45-49; 25:35-36; 27:7-14; 28:76-77; 29:39-40; 32:23-28; 37:114-122; 43:46-56; and 51:38-40. *Why would these twenty short stories of Moses be repeated throughout the Qur'an in the midst of short stories of other prophets?* Again, I believe it is simply to make the Qur'an a larger body of revelation. If the story of each prophet in the Qur'an is mentioned one time and one time only in its longer version, meaning the removal of all of the repetitious short stories, the Qur'an would be reduced to a much smaller size than what we have today.

Notice that the order of these short stories, as listed above, are in no logical or consistent order, much as we saw in the previous list of names. The story of Moses is always followed or preceded by the story of another prophet. For example, Mohammed mentioned the stories of such Muslim "prophets" as Noah, Abraham, David, Elijah, Ad, Themoud, and Alexander the Great. Again, this leaves us wondering if Mohammed understood the relationship or chronology of these biblical, historical, or fictional figures.

We will cover Moses' life, as written in Qur'an 28, but also draw on other versions of the story in Qur'an 7, 20, 26, and other portions of revelation as necessary to complete the story or show conflicts in

The Revelation of Error

the stories. Additionally, we will compare these stories in the Qur'an with the biblical account of Moses in Exodus.

The Birth of Moses and Killing of the Sons of the Israelites

In Qur'an 28, Mohammed gave us the story of the birth of Moses. According to verse 2: *²Those are the verses of the clear book;* this is not just a simple story but part of Mohammed's support for the veracity of his revelation. This statement is found throughout the Qur'an as Mohammed repeatedly maintained that the words of the Qur'an are *"clear." Was he trying to deceive us because he was keenly aware of how truly unclear the words were then and would be to us?*

Qur'an 28:2-6 contains a description of the status of the land of Egypt under the leadership of Pharaoh as he subdued the Jews who lived in the land by beheading their male children: *²Those are the verses of the clear book. ³We will recite to you some of the news of Moses and Pharaoh with the truth to the believing people. ⁴Surely Pharaoh exalted himself in the land and made its people into sects, weakening a group of them, slaughtering their sons, and sparing their women, surely he was of the vandals. ⁵And we desired to show favor to those who were weakened on the earth and to make them leaders and to make them the heirs ⁶and to establish them in the land, and we showed Pharaoh and Haman and their troops among them what they were fearing.*

This passage is in direct conflict with Moses' own account in Exodus 1:22 which records that the male children were not slaughtered as Mohammed said in the Qur'an but were drowned: **²²So Pharaoh commanded all his people, saying, "Every son who is born you shall cast into the river, and every daughter you shall save alive."**

In Ibn Kathir's interpretation, he wrote that Pharaoh abused the Children of Israel, causing them to do the worst and lowest type of work in the land, although they were the best of the people in the land.[7] He was killing their sons because the Children of Israel were studying the belief they inherited from Abraham, that from his descendants a young boy would be born and would destroy the king of Egypt. This news was so well known among the Children of Israel

---

[7] Ibn Kathir, *Stories of the Prophets*, 275.

that some of the Egyptian leaders mentioned this information to Pharaoh, which was why he was killing their male children.

In contradiction to this, Ibn Kathir stated that the Egyptians complained to Pharaoh that the shrinking number of male Israelites decreased the number of available workers; therefore, Pharaoh issued a new command to kill their male children on alternating years.[8] Therefore, it was said that Aaron was born in the year when they allowed Israelites to have sons while Moses was born in a year in which they killed the male children.

Does this make any sense if the reason that Pharaoh was killing the Israelites' sons was to kill the Savior who would grow up to kill the king of Egypt? Why would he let the sons born in alternating years live? Was the king of Egypt as foolish as Ibn Kathir? This is contradicted with what is written in Qur'an 7:127: **[127]And the leaders from the people of Pharaoh said, "Will you let Moses and his people to vandalize in the land and desert you and your gods?" He said, "We will kill their sons and spare their women, and surely we are dominant over them."**

Another question that we must ask is when did Pharaoh actually give the order for killing the sons of the Israelites? Was it when Moses was a baby or after Moses was a grown man? I ask this question because in Qur'an 28:7, Moses was a breastfeeding baby when this took place, but in Qur'an 7:127-128, Moses was a grown man. That is a great contradiction.

Where Did Haman Come From?

Another error in the preceding passage is in verse 6, where Haman is mentioned within the timeline of the story of Moses as being one of the contemporary Egyptians. Haman actually served under King Ahasuerus (Xerxes) who ruled Persia from 486 to 465 BC.[9] This was not only the wrong kingdom but a discrepancy of approximately a thousand years. No record of the name Haman can be found in Egyptian history during the period of Moses.

---

[8]Ibid.
[9]Richard L. Strauss, "The Story of Ahasuerus and Esther," *Bible.org.*, June 28, 2004, accessed November 8, 2011, https://bible.org/seriespage/such-time-this%E2%80%94i-story-ahasuerus-and-estheri.

Moses' Survival

Let us see how the Qur'an explains Moses' survival of Pharaoh's orders. In Qur'an 28:7-8, it is written: *⁷And we revealed to Moses' mother: "That breastfeeds him, so when you fear for him, so cast him into the river, and do not fear and do not grieve. Surely we will bring him back to you and make him of the messengers." ⁸So the family of Pharaoh picked him up so that he may become an enemy to them and a grief. Surely Pharaoh and Haman and their troops were khati'aeen.*[10]

Although the Qur'an does not mention a basket in these verses, Ibn Kathir's interpretation of this passage stated that Moses' family's home was on the river bank.[11] His mother made a basket and tied it with a rope with which she could pull him in to breastfeed him. She would send him back into the river when anyone came to threaten him.

However, the Bible records in Exodus 2:2-4: *²So the woman conceived and bore a son. And when she saw that he was a beautiful child, she hid him three months. ³But when she could no longer hide him, she took an ark of bulrushes for him, daubed it with asphalt and pitch, put the child in it, and laid it in the reeds by the river's bank. ⁴And his sister stood afar off, to know what would be done to him.*

This is where Ibn Kathir came up with the idea of a basket. However, notice that there was no rope attached to the ark, and Moses' mother did not pull him back. After placing him in the ark on the river, she let him go. Although the Qur'an does not mention Moses' mother's name, Ibn Kathir stated that her name was Ayarahk or Ayazhkt. According to the Bible, her name was Jochebed.[12]

Another conflict appears in Qur'an 28:9 where it is reported that it was Pharaoh's wife who adopted Moses. Ibn Kathir restated this when he said that "Pharaoh answered her by saying, 'I do not have need for him, but you have need of him.' They adopted him because they did not have any sons."[13]

On the other hand, the Bible teaches that it was really Pharaoh's daughter who discovered baby Moses. In Exodus 2:5-6: *⁵Then the daughter of Pharaoh came down to bathe at the river. And her*

---

[10] sinners, non-Arabic word of Syriac origin
[11] Ibn Kathir, 277
[12] Ibid.
[13] Ibid., 278.

maidens walked along the riverside; and when she saw the ark among the reeds, she sent her maid to get it. ⁶*And when she opened it, she saw the child, and behold, the baby wept. So she had compassion on him, and said, "This is one of the Hebrews' children."*

The Breastfeeding of Moses

Although the Qur'an does not give us any information of how Moses ended up in the house of Pharaoh, Mohammed gave us more details concerning the women who tried to breastfeed Moses and how he would not take any of their milk. Surprisingly, the sister of Moses appeared on the scene asking them if she could provide a house in which to take care of Moses; and that is how Allah returned Moses back to his own mother, for her heart was broken from losing her son.

This can be found in Qur'an 28:10-13: *¹⁰And the heart of Moses' mother became empty that she almost exposed him were it not that we tied on her heart that she will be of the believers. ¹¹And she said to his sister, "Follow him." So she watched him from alongside, and they did not feel. ¹²And we forbid him the breastfeeding [from other women] before that, so she said, "Will I point out to you the family of a house who will take care of him for you, and they will be an advisor to him?" ¹³So we returned him to his mother, so her eyes may be pleased, and she will not grieve; and she might know that the promise of Allah is true. But most of them do not know.* Ibn Kathir stated that the family of Pharaoh gave Moses to his sister and went with them to their home.[14] When his mother held him to breastfeed, he suckled from her; and they all rejoiced with a great joy. *Where did Ibn Kathir come up with this information?*

The preceding Qur'an verses and interpretations conflict with the following passage in Qur'an 20:37-39 when Allah spoke to Moses: *³⁷And indeed, we put on you a favor another time. ³⁸When we revealed to your mother what is revealed ³⁹that, 'Cast him into the ark, so cast him into the river, so the river will cast him to the shore. An enemy to me and an enemy to him will take him, and I will bestow love on you from me. And you will be made before my eyes.'* Did the basket have a rope? Did Moses' mother pull him in to breastfeed and push him back out into the river when

---

[14]Ibid., 278.

The Revelation of Error

danger was present? Or was he set loose upon the river and then washed ashore as in Qur'an 20:39?

Exodus 2:4-10 gives the original true account. Many of the Bible passages referred to in this section on Moses will be summarized and paraphrased. The reader is encouraged to read these Bible passages in their entirety.

According to verses 4-10, the sister of a baby boy, who at this point had been placed in a basket and hidden in the reeds on the river, watched to see what would happen to him. When the Pharaoh's daughter came to the river to bathe, she saw the basket and sent a maid to retrieve it and bring it to her. When she opened the basket, she saw the baby. The Pharaoh's daughter realized that it was one of the Hebrew children, yet she had compassion on him. Then the sister of the child asked Pharaoh's daughter if she could go find a nurse for this child. Pharaoh's daughter told her to do so.

The girl brought the baby's own mother to Pharaoh's daughter who told the woman to take the child and nurse him for her. Pharaoh's daughter also told her that she would pay her to do so. So the mother took her own baby home and nursed him. When he grew, she took him to Pharaoh's daughter where he became her son. Then Pharaoh's daughter named him Moses which means *because I drew him out of the water*.

When we read the story in the Qur'an, several women tried to breastfeed Moses. However, in the biblical account, it was his mother alone that breastfed him.

<u>The Killing of the Egyptian</u>

In Qur'an 28:14-21 we are told: *[14]And when he reached his strength and became settled, we gave him wisdom and knowledge; and likewise, we reward the doers of good. [15]And he entered the city at a time when its inhabitants did not notice him, so he found in it two men fighting, this is of his sect and this of his enemies. So he was called for help by the one of his sect against him who was of his enemies. So Moses struck him,[15] so he killed him. He said, "This is of satans' work. Surely he is an obviously misleading enemy." [16]He said, "My lord, surely I have done an injustice to myself, so forgive me." So he forgave him. Surely he is the forgiving, the merciful. [17]He said,*

---

[15] the enemy

"My lord, because you have graced on me, so I will not be a backer to the criminal."

[18] So he became fearful and vigilant in the city. So when the one that he helped the day before called out to him, Moses said to him, "Surely you are an obvious seducer." [19] So when he desired to seize the one who is an enemy to them, he said, "O Moses, do you desire to kill me as you killed a soul yesterday? Do you only desire to become a powerful in the land, and you do not desire to become of the good?" [20] And a man from the remotest part of the city came running. He said, "O Moses, surely the leaders are consulting to kill you. So get out! Surely I am an advisor to you." [21] So he got out from it in fear, vigilant. He said, "My lord, deliver me from the unjust people!"

Ibn Kathir interpreted these verses by stating that Moses was then forty years old, the age of prophethood.[16] (This statement is inconsistent with Muslims calling Jesus a prophet, as he *prophesied* from age thirty to age thirty-three.) He quoted Ibn Abbas as saying that "at the time when Moses entered the city, it was in the middle of the day." The Israelite asked Moses to help him kill his enemy, the Egyptian. Ibn Kathir said that Mujahid said that Moses punched the Egyptian with his fist. However, Ibn Kathir indicated that Qatadah said that Moses punched him with a rod.

In the continuation of his interpretations, Ibn Kathir indicated that the same Israelite whom Moses helped on the previous day called on Moses to help him against another Egyptian enemy.[17] However, this Egyptian went to Pharaoh, and this caused Pharaoh to summon Moses. Another man, full of compassion toward Moses, came to him by a shortcut and said, in Qur'an 28:20, *"...O Moses, surely the leaders are consulting to kill you. So get out! Surely I am an advisor to you."* According to Ibn Kathir, that is why Moses left Egypt, escaping to Midian.

When we look at this same part of the account in the Bible, we can find some similarities but significant differences. There were two confrontations in which Moses was involved. In Exodus 2:11-12 we learn of the first confrontation: **[11] *Now it came to pass in those days, when Moses was grown, that he went out to his brethren and looked***

---

[16] Ibid., 279.
[17] Ibid., 280.

The Revelation of Error

at their burdens. And he saw an Egyptian beating a Hebrew, one of his brethren. [12]So he looked this way and that way, and when he saw no one, he killed the Egyptian and hid him in the sand.

Notice that when Moses struck the Egyptian, there was no one else there, and he buried him in the sand. Therefore, at this time there was no reason for him to live in fear as suggested in Qur'an 28:18.

Notice also in Exodus 2:13-14, another error is found in the Qur'an in that the conflict was between two different Israelites, not between the same Israelite and another Egyptian: *[13]And when he went out the second day, behold, two Hebrew men were fighting, and he said to the one who did the wrong, "Why are you striking your companion?" [14]Then he said, "Who made you a prince and a judge over us? Do you intend to kill me as you killed the Egyptian?" So Moses feared and said, "Surely this thing is known!"*

Here in Exodus 2:14, Moses found out that the killing and burial of the Egyptian had become public knowledge, so he became afraid and said, **"Surely this thing is known!"** Pharaoh heard this news and sought to kill Moses, so Moses actually left Egypt and escaped to the land of Midian as recorded in Exodus 2:15.

Moses' Life in Midian

According to the Qur'an, Moses then fled Egypt because he was afraid that some of Pharaoh's people would catch him. He prayed that Allah might lead him since he had never been out of Egypt before, and he did not know where to go.[18] That was the interpretation of Ibn Kathir of Qur'an 28:21-24: *[21]So he got out from it in fear, vigilant. He said, "My lord, deliver me from the unjust people!" [22]And when he journeyed toward Midian, he said, "Perhaps my lord will guide me in the right way." [23]And when he arrived at the water of Midian, he found there a nation of people watering. And apart from them he found two women who were keeping back. He said, "What is [the matter] with you?" They said, "We will not water until the shepherds have left, and our father is a very old man." [24]So he watered for them, then turned away to the shade. So he said, "My lord, surely I am poor for whatever good you send down to me."*

Ibn Kathir also explained that the city of Midian was the city of the people of Shoaib and that this city was destroyed before the

---

[18]Ibid., 281.

lifetime of Moses.[19] There was a well there where Moses found two women separating their sheep, so they would not mix with other people's sheep. Ibn Kathir assured his readers that Moses' father-in-law had only two daughters and "whatever is written in the Bible (seven daughters) is false."

When Moses asked these two daughters why they were not watering their sheep, Ibn Kathir said that they answered that they were weak shepherds and that their father was an old man. Ibn Kathir further stated that the rock which was on the top of the well was very large, requiring ten men to remove it, but Moses was able to remove it by himself. After he watered their sheep, he put the rock back as it was. *If the rock information is true, how did the daughters of his future father-in-law get water for their sheep, especially if they were weak shepherds? Where did Ibn Kathir find this information?*

Ibn Kathir stated that Ibn Abbas said that Moses walked all the way from Egypt to Midian without eating anything except legumes and tree leaves.[20] Moreover, he had no sandals and his stomach was touching his back. That is to say, he was very hungry and needy. When Moses said, "*My lord, surely I am poor for whatever good you send down to me*," Ibn Kathir stated that the two women heard what he said.[21] They then went to their father who was surprised at their quick return.

When they told him about Moses, their father commanded one of them to go back and invite him to their home as is described in Qur'an 28:25-28: *[25]So one of them came to him, walking bashfully. She said, "Surely my father invites you so that he may reward you a wage for watering for us." So when he came to him and related to him the narrative, he said, "Do not be afraid. You are delivered from the unjust people." [26]One of them said, "O my father, hire him, surely he will be the best of whom you hired, the strong, the faithful." [27]He said, "Surely I desire that you have sex (marry) with one of these my two daughters, that you should be employed by me for eight years. So, if you fulfill ten, it is of your own doing,[22] for I do not desire a hardship for you. You will find me, if Allah wills, among the*

---

[19]Ibid.
[20]Ibid., 280.
[21]Ibid., 281.
[22]as a tip

good." ²⁸He said, "This is between me and you. Whichever of the two terms I fulfill, there will be no wrongdoing against me. And Allah is the guardian of what we say."

Ibn Kathir stated that scholars disagree on the identity of this *"very old man"* in Qur'an 28:23 who was to become Moses' father-in-law.[23] Some said that he was the Prophet Shoaib, explaining that he lived long years after the destruction of his people until the time he met Moses who married his daughter. Others said that he was the nephew of Shoaib, while others said he was Shoaib's cousin, and still others said that he was Jethro. However, Abu Obeida added that he was both Jethro and the nephew of Shoaib, and Ibn Abbas added that he was the companion of Midian.

What a wonderful collection of vastly different and distinct opinions! *How can Muslim scholars justify naming this man when he is not named in their Qur'an?* Ibn Kathir maintained that the Bible was wrong, even though the Qur'an does not have any information about this.[24]

Ibn Kathir said that when one of the daughters recommended that her father hire Moses, she praised Moses by saying he was "the strong, the faithful."[25] Ibn Abbas and others said that her father asked her how she knew this. She answered him that Moses had removed a rock from the well by himself that would have required ten men to remove it. Also, she reported that, when she began leading him to the house, he walked in front of her and asked her to walk behind him saying, "If I walk in the wrong way, lead me by throwing a small rock to the right or the left." They also did not walk close to each other or talk on the way. It is considered a sign of respect in the Muslim world for the man to walk ahead and not talk to a strange woman. *How did Ibn Abbas know this conversation took place between Moses' future father-in-law and his daughter?* This in itself was a greater miracle than the writing of the Qur'an, especially since Allah did not mention any of these details in his word.

Moses worked for his father-in-law, according to Ibn Kathir who wrote that Mohammed said, "Moses hired himself for eight years or ten years of living chastely for the honor of marrying his daughter and for food for his stomach."[26] Then Ibn Kathir stated that Ibn Abbas

---

[23]Ibn Kathir, 282.
[24]Ibid.
[25]Ibid., 283.
[26]Ibid., 283-284.

said that Mohammed said that he asked Angel Gabreel, "Which of the two terms did Moses serve?" Gabreel answered that Moses served and completed both of them. Then Mohammed said that he asked Gabreel, "Which of the two women did Moses marry?" The angel said, "It was the younger of the two of them." This question-and-answer session is not only confusing, but humorous. While unimportant aspects of the story are sometimes given in detail, Mohammed does not tell the names of some of the main characters or even key aspects of the life of Moses.

Ibn Kathir said when Moses decided to separate from Shoaib, he asked his wife to ask her father that he may give to her some of his sheep, so they may live on them.[27] So he gave her some of them, the ones with color that were born that year, for her father's sheep were black. So Moses got a stick, split it, put it in the depths of the watering trough, and then led the sheep toward it; and when each sheep went by it, he struck each sheep on the side. When the sheep gave birth, all, except for a few, of the lambs were colored.

On the other hand, Ibn Kathir said that Anas Ibn Malik said, "When Moses asked his companion (father-in-law) about the term of service agreed between them, he said to his companion, 'Every sheep which has birthed black goes to you.'" So Moses put a scarecrow above the water so that when the sheep saw it, they were frightened and subsequently gave birth to colored sheep, except for one. So Moses took all of the newborn sheep that year except one, *and Allah knows best.*

I would like to respond to this error and report the original and true account from the Bible. First of all, I personally believe that Mohammed and his scholars, as they usually did, confused and blended many stories of the Bible together. In this portion, Mohammed mixed the story of Jacob, son of Isaac, son of Abraham, with Moses in different portions. For example, Jacob worked for the marriage of his wife, not Moses. See Genesis 29:15 and 18: **[15]Then Laban said to Jacob, "Because you are my relative, should you therefore serve me for nothing? Tell me, what should your wages be?" ... [18]Now Jacob loved Rachel; so he said, "I will serve you seven years for Rachel your younger daughter."** As for Moses' case, there was no such thing as him working for years to marry his wife.

---

[27]Ibid., 284-285.

The Revelation of Error

Moses lived with his father-in-law for forty years, not eight or ten years as Mohammed and Gabreel claimed. As it is written in Exodus 2:20-21: *[20]So he said to his daughters, "And where is he? Why is it that you have left the man? Call him, that he may eat bread. [21]Then Moses was content to live with the man, and he gave Zipporah his daughter to Moses."*

Another example of the inaccuracy between Jacob's story and Moses' story was in the number of sisters. Laban, the father-in-law of Jacob, had two daughters, Leah and Rachel, as seen in Genesis 29:16: *[16]Now Laban had two daughters: the name of the elder was Leah, and the name of the younger was Rachel.* The father-in-law of Moses had seven daughters as recorded in Exodus 2:16: *"Now the priest of Midian had seven daughters. And they came and drew water, and they filled the troughs to water their father's flock."*

Another error was with the removal of the rock from the mouth of the well. In the story of Jacob, the rock exists, as written in Genesis 29:2-3: *[2]And he looked, and saw a well in the field; and behold, there were three flocks of sheep lying by it; for out of that well they watered the flocks. A large stone was on the well's mouth. [3]Now all the flocks would be gathered there; and they would roll the stone from the well's mouth, water the sheep, and put the stone back in its place on the well's mouth."*

In the story of Moses, however, there is no such rock to be removed. See Exodus 2:17: *[17]Then the shepherds came and drove them away; but Moses stood up and helped them, and watered their flock.* The problem in Moses' case was that other shepherds had driven away the daughters of the priest of Midian, not that a heavy rock was blocking the well.

One last error pertains to the sheep and their color. Moses did not require sheep from his father-in-law, nor did he take any sheep with him to Egypt as recorded in Exodus 4:20: *[20]Then Moses took his wife and his sons and set them on a donkey, and he returned to the land of Egypt. And Moses took the rod of God in his hand.* Therefore, there was no reason for Moses to manipulate the female sheep to cause them to give birth to lambs of different colors in order for him to acquire more of them for himself. However, these details are found in the story of Jacob. We encourage the reader to read Genesis 30 and 31 for the details.

For the sake of brevity, see Genesis 30:32, 38: *[32]Let me pass through all your flock today, removing from there all the speckled*

and spotted sheep, and all the brown ones among the lambs, and the spotted and speckled among the goats; and these shall be my wages.... [38] And the rods which he had peeled, he set before the flocks in the gutters, in the watering troughs where the flocks came to drink, so that they should conceive when they came to drink.
Therefore, when Jacob left his father-in-law, Laban, he took all of his goods as recorded in Genesis 31:18, but Moses did not take anything as mentioned above.

Perhaps the error with the sheep can be explained with the timing of God's call to Moses to go to Egypt through the experience with the burning bush. In the Bible, God called Moses while he was shepherding his father-in-law's sheep. None of his family was with him. However, in the Qur'an the experience of the burning bush occurred after Moses decided to leave his father-in-law to go with his wife and all his goods to visit his family, whom he missed, in Egypt. This is also in the interpretation of Muslim scholars.

The preceding comparison of the Qur'an stories of Moses and Jacob reveals the errors perpetuated by Islam. Now I would like to give the details of the original account of Moses from the Bible, beginning with events after he escaped from Egypt to the land of Midian.

First, according to the Bible it is the *land* of Midian, not a *city* as indicated in the interpretations of Muslim scholars as Ibn Kathir stated.[28] The first mention of this land is in Exodus 2:15: **[15] *When Pharaoh heard of this matter, he sought to kill Moses. But Moses fled from the face of Pharaoh and dwelt in the land of Midian; and he sat down by a well.***

As previously stated, in Exodus 2:16-17, the priest of Midian had seven daughters, and they had drawn their own water to give to their father's sheep. There was no rock to be moved as Mohammed claimed. The role of Moses was very clear. He delivered the daughters from the other shepherds who had driven them away.

If Muslims wish to understand the details of the story of Moses, they must read the biblical account. Again, as just stated in Exodus 2:20-21, Moses went and ate bread with his future father-in-law and married his daughter Zipporah. Exodus 2:22-23 tells of the birth of their son, Gershom, whom Moses so named because he said that "I

---

[28]Ibid., 280.

The Revelation of Error

have been a stranger in a foreign land." During this time the king of Egypt died, and the Children of Israel groaned under bondage to the Egyptians.

We again find the wife's name, Zipporah, as well as the first son's name, Gershom, and now the second son's name, Eliezer, along with the meaning of their names in Exodus 18:2-4. As just given above, Gershom means *I have been a stranger in a foreign land*, and Eliezer's name means *the God of my father was my help, and delivered me from the sword of Pharaoh.*

<u>The Experience of the Burning Bush</u>

According to Qur'an 28:29-32: [29]*So when Moses had fulfilled the term and departed with his family, he saw a fire on the mountainside. He said to his family, "<u>Stay, surely I see a fire. Perhaps I may bring you news from it or a brand from the fire, perhaps you will be warmed.</u>"* [30]*So when he came to it, he was called from the right side of the valley in the blessed spot from the tree: "That, O Moses, surely I am Allah, the lord of the worlds.* [31]*And throw down your rod." So when he saw it shake as if it were a jinn, he turned away and fled and did not return. "O Moses, come and do not be afraid, surely you are of the faithful.* [32]*Insert your hand into your pocket. It will come out white, without evil, and fold your wings toward you from the fear. So these are two proofs from your lord to Pharaoh and his leaders. Surely they were a transgressing people."*

Mohammed stated that after Moses completed the term of the agreement of the years of work, he took his family and went to Egypt. While they were on their way, on a dark and cold winter's night, as stated by Ibn Kathir, they got lost.[29] It was there on the right side of the west mountain that Moses saw the burning bush. He asked his family to sit there and wait while he went to investigate as to how he could find his way back to Egypt.

This incident is also described elsewhere in the Qur'an in 20:9-10: [9]*And have the sayings of Moses come to you?* [10]*When he saw a fire, so he said to his family, "<u>Stay, surely I perceive a fire. Perhaps I may bring you a lighted torch from it or find guidance at the fire.</u>"* Also, in Qur'an 27:7: [7]*When Moses said to*

---

[29] Ibid., 286.

his family, "Surely I have perceived a fire. I will bring you news from it, or I will bring you a blazing brand, perhaps you warm yourselves."

The wording of Moses' quotation in the three preceding passages is similar, and the differences would probably not be significant to the Western reader. It is important to point this out to the Muslim readers because they insist that one of the proofs that the Bible is corrupted is that minor variations appear in the wording of Jesus' or others' sayings in the Gospels. In other words, they are not all written exactly the same by the author of each Gospel. In the preceding case, the same quotation of Moses regarding the same incident is recorded three different ways despite the fact that they claim to have been communicated by one angel, Gabreel, to one man, Mohammed.

Now we ask a question. *What is the true account according to the Bible?* When we read Exodus 3, we discover that Moses was actually not yet on his way to Egypt when he was confronted by the burning bush. Rather, he was shepherding sheep for his father-in-law, and his family was not with him. There is no evidence to indicate that it was either a cold or a dark night or even that he was lost. Moses had been doing this work for forty years and was well familiar with the area in which he shepherded the sheep.

Also, the pronouncement of Allah is quoted differently in various locations. Qur'an 28:30-31a states: ^{30}So when he came to it, he was called from the right side of the valley in the blessed spot from the tree: "That, O Moses, surely I am Allah, the lord of the worlds. ^{31}And throw down your rod." ...

Qur'an 20:11b-18a says: ^{11}So when he came to it, he was called, ..."O Moses, ^{12}surely I am your lord. So take off your sandals. Surely you are in the holy valley of Tuwa. ^{13}And I have chosen you, so hear what will be revealed. ^{14}Surely I am Allah; there is no god except me, so serve me and perform the prayer for my remembrance. ^{15}Surely the hour is coming. I almost hid it, that every soul may be rewarded for what it strives. ^{16}So do not let those who do not believe prevent you from it and follow his desire so that you should perish. ^{17}And what is that in your right hand, O Moses?" ^{18}He said, "It is my rod which I lean on..."

Then Qur'an 27:8-10a says: ^{8}So when he came to it, he was called, "Blessed is he who is in the fire and those who surround *it, and praise be to Allah, the lord of the worlds. ⁹O Moses, surely I am Allah, the dear, the wise. ¹⁰And throw down your rod!"* ... We must ask another question. *Which of the previous quotations is actually what Allah spoke to Moses?* No Muslim can see these errors for two reasons. First, the Qur'an does not allow them to ask questions since the infallibility of Mohammed and the Qur'an is a basic tenet of Islam. Second, Muslims do not study the Qur'an to compare passages or perform any critical analysis.

Another error is in Ibn Kathir's statement "that according to the People of the Book (Jews and Christians) that Moses put his hand on his face because of the intensity of the light (coming out of the burning bush) and because of his fear of losing his sight. Then Allah spoke to him..."[30] However, when we read the Bible's account, we see no reference to Moses putting his hand on his face. The Bible, in fact, only states in Exodus 3:6 that he **hid his face,** and this was because he was afraid to look at God, not because of the intensity of the light from the burning bush.

I wish to challenge Muslims to read the Qur'an with the same level of examination they put into criticizing the Bible. For the full story of Moses and the burning bush, we look to Exodus 3 and 4. Here, we will only focus on key parts of the story in order to illustrate the error in the Qur'an.

Concerning the name of the mountain, Ibn Kathir says that the holy valley from which Allah called out to Moses was Tuwa.[31] However, when we compare this to Exodus 3:1, we see that Moses was not in a valley but rather on the mountain of God called Horeb: **¹Now Moses was tending the flock of Jethro his father-in-law, the priest of Midian. And he led the flock to the back of the desert, and came to Horeb, the mountain of God.**

Notice also the core of God's message to Moses is that he must go to his people, the Israelites, and lead them out of Egypt, for God has seen the conflict and heard the cry of the Israelites. The call was for Moses to take the Israelites out of Egypt and into the Promised Land which was full of milk and honey. This was the land which God promised Abraham, for the time had come for God to fulfill his promise because the sins of the original people of the land had reached full measure. (See Genesis 15.)

---

[30] Ibid., 280.
[31] Ibid., 287.

God told Moses that Pharaoh initially would not allow them to leave Egypt, but the punishment on Pharaoh and his land would be severe. Then Pharaoh would let them go, and they would not leave Egypt with empty hands but with riches of silver, gold, and clothes. This can all be found in Exodus 3.

Before we continue with the remainder of the story of Moses, I would like to point out, as you read the story in different portions of the Qur'an, for example Qur'an 20, 27, and 28, you will find many inconsistencies in the story. A side-by-side comparison might cause you to think there were different writers with different opinions of what took place in the life of Moses. For the sake of time and space, I will only highlight the portions with the most significant errors in the story of Moses. I encourage you to go back to the Qur'an and discover the numerous discrepancies for yourself.

Moses and Aaron

As we have previously covered from the Qur'an and the interpreters' versions of Moses' trip to Egypt, Moses had completed his years of work for his father-in-law and was on his way when he encountered Allah at the burning bush. When we read the following verses in Qur'an 28:33-35, we discover that there are four contradictions: *[33]He said, "My lord, surely I have killed a soul among them, so I fear they might kill me. [34]And my brother Aaron is more eloquent in speech than I. So send him with me as an assistant to affirm me. Surely I am afraid that they will deny me." [35]He said, "We will strengthen your arm with your brother, and we will give authority to both of you so that they will not reach to you. With our signs, both of you and whoever follows you are the victorious."* Ibn Kathir indicated that the response of Moses to Allah's command to go to Egypt was fear that the Egyptians might kill him since he had killed one of them.[32] Here is a question we must ask, which brings the first contradiction: *Why was Moses suddenly afraid to go to Egypt if he was already on his way there before Allah asked him to go to Egypt?* In Exodus 3 and 4, there is no mention of Moses being afraid to go back to Egypt as a result of killing one of the Egyptians.

This relates to the second contradiction that neither Mohammed nor his scholars had any idea of the actual length of time Moses had

---

[32]Ibid., 288.

The Revelation of Error

been away from Egypt and living in Midian before his return. They significantly compressed the timeline of events. However, in Acts 7:30 the Bible tells us: *[30]And when forty years had passed, an Angel of the Lord appeared to him in a flame of fire in a bush, in the wilderness of Mount Sinai.* This is supported by Exodus 7:7 which reveals that Moses was fourscore or eighty years old when he spoke to Pharaoh.

Third, Mohammed and his scholars believed that the same Pharaoh was ruling Egypt upon Moses' return as the one who was there when Moses fled Egypt. We find these words in Qur'an 26:18-19: *[18]He said, "Did we not see you as a child among us, and you stayed among us many years of your life? [19]And you did your act which you did, and you are of the infidels."* In his interpretation of these verses, Ibn Kathir said, "This proves that the Pharaoh which Allah sent Moses to was the same Pharaoh which Moses had fled from."[33] Additionally, we find these comments in Qur'an 26:22: *[22]And this is a grace that he has favored on me that has enslaved the children of Israel."*

Ibn Kathir explained this:
> Moses in his wording here shows appreciation to Pharaoh for his grace as he raised him and did good to him, but he reminded Pharaoh, 'You have done good to me as one Israelite man, but in exchange you have used the entirety of this great people and you have enslaved them in your work and your service.'[34]

This again shows that Mohammed and Ibn Kathir thought that the same Pharaoh still lived and ruled over Egypt when Moses returned. However, the Bible clearly says that not only Pharaoh but all those who wanted to kill Moses had died. In Exodus 4:19: *[19]Now the LORD said to Moses in Midian, "Go, return to Egypt; for all the men who sought your life are dead." [20]Then Moses took his wife and his sons and set them on a donkey, and he returned to the land of Egypt. And Moses took the rod of God in his hand.*

The fourth and final contradiction is revealed in the following question: *Did Moses ask Allah to send Aaron as a help to him as stated in Qur'an 28:34, or did God give Aaron to Moses after he asked God to send somebody else as indicated in Exodus 4:10-14?*

---

[33] Ibid., 289-290.
[34] Ibid., 290.

According to these verses, Moses said to the Lord that he was not an eloquent speaker but was instead slow of speech and tongue. Then the Lord reminded Moses Who had made man's mouth. The Lord told Moses to go and He would teach Moses what to say and He would be with him. Again Moses said to the Lord to send someone else. We see the response of the Lord in verse 14: *^{14}So the anger of the LORD was kindled against Moses, and He said: "Is not Aaron the Levite your brother? I know that he can speak well. And look, he is also coming out to meet you. When he sees you, he will be glad in his heart.*

I believe that the outcome of the communication with Pharaoh and the eventual exodus of the Israelites from Egypt had nothing to do with the eloquence of Aaron's speech, since it was God speaking through Aaron, not just the man Aaron. The Bible tells us in Exodus 4:15 that God will speak to Moses, Moses will speak to Aaron, and God will be with both: *^{15}Now you shall speak to him and put the words in his mouth. And I will be with your mouth and with his mouth, and I will teach you what you shall do."*

<u>Miracles (Signs) Proclaimed by Moses</u>

In Qur'an 20:17, Allah asks Moses from the fire, *^{17}And what is that in your right hand, O Moses?* This implies that Allah did not know what was in Moses' right hand. Let me ask a question here. *How many times did Allah ask questions in the Qur'an?* If Muslims knew, they would never denounce the Bible for errors every time God asks a question in the Bible, for many of the thousands of errors Muslims claim to be in the Bible occur when God simply asks questions. They maintain that Allah would not ask a question because he is "all knowing."

Let us look at Moses' answer to Allah's question in Qur'an 20:18: *^{18}He said, "It is my rod which I lean on and with which I beat by it^{35} to my sheep, and I have other uses for it."* According to Ibn Kathir's interpretation,^{36} Moses' statement to Allah was, "It is my rod, I lean on it, I depend on it in the case of walking; and when I feed my sheep, I shake the tree by it so the leaves may fall from it." Imam Malik stated that "the shaking of the tree causes the leaves and the fruit to fall, but it will not break the branches."

---

^{35}to bring leaves down from the tree for the sheep
^{36}http://quran.Al-islam.com/Page.aspx?pageid=221&BookID=11&Page =313, accessed November 27, 2011.

The Revelation of Error

As for the statement, "*I have other uses for it*," Miemon Ibn Mehran said that this rod brought light to Moses at night, and it used to shepherd the sheep for him when he slept. Miemon Ibn Mehran also said that when Moses stuck it in the ground, it became a tree to bring shade for him to sit under; these are some of the miraculous things. However, in the same sentence, Ibn Kathir denied this scholarly interpretation for he wrote that if this was true, then Moses should not have run away and feared it when the rod changed into a snake.

Some other scholars said this rod was the same rod which belonged to Adam, and others said this rod will be the animal which will come out on the day of resurrection. Ibn Abbas said, "Her name was Ma Sha Allah (whatever Allah will)." Ibn Kathir ended his interpretation with the statement, "*And Allah knows best* which of these interpretations is correct."

This question and its answer were not repeated in any other version of the story in the Qur'an when Allah commanded Moses to throw down his rod, although this story is repeated many times. After Moses threw his rod to the ground, it changed into a snake. Moses became afraid, but according to Mohammed's Qur'an, Allah gave differing orders in various locations to Moses as to how he should retrieve it. For example, in Qur'an 20:21 Allah said: *[21]He said, "Take it and fear not. We will restore it to the first state.* In Qur'an 27:10b Allah said: *"...O Moses, do not fear, surely the messengers will not fear in My presence..."* In Qur'an 28:31 Allah said: *[31]And throw down your rod." So when he saw it shake as if it were a jinn, he turned away and fled and did not return. "O Moses, come and do not be afraid, surely you are of the faithful."*

Again, the Muslim belief is that every word and letter in the Qur'an is accurate and infallible. *What did Allah actually say to Moses?* There cannot be three different versions of the same statement. We could go on and on with similar illustrations, such as the second miracle of Moses' hand being changed in Qur'an 20:22: *[22]And gather your hand to your wings,[37] it will come out white without evil as another sign.* And in Qur'an 27:12: *[12]And enter your hand into your pocket. It will come forth white, without evil, as one in nine signs to Pharaoh and his people, surely they*

---

[37] side

Chapter 16

were a transgressing people. Then in Qur'an 28:32: *³²Insert your hand into your pocket. It will come out white, without evil, and fold your wings toward you from the fear. So these are two proofs from your lord to Pharaoh and his leaders. Surely they were a transgressing people."* Ibn Kathir interpreted the condition of the hand of Moses: "That it became very bright like the moon in its whiteness without any evil; meaning without leprosy or any sickness."[38]

Exodus 4:6-7 contains this account: ***⁶Furthermore the LORD said to him, "Now put your hand in your bosom." And he put his hand in his bosom, and when he took it out, behold, his hand was leprous, like snow. ⁷And He said, "Put your hand in your bosom again." So he put his hand in his bosom again, and drew it out of his bosom, and behold, it was restored like his other flesh.***

According to the Bible, the hand had leprosy rather than a bright whiteness like the moon. Leprosy is a serious infectious disease that has been known since biblical times. It is characterized by disfiguring skin sores, nerve damage, and progressive debilitation.

Ibn Kathir continued by saying that these two miracles, meaning the miracle of the rod being changed into a snake and the miracle of the whiteness of the hand, were two of nine miracles serving as proof that Moses was sent by his lord to Pharaoh and his people. Five other miracles are written about in Qur'an 7:133: *¹³³So we sent on them the tūfān*[39] *and the locusts and the lice and the frogs and the blood, expounded signs, so they became proud. And they were a criminal people.*

Notice that we are still missing two of the so-called nine signs, as written in Qur'an 17:101-102: *¹⁰¹And indeed, we gave Moses nine clear signs. So ask the children of Israel when he came to them. So Pharaoh said to him, "Surely I think you are bewitched, O Moses." ¹⁰²He said, "Indeed, you know that nothing of those sent down except from the lord of the heavens and the earth as proof, and surely I think that you, O Pharaoh, are doomed."*

When you read these previous verses, you will discover that there were not actually nine miracles (which the Bible calls plagues) but only seven, and that is only when you add the white hand and the rod

---

[38] Ibn Kathir., 291.
[39] deluge, non-Arabic word of Hebrew/Syriac origin

becoming a snake to those mentioned in Qur'an 7:133. Notice that according to the Bible, there were not nine plagues but rather ten, and these ten do not include the hand, the rod, or the flood as Mohammed claimed in the previous verses.

When we read the story of Moses throughout the Qur'an, we will not find any other mention or explanation of the five signs or miracles listed in Qur'an 7:133. The flood, on one hand, was not mentioned outside of this verse throughout the Qur'an except in Noah's time which is known as Noah's Flood. As for those who may claim that Pharaoh and his army drowned in the flood, I would recommend to them to read the other stories in the Qur'an, for they do not say the word *tūfān*, but rather the word *allem*, which Muslims translate as *the sea* and at other times *river*.

How do Muslim scholars interpret the word tūfān? As usual, Muslim scholars disagree; this makes them appear foolish. For example, Ibn Kathir stated that Ibn Abbas said, "It is much rain which causes plants and fruit to be destroyed."[40] Al Dahak says, "It is lots of death." Mujahid says, "The water or disease, either one." Aisha said that Mohammed said, "It is the death." Yahya Ibn Yaman said, "It is a command of Allah to go around them, and he did it while they were asleep." Ibn Kathir ends his interpretation for Qur'an 7:133 by saying, "Tūfān is the water which covers the face of the earth and stays there to the point that the Egyptians could neither plow nor work the land for such a long time that they starved." Their difficulty in explaining this term possibly stems in part from the fact that tūfān is not an Arabic word; rather, it is of Hebrew/Syriac origin meaning *deluge*.

Mohammed and Muslim scholars did correctly identify some of the plagues, or miracles/signs as they were called, such as the lice. On the other hand, other so-called miracles mentioned, such as Moses' leprous hand and the rod which became a snake, are not among the ten plagues.

Therefore, all we can learn from the Qur'an so far was that there were only three plagues, but we cannot find anywhere in the Qur'an how these plagues happened, where they took place or when, in what order, or the reaction of Pharaoh or his people. Simply mentioning the names provides us no useful information. Add to that, these two miracles, the hand of Moses and the rod of Moses were used to prove to the Hebrews, not to Pharaoh, that Moses had met with the Lord as

---

[40]Ibn Kathir., 308.

written in Exodus 4:1-8. We will cover this in more detail when we study the ten plagues in the Bible.

Moses' Reunion with His Family

According to Ibn Kathir, after Moses was commanded by Allah to go to Pharaoh, he left the land of Midian and entered into his mother and brother's house in Egypt while they were eating dinner.[41] They were eating turnips, and Moses ate with them. One must say here that the amount of detailed information given by Ibn Kathir is laughable. *How did he know about the turnips since neither Allah nor Gabreel, who delivered Allah's Qur'an, appear to have known this detail?* Such improbable details will also be seen when we later discuss Moses and Aaron's meeting with Pharaoh.

According to the Bible, the meeting of Moses and Aaron did not take place at the mother's house over a dinner of turnips. Moreover, that scenario is made even more improbable since the mother would then have had to be over a hundred years old if she were still alive. Rather, they met at the mount of God as recorded in Exodus 4:27:
[27] And the LORD said to Aaron, "Go into the wilderness to meet Moses." So he went and met him on the mountain of God, and kissed him.

Moses and Aaron Meet with Pharaoh

Qur'an 20:40b-47 states: [40] *...Then you came as decreed, O Moses. [41] And I have made[42] you for myself. [42] Go, you and your brother, with my signs, and do not remember me less. [43] Go to Pharaoh, surely he has rebelled. [44] So [both] speak to him with gentle speech, perhaps he will remember or fear." [45] They said, "O our lord, surely we fear that he may exceed against us or he may rebel!" [46] He said, "Do not fear, surely I am with you. I hear and I see. [47] So you [both] go to him, so say, 'Surely we are messengers of your lord, so send with us the children of Israel, and do not torment them. Indeed, we have brought you a sign from your lord, and the peace is on who follows the guidance.'"*

The conversation above occurred between Moses and Allah after Moses had spent an unspecified number of years in Midian. Muslim scholars are in disagreement over the number of years. Some said the

---
[41] Ibid., 293.
[42] chosen

number was ten years, which is the length of Moses' dowry agreement with his father-in-law; others said it was twenty-eight years, when he worked ten years as a dowry and then eighteen more years until the birth of his son. *First, how did they come up with these years?* Second, they are obviously wrong as the Bible reveals in Acts 7:30 that it was forty years. This is supported by Exodus 7:7 which reveals that Moses was fourscore or eighty years old when he spoke to Pharaoh.

Ibn Kathir interpreted the previous verses by saying that Allah has chosen Moses and his brother to deliver his message, taking the great miracle as proof of their message.[43] Ibn Kathir said that Al Hasan said that he asked them to speak gently to Pharaoh, offering him the choice between (being a) god or the appointment (judgment) and that between his hands are the garden and the fire.[44] Ibn Kathir also explained that Pharaoh was mighty, aggressive, and a demon.[45] That is why Moses and Aaron were afraid to go and speak to him, but Allah strengthened them, asking them, as it is written in Qur'an 20:47, to send the Children of Israel with them and not to torment them as they took the signs of their lord with them as the great proof.

Ibn Kathir wrote: "Moses said to Aaron, 'Allah commands me and commands you to go to Pharaoh to invite him to serve Allah. So come with me.' They then went to the door of Pharaoh and behold the door was closed. And Moses said to the guardians of the door, 'Know that the messenger of Allah is at the door.' So they mocked and laughed at him."[46]

Some said that they were not given permission to enter the door until after a long wait. Mohammed Ibn Isaac said that they were given permission after two years, for no one had the boldness to ask permission for them, *and Allah knows best*. It was also said that Moses drew near the door and knocked at the door with his rod, so Pharaoh became very irritated and commanded them to enter. They stood before him and invited him to Allah as Allah had commanded.

This is in total disagreement with the Bible. In Exodus 4:29-31, Moses met with Aaron and then gathered the elders of the Israelites; he performed miracles before the people who believed in him and rejoiced, for God saw their affliction. They then bowed down and

---

[43]Ibn Kathir., 292.
[44]Ibid., 293.
[45]Ibid.
[46]Ibid.

worshiped God. In Exodus 5:1, the Bible records: *¹Afterward Moses and Aaron went in and told Pharaoh, "Thus says the LORD God of Israel: 'Let My people go, that they may hold a feast to Me in the wilderness.'"* Notice that Moses and Aaron did not invite Pharaoh to believe in God or to worship Him. That was not their mission. They were sent to ask Pharaoh to let the Israelites go worship God in the wilderness.

Let us go back to the story according to the Qur'an and Muslim scholars to see the details of the meeting between Pharaoh and Moses. Although the story is mentioned in many places throughout the Qur'an, with many inconsistencies, we will confine our attention to just two of these repeated stories which can be found in Qur'an 7 and Qur'an 26. Because of the many inconsistencies, we have chosen to place them in a side-by-side format to allow the reader to better visualize them.

Qur'an 7	Qur'an 26
¹⁰⁷So he threw down his rod. So behold, it became an obvious serpent. ¹⁰⁸And he drew out his hand. So behold, it was white to the onlookers. ¹⁰⁹<u>The leaders from the people of Pharaoh said</u>, "Surely this is a knowing sorcerer. ¹¹⁰He desires to get you out of your land, so what will you command?" ¹¹¹They said, "Delay him and his brother, and send gatherers into the cities. ¹¹²They will bring every knowing sorcerer to you."	³²So he threw down his rod, so behold, it is an obvious serpent. ³³And he drew out his hand, so behold, it was white to the onlookers. ³⁴<u>He said to the leaders around him</u>, "Surely this is a knowing sorcerer. ³⁵He desires to get you out of your land with his sorcery. So what do you command?" ³⁶They said, "Put him and his brother off for awhile, and send gatherers into the cities. ³⁷They will bring every knowing sorcerer to you."

Notice that the reading of these two portions of revelation is almost the same up to this point. The key difference is between Qur'an 7:109 and Qur'an 26:34. In the first case, the leaders of the people are speaking. In the second, it is Pharaoh who is speaking the words to the leaders. One must ask some questions. *Who actually said this statement, Pharaoh or the leaders? Or was it Pharaoh to his leaders?*

Additionally, what is meant by the statement *"He desires to get you out of your land..."?* According to the Bible, Moses was asking permission to take his people out of Egypt, not to displace the Egyptians from Egypt. We will discuss this discrepancy in more detail later.

Qur'an 7	Qur'an 26
[113]And the sorcerers came [to] Pharaoh. They said, "Surely we will have a wage if we were the victors." [114]He said, "Yes, and surely you will be of the nearer." [115]<u>They said, "O Moses, either you cast, or we will be those who cast."</u> [116]He said, "You cast." So when they cast, they bewitched the people's eyes and made them afraid, and they brought a great sorcery.	[38]So the sorcerers were <u>gathered on an appointed, known day</u>. [39]And it was said to the people, "Are you gathered? [40]Perhaps we will follow the sorcerers if they were the victors." [41]So when the sorcerers came, they said to Pharaoh, "Will we have our wage if we are the victors?" [42]He said, "Yes, and surely then you will become of the nearer." [43]<u>Moses said to them, "Cast down what you are casting."</u> [44]So they cast down their ropes and rods, and they said, "[We swear] by Pharaoh's might we will surely be the victors."

There is no mention in Qur'an 7 of the *appointed, known day* cited in Qur'an 26. In Qur'an 7:115 the sorcerers offer Moses the option of deciding who casts first, but in Qur'an 26:43 Moses takes the initiative, telling the sorcerers to cast their ropes and rods first. Even so, both versions are in conflict with the Bible. Exodus 7:10-11 reveals that it was actually Aaron who cast down his rod, not Moses. Exodus 7:10 states: [10]***So Moses and Aaron went in to Pharaoh, and they did so, just as the LORD commanded. And Aaron cast down his rod before Pharaoh and before his servants, and it became a serpent.*** It was after this that Pharaoh commanded the sorcerers to cast their enchantments. [11]***But Pharaoh also called the wise men and the sorcerers; so the magicians of Egypt, they also did in like manner with their enchantments.***

An item of disagreement among Muslim scholars is found in Ibn Kathir's book.[47] The number of the sorcerers whom Pharaoh gathered from throughout this country full of sorcerers was a multitude. It was said by Mohammed Ibn Kaab that there were eighty thousand sorcerers. Al Kasam Ibn Abu Bardah said that there were seventy thousand sorcerers. Al Saddi said there were thirty thousand plus. Abu Imamh said there were nineteen thousand. Mohammed Ibn Isaac said fifteen thousand. Kaab Al Ahbar said twelve thousand. Ibn Abbas said there were seventy men; and, elsewhere, that there were also forty Israelite young men whom Pharaoh had commanded to go to his sorcerers to learn sorcery from them. Ibn Abbas also said that Pharaoh, his leaders of his country, and the people of his city were all gathered to attend this great event, so they all came out as they (Pharaoh's people) said in Qur'an 26:40. Notice the numbers ranged from eighty thousand to forty sorcerers. This cast serious doubt on the scholarship and reliability of Muslim scholars.

Qur'an 7	Qur'an 26
[117]<u>And we revealed to Moses, "That cast your rod.</u>" So behold, it pecks what they fabricate. [118]So the truth was vindicated, and vain was what they were doing. [119]So they were defeated thereupon, and they were turned away humiliated. [120]And the sorcerers fell down worshiping. [121]They said, "We believed in the lord of the worlds, [122]the lord of Moses and Aaron." [123]Pharaoh said, "Have you believed in him before I give you permission? <u>Surely, this is a deception you have deceived in the city so that you may get its people out of it</u>, so you will know. [124]I will surely cut off your hands and legs on opposite sides. Then I will crucify you, all of you."	[45]<u>So Moses threw down his rod</u>, so behold, it pecks what they fabricate. [46]So the sorcerers fell down worshiping. [47]They said, "We believed in the lord of the worlds, [48]the lord of Moses and Aaron." [49]He said, "Have you believed on him before I gave you permission? <u>Surely he is your biggest who has taught you the sorcery</u>. So surely you will know I will cut off your hands and legs on opposite sides, and I will crucify you, all of you."

---

[47]Ibn Kathir, 295-296.

The Revelation of Error

In Qur'an 7:117 Allah revealed to Moses to cast his rod. In Qur'an 26:45 Moses took the initiative himself to throw down the rod. Both passages contradict the true account in the Bible. In Exodus 7:10 it was Aaron, and not Moses, who cast down his rod at the Lord's command. Although Qur'an 7 and 26 agree that the sorcerers became believers in and worshiped the lord of Moses and Aaron, they are both in conflict with Qur'an 10:83: *[83]So no one believed to Moses except an offspring from his people because of fear of Pharaoh and his leaders, lest he should seduce them....*

The Bible makes no mention of any sorcerers believing, but it does reveal that Pharaoh's heart was hardened. Exodus 7:12-13 says: **[12]For every man threw down his rod, and they became serpents. But Aaron's rod swallowed up their rods. [13]And Pharaoh's heart grew hard, and he did not heed them, as the LORD had said.**

Notice the difference in Pharaoh's comments between Qur'an 7:123 and Qur'an 26:49. In the first instance, Pharaoh accuses his sorcerers of deception to get the Egyptians out of the city. In the second, he states that Moses has taught the sorcerers the sorcery.

Qur'an 7	Qur'an 26
[125]They said, "Surely to our lord we will return. [126]And you do not take revenge on us, except because we believed on the signs of our lord when they came to us: 'Our lord, pour out patience on us and cause us to die Muslims.'" [127]And the leaders from the people of Pharaoh said, "Will you let Moses and his people to vandalize in the land and desert you and your gods?" He said, "We will kill their sons and spare their women, and surely we are dominant over them." [128]Moses said to his people, "Seek assistance with Allah and be patient, surely	*[50]They said, "It cannot harm us, surely we will return to our lord. [51]Surely we hope that our lord will forgive us of our sins, that we were the first of the believers." [52]And we revealed to Moses: "That go forth by night with my servants, surely you will be followed." [53]So Pharaoh sent to the cities gathering: [54]"Surely they are a small group. [55]And surely they are enraging us. [56]And surely we must be on guard together." [57]So we got them out of gardens and springs [58]and treasures and generous dwellings, [59]likewise, and we bequeathed it to the children of*

the earth is Allah's; he will bequeath it to whom he wills of his servants and the end to the fearer."	Israel. ⁶⁰So they followed them at sunrise.

Let us continue with the comparison in these two portions of revelation of the reactions of the sorcerers in the story. Notice that there is another inconsistency here. In 7:125 the sayings of the sorcerers do not match at all with the other passage. When one reads both passages, he will not realize that he is reading the same story. He will naturally assume these are two different stories. The bigger problem is, I believe, that Mohammed lost the main purpose of why Moses was sent to Pharaoh. As written in the pages of the Qur'an, we see that Mohammed assumed that Moses' goal was to conquer the land of Egypt and kick its people out. That is the opposite of what God and Moses' mission was. He was sent to Pharaoh to take his people out of Egypt and to the Promised Land, the land of Canaan. Egyptian people did not leave the land of Egypt, until 641 AD when Muslims invaded it; and Egyptian Christians there still live under persecution by Muslims.

In Qur'an 7:129: *¹²⁹They said, "We have been oppressed before you came to us and after you came to us." He said, "Perhaps your lord will destroy your enemy and will make you his viceroys in the land. So he will see how you do."* Ibn Kathir interpreted this verse by stating that even if the Egyptians begin to destroy Moses' people, they were to seek refuge from their lord and be patient; so if Moses' people become a fearing one, they will have the good end.[48]

The Plagues

The Qur'an does not mention the word plagues, but instead Mohammed uses the word *ayat* which means *signs* or *miracles*. The funny thing was that he describes them as a way for Pharaoh and his people to believe in Allah, not to punish Pharaoh, and force him to release the Children of Israel from slavery so that they could go to the Promised Land. The true number of plagues in the Bible is ten, and

---
[48]Ibn Kathir, 301.

The Revelation of Error

we will list them. As we stated previously, Mohammed only mentions five (Qur'an 7:130-133).

Let's first look at what is written concerning the plagues in the Qur'an. *[130]And indeed, we seized the family of Pharaoh with the years and less of the fruit, perhaps they may remember. [131]So when good fortune came to them, they said, "This is for us." And if evil befell them, they take Moses and who is with him as a bad omen. But surely their bird[49] is only with Allah, but most of them do not know. [132]And they said, "Whatever signs you bring us to bewitch us, we will not believe in you." [133]So we sent on them the tūfān[50] and the locusts and the lice and the frogs and the blood, expounded signs, so they became proud. And they were a criminal people.* Ibn Kathir stated that Allah has punished Pharaoh and his people for many years when they could not plant the land and had no fruit from the trees, but they did not learn any lessons from this punishment.[51] They continued to be disobedient and to be infidels. Then Ibn Kathir was confused about who Allah was talking to or who was receiving the punishment. "As it is written, when the good comes, they said this is for us; and if the evil befall them, they take Moses and who is with him as a bad omen."

Who are the ones who did plant and harvest the seed—the Egyptians or the Hebrews? If it was the Egyptians, why did they complain to Moses? And, if it was the Hebrews, why did Allah punish them with the plagues? Then, in verse 133, Allah continues to speak of the following plagues, which he had sent on the Egyptians as a proof of the continuation of the punishment on them, not the Hebrews who lived in the land.

As for mentioning the flood as one of the plagues, obviously Mohammed was confused between the flood of Noah and the story of Moses and Pharaoh. (See Genesis 7.) The ten plagues did not include a flood. (See Exodus 7:20-12:30.)

<u>The Reaction to the Plagues</u>

In Qur'an 7:134-135: *[134]And when the wrath fell on them, they said, "O Moses, call for us to your lord, according to that which he has covenanted with you. Surely, if you will take the*

---

[49] evil omen
[50] deluge, non-Arabic word of Hebrew/Syriac origin
[51] Ibn Kathir, 307.

scourge off of us, then we will surely believe you, and we will surely send the children of Israel with you." ^{135}So when we lifted the wrath from them for a period which they reached, behold, they broke [their oath]. Ibn Kathir meant that in the Qur'an Allah told us, concerning the infidels, that they continued to live in error, foolishness, and pride for not following the messenger of Allah and believing his great signs, even though they saw them with their own eyes and made it as evidence and proof.[52] Every time they saw one of these signs, they swore to Moses; if he removed such punishment, they would believe in him and send with him his people. However, after the sign was removed, they turned away from the truth. *Once again, we ask: Was it a series of signs or was it punishment?*

Then Allah sent on them another sign, which was much stronger than the preceding one. The cycle repeated itself over and over. Ibn Kathir went on and on through other passages in the Qur'an which ended with the same message.[53] In the following verse, Qur'an 7:137, the Qur'an states that the Children of Israel inherited the land of Egypt, not the Promised Land: *^{137}And we bequeathed to the people who were weakened the eastern and the western lands, which we had blessed; and the good word of your lord was fulfilled on the children of Israel because of their patience, and we destroyed what Pharaoh and his people were making and what they were building.* This scene is also repeated throughout the Qur'an.

The Ten Plagues

Now let's look at the actual ten plagues as documented in Exodus 7-11. In reviewing the plagues we will consider their relevance to the people of Egypt, their environment, and their gods.[54]

---

[52]Ibid., 309.
[53]Ibid., 310.
[54]See also http://en.wikipedia.org/wiki/Egyptiangods, accessed September 2, 2011.

The Revelation of Error

1. Water to Blood	Exodus 7:19: *¹⁹Then the LORD spoke to Moses, "Say to Aaron, 'Take your rod and stretch out your hand over the waters of Egypt, over their streams, over their rivers, over their ponds, and over all their pools of water, that they may become blood. And there shall be blood throughout all the land of Egypt, both in buckets of wood and pitchers of stone.'" ²⁰And Moses and Aaron did so, just as the LORD commanded. So he lifted up the rod and struck the waters that were in the river, in the sight of Pharaoh and in the sight of his servants. And all the waters that were in the river were turned to blood.*

At the very beginning of Egyptian history, the two parts of Egypt, Upper and Lower, were united as one, and Pharaoh was represented as the god of all Egypt. Of course, he was not the only god. Over the centuries, the priests and the Pharaohs invented all sorts of gods from objects of nature. Among them were animals, fish, and insects, but one of the most important was the Nile River.

The Nile was the very lifeline of Egypt, a long snake of a river along which all life existed. One can today literally step out of green, irrigated fields into the desert, but it was not always so. During the earliest Egyptian dynasties (shortly after the Flood), much of Lower Egypt was covered by water and the surrounding deserts were lush pastures with people living in them. In fact, the Nile valley was a jungle. Herodotus reported that priests told him that in earliest times there was no delta, and the coastline of the sea was near where Cairo is today. Since there had not been time for a delta to form in those early days, the Nile evidently had not been flowing for a long period of time after the great Flood. Since then, the climate has become increasingly dry, the land has dried up, and the Nile has become the source of life for Egypt. It was certainly this way by the time of the Exodus. In fact, by then the Nile had come to be revered in many ways by the Egyptians.

The Nile River was changed to blood. This plague was against the god Hapi, spirit of the Nile in flood and "giver of life to all men." The annual inundation was called "the arrival of Hapi."[55] The Nile water

---

[55]Carolyn Seawright, "Hapi, God of the Nile, Fertility, the North and South," *Thekeep.org,* August 21, 2001, accessed September 23, 2011,

was the transformed life-blood of Osiris. The fact that the Nile turned into blood, which was abominable to the Egyptians, was a direct affront to one of their chief gods. Although the fish goddess was Hatmeyt, all the fish in the Nile River died!

The Egyptians worshiped many gods who were each associated with different aspects of their lives. The Pharaohs were believed to be gods who were descended from gods. As we continue through the plagues, we will see that many of the plagues of the Exodus were directed against the gods of Egypt.

2. Frogs	Exodus 8:2-6: *²But if you refuse to let them go, behold, I will smite all your territory with frogs. ³So the river shall bring forth frogs abundantly, which shall go up and come into your house, into your bedroom, on your bed, into the houses of your servants, on your people, into your ovens, and into your kneading bowls. ⁴And the frogs shall come up on you, on your people, and on all your servants. ⁵Then the LORD spoke to Moses, "Say to Aaron, 'Stretch out your hand with your rod over the streams, over the rivers, and over the ponds, and cause frogs to come up on the land of Egypt.'" ⁶So Aaron stretched out his hand over the waters of Egypt, and the frogs came up and covered the land of Egypt.*

The land was filled with them so that they became objects of loathing. The frog-headed goddess, Hekt,[56] played a part in "creation." Hers was one of the oldest fertility cults in Egypt, but she could not control the fertility of these frogs! Through this plague they became a stench to the Egyptians.

---

http://www.thekeep.org/~kunoichi/kunoichi/themestream/hapi.html.
[56]Frank Alcamo, "Ten Egyptian Plagues For Ten Egyptian Gods and Goddesses," 2006, accessed September 28, 2011, http://www.freewebs.com/fjalcamo/tenplagues.htm.

3. Gnats or Lice	Exodus 8:16-17: *¹⁶So the LORD said to Moses, "Say to Aaron, 'Stretch out your rod, and strike the dust of the land, so that it may become lice throughout all the land of Egypt.'" ¹⁷And they did so. For Aaron stretched out his hand with his rod and struck the dust of the earth, and it became lice on man and beast. All the dust of the land became lice throughout all the land of Egypt.*
Some English editions of Scripture translate the Hebrew word kinim **as "gnats"; however, the root of this word implies a "fastening" insect. Strong's Concordance lists this alternatively as "lice."**[57]	

This plague was a direct affront to Thoth, at one time considered the god of magic.[58] Moreover, the Egyptian magicians, who were held in great awe, were unable to duplicate this plague. Helpless in the face of this challenge, they attributed the plague to "*the finger of God*" (Exodus 8:19), and they withdrew.

4. Flies or Swarms	Exodus 8:*21:* *²¹Or else, if you will not let My people go, behold, I will send swarms of flies on you and your servants, on your people and into your houses. The houses of the Egyptians shall be full of swarms of flies, and also the ground on which they stand.*
The more literal translation of the Hebrew word "'arob" is "swarms" although there is a general agreement that the plague consisted of stinging flies coming in a swarm.[59]	

Although it is not clear which insect the Hebrew word *'arob* refers to, this plague may have been against Khepri,[60] a scarab-headed god regarded as a manifestation of Atum or Ra.[61] It was supposed to

---

[57] James Strong, *The New Strong's Exhaustive Concordance of the Bible*, s.v. "kinim," (Nashville: Harper Collins, 1990).

[58] "What Egyptian Gods Were the Ten Plagues by God Attacking?" *Wiki.answers.com*, accessed January 4, 2012, http://wiki.answers/Q/What_Egyptian_gods_were_the_ten_plagues_by_God_attacking.

[59] *The Broadman Bible Commentary*, vol. 1, ed. Clifton J. Allen (Nashville: Broadman Press, 1969), 355-356.

[60] "Egyptian Gods: Khepri," *Egyptian Gods and Goddesses*, accessed February 7, 2012, http://egyptian-gods.org/egyptian-gods-khepri/.

[61] "The Egyptian Scarab Beetle God Khepri," accessed January 4, 2012, http://www.egyptian-scarabs.co.uk/khepri.htm.

be the god of the resurrection, perhaps because the dung ball it rolled around, and in which it laid its eggs, produced a new creation. Priests wore scarabs as charms.

5. Livestock Diseased (Pestilence)	Exodus 9:3: *³Behold, the hand of the LORD will be on your cattle in the field, on the horses, on the donkeys, on the camels, on the oxen, and on the sheep—a very severe pestilence.*

Murrain or Anthrax (Exodus 9:1-7): This judgment was against the bull god (which appeared in Egyptian writings as far back as the First Dynasty)[62] and the sacred cattle of Hathor,[63] the cow-headed love goddess. It was a special reproach to Pharaoh who worshiped Hathor, whose name means "house of Horus." Other gods associated with cattle were Ptah and Amon.

Great cemeteries of embalmed cattle have been excavated. The symbol of the bull was the symbol of Pharaoh himself. In the "Hymn to Amon,"[64] *it is difficult to distinguish the Pharaoh from the bull.* The title is "Adoration of Amunre (Amon-Ra), Bull of Heliopolis, chief of all gods, the good god, the beloved, who giveth life to all that is warm, and to every good herd."

6. Boils	Exodus 9:8-10: *⁸So the LORD said to Moses and Aaron, "Take for yourselves handfuls of ashes from a furnace, and let Moses scatter it toward the heavens in the sight of Pharaoh. ⁹And it will become fine dust in all the land of Egypt, and it will cause boils that break out in sores on man and beast throughout all the land of Egypt." ¹⁰Then they took ashes from the furnace and stood before Pharaoh, and Moses scattered them toward heaven. And they caused boils that break out in sores on man and beast.*

---

[62]Anita Stratos, "Divine Cults of the Sacred Bulls," *TourEgypt.net*, accessed January 24, 2012, http://www.touregypt.net/featurestories/bull.htm.

[63]Carolyn Seawright, "Hathor," *Wikipedia*, accessed January 24, 2012, http://en.wikipedia.org/wiki/Hathor.

[64]Wim van den Dungen, "Amun, the God: Hidden One and Millions," *Sophiatopia.org*, last updated April 12, 2010, accessed January 24, 2012, http://www.maat.sofiatopia.org/amun.htm.

The Revelation of Error

Boils (Exodus 9:8-12): This plague was against the god of healing, ImHotep,[65] an outstanding nobleman of the Old Kingdom, believed to be founder of ancient Egyptian medicine, who came to be considered a god and descendant of a god. Although not actually deified until later than the time of the Exodus, he was highly revered at this time, but he could do nothing to help the Egyptians.

7. Thunder and Hail	Exodus 9:18: *[18]Behold, tomorrow about this time I will cause very heavy hail to rain down, such as has not been in Egypt since its founding until now.* Exodus 9:22-24: *[22]Then the LORD said to Moses, "Stretch out your hand toward heaven, that there may be hail in all the land of Egypt—on man, on beast, and on every herb of the field, throughout the land of Egypt." [23]And Moses stretched out his rod toward heaven; and the LORD sent thunder and hail, and fire darted to the ground. And the LORD rained hail on the land of Egypt. [24]So there was hail, and fire mingled with the hail, so very heavy that there was none like it in all the land of Egypt since it became a nation.*

Hail (Exodus 9:13-26): The sky goddess Nut was "the mother of the sun-god Ra, whom she swallowed in the evening and gave birth to again in the morning."[66] She was especially culpable in this plague in that she was supposed to protect the land from destructions which came down from heaven. Exodus 9:31 mentions that the flax and barley were hit by the hail. Destruction of the flax was trying because it was used to wrap mummies and to make clothes.

---

[65]"Imhotep," accessed January 24, 2012, http://www.ancient-egypt-online.com/imhotep.html.
[66]Carolyn Seawright, "Nut, Sky Goddess: Mother of the Gods," accessed January 24, 2012, http://www.touregypt.net/featurestories/nut.htm.

8. Locusts	Exodus 10:4-5: *⁴Or else, if you refuse to let My people go, behold, tomorrow I will bring locusts into your territory. ⁵And they shall cover the face of the earth, so that no one will be able to see the earth; and they shall eat the residue of what is left, which remains to you from the hail, and they shall eat every tree which grows up for you out of the field.*

Grasshoppers or Locusts (Exodus 10:1-20): The locust-headed god was Senehem.[67] During the plague, the locusts were so thick that the "eye of the earth" was darkened (Exodus 10:5). One of the epithets of the sun-god Ra was "the eye of Ra." By causing darkness while the sun was shining, Ra was discredited.

9. Darkness	Exodus 10:21-22: *²¹Then the LORD said to Moses, "Stretch out your hand toward heaven, that there may be darkness over the land of Egypt, darkness which may even be felt." ²²So Moses stretched out his hand toward heaven, and there was thick darkness in all the land of Egypt three days.*

Darkness (Exodus 10:21-27): The Bible says that a three-day darkness fell next. One of the greatest gods of Egypt, next to the Pharaoh, was the sun. The sun-god Ra[68] was the principle deity of the pantheon. He made all growth possible. Pharaoh called himself *Son of the Sun*. With three days of darkness, this deity Ra was ridiculed.

10. Death of the Firstborn	Exodus 11:4-5: *⁴Then Moses said, "Thus says the LORD: 'About midnight I will go out into the midst of Egypt; ⁵and all the firstborn in the land of Egypt shall die, from the firstborn of Pharaoh who sits on his throne, even to the firstborn of the female servant who is behind the handmill, and all the firstborn of the animals.'"*

---

[67] David Livingston, "The Plagues and the Exodus," *Davelivingston.com*, 2005, accessed January 25, 2012, http://www.davelivingston.com/plagues.htm.
[68] "Amun," *Wikipedia*, last updated January 19, 2012, accessed January 25, 2012, http://en.wikipedia.org/wiki/Amun.

Death of the Firstborn: After the ninth plague, Pharaoh, under pressure from his advisors, now consented to the request made to let the people go; but he insisted that they must leave their animals behind. This was a totally unacceptable offer, as the animals were to be used as the actual sacrifice to the Lord. Moses had to refuse these terms and said in Exodus 10: *[25]...You must also give us sacrifices and burnt offerings, that we may sacrifice to the LORD our God. [26]Our livestock also shall go with us; not a hoof shall be left behind. For we must take some of them to serve the LORD our God, and even we do not know with what we must serve the LORD until we arrive there.*

Enraged by the refusal, Pharaoh pronounced the last deadly plague to be unleashed upon the land from his very own lips as he warns Moses in Exodus 10: *[28]...Get away from me! Take heed to yourself and see my face no more! For in the day you see my face you shall die! [29]So Moses said, "You have spoken well. I will never see your face again."*

At this point the passive obedience that the Children of Israel had shown was moved to a level of active obedience. They were given strict instructions to follow so that they would not also feel the judgment of this last plague sent by the Lord. These instructions provided the Israelites the protection of the Lord on this deadly night. For in all of the houses of Egypt, of both the Israelites and the Egyptians, if they did not offer a sacrifice and put its blood on the two door posts and on the lintel of their doors, the angel of the Lord would strike dead every firstborn human and animal in the land. These instructions are of eternal significance; Jesus serves as the sacrifice for Christians with His blood providing the ultimate salvation from spiritual death.

I believe Mohammed purposely did not mention this tenth plague, which is very important in Moses' writing, as Mohammed intentionally removed the mentioning of the offering of sacrifices throughout the rewriting of the stories of the Bible in the Qur'an. When Adam and Eve sinned, the Bible clearly states that God covered their nakedness with animal skin, and that was the first sacrifice, as recorded in Genesis 3:21. However, Mohammed did not mention this in his writings in the Qur'an. The sons of Adam each offered an offering. It was accepted from Abel, but it was rejected from Cain. Abel offered the blood sacrifice, but Cain offered the fruit of the land as seen in Genesis 4:3-5. Once again, Mohammed, when he rewrites the story of the sons of Adam, he disregarded these facts. So it was in Noah's story in Genesis 8:20-21.

The first thing Noah did when he came out of the ark was to build an altar and offer a sacrifice, but Mohammed disregarded this important section. So it was the case in the stories of Job, Abraham, Isaac, and Jacob as we read their accounts in the Bible. They always offered sacrifices, but Mohammed disregarded such worship which was a picture of the true sacrifice of our Lord and Savior, Jesus Christ.

This last plague was the foundation for the true delivering, not only for the Jewish people from the slavery of Egypt, but also for the delivering of humanity from the slavery of sin. It was on the day of Passover when Jesus was offered as the Passover Sacrifice for mankind. *Coincidence?* I think not. Sadly, our Muslims friends do not know Moses' Passover story or the fulfillment of the great event of Christ's sacrifice.

<u>The Crossing of the Red Sea and the Final Status of Pharaoh</u>
Although there are no details given in the Qur'an concerning the crossing of the Red Sea, Mohammed mentions this portion of the life of Moses and the Children of Israel in many places: Qur'an 7:136; 10:90-92; 20:77-78; 26:59-68; 28:39-40; and 51:40.

Qur'an 7:136 states: *[136]So we took vengeance on them, so we drowned them in the sea because they denied our signs, and they were unaware of them.* In Qur'an 20:77-78: *[77]And indeed, we revealed to Moses to walk with my servants at night, so strike a dry way in the sea. Do not fear to be overtaken, neither be you afraid. [78]So Pharaoh followed them with his troops, so covered them from the sea that covered them.*

Qur'an 26:59-68 continues: *[59]likewise, and we bequeathed it to the children of Israel. [60]So they followed them at sunrise. [61]So when the two groups saw each other, the companion of Moses said, "Surely we are overtaken!" [62]He said, "Certainly not, surely my lord is with me, and he will guide me." [63]So we revealed to Moses: "That strike the sea with your rod." So it split, so each side was as a great mound. [64]And we moved toward, then the others. [65]And we delivered Moses and all those with him. [66]Then we drowned the others. [67]Surely in this is a sign, and most of them were not believers. ⁶⁸And surely your lord is the dear, the merciful.*

Ibn Kathir interpreted this important event by saying that Allah mentioned this concerning the matters of Pharaoh and his troops and their drowning and how he took their pride, money, and souls.[69] Also, he bequeathed the Children of Israel their (Egyptian) money and their possessions, as it is written in 26:59: *⁵⁹likewise, and we bequeathed it to the children of Israel*. Ibn Kathir continued by stating that the king, his troops, his family, and his leaders were all destroyed.[70] There was no one left in Egypt except the general population. At this time, the women of Egypt had authority over their men because the wives of the princes married men from the general population. *Where did Ibn Kathir find this information?*

Ibn Kathir stated that the People of the Book said that the Children of Israel were commanded to leave Egypt during the first month of the year, and they were commanded to kill a lamb which they could share with a neighbor. They were also commanded, when they slaughtered it, to take its blood and put it on the threshold of their doors. Then they must roast the lamb over a fire, with its head, legs, and stomach. They were to consume it and not leave any of it until the morning. They must not break its bones or take any of it outside their homes. They also were to eat unleavened bread with it for seven days. When they ate it, they must tie their waists and have their sandals on their feet and their staffs in their hands. They must eat it in a hurry. Whatever was left of it, they must burn.

Where did Ibn Kathir come up with this information? Why did Mohammed not mention this information in his Qur'an? Maybe he excluded it because it included blood sacrifice which is the picture of the sacrifice of Christ as we mentioned earlier. We encourage the reader to read the entire account in the Bible in Exodus 12.

Ibn Kathir also stated that the People of the Book said on this night that Allah killed the firstborn of the Egyptians and the firstborn of their animals.[71] The sons of the Children of Israel left Egypt with all their money and their children while the Egyptians were weeping for their loss. The Children of Israel were hurrying to leave with their uncooked bread dough. Six hundred thousand men left Egypt where

---

[69] Ibn Kathir, *Stories of the Prophets*, 319.
[70] Ibid.
[71] Ibid., 320.

their families had lived for 430 years. Ibn Kathir described more of the story, including the crossing of the Red Sea and the celebration by Mary (Miriam) and the ladies of the drowning of Pharaoh and his soldiers, but we choose to stop here. However, what is amazing about the most important part of the story of Moses concerning the plagues, which Mohammed purposely refused to mention, is that it is not found in the Qur'an or the hadith.

One must ask these questions here. *What happened to Pharaoh? If he drowned, did he drown as an infidel or as a believer?* When we look at the verses of the Qur'an, we can see the huge contradiction because in Qur'an 10:90-92: *⁹⁰And we brought the children of Israel through the sea. So Pharaoh and his hosts followed them insolently and with enmity until, when he was about to drown, he said, "I believed that there is no god but him on whom the children of Israel believed, and I am of the Muslims." ⁹¹"Now, and indeed, you disobeyed before, and you were of the vandals. ⁹²So today we will deliver you with your body that you may become a sign to those who come after you, and surely most people are unaware of our signs."*

Ibn Kathir gave the interpretation of these verses, and one can see his struggle to correct the contradiction in the Qur'an, to show that Pharaoh's repentance was not accepted by Allah and it was too late for forgiveness.[72] Obviously, Ibn Kathir did not understand the nature of the true God who will forgive a truly repentant person, even at the last second of his life. Ibn Kathir gave a foolish hadith wherein Mohammed said when Pharaoh said, "I believed that there is no god but him on whom the Children of Israel believed, and I am of the Muslims." Angel Gabreel said to Mohammed that he took mud or silt from the bottom of the sea and put it in Pharaoh's mouth, for he was afraid that Pharaoh may receive mercy. *Really?*

In another hadith, Ibn Abbas said, "When Pharaoh was about to drown, he cried out, 'I believed that there is no god but him on whom the Children of Israel believed, and I am of the Muslims.' Then Gabreel was afraid that the mercy of Allah may come to him; therefore, he slapped Pharaoh by his wings."

Perhaps if Ibn Kathir or Ibn Abbas knew the true nature of the angels and of God, they would find that the angels of heaven would rejoice when one sinful man repents because God and his angels

---
[72]Ibid., 316-317.

desire that no one should perish but that all should come to the truth. There are two obvious conclusions. First, the prayer of Pharaoh is a fabrication and did not take place. Second, the Allah of Mohammed and his Angel Gabreel do not wish for any to be saved.

As for the interpretation of verse 92: *^{92}So today we will deliver you with your body that you may become a sign to those who come after you, and surely most people are unaware of our signs."* Ibn Abbas said that some of the people (Children of Israel) doubted the death of Pharaoh to the point that they said, "Surely he will not die." Therefore, Allah commanded the sea to lift Pharaoh to the top of the water, but others said that he was lifted near the shore. His shield was on him so they might know him. Therefore, they knew him from his clothes, and they knew for sure that he did drown. That is the proof to the Children of Israel that Allah had the power to destroy Pharaoh.

We must ask some questions of Ibn Abbas and Ibn Kathir. *What is the source of this knowledge concerning Pharaoh? How did they know that some of the Children of Israel doubted his death? What is the logic?* I believe they used too much imagination. Exodus 14:27-31 states that where Moses stretched his hand over the sea, the water returned to its strength and began flowing again. Then the Lord overthrew the Egyptians in the midst of the sea, and the water covered the chariots, the horsemen, and all the hosts of Pharaoh. The Scripture says that there remained not so much as one of them, not Pharaoh, not anybody. When the Israelites saw the Egyptians dead upon the seashore, they believed in the Lord and his servant Moses.

From reading this, we can conclude that not one of the Egyptians survived; they all drowned. I can find no justification for the scholars' statements. I believe the problem is found in Qur'an 10:90-92 which simply states that Pharaoh repented and Allah saved his flesh. There is no proof of the slap from the angel's wing or the mud in his mouth as mentioned above. This would contradict the following passage, Qur'an 28:39-40: *^{39}And he became proud with his troops in the land without the truth, and they thought that they will not return to us. ^{40}So we seized him and his troops, so we cast them into the sea. So see how was the end of the unjust.*

Ibn Kathir's interpretation was that they transgressed, they presumed to corrupt the land, and they believed there would be no resurrection and no return to Allah.[73] Therefore, their lord poured on them the torment. As for his interpretation of verse 40, "He drowned them in the sea in the morning, and he did not leave one of them alive. And that was the end of the unjust." The obvious interpretation of Ibn Kathir was that no one was saved. His fabrication for 10:90-92 was a needless and futile effort because the contradiction between these two passages is very clear.

Moses and the Children of Israel Asking to See God's Face

The story of the forty day meeting between Moses and God is very well known by Jews and Christians, as it is written in Exodus. We see, as a result of the length of this meeting, that the Children of Israel made a god because they did not think Moses was coming back. They did not know what happened to Moses. This story is also rewritten in Qur'an 7:142, and Mohammed amazingly broke it into two sessions, thirty days and ten days. As usual, Muslim scholars inserted their input to try to give good reasons for why it is written in such a way in the Qur'an. Here is the verse and its interpretation by Ibn Abbas: *[142]And we appointed for Moses thirty nights, and we completed with ten so that his whole time with his lord amounted to forty nights. And Moses said to his brother Aaron, "Be my viceroy among my people, and reform. And do not follow the way of the vandals."*

Ibn Kathir interpreted this verse by stating that Ibn Abbas and others said that Moses spent thirty days with his lord.[74] He was fasting and did not taste food the entire month. Because he desired to make his mouth smell good, he took the bark from a tree to chew on it. However, Allah commanded him to hold on for ten more nights. So it became forty nights as the hadith stated, "The mouth of one who is fasting in Allah's sight is better than the smell of the best musk (perfume)." Moses chose his brother Aaron to be in charge in his absence.

It is amazing that the *revelation*, as Muslims call it, in the Qur'an disregards so many important facts that exist in the original account of the Bible. On the other hand, extra fabrication, which is the opposite of the true account of the Bible, has been added to the story.

---

[73]http://quran.Al-islam.com/page.aspx?pageid=2218 BookID =11&page=390, accessed January 26, 2012.
[74]Ibn Kathir, 330.

The Revelation of Error

An example of this is that the Children of Israel asked Moses to see God's face.

Moses Seeks to See God's Face

First, let us look at Moses seeking to see God's face in Qur'an 7:143: *[143]And when Moses came at our set time and his lord spoke with him, he said, "My lord, show me, look to you." He said, "You will not see me, but look to the mountain. So if it dwells in its place, so you will see me." So when his lord tajallā[75] to the mountain, he made it dust, and Moses fell in a swoon. So when he was revived, he said, "Praise be to you. I repented to you, and I am the first of the believers."*

Ibn Kathir stated that Allah spoke to him from behind the veil. Allah talked to him and caused him to hear the conversation. Allah then caused him to be drawn near to him, and this is a very noble position. Because Allah gave him this very high position, he asked Allah to remove the veil.[76]

> And he said to the great one, who no sight can be aware of, 'Lord, show me, look to you.' He said, 'You will not see me.' Allah proved that Moses could not see him because even the mountain which is much stronger and bigger than men will not stand still when the merciful shows his glory. That's why Allah said, 'But look to the mountain. So if it dwells in its place, so you will see me.'

Ibn Kathir stated that in the earlier books, obviously he meant the two testaments of the Bible, no one can see Allah unless he dies. Ibn Kathir stated that Mujahid said that when Moses saw what happened to the mountain, he fell down, fainting before Allah, for the mountain had changed to dust.

So when Moses was revived, Ibn Kathir said that this was a proof that he was fasting. He said, *"Praise be to you. I repented to you."* He meant that he no longer asked Allah to see him. As for Moses saying, *"and I am the first of the believers,"* Ibn Kathir said that he meant no one can see Allah and live.[77] Ibn Kathir stated that Mohammed stated in the hadith that "no one should prefer me over Moses." This is from Mohammed's humility that he said this, and it

---

[75] appeared in glory, non-Arabic word of Syriac origin
[76] Ibn Kathir, 331-332.
[77] Ibn Kathir, 332.

has been abrogated, for he did not know then he was the best of the prophets. Because there is no doubt that the prayer of Allah and the peace of Allah are upon him, he is the "best of the creatures." As he himself said, "I am the master of the children of Adam on the day of resurrection and with no pride."

What about the true biblical account of Moses from Exodus 33:18-23? In Mohammed's usual way, he copied from the Bible and distorted it. Here we see, once again, there is missing information and extra fabrication. The Bible clearly stated that Moses asked God to allow him to see God's glory in Exodus 33:19. God responded to him that He will make all His goodness pass before him, He will proclaim the name of the Lord before him, He will be gracious to whom He will be gracious, and He will show mercy to whom He will show mercy.

Notice that God did not tell Moses that He will lead people astray or cause them to not understand His signs because they are not going to believe in them anyway, but God will simply show mercy and grace to those whom He chooses. As the love of God is given to all people, so it is in the case with His mercy. In His pre-knowledge, He knows who will believe and who will reject, but He will never lead anyone astray as we read in Exodus 33:18-23.

As for the fabrication of Mohammed that the mountain turned to dust, there is no such thing mentioned in the Bible. Mount Sinai still exists today in Arabia.

As to what is written in Qur'an 7:144: **[144]*He said, "O Moses, I have chosen you above all people with my messages and with my words,"*** Ibn Kathir said Allah meant that Moses was the best in Moses' day. *How did Ibn Kathir know what Allah meant? Did Ibn Kathir talk to Allah?* It's amazing how the extreme arrogance of Muslim scholars like Ibn Kathir can fabricate such a ridiculous *proof* for a claim that Abraham was greater than Moses before Moses and that Mohammed is greater than Abraham and Moses after Moses. The honor he was given is *proven* by Mohammed's ascendance to the seven heavens, and he was above all the messengers and the prophets. I will discuss this later in the section on Mohammed and prove that the story of Mohammed ascending to the seven heavens is a big lie. As for the saying, "so take what I have given to you and be of the thankful," Ibn Kathir said he meant to be thankful for what Allah gave him of the worlds and that he will not ask for more than that.

In Qur'an 7:145: *[145a]And we wrote for him in the alwah[78] from everything, a sermon and an exposition of everything...* In the hadith, Ibn Kathir stated that Allah wrote by his own hand and gave to Moses the Torah, which includes all the preaching and details of all they needed concerning what was lawful and what was forbidden.

Notice that the word *alwah*, according to Arabic grammar, is plural and means three or more tablets, unlike English grammar in which the plural meaning is two or more. In the true account found in Exodus 31:18, the Ten Commandments were written on two tablets. Notice that the tablets in the Qur'an version included not only the Ten Commandments but also contained many other things. Note that the word *alwah* also means wooden boards or planks, not stone as described in the Bible.

Ibn Kathir interpreted Qur'an 7:145: ...*[145b]So take it with strength and command your people to take the best part of it. I will show you the home of the transgressors*, by stating that it means "with good determination and the best and most beautiful respect."[79] Allah said that he will show Moses the punishment of those who disobey and who are calling his messengers liars.

Finally, Ibn Kathir closed this session by simply interpreting the following verses in Qur'an 7:146-147: *[146]I will turn away from my signs those who are proud on the earth without the truth, and if they see every sign, they will not believe in it. And if they see the way of guidance, they will not take it a way. And if they see the way of error, they will take it a way. This is because they denied our signs, and they were unaware of them. [147]And those who denied our signs and the meeting of the hereafter, their work will be in vain. Will they be rewarded, except for what they were doing?"*

He interpreted these verses by stating that it is Allah who causes the proud one to not understand or comprehend the meaning of the signs. Even if they see all of the signs, how wonderful and powerful they are, they will not be led by the signs, and they will not believe. For Allah himself turned them away from the signs because they did not believe them, and they disregarded them. Allah turned them away from thinking of their meaning so they would not obey what is in the signs.

---

[78] boards, non-Arabic word of Aramaic origin
[79] Ibn Kathir, 333.

I cannot imagine how Muslims can accept the nature of Allah or how cruel he is. Muslims like Ibn Kathir and others could not see anything wrong in such a description of Allah. Because *Allah knows best,* they will not believe the signs; that is why Allah makes them turn away from them and misunderstand them. He leads people astray because he knows they are not going to believe. What a "just" god! *Where is the patience and guidance in such a god? Who then can be led to the truth?* For all have sinned and are not good, not even one.

The Children of Israel Seek to See God's Face

Another contradiction can be found between both texts, the Bible and the Qur'an, as shown clearly in the following two passages. In Qur'an 2:55, Mohammed claimed that the Children of Israel asked Moses to see God's face or they would not believe in him (Moses). *[55]And when you said, "O Moses, we will not believe you until we see Allah openly." So the thunderbolt seized you while you were looking on.* The opposite account can be found in the Bible, for the Children of Israel were afraid when they saw the lightning, heard the thunder and the sound of the trumpet, and saw the mountain smoking. They stood far away, and according to Exodus 20:19:
[19]Then they said to Moses, "You speak with us, and we will hear; but let not God speak with us, lest we die."

The Worship of the Magic Cow

In Qur'an 7:148-154 and 20:83-100, Mohammad's story of the Golden Calf is recorded and repeated. As usual, when Mohammed repeats a story, words change which is a great proof that the words of the Qur'an were invented and are counterfeit stories adapted from the Bible. Ibn Kathir presented this story and its interpretation in his book.[80] This story is repeated in two sections, Qur'an 7:148-156 and 20:83-98. First, I would like to quote what is written in Qur'an 7:148-149: *[148]And Moses' people took, after him, from their ornaments a calf, a body which gave a mooing sound. Did they not see that it could not speak to them, nor guide them a way? They took it, and they were unjust. [149]And when it fell in their hands and they saw that they had gone astray, they said, "If our lord will not have mercy on us and forgive us, we will surely be of the losers."*

---

[80] Ibn Kathir, 333-341.

The Revelation of Error

Notice that Moses' anger, in the following verses, over Aaron and the absence of the Samaritan proves that Aaron was behind the creation of the golden calf. Notice that the boards (tablets) were never broken. This is a contradiction to the biblical account as written in Exodus 32:19: **[19]*So it was, as soon as he came near the camp, that he saw the calf and the dancing. So Moses' anger became hot, and he cast the tablets out of his hands and broke them at the foot of the mountain.***

In Qur'an 7:150-156: [150]*And when Moses returned to his people, wrathful, sorrowful, he said, "Evil is what you have done following my departure. Would you hasten the command of your lord?" And he threw down the boards and seized his brother by the head and dragged him to himself. He said, "Son of my mother, surely the people weakened me and had almost killed me. Therefore, do not make the enemy rejoice at me, and do not place me with the unjust people."* [151]*He said, "My lord, forgive me and my brother and admit us into your mercy. And you are the most merciful of the merciful."* [152]*Surely those who took the calf will receive wrath from their lord and humiliation in the world's life, and likewise, we reward the forgers.* [153]*And those who did the evils, then repented after it and believed; surely your lord, after that, is forgiving, merciful.* [154]*And when the wrath of Moses was calmed, he took up the boards, and in their writing was guidance and mercy for those who are terrified of their lord.*

[155]*And Moses chose his people, seventy men, for an appointed time. So when the quake seized them, he said, "My lord, if you will, you had destroyed them before and me. Will you destroy us because of what the fools did among us? It is only your sedition. You will mislead by it whom you will and guide whom you will. You are our friend, so forgive us and have mercy on us, and you are the best of the forgivers.* [156]*And prescribe for us in this world good, and in the hereafter, surely our guidance is toward you." He said, "I will afflict my torment on whom I will. And my mercy embraces all things, so I will prescribe it to those who fear and bring the legal alms and those who believe in our signs.*

The following story is about the Samaritan and Moses' people, even though the Samaritans did not exist as a people until hundreds of years later. This story contradicts the Bible which clearly teaches that

Chapter 16

it was Aaron, not the Samaritan, who fashioned the golden calf. (See Exodus 32.) Mohammed confused Hosea 8:5-6 with the calf of the Exodus rebellion!

This second section that mentions the mooing calf is found in Qur'an 20:83-98: *[83]"And what has hastened you from your people, O Moses?" [84]He said, "They were following me closely, and I hastened to you, my lord, that you may be pleased." [85]He said, "So surely indeed, we seduced your people after you, and the Sāmirī[81] led them astray." [86]So Moses returned to his people, wrathful, sorrowful. He said, "O my people, did not your lord promise you a good promise? Was the covenant so long to you, or you desired that wrath from your lord should fall on you so that you broke your promise to me?" [87]They said, "We did not break your promise by our choice, but we carry loads of the people's trinkets, so we threw them, so likewise, the Samaritan threw." [88]So this gave forth a calf to them, a body which had a mooing sound, so they said, "This is your god and the god of Moses." So he forgot. [89]"Do they not see that it does not return to them saying and it does not have for them a harm or benefit?"*

[90]And indeed, Aaron said to them before that, "O my people, surely you are only seduced by it, and surely your lord is the merciful. So follow me, and obey my commands." [91]They said, "We will not stop worshiping it until Moses returns to us." [92]He said, "O Aaron, what hindered you when you saw them go astray? [93]Will you not follow me? Did you disobey my command?" [94]He said, "O son of my mother, do not seize me by my beard nor by my head. Surely I feared, lest you should say, 'You divided between the children of Israel, and you did not watch my word.'"

[95]He said, "So what is the affair with you, O Samaritan?" [96]He said, "I saw what they have not seen, so I took a handful of dust from the path of the messenger, so I made it. And likewise, my soul prompted me to do." [97]He said, "So be gone, so surely to you in this life that you say, 'No touch.' And surely you have a promise that you will not break. And look at your god whom you continue worshiping. Surely we will burn him; then we will blast it into the sea, blasting. [98]Surely your god is

---

[81]Samaritan, non-Arabic word of Hebrew/Syriac origin

only Allah; there is no god except him. His knowledge surrounds all things.

Ibn Kathir began his interpretation by giving the location of this event. This is about the Children of Israel when Moses met with Allah at the mountain. He was calling on his lord, asking him about many things, and Allah was answering him.

We must ask questions here. *How did Ibn Kathir know this was the setting here? What was Moses' question? What was the answer?* Ibn Kathir did not know, *and Allah knows best.* Perhaps he read Exodus 19 through 32. It is a total of fourteen chapters in the Torah which Muslims believe without knowing anything about them. Ibn Kathir summarized these chapters in the following sentence: "Moses was asking Allah, and Allah was answering him."

If Muslims would simply read the book of Exodus, they would discover that Ibn Kathir and others were ignorant of the truth. I do not blame Ibn Kathir or any other Muslim scholar, for neither Mohammed their prophet nor Gabreel his angel knew any of the details and only a few facts about Moses' life. That is why we always encourage the reader to go back to the Bible.

Ibn Kathir continued by stating one of their men was called Aaron the Samaritan. Here Ibn Kathir reconciled both of the above passages of the Qur'an as he smoothly fixed a problem which Mohammed falls into by adding the name of Aaron to the word Samaritan. That was a very deceptive way to fix an error in the Qur'an, for the truth is that there was no such man in Moses' day by the name of Aaron the Samaritan.

In Qur'an 7:148-154, Mohammed forgot to mention the Samaritan; he mentioned Moses' brother which causes a person to believe that it was Moses' brother who made the golden calf, exactly as it is written in the Bible. On the other hand, Mohammed in Qur'an 20:83-98 mentioned the Samaritan as the one who did it. Although the Qur'an does not mention a name for the Samaritan, Ibn Kathir came up with the name Aaron. *How did Ibn Kathir know this name?*

Ibn Kathir said that Aaron the Samaritan borrowed some of the ornaments, shaped it as a calf, and put inside it some of the dirt which he took from the path of the horse of Gabreel when he saw him the day Allah drowned Pharaoh.[82] When he put dust into the calf, it began to moo just like a real calf. Ibn Kathir said that Qatadah said that the

---

[82] Ibn Kathir, 334.

golden calf literally changed into a real calf with flesh and blood. Ibn Kathir also stated that it was said that when the wind used to go in from the butt of the calf to his mouth, this was when he made the mooing sound.

Ibn Kathir said, "The Jews stood and danced and rejoiced around the golden calf. That is why they said, 'This is your god and the god of Moses.' So he forgot (meaning Moses forgot his lord with the Jews) seeking him, and Allah was there." Ibn Kathir proved that they were wrong, for this god was nothing but an animal and a *stoned Satan*. (This is an expression which means Allah cursed Satan and caused Muslims to throw stones at him.)

That is why Allah said in Qur'an 7:148, *[148]And Moses' people took, after him, from their ornaments a calf, a body which gave a mooing sound. Did they not see that it could not speak to them, nor guide them a way? They took it, and they were unjust.* Ibn Kathir interpreted this verse by saying that this was "an animal that did not talk or answer and did not have evil or good, who did not guide, and that they were unjust themselves for what they had done, for what they were doing was vanity resulting from ignorance and error."

Then Ibn Kathir quoted Qur'an 7:149: *[149]And when it fell in their hands and they saw that they had gone astray, they said, "If our lord will not have mercy on us and forgive us, we will surely be of the losers."*[83] He interpreted this by saying that when Moses returned to them and saw what they were doing in worshiping the calf, he threw the boards which were in his hands. On these boards was the Torah. When he threw the boards, it was said that he broke them, as it is believed by the People of the Book, and Allah had given him another one. That is not true, for the reading of the Qur'an does not indicate that at all.

Ibn Kathir continued that the People of the Book claimed that there were two boards, but he stated that the language of the Qur'an clearly teaches that there were lots of boards.[84] Obviously, Ibn Kathir did not know what he was writing about, for as he stated above: "on these boards the Torah was written." Five books is a lot of material, and you cannot put them on two boards. What Ibn Kathir did not know was that what was written on those two boards was not the

---

[83]Ibid., 335.
[84]Ibid.

The Revelation of Error

Torah but the Ten Commandments which could be written on two boards. As recorded in Exodus 32:15-16, the Ten Commandments were written on two tablets. In verse 19, it is written that Moses broke the two tablets.

Throughout the history of Islam, whenever any given fact disagrees with what they believe, the scholars or the lay people immediately accuse others of lies and infidelity. In their belief, they are right and everyone else is wrong. Although the Qur'an gives no details at all about Moses or his life and, even though thousands of manuscripts dated before Mohammed was born are in agreement that there were two tablets and they were broken when Moses threw them to the ground, Muslims contest the story. In other words, Ibn Kathir argued with historical documents without knowing their contents.

Then Ibn Kathir stated that Moses angrily rebuked the Children of Israel for the evil wicked thing they had done, so they apologized to him.[85] They explained by stating in Qur'an 20:87: *[87]They said, "We did not break your promise by our choice, but we carry loads of the people's trinkets, so we threw them, so likewise, the Samaritan threw."*

Ibn Kathir chose to interpret the same passage from Qur'an 7:151, and he stated that Jewish people were embarrassed by having the jewelry of the family of Pharaoh. Allah had commanded and allowed them to take the jewelry. However, they were not embarrassed about their foolishness in worshiping a golden calf, with a mooing sound, along with Allah, the one, the absolute, the dominator. *Why were the Jewish people embarrassed to wear the Egyptian people's jewelry?*

Then we read that Moses came to Aaron and said to him in Qur'an 20:92-94: *[92]He said, "O Aaron, what hindered you when you saw them go astray? [93]Will you not follow me? Did you disobey my command?"* Aaron's response was: *[94]"...Surely I feared, lest you should say, 'You divided between the children of Israel...'"* Ibn Kathir interpreted this by stating that Moses came to Aaron and asked Aaron why he had not come to him immediately to inform Moses about what they had done. Aaron said, "How can I leave them and come to you while you left me to watch over them?"

Then Ibn Kathir referred to Qur'an 7:151: *[151]He said, "My lord, forgive me and my brother and admit us into your mercy. And*

---

[85]Ibid.

you are the most merciful of the merciful." He interpreted that Aaron had rebuked them and forbidden them from this very evil act.

It was Aaron who said to them in Qur'an 20:90: *⁹⁰And indeed, Aaron said to them before that, "O my people, surely you are only seduced by it, and surely your lord is the merciful.* That means Allah allowed the worshiping of the cow to take place and caused the calf to make a mooing sound to tempt them. Aaron said to the people, "So follow me and obey my command." But they did not obey him, and they did not follow him. Then Moses came to the Samaritan saying, "So what is the affair (matter) with you, O Samaritan?" The interpretation is that he meant what caused you to make the golden calf.

In Qur'an 20:96: *⁹⁶He said, "I saw what they have not seen…"* He meant that he saw Angel Gabreel riding the horse. So he took a handful of dust from the path of the messenger from the trail of Angel Gabreel's horse. *Where did Ibn Kathir come up with this information?* I did not know that Angel Gabreel rode on a horse; I thought that he flew by his wings. The Bible never mentions Angel Gabreel, not in this time period of the Children of Israel, not riding on his horse, nor even flying by his wings. This entire story is a fabrication.

Ibn Kathir stated that some said the Samaritan was following the horse and was picking up the dirt from the footprints of the horse.[86] When he put this dirt inside the calf, the dirt caused it to make the mooing sound. Then Moses said in Qur'an 20:97: *⁹⁷He said, "So be gone, so surely to you in this life that you say, 'No touch.' And surely you have a promise that you will not break. And look at your god whom you continue worshiping. Surely we will burn him; then we will blast it into the sea, blasting.*

Ibn Kathir interpreted *no touch* to be a curse on him that he will not touch anyone as a punishment for him in this world's life and in the hereafter. Ibn Kathir continued by stating that Moses went to this calf, burned it with the fire, and then spread it in the sea as it is written with the People of the Book. Then he commanded the Children of Israel to drink it.

So when they drank the water, all those who worshiped the calf had gold clinging on their lips, but others said their color turned to yellow. It was said that same day those who did not worship the calf

---

[86]Ibid., 335-336.

The Revelation of Error

took the swords in their hands. Then Allah sent the fog on those who worshiped the calf to the point that no one could know his own family or his neighbor. So those who had the swords killed the ones who worshiped the calf, and they killed seventy-one thousand that morning.

Then Allah said in Qur'an 7:154: *154And when the wrath of Moses was calmed, he took up the boards, and in their writing was guidance and mercy for those who are terrified of their lord.* Ibn Kathir interpreted this verse by stating that some concluded from the words *in their writing* that the original boards were broken, but the wording does not prove such a thing, *and Allah knows best.* It is very amazing, as we have seen above, how Ibn Kathir mixes information from the Bible with the nonsense of the verses of the Qur'an to tell the story of Moses. I wonder if, when Muslims read Ibn Kathir's interpretation, they ever question the source of this information. *In other words, do they know that he is quoting the Bible to make sense out of the nonsense of the Qur'an?*

Ibn Kathir stated that Ibn Abbas said that they worshiped this golden calf just after they crossed the sea.[87] It is written in Qur'an 7:138: *138And we caused the children of Israel to cross the sea, so they came on a people who were devoted to their idols. They said, "O Moses, make us a god as they have gods." He said, "Surely you are an ignorant people."* Ibn Kathir continued that, according to the People of the Book, the Children of Israel worshiped the calf before they entered the Promised Land. When they were commanded to kill those who worshiped the calf, they killed three thousand people. Moses then went to seek forgiveness for them, and Allah forgave them with one condition, that they must enter the Holy Land.

As we have seen above, Ibn Kathir with his cleverness went back and forth between Qur'an 7 and Qur'an 20, skipping many passages and ignoring the contradictions in them. *What about the Muslims who count on his knowledge and his scholarship to discover the truth about Moses and the Children of Israel?* Once again, I will not waste time or space; I will just point to one of many contradictions in these two passages. Then I will take us through a quick tour of the true account in the book of Exodus.

---

[87] Ibid., 336.

Qur'an 7:150-151	Qur'an 20:92-94
[150] And when Moses returned to his people, wrathful, sorrowful, he said, "Evil is what you have done following my departure. Would you hasten the command of your lord?" And he threw down the boards and seized his brother by the head and dragged him to himself. He said, "Son of my mother, surely the people weakened me and had almost killed me. Therefore, do not make the enemy rejoice at me, and do not place me with the unjust people." [151] He said, "My lord, forgive me and my brother and admit us into your mercy. And you are the most merciful of the merciful."	[92] He said, "O Aaron, what hindered you when you saw them go astray? [93] Will you not follow me? Did you disobey my command?" [94] He said, "O son of my mother, do not seize me by my beard nor by my head. Surely I feared, lest you should say, 'You divided between the children of Israel, and you did not watch my word.'"

Notice the two versions of this story are completely different. *Did Aaron say, "Son of my mother, surely the people weakened me and almost killed me"? Or, did he say, "Son of my mother, do not seize me by my beard or by my head; surely I feared, lest you should say, 'You divided between the Children of Israel, and you did not watch my word'"? Did Moses seize his brother by his head and drag him to himself, or did he seize him by his beard and his head? Why does the Samaritan not exist in Qur'an 7 but exists in Qur'an 20? Was there any Samaritan at all in the time of Moses?*

Obviously, Ibn Kathir was ignorant historically just like Mohammed was. The Samaritans, as a people, were a mix between Jews and Gentiles, and they did not exist in Palestine at the time of the Exodus of the Children of Israel from Egypt. The city of Samaria was built in 883 BC. *So how can a Samaritan make such a calf if no Samaritans existed for at least another six hundred years?* This is an unacceptable historical error by Mohammed in his Qur'an.

Now let us go to the true account of the worship of the calf written in Exodus 32. The Children of Israel never asked Moses to make a god for them as is claimed in the Qur'an. The truth is in

The Revelation of Error

Exodus 32. Because Moses delayed coming down from the mountain, the people asked Aaron, not a Samaritan, to make a god for them. This took place three months after they left Egypt (Exodus 19:1-3), not as Ibn Kathir claimed that the People of the Book said it was just before they entered the Promised Land.

If we could ask Mohammed or any of his scholars when the Jews entered the Promised Land, they would not be able to answer. The fact is the Bible states it was forty years after they left Egypt. *Did you just notice the Qur'an is in agreement with the Bible in that the Jews took the Promised Land of Israel in 1500 years BC?* That would make Israel the one and only country given by God Almighty to His chosen people, the Jews.

I remember meeting with a Muslim friend from Palestine during my traveling in the United States in 2011. He was a Muslim believer. Before I met with him, a mutual friend told me this Muslim friend hated Israel. As I sat and had a coffee with him in a coffee shop, I asked him why he did not like the Jews. His answer was very simple: Israel occupies his homeland. I asked him how he knew that. He said that the country is called Palestine, and it belongs to his people. The Jews have occupied this land since 1948. I asked him, "Really? Do you believe in the Qur'an?" He said, "Sure."

I then took him to these passages where we read that the Promised Land was given to Moses and his people. This Muslim friend was astonished to see this fact in his Qur'an. Then I asked him, "Do you know when Moses lived?" He smiled and answered, "Some time ago." I smiled back at him and said that it was much earlier than 1948. It was actually 1500 BC when the Israelites lived there. I ended my conversation with him by stating that this was the only piece of land with a written deed found in the Bible which was written by Moses' hand 3,500 years ago. It is also registered in the book of the Qur'an written 1,400 years ago. My Muslim friend was totally shocked to hear this fact.

In 2012, during the primary election debates among the Republican Party, former Speaker of the House, Newt Gingrich, made a statement that the Palestine state was a made-up state. The entire leadership of America, along with the leadership of CAIR and other Muslim jihadists in America who wear suits and ties, attacked the Speaker for his statement, which shows the level of ignorance among liberals in the United States of America. I wonder if the American liberals know anything about the history of their baby country,

America. The level of ignorance among liberal Americans concerning the Israel and Palestine situation, in my opinion, is a much deeper history to comprehend, especially for those who cannot remember what took place in America on September 11, 2001.

Israel is the Promised Land and is the Jews' home country. It was their land before there were Arabs, Islam, or Christianity. As a matter of fact, it was given to them when God promised it to Abraham in 1900 BC before Abraham had any children. As it is written in Genesis 15:13-16, there was a great prophecy wherein God told Abraham that his children would be in slavery for four hundred years and that they would leave with great substance. God did not give Abraham the land at the time at which He swore that He would give it to Abraham because the sin of the original inhabitants, the Amorites, was not yet fulfilled. Notice the original people of the land were not Palestinians, the Arabs that we know of today, but rather the Amorites. They are also known as Canaanites, the descendants of Canaan, son of Ham, who existed in the land 2400 BC.

We encourage the reader to read the entire account in Exodus 32, but in simple words I would like to paraphrase what is written there. Aaron asked the people to remove the gold from their ears and give it to him. He made a molten calf which he shaped with engraving tools, and they said *these are your gods, O Israel*. There Aaron built an altar before this god. Early in the morning, they offered burnt offerings and peace sacrifices. The people ate and drank, and then they played.

Then God told Moses to go down for the people had sinned. They had made a molten calf and worshiped it. Then God desired to wipe out the entire people, but Moses begged God to spare them for he said to Him, "What will the Egyptians say? That God brought them out to destroy them? You have promised Abraham, Isaac, and Israel that You will bless them and make them more than the stars. You will give them the Promised Land, and they will inherit it forever." Then God relented of the evil which He was about to do to them. Moses came down with the two tablets in his hand. Joshua heard the voice of the people and told Moses it was the voice of war in the camp, not knowing that Moses knew what the noises were about.

Moses said it was the noise of singing. When he saw the calf and the dancing, he was angered and threw the two tablets down and broke them. Then he burned the golden calf, ground it into powder, spread it on the water's surface, and made the Children of Israel drink it. Then Moses spoke to Aaron, not some fictional Samaritan: "What

The Revelation of Error

did the people do unto you that you have let the people sin this great sin?" Then Aaron confessed all that had taken place. Moses saw the people were naked.

Then he stood in the gate of the camp and said, "Who is for the Lord, come to me." So the Levites gathered to him, and he commanded them to carry their swords by their sides and asked them to go from one gate to the other gate and for each one to kill their brother and their companion and their neighbor. Then the children of Levi killed that day three thousand men. The following day, Moses spoke to the people and said, "You have sinned a great sin against God." Moses interceded on their behalf, but the Lord sent a plague upon the people because of their sin.

To continue our study of the story of Moses, we read in Qur'an 7:155-156: *155And Moses chose his people, seventy men, for an appointed time. So when the quake seized them, he said, "My lord, if you will, you had destroyed them before and me. Will you destroy us because of what the fools did among us? It is only your sedition. You will mislead by it whom you will and guide whom you will. You are our friend, so forgive us and have mercy on us, and you are the best of the forgivers. 156And prescribe for us in this world good, and in the hereafter, surely our guidance is toward you." He said, "I will afflict my torment on whom I will. And my mercy embraces all things, so I will prescribe it to those who fear and bring the legal alms and those who believe in our signs."*

Ibn Kathir made a fool of himself and other Muslim scholars by interpreting the verses to say that Al Saddi and Ibn Abbas and others said these are the seventy scholars of the Children of Israel and with them were Moses and Aaron and Yosha (Joshua) and Nadab and Abihu.[88] They went to Moses to apologize on behalf of the Children of Israel for their worship of the calf. They were commanded to be washed, purified, and cleansed. When they went with him and drew near the mountain, the cloud surrounded him and the pillar of fire was shining. Moses went up to the mountain. Then the Children of Israel remembered they had heard the word of Allah, and some of the interpreters agreed with them. That is what Allah said in Qur'an 2:75: *75Do you hope that they will believe in you? And indeed, a group of them were hearing the words of Allah; then they*

---

[88] Ibn Kathir, 337.

altered it after they had understood it, and they know. This is an amazing "proof" that the Jews corrupted the words of Allah.

Once again, Ibn Kathir made an error to correct an error in the Qur'an, for his interpretation of the verses has nothing to do with the verses of the Qur'an. His interpretation is actually a fabrication, and I place the blame on his Allah, Gabreel, and Mohammed.

The error is in the Qur'an, for Qur'an 7:155-156 should have come before Qur'an 7:148-154. *So, what are the sources these Muslim scholars used to bring such interpretations?* The verses of Qur'an 7:155-156 do not mention the names of Yosha, Nadab, and Abihu. What these verses say is that Allah is a deceiver. He seduced the Jews to sin, and he led them astray. Moses sought forgiveness from Allah. *So, how could Allah punish Moses and the faithful ones with those who had sinned and worshiped the calf, the foolish ones?*

Today's Muslim scholars can easily say this took place after the quake, and they will tie the story of Qur'an 7:155-156 with Qur'an 2:75 to prove that the Jews corrupted the Bible. *How can a person use a corrupt book (the Qur'an) to prove that the Bible is corrupted?* To understand the true story, one must go back to Exodus 24. Once again, we encourage the reader to read the entire account in Exodus. God asked Moses to choose seventy of the elders of the Children of Israel, along with Aaron, Nadab, and Abihu, to come and worship God at a distance, while Moses was to approach God alone.

Notice that Joshua was not among this group, but later Joshua and Moses were sent together to the Mountain of God. This took place before the building of the altar and the sacrifices of peace offerings which Moses offered and the sprinkling of the blood on the people, the blood of the covenant. All this took place before Moses and his servant Joshua went to the top of the Mountain of God. Moses spent forty days there, and that is when the people worshiped the golden calf.

Mohammed and the scholars got the whole story wrong. Exodus 24 shows that the selection of the seventy men was before, not after, the worshiping of the golden calf.

Ibn Kathir continued his fabrication by quoting Mohammed Ibn Isaac who clearly stated that the seventy men were purified and wore purified clothes and were fasting.[89] Moses took them to Mount Sinai, and they all went inside the cloud. They all fell down worshiping.

---

[89]Ibid.

They heard the voice of Allah speaking to Moses, forbidding and commanding him what to do or not to do. Then when the cloud was gone, they told Moses they would not believe in him until they saw God face to face. Then, when the quake took them, it was a shocking strike of lightning. They all died, and their souls met together. Then Moses prayed to Allah and asked Him not to destroy them with the foolish ones. However, Ibn Abbas had a different opinion, for he stated that they were killed because they did not forbid their people from worshiping the calf.

As for the saying, *"It is only your sedition,"* Ibn Kathir interpreted it as *it is your test*. Other Muslim scholars said that Allah is the one who estimated and created the test of the golden calf. As for the saying, *"You will mislead by it whom you will and guide whom you will,"* Ibn Kathir said it meant whomever Allah wishes to lead astray by this test, he will lead astray; and whomever Allah will guide with this test, he will guide and to Allah alone the judgment and the will. No one can hinder him, and no one can change what Allah judges or ordains.

As for the saying, *"[155]...You are our friend, so forgive us and have mercy on us, and you are the best of the forgivers. [156]And prescribe for us in this world good, and in the hereafter, surely our guidance is toward you,"* Ibn Kathir interpreted this by saying that Moses said that we repent to you and we return to you. As for the saying, *He said, "I will afflict my torment on whom I will. And my mercy embraces all things..."* Ibn Kathir said this meant Allah will torment whom he will by this thing which he created and measured.

Finally, Ibn Kathir interpreted *"so I will prescribe it to those who fear and bring the legal alms and those who believe in our signs,"* by stating that here Allah means these were the people of Mohammed as Allah showed and taught Moses through the dialogue between Allah and Moses.

What Was on the Tablets

Obviously, neither Mohammed nor his scholars knew what was on the tablets, for they claimed there were many tablets because the word the Qur'an used in the Arabic text means three or more, causing the scholars to be confused. As for the saying in Qur'an 7:145: *[145]And we wrote for him in the alwah[90] from everything, a*

---

[90]boards, non-Arabic word of Aramaic origin

sermon and an exposition of everything, the word *everything* of "sermon and an exposition of everything" causes Muslim scholars to believe it was a huge book with many tablets, as described previously. However, as we explained before, there were only two tablets. The only things written on them were the Ten Commandments.

Here is another proof that Muslim scholars erred and lied. Qatadah made up the following conversation as described by Ibn Kathir.[91] The conversation took place between Moses and Allah; for the sake of time, I will shorten it.

> Moses said, "O lord, I see in the 'tablets' the best nation on earth, command what is right and forbid what is evil, make them my nation." Allah answered, "This is the nation of Ahmed." Moses said, "The last in the creation and the first to enter the Paradise, who believe in the book, the first book and the last book, who engage in war with others who will be misguided until they kill the one-eyed liar, the Antichrist, make them my nation." Allah said, "These are the nation of Ahmed." Moses said, "If one of them decides to do a good deed then he did not do it, it will be accounted to him as a good deed. However, if he does do it, you account it to him as ten good deeds or up to seven hundred fold (times) good deeds." Allah said, "These are the nation of Ahmed."

Qatadah repeated other things Moses saw on the tablets, but for the sake of time and space, we will not repeat all of these made-up teachings. Obviously, what Muslim scholars meant by Ahmed was Mohammed. Qatadah mentioned in the end that Moses renounced the tablets, and he said, "O Allah, make me of the nation of Ahmed."

The Cow and the Children of Israel

This story comes from Qur'an 2:67-73. Let us begin with verse 67: *⁶⁷And when Moses said to his people, "Surely Allah commands you to slaughter a cow." They said, "Do you take us as a scoff?" He said, "I seek refuge from Allah that I be of the foolish."* It is because of this portion that Qur'an 2 is named "The Book of the Cow," for every portion of revelation carries a name which naturally comes from a story, a verse, or a word in the portion of revelation. Ibn Kathir interpreted these verses by stating that Ibn Abbas and other Muslim scholars said there was a wealthy old man

---
[91]Ibn Kathir, 338.

The Revelation of Error

among the Children of Israel who had nephews who wished him dead so they could have his inheritance.[92] One of them purposely killed him at night, and they threw his body onto the crossroads. It was said the body was in front of the door of a man among them.

What an amazing contradiction in one sentence. *Where was the body left*? The answer is that it was in front of the door of a man among them. Normal common sense says that if someone kills a person, the body would be put far away from the door, not right in front of it.

When they woke up in the morning the people disagreed. His nephew shouted and complained, so they said, "Why do you disagree? Why don't you come to the prophet of Allah?" His nephew came and complained to the messenger of Allah, Moses. So Moses sought for any witness concerning this murder, but they could not find anyone with knowledge of this crime among them. Then they asked Moses to seek an answer from his lord. Therefore, Allah commanded them to sacrifice a cow. That's when Allah said, "Surely Allah commands you to sacrifice a cow." They said, "Do you scoff at us?" They meant *we ask you concerning this murder and you tell us that (to kill a cow)*.

Moses said, "I seek refuge from Allah that I be of the foolish ones." This meant that he was only telling them what was revealed to him, what Allah had told him when he asked him their question. Ibn Abbas stated that if they had killed any cow, they would get the answer, but because they demanded details, Allah gave exact information and requirements for the type of cow.

Then Qur'an 2:68-71 continues with: *[68]They said, "Call on your lord for us that he would inform us what it is." He said, "Surely he said, 'Surely it is a cow, neither old nor young, between the two,' so do what you are commanded." [69]They said, "Call on your lord for us that he would inform us what is its color." He said, "Surely he said, 'Surely she is a yellow cow. Her color is bright; she pleases the beholders.'" [70]They said, "Call on your lord for us that he would inform us what she is. Surely the cows are alike to us, and surely, if Allah wills, we will be guided."*

[71]He said, "Surely he said, 'Surely she is a cow not worn by plowing the earth or watering the field, submissive, no blemish

---

[92]Ibid., 342-343.

in her.'" They said, "Now you come with the truth." So they slaughtered her, and they almost did not do [it].

These qualities are more detailed from the previous command of Allah to simply kill a cow. It was said they could not find a cow of this description except with a righteous man among them, and when they asked him to give them the cow to be sacrificed, he refused. So they asked him if they could buy it from him by its weight in gold, but he refused until they gave him ten times its weight in gold. Then Moses ordered the people to slaughter it. Then they killed it. However, they almost did not do it, meaning they were reluctant to do it.

Then Allah commanded them to strike the person who had been killed with some part of the cow. Notice the details of the words of Allah in the Qur'an concerning the description of the cow. Also, notice the exceptional details Mohammed provided about the cow, although none of this information exists in the true account of the Bible. Mohammed typically provided copious information and precise details only when he was attempting to prove that he was not lying about something. Moreover, such details are usually about relatively insignificant things.

I can only imagine Moses speaking to his people when they asked him tedious and insignificant questions about the exact description of the cow. Moses went up to the top of the mountain and asked Allah about this specific description of the cow. Allah answered his question, and Moses came down from the mountain. Then the Jewish people asked him another question. Moses went back up the mountain again and asked Allah this particular question. This continued until all of these individual questions were answered by Allah in this story.

We must ask some questions here. *Does the Allah of Mohammed know the future? Did he know all of the questions that the Jewish people would ask Moses? If so, why did he not give a detailed complete description of the cow before the Jewish people had asked all of these questions?* Perhaps if Mohammed or those who helped him to make up this story in the Qur'an had read the account carefully in the Bible, we would not have this poor writing style, along with the many errors and mistakes found throughout this story in the Qur'an. A good example of an error is the color of the cow. As Mohammed clearly stated it was a bright yellow. Another huge error is the purpose of killing the cow. These errors will be revealed as we compare the Qur'an verses to the account in the Bible.

The Revelation of Error

Also, Muslim scholars disagree about which part of the cow was used to strike the dead man.[93] Some said it was the meat of the thigh, some said it was with some bones of the cow, and some said it was with the spine which is between the two shoulders. When they struck the dead body with the part of the cow, Allah raised the man back to life. Then he stood up, and Prophet Moses asked the man who killed him. So the man said, "My nephew killed me." Then the man died again.

As it is written in Qur'an 2:72-73: *[72]And when you kill a soul and disagree among yourselves about it, and Allah brings forth what you were hiding. [73]So we said, "Strike him with part of it." Likewise, Allah gives life to the dead and shows you his signs, perhaps you may understand.*

One must ask some questions here. *What is the source for Muslims to come up with this story? Does the reader, Muslim or not, get the sense that this is a fairy tale?* The source of this account is the Bible in Deuteronomy 21:1-9. We encourage the reader to read the entire chapter and learn what the Lord said to Moses concerning future events, not about the murder of a specific uncle.

Deuteronomy 21 clearly teaches that if a person was found murdered on a farm and no one knows who killed him, there was a specific procedure to follow. Notice it is a farm, not a crossroad or in front of someone's door where the person was found murdered. The elders and judges of this land would measure (the area) between the crime scene and the nearest city. Then they would take a heifer (a young cow) from the nearest city which had never been used for labor. The elders of this city would take this heifer into a valley which had never been used for farming, and there they would break this heifer's neck. The priests, the sons of Levi, would draw near to the sacrifice, and the elders of this city would come out and wash their hands over the heifer, as they would state that they had not shed this blood and their eyes had not seen the crime committed. Then they would say, "Be merciful to your people Israel and lay not innocent blood onto your people." Then the bloodshed would be atoned, the guilt would be put away of the murder, and the Children of Israel would be forgiven.

As for the bright yellow cow, I have investigated to determine if a cow of bright yellow could be bred. I was informed by a professional

---

[93]Ibid., 343.

breeder, with expertise in genetics, that there has never been a cow with such a color because genetics do not permit it. Genetic research supports this.[94] I learned that there are several genes that will wash out the basic coat color. The Dilute genes (there are apparently several of these which do slightly different things) are incompletely dominant — one copy turns red to light red or orange, black to grey, or brown to lighter brown. <u>Two copies turn the animal lighter still — red to yellow or cream</u>, black to light gray, brown to dun. One variant of this gene in Charolais turns cattle nearly white in its homozygous form. Note the only yellow is a faded red or cream color, not a bright yellow.

The only place in the Bible where God asked Moses to kill a specific color cow (heifer) is found in Deuteronomy 19:2. The Bible said it was to be a red heifer without spot, without any blemish, and which had never been yoked. This red heifer was to be burned for purification. We encourage the reader to read the entire chapter.

<u>The Rejection from Entering the Promised Land</u>

Ibn Kathir stated that the prophet of Allah, Moses, reminded the Children of Israel of the grace of Allah and his goodness to them.[95] He commanded them to perform jihad for the sake of Allah and fight the enemy of Allah. That is when he said, in Qur'an 5:20-21: *[20]And when Moses said to his people, "O my people, remember the grace of Allah on you when he made prophets among you. And he made you kings, and he gave you what he did not give anyone of the world. [21]O my people, enter the holy land which Allah has prescribed for you, and do not turn away on your backs so you will be turned back losers."* This means not to retreat in the fight with the enemy that they may not lose after winning and be reduced after being perfect.

The response of his people was in Qur'an 5:22: *[22]They said, "O Moses, surely in it are powerful people, and surely we will not enter it until they come out of it. So if they come out of it, so surely we will enter."* Ibn Kathir interpreted this verse by saying that they were afraid to fight these giants, even though they had seen the destruction of Pharaoh who was more powerful and had more

---

[94]"Coat Color in Cattle," *Fern Hill Farm,* accessed January 24, 2012, http://www.sss-mag.com/fernhill/cowcolor.html.
[95]Ibn Kathir, 323.

The Revelation of Error

soldiers. Therefore, no such excuse could be given to them for not fighting the enemy.

Ibn Kathir continued with the exaggeration that the people of the land were so big that one of them put the twelve messengers in his sleeves. He said these were myths and there was no truth in them. The king sent with them a cluster of grapes. Each grape in the cluster was enough for a man to be satisfied. This teaching is not true.

They also mentioned there was a man by the name Aog Ibn Onk who was 3333.3 cubits, and this teaching is also untrue. The proof that these teachings are false is that Ibn Kathir said that Mohammed said when Allah created Adam, Adam was sixty cubits and from the days of Adam "until now people are getting shorter." It was said that Aog picked up the top of the mountain and threw it on the army of Moses, but a bird punched a hole in it so it became like a ring around his neck. Then Moses jumped on him in the air and with a rod in his hand, he killed him.

Ibn Kathir stated that this is from the Israelite teaching which includes much foolishness and lies.[96] It is amazing that Ibn Kathir saw myths in these stories, but he then cannot see that Mohammed saying that Adam was ninety feet tall is a myth.

Ibn Kathir continued by interpreting the following verse in Qur'an 5:23: *[23]Two men among the fearers, Allah graced on them, said, "Enter on them the door. So when you enter it, so surely you will be victorious. And on Allah, so depend, if you were believers."*[97] Here he said these two men fear Allah and Allah has graced on them by Islam, faith, obedience, and courage. They said if you depend on Allah and seek his help, you will have victory over your enemy.

However, the Children of Israel said in Qur'an 5:24: *[24]They said, "O Moses, surely we will never enter it as long as they are in it. So go, you and your lord. So engage in war. Surely we are sitting down right here."* Here they refused to perform the jihad and that was a very great weakness. Also, it was said that Joshua and Caleb, when they heard these words, tore their clothes. *How did Ibn Kathir know these two names, Joshua and Caleb?*

Then Moses said, in Qur'an 5:25: *[25]He said, "My lord, surely I do not own anything except myself and my brother, so separate*

---
[96]Ibid., 323.
[97]Ibid., 324.

between us and the transgressing people." Ibn Kathir said that Ibn Abbas said it means "judge between us and the people." Then Allah said, in Qur'an 5:26: *[26]He said, "So surely it[98] is forbidden to them forty years; they will be lost on the earth. So do not grieve on the transgressing people."* Ibn Kathir said this means that they were punished by being lost in the land traveling without a purpose or a goal, night and day, morning and evening, until all of them died during the forty years, except Joshua and Caleb.

Ibn Kathir closed this section by emphasizing the statement, *"So go, you and your lord. So engage in war."*[99] By quoting many hadith, the believers in Mohammed made the same statement to Mohammed by saying, *"*We will not say, 'So go, you and your lord. So engage in war.'" The Children of Israel said to Moses that they would fight along with him. They would be on his right hand, left hand, and between his hands. They would be in front of him and behind him. There the face of Mohammed was shining, and he was very pleased. What a loving, peaceful prophet.

Ibn Kathir told the story of the Children of Israel's disbelief concerning the taking of the Promised Land. Obviously, he misunderstood the story because he made many errors. I will not blame him for this because the information is missing in the Qur'an; he simply tried to complete the story without taking the entire story from the Bible.

He was able to fill in the names of Joshua and Caleb, but he forgot to mention the rest of the twelve spies, which one can find in the book of Numbers 13:4-15. He did not tell the complete true story of the twelve spies' mission to the land of Canaan as commanded of Moses by God. He did not give the full report which the twelve spies gave of their mission. He made fun of the grapes and added a fabricated story, with no facts, concerning the people of the land. The truth of the report of the spies was that the cluster of grapes was huge, and it was carried on staffs between two men. The land was filled with milk and honey. However, the people of the land were strong; and, because of that, ten of the spies did not believe they could take over the land. They described themselves as if they were grasshoppers in their own eyes.

---

[98] the Promised Land
[99] Ibn Kathir, 324.

The Revelation of Error

When the people (Jews) heard the report, they lifted up their voices and cried, "We wish we would have died in the land of Egypt." They grumbled against Moses and Aaron. Moses and Aaron fell on their faces before the assembly. Joshua and Caleb tore their clothes, and they tried to encourage the people to take the land for they believed the Lord would give it to them. This land was very good. So because of their doubt, God desired to destroy the entire people of the Children of Israel by striking them with disease. However, Moses cried out to God and pleaded for God not to do it. He begged God to forgive the sin of the people. Therefore, God said that all men of the age of twenty and older would never see the Promised Land, except for Caleb and Joshua.

As for the men who spread the rumors to scare the people from taking the Promised Land, they died from the plague. The following morning the people tried to take the Promised Land. Moses said, "Do not go, for it will not prosper," but they went anyway. Then the Amalekites and Canaanites who lived on the mountain came down and smote them. We encourage the reader to read the entire account and its details in Numbers 13 and 14.

The Children of Israel Lost in the Wilderness

When we read the Bible's account of what took place in the lives of the Children of Israel, there is so much recorded in the Torah, the first five books, and in the book of Joshua, that this would be a large book in itself. As usual, the story is not included in the pages of the Qur'an except for a few sentences. Ibn Kathir filled in the missing information by adding it from the Bible's account. It is ironic that Ibn Kathir and other Muslim scholars criticized the Bible for being corrupted, while they repeatedly took information from the Bible and corrupted it in a desperate attempt to explain and correct the many fallacies of the Qur'an.

For example, Ibn Kathir stated that Joshua prepared Moses to fight some of the infidels.[100] Moses and Aaron and Khor sat on top of a hill. Every time Moses lifted up his staff, Joshua was prevailing; but every time his hand went down from exhaustion, Joshua began to lose until Aaron and Khor supported his hands on the left and on the right. Then the group with Joshua won the battle. This story is taken from Exodus 17 which obviously took place before the forty years in the

---

[100]Ibid., 326.

wilderness. Here Ibn Kathir presented the story as if it took place after the forty years in the wilderness. Obviously, this story is missing a lot of information. For the sake of time and space, I will not write the rest of the story as Ibn Kathir put it, but we encourage the readers to read the entire account in the Bible.[101]

I would like to share another example of the abridged story in Qur'an 20:80-82: *[80]"O children of Israel, indeed, we have delivered you from your enemy. And we made a covenant with you on the right side of the mountain, and we caused the manna and the quail to descend on you. [81]Eat of the good things which we provided to you, and do not rebel in them, lest my wrath falls on you. For on whom my wrath does fall, so indeed, destroyed. [82]And I am surely forgiving to who repented and believed and did good deed, then guided."*

How much information has been given on this passage? Hardly any! None of this information gives any details to help the reader to know what in the world Mohammed was talking about. For example, Allah saved the Children of Israel from their enemy. *What enemy? When did he save them? How did he save them? Why did he save them? Where did he save them?* Another example is the statement, **"we made a covenant with you."** *What covenant?*

Wow, the right side of the mountain? Which right side? Another example of the lack of information is, "we descend on you the manna and the quail." *What is the real story behind the manna and the quail? How did it descend? What is manna? How much did they take on Monday? How much did they take on Friday?*

That is how the Qur'an is written. It is a much abbreviated book. It is a foolish counterfeit of the Bible. Not only is there very little information given, but when the information is given, it is almost always wrong. I am not talking about doctrine, but the simple history and facts are missing. That's why I believe it is very important for our dear Muslim friends to read the Holy Bible and compare it to *The Generous Qur'an*.

I would like to share an example here when Ibn Kathir quoted Qur'an 2:60-61: *[60]And when Moses gave drink for his people, so we said, "Strike the rock with your rod." So gushed from it twelve springs; indeed, all humans knew their drinking place: "Eat and drink from Allah's provision, and do not act wickedly in*

---

[101]Ibid., 326-327.

the land, vandalizing." [61]And when you said, "O Moses, we will not be patient with one food, so pray to your lord for us that he would bring forth for us of that which the earth grows: its herbs and its cucumbers and its garlic and its lentils and its onions." He said, "Do you exchange that which is worse for what is better? Go down into Egypt, so surely you will have what you have asked." And the humiliation and poverty were struck on them, and they returned with wrath from Allah because they were infidels with the āyat[102] of Allah; and they killed the prophets unjustly because they disobeyed, and they were transgressors.[103]

It would be better if Mohammed just said in the Qur'an, "We give you a drink." Instead, he gets himself in trouble by adding more information; the more Mohammed said in the Qur'an, the more errors he made. The interpretation by Ibn Kathir is much worse than the verse because he made the story worse than it already was.

We will only concentrate on verse 60, and we advise the reader to go back to the Bible and read the true account in Exodus 17:6 and Exodus 15:27. According to the Qur'an, Moses struck the rock with his rod and twelve springs of water came gushing out of the rock for the Children of Israel.

Now let us look at the interpretation of Ibn Kathir. Moses used his rod to strike the rock which the Israelites used to carry. When we read the interpretation of Ibn Kathir to find the source of the rock which brought all the water for the Children of Israel, we notice the exact number of springs that gushed out from this rock were twelve springs. Not eleven. Not thirteen. *I wonder how big this rock was which the Children of Israel "used to carry." How many of the children did it take to carry the rock? How much water was gushing from the springs?*

Now I would like to correct the record. The twelve wells of water are found in Exodus 15:27 and were located in the land of Elim. There were also seventy palm trees. There was no rod, and Moses did not hit the rock.

How about the real account of the rock and the rod of Moses? We can find the answer in Exodus 17:1-7. The Children of Israel were traveling in the Wilderness of Sin, they were specifically in

---

[102]signs, non-Arabic word of Syriac/Aramaic origin
[103]Ibn Kathir, 328.

Rephidim. Notice the Bible gives the exact location where the story took place. The people chided Moses and were in conflict with him because they were thirsty. The people said, "Why did you get us out of Egypt, to cause us and our children and our cattle to die of thirst?" Moses cried out to God, "What should I do with these people; they are almost ready to stone me?" Then God answered Moses and said, "Go before the people. Take with you the elders and the rod in your hand. There I will stand before you upon the rock in Horeb."

Notice that God would stand upon the rock and that no one carried the rock! Exodus 17:6 states, "So you smite the rock and the water will come out of it, so that all the people will drink." Notice that it was not twelve springs, but the water simply came out of the rock. Then Moses called this place Massah and Meribah which means "Is the Lord among us, or not?" *Do you see, dear reader, the difference in the account of the Bible and the error of the Qur'an with the ridiculous interpretations of the Muslim scholars?*

The Story of Moses and the Khidr (The Green Prophet)

This story is found in Qur'an 18:60-82. Let us examine these verses beginning with verse 60: **⁶⁰And when Moses said to his young man, "I will not stop until I reach the confluence of the two seas, or I will be traveling for years."**

Who was this Moses? Ibn Kathir claimed that the People of the Book (Jews and Christians) said or believed that he was Moses Ibn Mesha, Ibn Joseph, Ibn Jacob, Ibn Isaac, Ibn Abraham.[104] My response is very simple. This is just a fabrication for neither the Jews nor the Christians believe this. A simple study of the book of Genesis will prove that Joseph son of Jacob did not have any sons by the name of Mesha or a grandson by the name of Moses; therefore, I could not find proof of this genealogy. Ibn Kathir corrected the "false teaching" of the People of the Book by assuring the reader that this Moses of this story is Prophet Moses, son of Amran, the companion of the Children of Israel.

Ibn Kathir quoted the hadith of Mohammed to prove that it was Moses the prophet of the Children of Israel by stating that Mohammed said, "Moses stood up to preach to the Children of Israel. So he was asked who is the most knowledgeable of the people. He said, 'I am.' Allah corrected him and sent Moses to another servant

---

[104]Ibid., 344.

who had more knowledge than he. Allah told him that he would meet this man at the confluence of the two seas. So Moses asked Allah, 'How can I recognize him?' Then Allah told him to 'take a whale (Mohammed used the wrong word; I'm guessing he meant *fish*) with you and put it in Mektel (a bag). Wherever you lose the whale, that is where you will find him.'"

This is found in the following verses: *[61] So when they reached their confluence, they forgot their whale. So it got its way into the sea going away. [62] So when they had gone farther, he said to his young man, "Bring our lunch to us, indeed, we have incurred weariness from this our traveling." [63] He said, "Did you see when we took refuge in the rock, so surely I have forgotten the whale. No one causes me to forget to mention it except Satan, and it has taken its way in the sea wondrously."*

Ibn Kathir interpreted the previous verses by explaining that Moses took a whale and put it in a Mektel (the Qur'an said that he forgot the whale), and he traveled with it.[105] He also took a young man, Yoshaa Ibn Noon. He meant Joshua. They traveled together until they came to a rock. They put their heads on it, and they slept. The whale became anxious inside the Mektel and came out of it and went into the sea. When they woke up, his companion forgot to tell Moses about the whale, and they continued to travel the rest of the day and the night until the following day. Moses said to his young man, "Bring our lunch to us, indeed we have incurred weariness from this our traveling."

Moses did not find the monuments until they passed the place to which Allah commanded him to go. Then his young man told him, "Did you see when we took refuge in the rock, so surely I have forgotten the whale. No one causes me to forget to mention it except Satan, and it has taken its way in the sea wondrously." Moses and the young man were surprised because now the whale was with a whole pod of whales.

[64] He said, "It is this we were seeking." So they went back retracing their footsteps. [65] Then they found a servant from our servants whom we had given mercy from us and whom we had instructed with our knowledge. Ibn Kathir said they went back until they arrived at the rock and there was a man lying down in a gown. So Moses said, "Peace be on you." Then Moses asked him to teach

---

[105] Ibid., 345.

him and give him guidance. Ibn Kathir continued by stating that this man told Moses that "you will not have patience with me." But Moses said, "By Allah's will you will see me patient, and I will not disobey you." As it is written in the Qur'an: *[66]And Moses said to him, "Will I follow you so that you will teach me guidance from what you have been taught?" [67]He said, "Surely you cannot have patience with me. [68]And how can you be patient in that you do not have knowledge of?" [69]He said, "You will find me patient if Allah wills, and I will not disobey your command." [70]He said, "So if you follow me, so do not ask me about anything until I mention to you something about it."*

Ibn Kathir interpreted the following verses: *[71]So they went on until they embarked in a safīna,[106] and he made a hole in it. He said, "Have you made a hole in it so that you may drown its people? Indeed, you have done an idiotic thing!" [72]He said, "Did I not tell you that you surely would not have patience with me?" [73]He said, "Pardon me for my forgetfulness, and do not overburden me of my difficult affair."*[107] His interpretation was, "So they both got out of the ship walking again on the shore."

Then Ibn Kathir continued the story by interpreting the following verses: *[74]So they went on until they met a young man, so he killed him. So he said, "Have you killed a pure soul, without a soul?[108] Indeed, you have done a horrible thing!" [75]He said, "Did I not tell you that surely you would not have patience with me?" [76]He said, "If I ask you about anything after this, so do not accompany me. Indeed, you have received an excuse from me." [77]So they went on until they came to the people of a village. They asked these people for food, but they refused to host them. So they found in it a wall that was about to fall so he set it upright. He said, "If you had willed, you might have obtained a wage for this."*

[78]He said, "This is the parting between you and me. But I will first tell you the interpretation of that with which you could not be patient. [79]As to the ship, so it was owned by poor men who worked on the sea, and I was minded to damage it, for in their rear was a king who seized every ship by force. Ibn Kathir

---

[106]ship, non-Arabic word of Aramaic origin
[107]Ibn Kathir, 345.
[108]who did not commit murder

The Revelation of Error

interpreted these verses by adding that if the wicked king came by the ship and saw it had a defect, he would not take it, but rather leave it.[109] Then, after the king leaves they would be able to fix it.

⁸⁰And as to the young man (Ibn Kathir added that he was an infidel), *so his parents were believers so we feared lest he should trouble them by rebellion and infidelity.* That is, he may lead them to follow his religion because of their love for him. *⁸¹So we desired that their lord might exchange in his place, better than he was in virtue and closer in mercy. ⁸²And as to the wall, so it was owned by two young men, orphaned in the city, and under it was a treasure to them. And their father was a righteous man, so your lord desired that they should reach the age of strength and take forth their treasure as a mercy from your lord. And I did not do it of my own affair. This is the interpretation of that which you could not have patience."*

Ibn Kathir stated that Al Sohale said that these two young men were Asrum and Srem, sons of Kashah. "And under it was a treasure to both of them." It was said by Akramah that it was gold, but Ibn Abbas said it was knowledge. Ibn Kathir said perhaps it was a board of gold that has knowledge on it, and their father was a righteous man, so their lord desired that they should reach the age of strength and take forth their treasure as a mercy from their lord. The Green said to Moses, "This is the interpretation that Moses could not have patience."

There is a long history of disagreement among Muslim scholars concerning this story. For the sake of time and space, we have decided to abbreviate the commentary.

<u>The Building of the Tabernacle</u>

Although neither the Qur'an nor the hadith mention anything about the building of the Tabernacle, Ibn Kathir gave some information concerning the Tabernacle, the material used to build the Tabernacle, the Ark of the Covenant with the details of its description, and all the tools used for the altar. Then he inserted Qur'an 2:248: *²⁴⁸And their prophet said to them, "Surely the sign of his kingdom will be that the tābūt*[110] *will come to you. In it is tranquility from your lord and the relics left by the family of*

---

[109] Ibn Kathir, 347.
[110] ark, non-Arabic word of Egyptian origin

Moses and the family of Aaron. The angels will carry it. Surely in this is a sign to you if you were believers."

Ibn Kathir continued that in their books there are long details to the laws and the judges, the description of the offerings, the Ark of the Covenant, and the Tabernacle. He claimed all these were there before the worship of the golden calf, for he was deceitfully trying to make the Jews look bad because, although they had the true guidance for worship in their books, they turned away from true worship to worship the golden calf. He continued by stating that Moses used to enter the Tabernacle, the pillar of cloud would come to its door, and all the Jews would come to bow down to worship Allah.

I would like to correct some of Ibn Kathir's errors. The Tabernacle was not built before the worship of the golden calf but after it. As we read in the book of Exodus in chapter 35, the Tabernacle did not yet exist when Moses asked the people to give gifts to the Lord of gold, silver, brass, and other material to build the Tabernacle. As to the descriptions, we would encourage the reader to read Exodus 25 through 31.

Ibn Kathir continued by stating that Allah spoke to Moses from a pillar of cloud which is light.[111] Allah spoke to him, then commanded him and forbade him while he was standing by the Ark of the Covenant. Then Moses spoke to the Children of Israel concerning whatever Allah revealed to him, and whenever a situation arose for which Moses had no answer, he would go stand by the Ark of the Covenant until Allah gave him an answer. Ibn Kathir stated that it was lawful at that time for them to use gold, silver, and jewelry in their temple, but he stated that in Islamic Law it was forbidden for the decoration of the mosque and the ornaments in it, as they could distract those who pray.

As Mohammed told Omer when he enlarged the Mosque of Mohammed, "Build to the people. I forbid you the red and the yellow (he meant not to decorate or paint with colors) because it could tempt the people." However, amazingly, there are hundreds of colorful and very ornate mosques which exist today.

Ibn Kathir concluded that the Tabernacle existed during the Children of Israel's travel in the wilderness.[112] It was their place of prayer because they used to pray towards it. It used to be their Kaaba,

---
[111] Ibn Kathir, 360.
[112] Ibid.

The Revelation of Error

Moses was their imam (meaning leader), and Aaron was the one who offered up the offering for them. After Moses and Aaron died, the children of Aaron continued to perform the offering from then until now. As for the prophethood duty following Moses' death, it was fulfilled by Yosha (he meant Joshua) until they entered the Holy Land. There he put the Tabernacle on the Dome of the Rock.

So it was the Qiblah (direction of prayer) for the prophets until the time of Mohammed, and Mohammed prayed toward it until his emigration to Medina. He was commanded to continue to pray toward it for sixteen or seventeen months, and then he changed the direction of the prayer toward the Kaaba, as it is written in Qur'an 2:142-144:

142 The fools among the people will say, "What has turned them from the direction[113] which they were?" Say, "The east and the west to Allah. He guides whom he wills into a straight way." 143 And likewise, we have made you a central nation that you may be witnesses against the people and that the messenger may be a witness against you. And we did not appoint the direction which you were on except that we might know who follows the messenger from him who turns on his heels. And it was a big[114] except to those whom Allah guided. And Allah was not to let your faith be lost. Surely Allah, to the people, is compassionate, merciful. 144 Indeed, we have seen you turning your face toward the heaven. So we will have you turn to a direction which will please you. So turn your face toward the forbidden mosque.[115] And wherever you are, so turn your faces toward that place. And surely those who have been given the book know for sure that this is the truth from their lord. And Allah is not unaware of what they were doing.

It would have been better for Ibn Kathir, in my opinion, if he had not mentioned anything concerning the Tabernacle and the Jewish worship. He opened a can of worms which he could not handle, and then he purposely ignored the most important thing about the Jewish faith, the sacrifice. Just as Mohammed in his Qur'an purposely ignored these facts, so did Ibn Kathir. That is why we encourage the reader to study these facts from the biblical account with its interpretation by Jewish and Christian scholars so he may see for

---

[113] of prayer
[114] a difficult task
[115] Masjid ul Haraam at Mecca

himself the details of information about the size of the Tabernacle, its measurements, the materials used to build it, the colors, what each large and small part represented as a symbol, and how all this has been fulfilled by our Lord and Savior Jesus Christ through His life, death, and resurrection.

When Jesus fulfilled all of the above, the veil in the temple was torn apart from top to bottom (Matthew 27:51). This demonstrated that there was no longer any need for the physical Tabernacle to exist as a place of God's dwelling on earth because of the death of Jesus Christ on the cross and the shedding of His blood, which was the perfect sacrifice for all time and eternity. This opened the way for God to dwell in the hearts of men.

The Mysterious Egyptian Believer

Although Mohammed left out many important parts of the story of Moses, we find in the following passage that Mohammed added this story which has no details to attempt to prove its existence in the life of Moses, for we have no evidence of it in the true biblical account. That is why I chose the subtitle, "The Mysterious Egyptian Believer." No name has been given to this character. Ibn Kathir stated that he was returning to the advice, the preaching, and the objection of this mysterious believer.[116]

As it is written in Qur'an 40:28-29: *28And a believing man from the family of Pharaoh, who was hiding his faith, said, "Will you kill a man because he is saying, 'My lord is Allah'? And indeed, he came to you with the proofs from your lord. And if he is a liar, so his lie is against him. And if he is truthful, some of what he promises will fall on you. Surely Allah will not guide he who is extravagant, a liar. 29O my people, the kingdom is yours today. [You are the ones who] appeared on the earth. So who will help from the torment of Allah, if it comes to us?" Pharaoh said, "I will not let you see except what I see, and I will not guide you except to the right way."* Ibn Kathir explained that this mysterious believer was the cousin of Pharaoh, and he hid his belief because he was afraid that the Egyptians would kill him. Then Ibn Kathir inserted the second opinion that he was from among the Jews for he was an Israelite, stating that this was not true because it did not

---

[116]Ibn Kathir, 361.

fit with the wording of the sentence. He ended by stating, *and Allah knows best*.

Ibn Kathir stated that Ibn Abbas said that not one of the Egyptians, except for two, believed in Moses. These were a man who came from the far end of the city and Pharaoh's wife. When Pharaoh decided to kill Moses, he took counsel from his people. This believer feared for Moses' life, so he spoke to Pharaoh to calm him. Then he ran into Moses far away from the city and told him that the people of the city desired to kill him and advised him to leave Egypt.

We can find this story in Qur'an 28:19-21: *[19]So when he desired to seize the one who is an enemy to them, he said, "O Moses, do you desire to kill me as you killed a soul yesterday? Do you only desire to become a powerful in the land, and you do not desire to become of the good?" [20]And a man from the remotest part of the city came running. He said, "O Moses, surely the leaders are consulting to kill you. So get out! Surely I am an advisor to you." [21]So he got out from it in fear, vigilant. He said, "My lord, deliver me from the unjust people!"* I do not see how Ibn Kathir or any other Muslim scholar could have tied these verses to Qur'an 40:28-29. Obviously, neither Mohammed nor his Muslim scholars had any concept of the time and history of the life of Moses because a simple reading of the Bible will bring us to the conclusion that the time of Moses leaving Egypt and the time of his returning to lead the Hebrews out of Egypt was forty years, as we mentioned previously. This Pharaoh that Moses met with was a completely different Pharaoh. The first Pharaoh had died, as is found in Exodus 2:23.

Ibn Kathir stated that this mysterious believer said to Pharaoh and his people, "Will you kill a man who says Allah is my lord? And indeed, he came to you with proof from your lord." He was referring to the wonderful miracles Moses performed. I do not see where this man was hiding his belief if he spoke to Pharaoh about Moses with such words. From the rest of verses 28 and 29, I can clearly say he is no longer a believer in secret but openly, unless Pharaoh and his people were mentally deficient, especially when he said, "Who will give us victory from the torment of Allah?"

No Egyptian believed in Allah, and here he was speaking about the power of Allah. Not only did this believer believe in Moses, but he also believed in all of the stories of the Qur'an, which did not even exist. From the contents of his speech in verses 30-33, I believe he was an imaginary Muslim believer who believed in Mohammed and his made-up stories. For the Qur'an stated: *³⁰And the one who believed said, "O my people, surely I fear for you, like the parties day. ³¹Like the habit of the people of Noah and Ad and Themoud and those who came after them, and Allah does not desire injustice to the servants. ³²And, O my people, surely I fear for you the summoning (resurrection) day. ³³A day you will turn your back, retreating, you will not have any defender against Allah, and whomever Allah leads astray, so he does not have a guide.*

This mysterious believer, as we saw in the above verses, believed in the fabricated stories of Mohammed and the day of parties which is Qur'an 33 and the story of Ad and Themoud. He also believed in the Allah of Mohammed, the one who leads people astray (Satan). Also, in the following verses, in Qur'an 40:34-35: *³⁴And indeed, Joseph brought to you the proofs before. So you are still in doubt from what he brought you until, when he perished, you said, 'Allah will not send a messenger after him.' Likewise, Allah leads astray who is extravagant, a doubter. ³⁵Those who dispute in the verses of Allah without authority he gave them, bigger wrath is with Allah and with those who believed. Likewise, Allah seals on the heart of every proud powerful."* Neither Jews nor Egyptians ever believed that Joseph was a prophet; only Mohammed believed so. That is why I believe that this mystery man was an imaginary Muslim believer.

Moses and Qūrūn

Qūrūn is mentioned in the Qur'an in three different locations. His full story is discussed in Qur'an 28:76-83, but his name is mentioned in two other locations, 29:39-40 and 40:23-24. Let us first begin with Qur'an 40:23-24: *²³And indeed, we sent Moses with our signs and with manifest authority ²⁴to Pharaoh and Haman and Qūrūn. So they said, "A lying sorcerer."* This is one of the passages where Mohammed erroneously put three people together who have nothing to do with each other. Ibn Kathir mentioned these two verses, but he did not give any interpretation or explanation for them.[117] Pharaoh was the king of Egypt, Haman lived in the kingdom of Ahasuerus approximately eight hundred years after Pharaoh, and

---

[117]Ibn Kathir, 364.

then Mohammed added Qūrūn to the group. One can come to the obvious conclusion from this verse that Qūrūn was one of the Egyptians. The agreement among these three men, Pharaoh, Haman, and Qūrūn, was that they disbelieved Moses and called him a sorcerer.

A similar conclusion concerning Qūrūn being an Egyptian can be found in the following verses, Qur'an 29:39-40: *[39]And Qūrūn and Pharaoh and Haman, and indeed, Moses came to them with the proofs. So they became proud on the earth, and they were not ahead. [40]So we seized each one with his sin. So some of them we sent on him a hailstorm, and some of them were seized by the shout. And some of them we sank him into the earth, and some of them we drowned. And Allah was not to treat them unjustly, but they were treating themselves unjustly.* Ibn Kathir simply wrote that the one whom Allah sunk into the ground was Qūrūn and the ones who drowned were Pharaoh and Haman and their troops.

Now let's go to the major portion of revelation which discusses the story of Qūrūn and is found in Qur'an 28:76-83. Beginning in verse 76: *[76]Surely Qūrūn[118] was one of Moses' people, so he rebelled against them. One must ask who Qūrūn was and what was his relationship to Moses?* Ibn Kathir gave an answer which obviously contradicts the previous verse.[119] He stated that Qūrūn was one of Pharaoh's people. Ibn Kathir stated that Ibn Abbas and others said that Qūrūn was a cousin of Moses. They stated that his name was Qūrūn, Ibn Ysher, Ibn Kahes. Moses' name was Moses, Ibn Amran, Ibn Kahes. On the other hand, Ibn Isaac said he was Moses' uncle.

I wonder how these Muslim scholars knew that he was Moses' cousin by giving these names if other scholars called him Moses' uncle. *Were they fabricating these names?* Obviously, the answer is *yes*, for when we read from the Bible in Exodus 6:20, we can find that Moses' father's name was Amram not Amran. Amram was the son of Kohath, son of Levi. On the other hand, to study the genealogy of Korah, which is the correct name for Qūrūn, one must read the source of this information which can be found in the book of Numbers in chapter 16. This story is obviously the source of Mohammed's Qūrūn story since much of the information of these two characters match.

---

[118]Korah, non-Arabic word of Hebrew origin and modified
[119]Ibn Kathir, 361.

Chapter 16

Numbers 16:1 tells us that Korah was the son of Izhar, the son of Kohath, the son of Levi. The real name in Arabic of the grandfather of both Moses and Korah is Kahat not Kahes as stated in error by Muslim scholars, and the real name of Korah's father in Arabic is Yshar not Ysher. Obviously, Muslim scholars read both of these passages from the Bible in Exodus 6:20 and Numbers 16:1. That is how they know about the family names; however, they did not correct the spelling in the Qur'an, but wrote them incorrectly to confirm Mohammed's errors.

Ibn Kathir stated that Qatadah said that Korah used to be named Al Monawar (the one who sheds light) for he used to have a beautiful voice reciting the Torah.[120] He was deceived by his wealth because he used to have many treasures. The keys to these treasures were so heavy that none of the strong men were able to carry them, as it is written in Qur'an 28:76: *[76]Surely Qūrūn[121] was one of Moses' people, so he rebelled against them. We gave to him of the treasures what surely its keys would have burdened a strong, substantial company. When his people said to him, "Do not rejoice, surely Allah does not love the rejoicing.*

It was said that the treasure was put into animal skins and used to be carried on sixty mules, *and Allah knows best*. The wise one among his people advised him not to be happy, not to rejoice, because Allah does not love the rejoicing one. They also advised him not to forget his share of this world, and he should enjoy himself with what is lawful and good and that he may do good with his treasure as Allah did good to him. Also, they continued to advise him not to seek mischief in the land and not to do evil to them so Allah may not punish him and take what he has given him of wealth. For Allah does not love a mischievous one as it is written in Qur'an 28:77: *[77]And seek in what Allah has given you, the home of the hereafter, and do not forget your portion from this world. And do good as Allah has done good to you, and do not seek the vandalizing in the land. Surely Allah does not love the vandals."*

Ibn Kathir said his answer to this advice was, "Surely I have been given it only because of the knowledge that I possess." He meant, "I do not need your advice for Allah has given me this wealth because he knows I deserve it, and I am worthy. If it was not that he loves me

---
[120]Ibid.
[121]Korah, non-Arabic word of Hebrew origin and modified

and my luck is with him, he would not have given me what he has given me."

Ibn Kathir stated in his interpretation of verse 78 that Allah's response to Qūrūn was: *Did he know that Allah indeed destroyed before him some generations that were mightier than he in strength and more gathering,*[122] *and the criminals will not be asked about their sins.*[123] Some claim the interpretation of Qūrūn's statement was that he gained his wealth from his knowledge because Qūrūn was a chemist. That was how he became rich.

Then Allah said in Qur'an 28:79: *[79]So he went forth to his people in his adornment.* (Many interpreters have said *adornment* means dressing with great adornment for his servants.) *So those who desire the world's life said, "Oh, we wish we had the like of that which has been given to Qūrūn, surely he has a great luck."* And then in 28:80-81: *[80]And those who have been given the knowledge said, "Woe to you! The reward of Allah is better for him who believed and did good deed..."* (meaning Allah's reward in the hereafter is better, lasting, and higher). Then Allah said, *"... and no [one] will receive it, except the patient." [81]So we sunk him and his home into the earth. So there was not any group to help him without Allah, and he was not of the helped.*

Ibn Kathir stated that Ibn Abbas said that Qūrūn gave some woman some money so she could accuse Moses in front of all the people of what he had done to her.[124] So it was said she did do that. So lightning struck. Then Moses prayed by kneeling twice. When he came back to her, he asked her to swear concerning what she had said and tell him who made her say that. She said it was Qūrūn who had asked her to say that. Then she sought Allah's forgiveness and repented. Moses worshiped Allah and called out to Allah against Qūrūn. So Allah revealed to him, "Surely I have commanded the earth to obey you." Then and there Moses ordered the earth to swallow Qūrūn and his house. So it was, *and Allah knows best*.

Other scholars have different stories about how this took place which we will not mention here for the sake of time. Ibn Kathir also wrote that Qatadah said that Qūrūn sinks into the earth every day until

---

[122] richer
[123] Ibn Kathir, 361-364.
[124] Ibn Kathir, 363.

the day of resurrection. Ibn Abbas said that Allah sunk Qūrūn into the seventh earth.

Ibn Kathir wrote that when the people saw what had happened to Qūrūn, his money, and his possessions, they gave thanks to Allah for his will in the life of his servants. That is when they said in Qur'an 28:82-83: *[82]And those who desired his position yesterday were saying, "No wonder that Allah expands and measures the provision to whom he wills of his servants. Were it not for Allah's grace on us, he may sink us! No wonder that the infidels do not prosper." [83]This is the home of the hereafter. We made it for those who do not desire exaltation on the earth nor vandalization, and the end is to the fearer.*

When comparing this story, as it is written in the Qur'an and the interpretation of the Muslim scholars to the true account which is written in Numbers 16:1-40, one can see how many errors were made in one simple story. We encourage the reader to read the entire chapter of Numbers 16.

However, here is a summary. Korah, son of Izhar; Dathan and Abiram, the sons of Eliab; On, the son of Peleth, the son of Reuben; and 250 other men from the Children of Israel grumbled against Moses. They rejected his leadership over them. When Moses heard this, he fell upon his face for his heart was broken. Then he put a test before the Lord to see if God would choose these others as leaders or choose himself and Aaron.

The Lord spoke with Moses and Aaron, asking them to separate from the Children of Israel for God desired to destroy the Jews who had complained against Moses. This happened twice, first in verse 21 and then again in verse 45, but Moses fell upon his face interceding on their behalf asking God not to destroy them. Moses told the people that if these men die in a normal way, then the Lord had not sent Moses. However, if these men die in an unusual way by the earth opening up and swallowing them and all their families and possessions, then the people would know that these men had rejected the Lord. Moses asked the congregation to separate from Korah and his company so the congregation would not be harmed because of the sin of Korah and his followers. When Moses finished speaking, the earth swallowed them just as he had said. Fire came out from the Lord and consumed the 250 men who had complained against Moses.

The next day a second complaint arose by the rest of the people of the congregation in saying that Moses and Aaron had killed the people of the Lord. This can be found in verse 41. This time the Lord caused a plague to kill 14,700 people from among the Children of Israel because of the sin of Korah. When Aaron and Moses interceded on their behalf, the plague was stopped.

Ibn Kathir continued to write about Moses and his character, as well as his visit to Mecca.[125] He described him to be a sincere man, a prophet, and a messenger, as he was chosen above the people by the words and the message of Allah. Somehow Mohammed used his imagination to see him somewhere in a valley near Mecca in Saudi Arabia; therefore, he was considered to be a person who performed the Hajj. Also, Mohammed described Moses' appearance when he met with him on his trip to the seven heavens. I do not find any importance in these writings, so I will not elaborate any further.

The Death of Moses

Ibn Kathir quoted Bukhari who quoted Abu Horyrah:
> The angel of death was sent to Moses (meant to take his soul), but he refused to give up his soul. So he said to Allah that you have sent me to a servant who does not desire death. So Allah said return to him and say to him to put his hand on top of an ox. He will have whatever numbers of hairs under his hand as years to live. Then the angel of death said, 'So what then, my lord?' Allah said, 'Then the death.'[126]

In another hadith, according to Ibn Kathir by Imam Ahmed who said that Abu Horyrah said that when the angel of death came to Moses to take his soul, Moses slapped the angel of death.[127] He knocked his eye out. So the angel of death came back to Allah saying that he had sent him to a servant who does not desire death and that Moses had poked out his eye. Then Allah returned his eye back to him. The rest of the hadith is like the previous one.

There is no similar story in the Bible. However, it may have been inspired by a battle described in Jude 1, not between Moses and the angel of death, but between Michael the Archangel and Satan. Jude 1:9 reads: *⁹**Yet Michael the archangel, in contending with the devil, when he disputed about the body of Moses, dared not bring against him a reviling accusation, but said, "The Lord rebuke you!"***

---

[125] Ibid., 365-369.
[126] Ibid., 370.
[127] Ibid., 371.

There are some obvious questions that need to be asked. *Why would Michael the Archangel want to keep Moses' body away from Satan? What would Satan do with his body?* The answer is found in the Bible in Exodus 20:13: *¹**And God spoke all these words, saying:** ²**"I am the LORD your God, who brought you out of the land of Egypt, out of the house of bondage. ³You shall have no other gods before Me."*** This is the first of the Ten Commandments, which states that we are to have no other gods before the true God.

Satan would have made the body of Moses and his grave an object of worship, just as he does with so many things in this world. Israel had formally been guilty of worshiping the golden calf. The body and tomb of Moses, the revered leader of the nation, would have been a constant place of visit by the people of Israel had they known where his body had been interred. God wants our worship to be only of Him, instead of some shrine to remind us of the past.

Ibn Kathir gave the details of Aaron's death.[128] He stated that Al Saddi and other scholars said that Allah revealed to Moses that Allah would cause Aaron to die.

> Allah asked Moses to take him to some mountain. Moses and Aaron went to the mountain, and behold, they were by a tree unlike any other. Behold, they were in a built house. They were on a bed which had covers and had a beautiful fragrance. When Aaron saw the mountain and the house and what was in it, he liked it. Then he said to Moses, 'I would love to sleep in this bed.' Then Moses said, 'So sleep on it.' But Aaron said, 'I am afraid that the lord of this house will come, and he will be angry at me.' Then Moses said, 'Do not be afraid; I will take care of the lord of the house. Just go to sleep.' Then Aaron said to Moses, 'Sleep with me, so if the lord, the owner of this house, comes, he will not get angry with both of us.'
>
> So when they both slept, Aaron was taken by death. So when he found his senses, he said to Moses, 'O Moses, you tricked me.' So when Aaron died, the house, the tree, and the bed were lifted to heaven. So when Moses returned to his people and Aaron was not with him, they said Moses killed Aaron because he envied the love of the Children of Israel.

---

[128] Ibid., 372.

This was said because Aaron was easy and soft with them, but Moses was rough and mean to them.

Then Moses said, 'Woe to you. You accuse me unfairly.' So he stood up, prayed, and kneeled twice. Then he called on Allah. So Allah sent down the bed from heaven, until all of them saw the bed between the heaven and the earth, meaning they saw Aaron sleeping on the bed.

Where did Ibn Kathir come up with this information? The true account of Aaron's death is found in the Bible in two different locations in the book of Numbers in 20:22-29 and 33:38-39. From Numbers 33 we discover Aaron died forty years after the Exodus from Egypt and that he died on the first day of the fifth month. He was 123 years old when he died. As for how he died, we must go to the record in Numbers 20:22-29, and we encourage the reader to read the entire chapter.

On the top of Mount Hor, God asked Moses to take Aaron and Eleazer his son to the top of the mountain. There Moses stripped the garment off Aaron and put it on Eleazer. When they went up to the mountain, it was in sight of the people. There on the mountain Aaron died and was buried. Then Moses and Eleazer came down from the mountain, and all the people mourned for Aaron for thirty days. What a great difference between the true biblical account and the erroneous fairy tale of the Muslim scholars.

Ibn Kathir continued by stating that when Moses was walking with his servant Yoshaa (which is a wrong name, he meant Joshua) a black wind came through. So Yoshaa thought it was the hour (of death) so he held onto Moses because he said if the hour comes, "I will be with Moses, the prophet of Allah." Then Moses was pulled out from under the shirt and left the shirt in the hands of Yoshaa. So when Yoshaa brought the shirt, the Children of Israel took the shirt; and they said, "You killed the prophet of Allah." Yoshaa said, "I swear by Allah, I did not kill him. He was pulled from me." But they did not believe him, and they decided to kill him. So Yoshaa said, "Delay me three days." So he called on Allah. So Allah came to all the men who were guarding him while he was sleeping (he was imprisoned). Allah told them that he did not kill Moses, but "I lifted him up to me." After Allah clarified that Yoshaa did not kill Moses, all those who refused to take the village of the giants had died. However, Yoshaa did not see the invasion, *and Allah knows best.*

Chapter 16

As for the true account of the death of Moses, one can read about it in Deuteronomy 34:1-8. Moses went to the top of Nebo, and there the Lord showed him the Promised Land. The Lord said to him, "This is the land that I swore unto your forefathers to give to them." Moses died there. He was buried in a grave by God, and no one knows even to this day its location. Then the Children of Israel wept and mourned for thirty days. The error concerning the shirt obviously was that Muslim scholars confused this with the story of Elijah and Elisha found in the book of 2 Kings 2:13-14. Joshua was not near Moses when he died.

Ibn Kathir continued by stating that none of the people of Moses who were in the wilderness entered the Promised Land except Yoshaa Ibn Noon and Caleb Ibn Yokona, and Yoshaa was the husband of Miriam the sister of Moses and Aaron.[129] They were the two men who indicated to the Children of Israel to enter the Promised Land.

Where did Ibn Kathir come up with this information? None of this information is in the Qur'an. Moreover, he is in apparent error about Miriam being the wife of Yoshaa. Miriam was actually the older sister of Moses and Aaron who was a strong influence in Moses' life beginning with her watching over him while as an infant he was hidden in the reeds, reuniting him with his mother by approaching the daughter of Pharaoh after he was found in the reeds, and offering to find a wet-nurse for him (Exodus 2:3-4).

Josephus, the first century Jewish historian, in *Antiquities of the Jews* states that Miriam was the wife of Hur, who is mentioned in Exodus as a close companion of Moses.[130] He was also a member of the tribe of Judah.

Ibn Kathir stated Whab Ibn Monabah said that Moses was walking by a group of angels who were digging a grave. He had never seen such a beautiful grave. So Moses said, "O angels of Allah, for whom are you digging this grave?" They said, "To a generous servant of Allah. So if you would love to be that servant, so enter this grave and stretch in it and go to your lord and breathe easier breathing." Moses did that, and so he died. All the angels prayed over him and then buried him. Ibn Kathir ended by stating a fact that the People of the Book said Moses died when he was 120 years old.

---

[129] Ibn Kathir, 372.
[130] Josephus, *Antiquities of the Jews*: Book 3, accessed January 24, 2012, http://sacred-texts.com/jud/josephus/ant-3.htm.

The Revelation of Error

Jews Are Monkeys and Swine

In three locations throughout the Qur'an, Mohammed claimed that Allah turned the Jews into monkeys. In Qur'an 2:65-66 Allah said it was because the Jews did not keep the Sabbath, he cursed them to become monkeys: *⁶⁵And indeed, you know those of you who transgressed in the Sabt;[131] so we said to them, "Become despised monkeys." ⁶⁶So we made that[132] an example to what is between her hands[133] and what is behind her[134] and a sermon to the fearers.*

Mohammed also stated in the following verse that Allah had changed some of the Jews into monkeys and swine. Qur'an 5:60: *⁶⁰Say, "Will I inform you of evil than that as punishment from Allah?" They whom Allah has cursed and on whom he has poured forth his wrath, some of them[135] he changed into monkeys and swine; and they who worship the idolatry, those are in an evil place and have gone astray from the right way.*

In the following verses, the Qur'an states that some of the Jews were cursed and became monkeys until the resurrection. Qur'an 7:163-167: *¹⁶³And ask them about the village which was present by the sea, when they transgressed on the Sabbath (Saturday), when their whales came to them appearing openly on their Sabbath day; and the day they did not have Sabbath, they (their whales) did not come to them. Likewise, we tempted them because they were transgressors.*

¹⁶⁴And when one nation of them said, "Why preach to people whom Allah will destroy or torment them with severe torment?" They said, "[As] an excuse for your lord, and perhaps they may fear." ¹⁶⁵So when they forgot what they had been reminded of, we delivered those who had been forbidden from the evil, and we seized those who did injustice with an evil torment because they were transgressors. ¹⁶⁶So when they revolted against what they were forbidden to do, we said to them, "Become despised monkeys." ¹⁶⁷And when your lord decided to send against them who will subject them to the evil

---

[131] Saturday, non-Arabic word of Aramaic/Hebrew origin
[132] that, i.e. Allah's punishment
[133] now—the present time
[134] the following generations
[135] Jews

torment until the resurrection day, surely your lord is hasty in the punishment, and surely he is forgiving, merciful.

It is written above that Allah tempts with evil. This contradicts the Bible which clearly teaches that God does not tempt anyone. See James 1:13-14: *¹³**Let no one say when he is tempted, "I am tempted by God"; for God cannot be tempted by evil, nor does He Himself tempt anyone. ¹⁴But each one is tempted when he is drawn away by his own desires and enticed.***

The Story of Joshua

Who was Joshua? Ibn Kathir stated that he was Yoshaa Ibn Ephraseem (Ephraim), which was the wrong name, for he meant Joshua, who was the son of Joseph, son of Isaac, son of Abraham.[1] Then he said, according to the People of the Book, he was Joshua, the cousin of Houd. Obviously, Ibn Kathir, as in the case of Mohammed concerning such names, took no heed of historical timelines. Ibn Kathir thought Joshua to be the grandson of Joseph, who was the grandson of Isaac, son of Abraham, which was a great error. When we read the Bible, we discover that between Joshua and Joseph there were four hundred years, not just one generation. The error here obviously results from the silence in the Scriptures of what happened during the intervening years. There were four hundred years of silence in the Bible while the Jews were living in Egypt.

Muslim scholars like Ibn Kathir do not read between the lines of the Scripture. We read in the last verse of Genesis 50:26 that Joseph died when he was 110 years old. He was mummified and put into a coffin in Egypt. He had seen, in his life, the third generation born to his sons, Ephraim and Manasseh, as written in verse 23. When we move to Exodus, Moses wrote the names of the sons of Jacob who came to Egypt. He numbered them to be seventy souls who came out of the loins of Jacob (Exodus 1:1-5). Once again, he mentioned the death of Joseph and all his brothers (Exodus 1:6), and here is what is written which Ibn Kathir and other Muslim scholars missed.

But the Children of Israel were fruitful and increased abundantly, multiplied and grew exceedingly mighty; and the land was filled with them (Exodus 1:7). We must ask a question here. *What was the length of time that it took for this verse to be fulfilled?* The answer can be found in the pages of the Bible. It was four hundred years. Therefore, Joshua cannot be the grandson of Joseph, because Joshua existed more than three hundred years after Joseph's death. As it is written, the proof of that can be found in the prophecy which God gave to Abraham in Genesis 15:13-14: ***[13] Then He said to Abram: "Know certainly that your descendants will be strangers in a land that is not theirs, and will serve them, and they will afflict***

---

[1] Ibn Kathir, *Stories of the Prophets*, vol. 1, Abo Al Fida Ishamail Ibn Kathir Al Kurashi Al Damashce (Beirut: Dar Al-Arab Heritage, 1408 AH, 1988), 373.

them four hundred years. ⁱ⁴and also the nation whom they serve I will judge; afterward they shall come out with great possessions."

I believe the real reason for the confusion of Ibn Kathir is because he was trying to make a story out of nothing, for there is no mention of Joshua in the entire Qur'an. All that is written there is "his young man." This can be found in Qur'an 18:60: *When Moses said to **his young man*** and 18:62: *He (Moses) said to **his young man**. How can he get such a long story from these three words?* The story of how Moses and his young man and the whale, the one where they were traveling and forgot their whale (their lunch), was made up. This is a comedy. Actually, we have already covered this in the story of Moses. When comparing this information to the biblical account, not only do we discover that there are twenty-four chapters in the book of Joshua, but Joshua himself exists throughout the early pages of the Bible. His name is found in the following books: Exodus, Numbers, Leviticus, and Deuteronomy. There are 228 verses that refer to Joshua throughout the Bible, and we encourage the reader to read about Joshua in these verses to know the true account of his life.

As for Ibn Kathir's claim that the People of the Book said that he was the cousin of Houd, there is no such statement or belief in the Bible. As we discussed previously, the entire story of Houd was made up by Mohammed.

Ibn Kathir continued in his book, quoting from the hadith that the People of the Book agreed that Joshua was a prophet.[2] However, a group of them who were called Samaritans did not believe anyone except Joshua, who came after Moses, was a prophet. May the curses of Allah be upon them until the day of resurrection. Ibn Kathir stated that Ibn Jarir said the prophethood had turned from Moses to Joshua in the last days of Moses, as when Moses used to meet with Joshua and ask him, "What is the new command and forbidden things Allah has given to you?" Then Joshua answered him, "When Allah used to reveal to you, I did not ask you until you told me yourself." At this point, Moses hated life and loved death. He wished to die. *Where did Ibn Kathir come up with this fabrication?*

Then Ibn Kathir contradicted himself in the story by stating there was doubt in the hadith, for Moses used to receive revelation until

---

[2]Ibid.

Allah caused him to die, as we saw in the story of Moses.³ Ibn Kathir quoted the Bible, by stating the following:

> It is written in the third portion (he meant the third book, Leviticus), that a law commanded Moses and Aaron to prepare the Children of Israel and appoint a prince or a captain over each one of the twelve tribes so they could prepare to fight after they got out of the wilderness in which they were lost. This was near the end of the forty years.

Ibn Kathir stated this was similar to the case of Mohammed when he prepared the army of Osama to fight the People of the Book (Christians and Jews), as it is written in Qur'an 9:29: *²⁹Engage in war with those who do not believe in Allah nor in the last day. Nor forbid what Allah and his messenger forbid, nor believe in the religion of the truth⁴ among those who have been given the book until they pay the jizya⁵ out of hand and they are subdued.*⁶ After Mohammed prepared the army of Osama, Osama died, and his best friend (and father-in-law), the first caliph, Abu Bakr, prepared the army. He sent them to invade the land of Byzantine.

He continued by quoting Qur'an 5:12: *¹²And indeed, Allah took a covenant with the children of Israel, and out of them we raised up twelve chiefs, and Allah said, "Surely I am with you. If you performed the prayer and brought the legal alms and believed in my messengers and 'azzara⁷ them and lend Allah a good loan, I will surely atone for you your evils, and I will admit you into gardens, below them the rivers flow. So whoever of you becomes an infidel after that, so indeed, he has gone astray from the right way."*

Ibn Kathir interpreted this verse by stating that Allah said to them, if they did what they were commanded (fight or engage in war) and not retreat from the war, Allah would make the good deed of this war as a propitiation to what had fallen on them from previous punishments.⁸ Here, once again, Ibn Kathir compared Mohammed

---

³Ibid., 374.
⁴Islam
⁵tribute, non-Arabic word of Aramaic origin
⁶Ibn Kathir, 374.
⁷help, non-Arabic word of Hebrew origin
⁸Ibn Kathir, 374.

and his talk to his Muslim followers in the Qur'an to that of which he claimed took place between Allah and the Children of Israel, as he talked about the Battle of Al-Hudaibiya. That is when Mohammed claimed that Allah said in Qur'an 48:16: *[16]Say to those Bedouins who lagged behind [in battle], "You will be called to [face] a people of substantial mighty valor. You will engage in war against them, or they will become Muslims. So if you obey, Allah will give you a good wage; and if you turn away, as you turned away before, he will torment you with a painful torment.* Likewise, Ibn Kathir said that Allah said to the Children of Israel in Qur'an 5:12: *"[12]...So whoever of you becomes an infidel after that, so indeed, he has gone astray from the right way."[9]*

Then Allah condemned them for their evil deed, as he also condemned the Christians after them, for the difference in their beliefs (denominations). Ibn Kathir stated that Allah commanded Moses to write down the names of the fighters from the Children of Israel, those who could carry the arms and were twenty years or older.[10] He placed an officer over each one of the tribes. Then Ibn Kathir mentioned the twelve tribes by their names, the number of fighters, and the name of the officer over each tribe. Obviously, he was copying this information from the Bible. This came directly from the book of Numbers in chapter 1, and as usual, Ibn Kathir included some errors.

First, all of the leaders and those twenty years and older whom Moses counted in Numbers 1 had died and thus could not go with Joshua to fight and take the Promised Land. Second, there was no such thing as the tribe of Joseph, for in Numbers 1:32 (see also Joshua 13-14:4), the sons of Ephraim were considered to be a tribe of themselves and the sons of Manasseh were also a separate tribe, but the tribe of Levi was not counted among those who went to fight. They dwelled at the Tabernacle and took over the work of the ministry of the house of the Lord. This obviously caused an error in the numbers which Ibn Kathir mentioned.[11] As for making Joshua the leader of the tribe of Joseph, Ibn Kathir tied this error to his previous lies.

---

[9]Ibid.
[10]Ibid.,375.
[11]Ibid.

The Revelation of Error

The fact is that Joseph had two sons who founded two tribes. The leader of the children of Ephraim was Elishama, the son of Ammihud; and the leader of the children of Manassah was Gamaliel, the son of Pedahzur. Ibn Kathir added the name of another tribe named Mesha, claiming that their number was 31,200 and the leader was Gamaliel, the son of Pedahzur, who just happened to be the leader of the tribe of Manasseh. However, the numbers of those who belonged to this tribe were not 31,200, as Ibn Kathir stated, but were 32,200. Ibn Kathir stated that there were errors in the totals of the number of men who were twenty years and older, for he stated that the total of those who fought, except the children of Levi, were 571,656; but Ibn Kathir stated that some said the Children of Israel were 603,555, *and Allah knows best.*[12] This last number is a correct number according to the Bible in Numbers 1:46. The fact is Joshua was not the leader of any tribe.

An amazing thing is Ibn Kathir ended this portion of his book by stating, "This is the text of their book which is in their hand, *and Allah knows best.*" Sadly, that was a lie, and as we have already seen above, this information was not written in the Bible. It was copied and mixed with error.

Although Ibn Kathir supposedly is writing on these pages the story of Prophet Joshua, so far he has told us hardly anything about Joshua. He moved on to another story which had nothing to do with Joshua.[13] He stated that Ibn Isaac claimed Moses was the one who invaded the holy house (Jerusalem), but Ibn Kathir stated that "the fact was it was Joshua."

Ibn Isaac mentioned on their way to Jerusalem the story of Balaam, Ibn Beor. Ibn Kathir inserted three verses from Qur'an 7:175-177, which I believe have nothing to do with Balaam. The verses state: *[175]And recite to them the news of him to whom we gave our verses, so he departed from it, so that Satan followed him, so he was of the seduced. [176]And if we will, we would lift him up with it, but he clung to the earth and followed his desire, so his parable is like the parable of the dog which pants if you chase him or pants if you leave him alone. Such is the parable of those people who denied our verses. So narrate the stories, perhaps they may reflect. [177]Evil is the likeness of those people*

---

[12]Ibid.
[13]Ibid., 376.

who denied our verses, and they were treating themselves unjustly.

Ibn Kathir interpreted these verses by stating that Ibn Abbas said that Balaam knew the great name and his people asked him to curse Moses and his people.[14] However, he refused; and when they nagged him, he rode on his donkey and went toward the camp of the Children of Israel. When he drew near to them, the donkey refused to move on, so Balaam kicked the donkey. Then the donkey moved. However, the donkey stopped moving again, so he kicked her harder the second time. Then she roused and stopped a third time, so he kicked her again. Then she said to him, "O Balaam, where do you want to go? Can't you see the angel in front of me? Will you go to the prophet of Allah and the believers to curse them?"

So he did not give up from beating the donkey until they arrived at the top of the mountain. When he looked at the camp of the Children of Israel, he began to curse them; but his tongue did not obey him, except to bless Moses and his people and to curse his own people. So they blamed him. He apologized by telling them that his tongue could only do that. His tongue stuck out until he fell on his chest.

Then he told his people, "Now I lost the life of this world and the hereafter, and nothing is left except cunning and deception." Then Balaam ordered his people to beautify the females and send the women with goods (from the market) so that they could show them and sell them to the people. Perhaps they would cause the Children of Israel to commit adultery with the women so then Balak could have victory in battle. So they did, and one of their women by the name Kastee met with one of the great men from the Children of Israel, Zimary son of Shalom. It was said that he was leader of the tribe of Simeon, Ibn Jacob. So when he committed adultery with her, Allah sent a plague on the Children of Israel, and it spread among them.[15]

So when the news arrived to Phinehas, Ibn Eleazar, Ibn Aaron, he took his spear, which was made out of iron, and killed the man and the woman in their tent. That's how the plague was ended.[16] Ibn Kathir ended the story by stating that the number of those who were killed by the plague was seventy thousand. The smallest number

---

[14]Ibid.
[15]Ibid.
[16]Ibid., 377.

The Revelation of Error

mentioned was twenty thousand, but then Ibn Kathir stated that perhaps this story of Balaam took place when Moses' army entered Jerusalem for the first time after he left Egypt, *and Allah knows best.* Ibn Kathir also stated that the story of Balaam took place while they were wandering in the desert, *and Allah knows best.* Remember, none of this story is in the Qur'an. Everything was copied from the Bible and rewritten with many errors.

What really happened, according to the biblical account in Numbers 22-25? First, after the Children of Israel settled near Moab, Balak, son of Zipporah, was so afraid of the large number of the Children of Israel that he asked the elders of Midian to send and ask Balaam, son of Beor, to go and curse the Children of Israel. However, Balaam refused to go with the elders and do so, as God commanded him not to, for God explained to him that these people were blessed. However, Balak sent the elders once again. The response of Balaam was, even if Balak would give him his house full of silver and gold, he would not disobey the word of the Lord his God. He asked the elders to wait that night so that he could seek the advice of the Lord. Then God said he could go, but he could only do what God commanded. Balaam rode his donkey, and on his way to the Children of Israel, the angel of the Lord appeared, and the donkey saw it. The donkey stopped and turned aside into a field because the angel, with his sword drawn, blocked the way. Balaam beat the donkey, and then she started moving. The second time the angel stood in the path, the donkey crushed Balaam's foot against the wall of a vineyard, so he struck her again. Then when the donkey saw the angel of the Lord for the third time, she fell down under Balaam. That is when Balaam became angry.

Then the Lord opened the mouth of the donkey, and the donkey asked what she had done to him that he had to hit her three times. Balaam said that if he had a sword in his hand, he would have killed the donkey. Then the Lord opened the eyes of Balaam, and he saw the angel of the Lord. So he fell flat on his face. Then the angel of the Lord told Balaam to go and say only what He commanded him to say. Balaam then met with Balak. They arrived at the village of Kirjath Huzoth. There Balak offered a sacrifice, and instead of cursing the Children of Israel, Balaam blessed them.

You can read the blessing of Balaam in Numbers 23. When Balak required him to curse the Children of Israel, he could not; he could only bless them. This took place three times. Read about this in

Chapter 17

Numbers 24. Then he prophesied to Balak what would take place in his land, for the land would be completely given to the Children of Israel and none of his people would live. Then, in the end, Balaam arose and departed from Balak, and each went his own way.

As for the fabricated story by Ibn Kathir concerning the adulterous relationship between the Children of Israel and the daughters of Moab, there is no connection between Balaam and such a story.[17] We can read the entire true account in Numbers 25. The Children of Israel committed adultery with the Moabite women on their own. The number of people who died was twenty-four thousand, not twenty thousand nor seventy thousand, as we can see in verse 9. The plague did not end until Phinehas intervened by killing Zamari, the son of Salu, and a Midianite woman whose name was Cozbi, the daughter of Zur. The plague ended, and God gave his descendants a covenant of the everlasting priesthood because Phinehas, the son of Eleazar, the son of Aaron the priest, was zealous for his God and made atonement for the Children of Israel.

Let us go back to the story of Joshua.[18] Ibn Kathir stated that it was Joshua who took the Children of Israel across the Jordan River to the city of Jericho, the city with the high walls and great castle. He surrounded the city of Jericho for six months. One day they surrounded it and blew their trumpets and shouted "Allah Akbar" with the voice of one man and the wall fell down. They took all the spoils and killed twelve thousand men and women. *Where did Ibn Kathir come up with these lies?*

The true story of the capture of Jericho can be found in the book of Joshua in chapter 6. The Lord told Joshua to go around the city of Jericho, for the city was completely shut up. Six days they went around the city quietly. However, on the seventh day, the Children of Israel went around the city six times quietly; and then on the seventh time they went around the city, the priests blew the trumpets and their people shouted. Notice that the people did not shout "Allah Akbar," for the Jewish people did not have such a shout, but they simply made noise.

Everybody in the city was cursed by the Lord except Rahab the harlot. She and all her household would live because she had hidden the spies earlier when they came to Jericho. As for the silver, gold,

---

[17] Ibid.
[18] Ibid.

brass, and iron taken from the city of Jericho, it would be holy to the Lord and would have been given to the treasury of the Lord. The city was burned to the ground. Every animal, man, and woman was killed. Joshua swore by God that any man who would rebuild the city would be cursed. The Lord was with Joshua, and he became famous throughout all the land.

Ibn Kathir went on in his book to tell us more about Joshua, for he stated that Joshua waged war against many kings.[19] Then he told the story of Joshua praying to hold the sun and the moon still, *and Allah knows best*. He implied that Allah knows better than anyone. This story is not in the Qur'an, the hadith, nor in any other writing. It is only in the Bible, which is the only source Ibn Kathir used to make up his story. As Mohammed was, so was Ibn Kathir. Mohammed used to copy and then change and fabricate stories based on information he took from the Bible, and then so did his follower, Ibn Kathir.

Ibn Kathir stated that Abu Horyrah said that Mohammed said one of the prophets invaded, so he said to his people, "No one follow me if he just got married to a wife and he desires to have children with her or if he built a house and he did not finish his roof or if he bought sheep and he is waiting for the babies."[20] So this prophet went to invade a village and prayed the prayer, so he said to the sun, "You are commanded and I am commanded. O Allah, imprison the sun for me for a while." So Allah imprisoned it. So they won and gathered the spoils. Then the fire came to consume it, but the fire refused to consume it. The prophet said, "Some iniquity is in you. Who among you will pledge allegiance?" A man's hand stuck to his hand. Then he said, "Some iniquity is in your people." So he pledged his people and [something] stuck to the hand of two or three of his people. So he said, "Iniquity is among you." Then they brought out to him the head of a cow made of gold, and when they put it with the money, the fire came and consumed the spoils.

Perhaps if Mohammed had read the true account in the Bible correctly, he would not have made so many errors as we have just seen in the nonsense above. As for the part where God commanded His people concerning those who should not go out to fight, as in the

---

[19]Ibid.
[20]Ibid., 378.

case of a newly wedded husband, it was given to Moses, not to Joshua as we see in the Torah in Deuteronomy 24:5.

As for the sin of the people, we can find the true account concerning what was forbidden to keep of the spoils in its entirety in Joshua 7; for it was one of the Children of Israel, son of Achram from the tribe of Judah, who actually took a goodly garment, two hundred shekels of silver, and a wedge of gold of fifty shekels weight, but not the gold head of a cow as erroneously stated by Mohammed. He also hid these spoils under the middle of his tent. Because of this man's sin, the Children of Israel lost a battle against Ai. We encourage the reader to read the entire account in the Bible to see how this man and his entire household were stoned and burned with fire.

Mohammed's confusion in this hadith is very clear, for the spoil in the first battle of the city of Jericho was forbidden. The purpose of this battle of Jericho was not for the Children of Israel to take spoils at all. All the gold, silver, and iron taken from the city were taken to the house of the Lord. The story of Achan took place afterwards, not at the same time as the invasion of Jericho.

Ibn Kathir quoted Qur'an 7 and Qur'an 2 to somehow try to attach these verses to the story of Prophet Joshua.[21] Qur'an 7:161-162 states: *[161]And when it was said to them, "Dwell in this village and eat what you will from there and say forgiveness and enter the door worshiping, we will forgive your sins; we will increase the doers of good." [162]So the unjust among them replaced that word with another, not the same which had been said to them, so we sent a wrath over them from the heaven because they were unjust.*

Then Qur'an 2:58-59 says: *[58]And when we said, "Enter this qarya,[22] so eat there plentifully whatever you will and enter the bāb[23] with worship, and say, 'Hitta.'"[24] We will forgive you your sins, and we will increase the doers of good. [59]So those who were unjust changed the saying to what had not been said to them, so we sent down on those unjust a rujz[25] from the heaven because they were transgressors.* I could not find any connection between these verses and Joshua, for the truth must be

---

[21]Ibid., 379.
[22]village, non-Arabic word of Syriac origin
[23]door, non-Arabic word of Aramaic origin
[24]forgiveness, non-Arabic word of undetermined origin
[25]wrath, non-Arabic word of Syriac origin

told that this conversation about entering the door never took place in the life of the Children of Israel. Such a story is made up by Mohammed just to add more sentences to his poetry in *The Generous Qur'an*.

Ibn Kathir ended the story of Joshua by stating that when the Children of Israel settled in Jerusalem, Joshua continued to be among them, judging between them with the book of Allah, the Torah, until Allah took his spirit when he was 127 years old.[26] Therefore, he lived 27 years after the death of Moses. *Where did Ibn Kathir get this information concerning the death of Joshua?* The only source for the answer is found in the Bible.

As for the true account of Joshua in the Bible, it can be found in the book of Joshua. As for the death of Joshua, son of Nun, he was 110 years old, not 127 as Ibn Kathir erroneously stated. He was buried on the border of the city of his inheritance in Timnath Serah, which is located on the mountain of Ephraim, on the north side of the hill of Gaash. This can be found in Joshua 24.

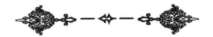

---

[26]Ibn Kathir, 380.

18 The Story of Al Kadar (The Green Prophet)

Ibn Kathir introduced the story of The Green by stating that this was the man that Moses traveled to seek knowledge from, as Allah narrated their news in *The Book of the Cave* in Qur'an 18, as mentioned earlier in the story of Moses.[1] There are different opinions about the identity of The Green, his name, and his genealogy. *Who was Al Kadar?* This is not a biblical name. It means *The Green*, but there is no character called The Green Prophet in the Bible. I believe that this is another made-up story.

Ibn Kathir said that "Al Kadar was Ibn Adam, and he came from his backbone. He will live until the antichrist comes, and The Green will call the antichrist a liar."[2] The second opinion came from Abu Hatem who said that Al Kadar was the oldest living son of Adam and his name was Khaddron, Ibn Kabeel (he meant Cain), Ibn Adam.

Ibn Isaac said that when it was about time for Adam to die, he told his children that the flood was about to happen and advised them to carry his body with them in the ship. He also told them where to bury him afterwards. When the flood took place, they carried his body with them.[3] Then, when they landed back on the land, Noah commanded his sons to bury Adam's body where he told them. So they said to their father, "The earth is not safe, for on it is desolation." Noah then provoked them to bury Adam, telling them that Adam had called upon Allah, and whoever buried him would have long life. They kept the body until The Green arrived and took responsibility for burying him. Allah gave him what he promised, which is that "Allah gives life to whom he wills."

Ibn Kathir said Ibn Qatadah said that The Green (man)'s name was Baleah or Elijah, Ibn Malkan, Ibn Faleg, Ibn Aabr, Ibn Shalik, Ibn Arfakshas, Ibn Shem, Ibn Noah.[4] Therefore, I can surely say he was not Ibn Adam or Ibn Cain. However, Ibn Kathir said that Ishmael, Ibn Oayes said he was Al Moamar, Ibn Malik, Ibn Abulah, Ibn Nsar, Ibn Lazd. Then Ibn Kathir also stated that others said that

---

[1] Ibn Kathir, *Stories of the Prophets*, vol. 1, Abo Al Fida Ishamail Ibn Kathir Al Kurashi Al Damashce (Beirut: Dar Al-Arab Heritage, 1408 AH, 1988), 381.
[2] Ibid.
[3] Ibid.
[4] Ibid.

he was Khaddron, Ibn Amyaeel, Ibn Alyfz, Ibn Alise, Ibn Isaac, Ibn Abraham. Ibn Kathir stated that it was said that he was Jeremiah, Ibn Khalkya, *and Allah knows best.*

Ibn Kathir also stated it was said The Green was Ibn Pharaoh, the king of Egypt, in Moses' days.[5] It was said he was Ibn Malik, the brother of Elijah, and it was said he was born before Ze Al Qarnain (Alexander the Great). It was said that he was one of those who believed in Abraham and emigrated with him. It was also said that he was a prophet in the time of Bastesp, Ibn Harasp. There are many more opinions, but the conclusion is that nobody knows who this man was. This is my proof that this is a made-up story by Mohammed.

Ibn Kathir stated that when The Green was passing by a monastery that he looked upon the monk and taught him Islam. One must ask some questions. *Was The Green man a Jew, a Muslim, or a Christian?* Monks and monasteries did not even exist until late in the fourth century. *So, how could this event have occurred thousands of years prior to the existence of Christians, Muslims, monks, and monasteries?* This is further evidence that neither Mohammed nor Muslim scholars had any grasp of the timeline of the biblical characters they try to appropriate.

Ibn Kathir stated that Abu Zarah wrote in his book, *The Proof of the Prophethood,* that Ibn Abbas said Mohammed said in the night when Mohammed was taken to the seventh heaven, he smelled a good smell, so he asked Gabreel what that good smell was. Gabreel answered, "This was the smell of the wind from the tomb of the hairdresser, her daughter, and her husband."[6] He continued by saying it was the start of The Green and that he was from the honorable of the Children of Israel.

Gabreel went on to tell Mohammed that when The Green became mature, his father married him to a woman and he taught her Islam and he told her not to tell anyone. The Green was not of those who have sex with women, so he divorced her. His father married him to another one, and he taught her Islam and told her not to tell anyone. Then he divorced her also.

One of the women kept her Islam faith secret, but the other one told about her Islam faith. The Green escaped to an island in the sea.

---

[5] Ibid., 382.
[6] Ibid.

Two men were collecting wood and saw him. One of them kept it secret, and the other one told about it.

He (the one who did not keep the secret) said, "I saw Aezzqil." Some people asked him, "And who saw him with you?" He said, "It was so and so." So they asked the man who kept the secret. Since it was in their religion that whoever lies will be put to death, he was killed. Before his death, the man who kept the secret had been married to the woman who kept the secret.

Then Angel Gabreel said when she, the women who kept the secret, was combing the hair of Pharaoh's daughter, the comb fell from her hand. She said Pharaoh dozed, so she told her father. The woman had two sons and a husband. So Pharaoh sent to them asking them to leave their religion. They refused to leave their religion. Pharaoh said, "I will surely kill you both (husband and wife)." So they said, "If you kill us, do us a favor and bury us in one tomb." So he buried them in one tomb. So he said, "I did not find any better fragrance than from them, and indeed they entered the garden." Ibn Kathir stated that this story is also mentioned by Ibn Kaab and Ibn Abbas, *and Allah knows best*. This story is a great example of Mohammed's nonsense which was continued by his scholars because we do not know who The Green was or even who was speaking at times during the above dialogue.

Why was he called The Green? There are many opinions about this.[7] Abu Horyrah said that Mohammed said it was because he sat on a white *frawah* (sheepskin). "So, behold, it was shaking from behind him, green." Abd Al Razak said that the frawah was the white grass or what looks like it, meaning the dry grass. Others said that the frawah was the land which does not grow plants. The head frawah was the skin of the head with all the hair on it.

Al Qurtobi said that he was named The Green because of his goodness and his shiny face. Mujahid said that he was named The Green because wherever he stood to pray, everything around him turned green. The simplest and most obvious explanation for this fictitious person being The Green, if in fact there was one, was simply that green was well known to have been Mohammed's favorite color. Perhaps Mohammed invented the person on a whim when he happened to think of his favorite color. The story of Moses and

---

[7] Ibid., 382-383.

Yoshaa meeting with The Green man has already been covered in Qur'an 18 in our section on Moses.

Ibn Kathir gave the proof that The Green was a prophet. The first proof was Allah calling him "our servant." The second proof was his position as shown by the manner in which he addressed Moses as *the great prophet and generous messenger*. Because Moses was a humble messenger, searching for him for eight years was another proof that The Green was a prophet. His knowledge and his secret knowledge were even more proof he was a prophet.

When The Green killed the young man, it was a revelation from the angel, the knower, for no one would kill a soul simply because a thought comes into his head. (This is not true. *Didn't Cain kill Abel? And have you watched the news lately?*) The Green killed this young man, who was still a child, because he knew that if he grew up, he would become an infidel and would cause his parents to sin because of their love for him. The killing of this young man was a great good. That was their proof that The Green was a prophet.

I cannot see anything more foolish than this. *What kind of prophet would kill a child before the age of puberty because he will sin? What kind of god would send such a prophet?* If this were true, then there should not be one person left living, for the Scripture teaches that all have sinned. The final proof The Green was a prophet was that he did not do any of these actions by his own choice, but because it was Allah's command. When he interpreted it, Moses realized that he was a great prophet as written in Qur'an 18:82: [82]"*...And I did not do it of my own affair...*"

Some also said The Green was an angel. Ibn Kathir thought this was very strange, especially when there was enough evidence that he was a prophet. I wonder why Ibn Kathir thought that The Green being an angel was very odd, especially since the whole story is very strange.

Ibn Kathir stated also that there are disagreements among Muslim scholars about why The Green Prophet is still alive today.[8] Some said it was because he buried Adam, and Allah answered Adam's prayer. Others said it was because he drank from the spring of life and that there are many *proofs* that he is still alive today. *Where are these many proofs?* As for when Moses asked for his advice, he advised

---

[8]Ibid, 384.

Moses by telling him, "Be useful, and do no harm. Be content, and do not be angry. Do not rush into evil. Do not walk in need."

In another story, it was said that The Green advised Moses not to laugh, except in wonder. Muslim scholars added many more pieces of advice, as written in many hadith by Mohammed. They are very lengthy and like a fairy tale. I wonder how Mohammed could know all these facts about The Green and about Moses, but he never mentioned them in the Qur'an. Ibn Kathir ended these stories by saying these are made-up stories by Zachariah Ibn Yahya, the Egyptian.[9] Others have said that he was a liar.

Ibn Asakir mentioned that The Green and Elijah fasted the month of Ramadan every year.[10] They performed the Hajj every year and drank from the Zamzam (a famous well in Masjid Al Haram, the forbidden mosque in Mecca) once a year, which satisfied their need for water until the following year.

Ibn Asakir also stated that Al Waled, Ibn Al Melek, Ibn Marwan, the one who built the mosque of Damascus, prayed in the mosque alone one night. He commanded the people to leave the mosque, so they did. When it was evening, he entered the mosque and found a man standing to pray, so he said to the people, "Have I not commanded you to leave the mosque?" They said, "Yes, O Prince of the Believers, this is The Green. He comes every night to pray."

This was one of the so-called proofs that he was still alive in the days of the Prince of the Believers. There are many stories as mentioned above that Ibn Kathir used in his book to try to prove the existence of The Green, and many stories were given to prove he is still alive today. Ibn Kathir inserted many stories about The Green which he declared may not be true, *and Allah knows best.*

Mohammed said that the antichrist will come near the city, but he will not be able to enter the city, so on that day a man will come out to him who is the best of the people. He will say to him, "You are the antichrist, which the apostle of Allah, Mohammed, told us about." So the antichrist will say, "Will you see if I kill this man and bring him back to life? Will you doubt on the matter?"

They will say *no*, so the antichrist will kill him and bring him back to life. Then the man who was killed and came back to life will say to him, "I swear by Allah, now I see you even better." So the

---

[9]Ibid.
[10]Ibid., 390.

antichrist will desire to kill him again, but he will not be able to. Moamar said that he was told, "He will put a sheet of brass on his throat, and he knows that he is The Green, which the antichrist will kill and bring to life." Many Muslim scholars agreed that he was The Green who will be alive until the time of the coming of the antichrist, which will come at the end of time. However, other scholars believe that The Green will die like everybody else, as written in Qur'an 21:34 which states: *And we did not make it for humans before you to dwell forever.*[11] Therefore, if The Green was a human, he must die, that is, unless we have another proof.

Ibn Kathir stated, "If all the prophets in Mohammed's day were alive, they would be responsible to be Mohammed's followers, obey his commands, and follow his laws, which took place when he was lifted up to the seventh heaven.[12] He was raised up above all the prophets, and Gabreel commanded him by the command of Allah to lead all the prophets in the prayer, which is a proof that he was the great imam and the respected seal of the prophets; prayer and peace be upon him and all the prophets."

All Muslim believers know that, if The Green were alive in Mohammed's day, he would surely have followed Mohammed's law. Even 'Isā (Jesus) will follow when he comes back at the end of time. He will follow the purified laws of Mohammed; he will not turn away from them. Ibn Kathir inserted another proof that The Green was not alive after Mohammed by saying, if he had been alive, he would have notified the people about the sayings of Mohammed and the verses of the Qur'an.[13] He would deny the false sayings about Mohammed, deny the heretics and liars, and would engage in war alongside the Muslims in their invasions.

Mohammed also said in the hadith, "Do you see this night? For sure, a hundred years from now, not one person here now will be alive on this earth." That prophecy was true because people in Mohammed's day did not live past a hundred years; and, of course, anyone could have prophesied that. Today, however, the prophecy is not true due to modern day medicine which enables some people to live past the age of one hundred.

---

[11]Ibid., 391.
[12]Ibid., 392.
[13]Ibid., 393.

In conclusion, I personally believe that the story of The Green Prophet is simply a made-up story by Mohammed, and its interpretation is an even greater fantasy by Muslim scholars. The Green Prophet never existed, not in Adam's day, not in Moses' day, not in Mohammed's day, and for sure, not in our day. Many other stories were written about The Green, but I do not see any benefit in including more of them in my book.

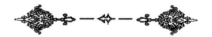

19 The Story of Elijah

The name Iliyas (Elijah) is mentioned in the Qur'an twice; this is obviously the wrong name, for the name Elijah in the Arabic language is Elaya not Iliyas. The first time this prophet is mentioned is in Qur'an 6:85 and then only by his name with no details. The story of Iliyas is found in Qur'an 37:123-132 in forty-two words. As usual, Mohammed copied the story from the Bible condensing it into these very brief words.

Here are the verses of Qur'an 37:123-132: *[123]And surely Iliyas[1] is one of the messengers. [124]When he said to his people, "Will you not fear? [125]Do you call on Bual[2] and forsake the best of the creators, [126]Allah your lord and the lord of your ancient fathers?" [127]So they denied him, so surely they will be brought, [128]except the faithful servant of Allah. [129]And we left for him among the others. [130]Peace be on the family of Yaseen.[3] [131]Likewise, we surely reward the doers of good. [132]Surely he is among our believing servants.*

The biblical account of Elijah is given in the following chapters: 1 Kings 17-21; 2 Kings 1-10; 1 Chronicles 8; 2 Chronicles 21; Ezra 10; Malachi 4; Matthew 11, 16, 17, and 27; Mark 6, 8, 9, and 15; Luke 1, 4, and 9; John 1; Romans 11; and James 5. We encourage you to read about Elijah in the Bible so you may see for yourself how the story was rewritten in the Qur'an with many errors.

I will begin by asking the question. *Who was Elijah?* Ibn Kathir answered this question by giving different opinions.[4] First, he said the scholars of genealogy said he was Iliyas of Tishbite. *Where did the scholars of genealogy get this name? Did they ask Mohammed, or did they meet with Angel Gabreel?* Obviously not. All they did was to look in the Bible in 1 Kings 17:1.

Ibn Kathir continued by stating it was said he was Ibn Yaseen, Ibn Finhas, Ibn Alayzar, Ibn Aaron. It was also said he was Iliyas Ibn Alazr, Ibn Alayzar, Ibn Aaron, Ibn Amran. The Bible does not give

---

[1] wrong name, he meant Elijah
[2] Baal, non-Arabic word of Syriac origin
[3] another mistake for the name Elijah
[4] Ibn Kathir, *Stories of the Prophets*, vol. 1, Abo Al Fida Ishamail Ibn Kathir Al Kurashi Al Damashce (Beirut: Dar Al-Arab Heritage, 1408 AH, 1988), 394.

any information about his ancestors. Muslim scholars did not know who his ancestors were, but they constructed a confusing genealogy for him anyway. Even though the Bible does not give his genealogy, it is clear that he lived during the reign of King Ahab in 900 BC. However, the list of names mentioned by Ibn Kathir's scholars lists four or five generations between Moses and Aaron's day and Elijah's. There is no way that five generations could cover six hundred years because Aaron and Moses lived in 1500 BC.

It was said that he was sent to the people of Baalbek, west of Damascus, and he called them to Allah so that they would leave the idol they worshiped. This idol's name was Baal. It was said this idol was a woman. This is strange, since Baal is a Semitic word signifying the lord, master, owner (male), keeper, or husband. In fact, there are frequent references to the wife of this god. In historical references, Baal is <u>always</u> a male. Ibn Kathir said that [calling them to leave Baal] was why Iliyas said to them, *"Will you not fear?* Qur'an 37:125-126 states: *^{125}Do you call on Baal[5] and forsake the best of the creators, ^{126}Allah your lord and the lord of your ancient fathers?"* Ibn Kathir interpreted these verses by saying that they called him a liar, they disobeyed him, and they desired to kill him. It was said he escaped and hid from them. *How did Ibn Kathir come up with such an interpretation for this verse which simply said, "So they called him a liar..."?*

One must ask another important question. *How many creators are there?* The Qur'an teaches that Allah is the best creator. This is obviously another error in the Qur'an. If he is the best, then obviously there must be others. To add further confusion, Ibn Kathir said that Abu Yakob said Iliyas hid from the king of his people in a cave which was below the blood ten years (no idea what is meant by this term), until Allah destroyed this king and put another one in his place. Iliyas then came back to him and offered him Islam, so he became a Muslim.

A large number of his people became Muslim with him, except ten thousand people; so he ordered those to be killed, every last one of them. However, Ibn Kathir said that Ibn Abu Al Donya said Iliyas escaped and continued to be away from his people in a cave for twenty nights. Others said it was forty nights, and the ravens used to come to him with his provisions.

---

[5]Baal, non-Arabic word of Syriac origin

The Revelation of Error

Ibn Kathir said that Makhol said there were four prophets alive, two on earth, Iliyas and The Green, and two in heaven, Adryes (Enoch) and 'Isā (Jesus), even though Ibn Kathir disagreed with him.[6] Ibn Kathir stated:

> Wahab Ibn Monabah and others said that when Iliyas's lord called him to take his spirit, that is when his people called him a liar and caused him harm. Then a beast, colored like the color of fire, came to him, and he rode on it. And Allah made him to have feathers and dressed him in light and removed from him the enjoyment of food and drink, and he became an angel--an earthly, heavenly human angel. And he gave advice to Iliyas Ibn Aktob (wrong name, he meant Elisha the son of Shaphat).

We understand this writing makes no sense, but this is what Ibn Kathir wrote in his book. Ibn Kathir doubted this story because it was an Israelite story, but he said that we cannot deny it and we cannot believe it. What we learn from the story is that it is not true, *and Allah knows best.*

What about the true account in the Bible? The Bible teaches that Elijah was not sent to some foreign people but to his own people. He stood boldly against King Ahab, as stated in 1 Kings 17:1: ***As the LORD God of Israel lives, before whom I stand, there shall not be dew nor rain these years, except at my word.*** This was one of seven miracles he performed which was proof of his prophethood. Then Elijah left there and went to Brook Cherith, which flows into the Jordan River, not near Damascus as stated by Ibn Kathir. There God provided the ravens to feed him.

When the brook dried up, he went and lived with a widow whom he asked to make him a cake. Although it was the last of her flour and the last of her oil, Elijah told her to make him a cake first. He promised her that the flour would not waste and the oil would not fail until the Lord of Israel gives rain back on the face of the earth. This was Elijah's second miracle (1 Kings 17:7-16).

Her son became sick and died, but Elijah raised him back to life. Then the widow told Elijah she now knew that he was a man of God. This was the third miracle, and it can be found in the book of 1 Kings 17:17-24.

---

[6] Ibn Kathir, 395.

Chapter 19

Then in 1 Kings 18, after three years, the Lord asked Elijah to go and meet with King Ahab. There Elijah commanded the rain to come. When Jezebel killed the prophets of God, a man named Obadiah hid one hundred of the prophets of God in a cave. King Ahab asked Obadiah to search for water and some grass so the horses and the mules and beasts would not all die. On his way to do so, he met with Elijah. Elijah asked him to go and tell the king that Elijah was back.

At first, Obadiah was afraid to go to the king to ask for a meeting with Elijah the prophet of God, but then he went. Elijah explained to the king that the famine was the result of the Children of Israel leaving the Lord and worshiping Baal. Elijah asked the king to bring all the prophets of Baal and the prophets of Asherah to Mount Carmel. There Elijah challenged the people of Israel. This would be a great test to prove who the true God of Israel was.

They offered two bullocks, one for the false prophets and one for Elijah. The false prophets chose a bullock, prepared it, and put it on the wood. No fire was to be started. Instead, the false prophets were to call on their god, and if he was the true god, then he would bring a fire to consume the bullock. They called on their god from early morning till afternoon and nothing happened. Elijah made fun of them. He told them to shout louder, that perhaps their god was on a journey or perhaps he was asleep. They shouted louder and cut themselves until they bled, but nothing happened.

Then Elijah took twelve stones, according to the number of the tribes of Israel, and repaired the altar of the Lord. After he put the wood on the top of the altar, he cut the bullock into pieces and placed the pieces on the wood of the altar. Four full barrels of water were poured on the sacrifice. This was repeated three times. Then he prayed to the Lord, the God of Abraham, Isaac, and Israel that the people of Israel would know that he was the Lord's servant and that they must turn back to Him. God answered his prayer, for the fire of the Lord fell and consumed the sacrifice, the wood, the stones, the dust, and even licked up the water which was in the channel around the altar. Then the people fell on their faces and declared, "The Lord is God!" Then they captured the nine hundred false prophets and slew all of them by the Brook of Kishon. This was the fourth miracle (1 Kings 18:16-40).

Then Elijah prayed, and the rain came back. This is found in 1 Kings 18. Jezebel got mad and sent a message to Elijah. She threatened his life because she decided to kill him as he had killed her prophets. He walked in the wilderness for a day, sat under a juniper tree, and requested to die. The Lord sent an angel to him and gave him cake and water. The angel asked Elijah to eat and to drink. Then Elijah slept. Then the angel returned and told him once again to eat, so Elijah ate, drank, and walked with the strength from this meal for forty days and forty nights until he arrived at the Mountain of Horeb, the mountain of God, where he entered a cave.

Then the Lord spoke to him, and Elijah thought that he was the only prophet who was left alive, so the Lord told him to go stand on the mountain of the Lord. Then a loud wind went before the cave and then an earthquake, but the Lord was not in these. Then a fire followed after the earthquake, and the Lord was still not there yet. After the fire came a calm, still, small voice. The Lord spoke to Elijah and said, "What are you doing here, Elijah?" Once again Elijah answered the Lord that he had been very zealous for the Lord because he thought that he was the only prophet left. Then the Lord asked him to return by the way of the wilderness of Damascus and anoint Hazael to be a king over Syria, Jehu to be the king over Israel, and Elisha, the son of Shaphat of Abelmeholah, to be a prophet in Elijah's place.

Then God told Elijah that the sword of Hazael and Jehu and Elisha would slay all those who disobeyed His command. Then God gave him the good news that there were seven thousand knees who had not bowed down to Baal. Thus, all that was said was fulfilled according to 1 Kings 19. As for the rest of the story, we encourage the reader to read 1 Kings 20, 21, and 22.

Notice when I paraphrased the account as written above, I did not give any fabrication, but simply told the story as it is written in the Bible. I gave the references from where this information came, not as in the case of Muslim scholars who literally fabricate stories and plagiarize much information from the Bible and other books without giving any references, as if they were receiving revelation from Allah, but they only copied Mohammed.

In 2 Kings 1, we read about the story of Ahaziah falling out of a window, his injury, and sending messengers to ask Baalzebub whether or not he would be healed of his injury. He did not ask the Lord of Israel; therefore, the Lord told Elijah to go up to meet the messengers of the king and prophesy to them that the king would die. When they returned to the king and gave the description of the prophet to him, Ahaziah knew it was Elijah. He then sent fifty men with their leader, and the leader told Elijah that the king sought him.

Elijah told them if he was the man of God, to let fire come down from heaven and consume the leader and all fifty men with him. Then fire from heaven fell and consumed the men. The king sent a second group of fifty men and their leader with the same result. The king then sent a third new group of fifty men with their leader. However, this leader fell before Elijah and asked him to have respect for their lives. On this third time, the angel of the Lord asked Elijah to go with the men. Elijah went and met with the king and told the king again that he would not leave his bed again. Ahaziah died as Elijah said. This was the fifth miracle.

As for the sixth miracle which Elijah performed, we can read of it in 2 Kings 2:8: the miracle of the crossing of the Jordan River. That was when Elijah took his mantle and wrapped it together and smote the river with it. The water divided, and Elijah and Elisha crossed the river.

As for the story of the ascension of Elijah to heaven, it was not by riding on a beast the color of fire as claimed by Muslim scholars. It was a chariot of fire. We can read the entire account in 2 Kings 2:1-12. Elisha requested to have a double portion of the spirit of Elijah. Elijah replied that if Elisha saw him being taken up, he would receive a double portion. While they were both walking, a chariot of fire with horses of fire came between them, and Elijah was taken up by a whirlwind into heaven as Elisha watched. Elisha shouted, "My father, my father," and he saw him no more. This was the seventh and last miracle Elijah performed.

This was a summary of the Prophet Elijah. One important thing must be recognized from his life here. He prophesied and his prophecies were fulfilled. He also performed miracles, and these are the signs as a proof of a true prophet.

To see the level of foolishness of Muslims' deception and lies, we read what Ibn Kathir said concerning Anas Ibn Malik who said that he was with Mohammed and they came to a house and there was a man in the valley who said, "O Allah, make me of the people of Mohammed."[7] So Anas said he looked out to the valley and beheld a man whose length was 300 cubits (450 feet) who said to me, "Who are you?" Anas said, "I am Anas Ibn Malik, the servant of the Apostle of Allah." So he said, "Where is he?" Anas said, "He hears your

---

[7] Ibn Kathir, 395.

words." So he came to Mohammed and gave the greetings of peace, and he said to him, "Your brother Elijah sends you his greetings."

So Mohammed met with him (Elijah), and they sat together, talking to each other. This was also the day he ate, for he only ate one day a year. He said a table came down from heaven on them and on it there was bread, whale, and celery. So they ate and gave Anas some food, and he ate. They prayed the afternoon prayer together. Then Elijah said good-bye to him as he went through the clouds to heaven.

Ibn Kathir disagreed with this hadith because Mohammed said in another hadith that Adam's height was sixty cubits (ninety feet) and he was the tallest man. I personally believe if anyone believes the fairy tale of Mohammed that Adam was ninety feet tall, then he could believe any other number. The other reason Ibn Kathir refused this hadith is that Mohammed went to Elijah rather than Elijah to Mohammed and that is not acceptable, for Mohammed is the *seal* (last and final) of the prophets. Also, Allah removed from Elijah the desire to eat and drink as was shown in this hadith.

Because there was contradiction, the hadith was rejected by Ibn Kathir. The hadith was repeated in different words with different information as Ibn Kathir repeated the story.[8] As for the saying in Qur'an 37:127: [127]*So they denied him, so surely they will be brought,* this meant the torment in this world's life and in the hereafter or in the hereafter alone, but the interpreters and scholars believe it will be in this world and the hereafter. As for his interpretation of Qur'an 37:128: [128]*except the faithful servant of Allah,* he meant those who believed among them. Then for the saying in verse 129: [129]*And we left for him among the others,* Ibn Kathir interpreted this by saying "we left after him a good mention for him in the world. So he will only be spoken of with good." Then Allah said in Qur'an 37:130: [130]*Peace be on the family of Yaseen.*[9] Ibn Kathir interpreted the name Yaseen as Iliyas (he meant Elijah). Ibn Kathir fabricated an answer for this error in the Qur'an when he said that Arabs add the letter *n* to many of their words. For example, Asmaayl was renamed Asmaayn, Israel was Israen, and Iliyas to be Yaseen. I personally believe this was just a good fabrication for Allah's error in the Qur'an, for the speaker here was neither Mohammed nor an Arab but Allah himself.

---

[8]Ibid., 396.
[9]another mistake for the name Elijah

Even if all the Arabs do not know Arabic, Allah himself should know Arabic. Just because some people in the street do not know proper Arabic, it does not mean that the professor should not speak or know correct Arabic. To conclude, I would like to say how sadly unreasonable this story is, as told by Mohammed and his Angel Gabreel, especially when it is compared to the true original account. Perhaps if my Muslim friends will read the true account in the Bible, they will realize this is another error of the Qur'an.

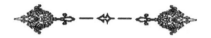

What will you do with Jesus?

It is no accident that you are reading this particular page at this particular moment in time. The Library of Congress contains nearly 30 million books on over 500 miles of shelves, receiving nearly 20,000 new items per day. Adding all other printed materials, the number would surely climb into the hundreds of millions. Yet, today, at this moment, you are reading this. Is it an accident? I say *NO*.

When it comes to ultimate questions, there are three basic issues that we all need to answer. First, "Who am I?" Second, "Is there a purpose in life?" And finally, "Where am I going when I die?" These are the real questions that we hear deep down inside, during quiet moments, moments when we stop the background noise of the distractions of the day. Many people run from these questions, but *don't*. Let's take a few minutes and *think*.

RANDOM CHANCE OR INTELLIGENT DESIGNER?

Atheism, a belief system that denies that there is a God, tries to dismiss these deep questions by speculating about a universe with no cause, no purpose, and no Creator. Atheism defines our existence as an incredibly improbable cosmic accident: a galactic fluke, a nearly limitless chain of biological mutation miracles, called evolution, to arrive at the beauty and complexity of life that we see all around us. However, recent research into DNA, the building code of life, shows that evolution is not only *mathematically* impossible in terms of time, number of mutations, and specified complexity, it is *genetically* impossible due to built-in error correction in our DNA.

Some skeptics will say, "Well, the universe could be billions of years old, so surely it could have happened!" Considering the possible age of our universe and the age of our planet, doesn't it sound reasonable to think there might be enough time for almost anything to occur by chance? Using statistics, the mathematical science of probability and chance, is this within the realm of possibility? The answer is an overwhelming *NO*! It is not even *close*.

Mathematicians who study probability say that any event with a chance less than 1 in 10^{50} is effectively ZERO. Life by chance is not 1 in 10^{50} but *quadrillions* of times far less likely than that. In other words, ZERO chance. In 1991, John Horgan, an atheist and senior staff writer for *Scientific American*, after reviewing the status of *all* existing scientific theories for the origin of life, said that there is *still no plausible way life could have begun by chance*.

The only logical conclusion is that an intelligence far beyond our own has *designed life*.

Eminent scientist and British mathematician Sir Fred Hoyle had this to say about the evidence: "A common sense interpretation of the facts suggests that a *super intellect* has monkeyed with physics, as well as chemistry and *biology*, and that there are no blind forces worth speaking about in nature" [emphasis mine] ("The Universe: Past and Present Reflections," *Annual Reviews of Astronomy and Astrophysics* 20, 1982, 16). He also says: "The notion that not only the biopolymer but the operating program of a living cell could be arrived at by chance in a primordial organic soup here on the Earth is evidently *nonsense* of a high order" [emphases mine] ("The Big Bang in Astronomy," *New Scientist*, 19 November 1981, 527).

IN THE BEGINNING…NOTHING?

But atheism's problems go much farther than just concerning the nearly unimaginable intricacies of life. In defiance of logic and science, atheism imagines that the entire universe either exploded out of nothing for no reason or that it has always existed (eternal). Both of these scenarios are now being rejected due to recent discoveries. Robert Jastrow (Ph.D. in physics), former head of NASA's Goddard Institute for Space Studies, proclaimed: "Astronomers now find they have painted themselves into a corner because they have proven, by their own methods, that the world began abruptly in an act of creation… That there are what I or anyone would call supernatural forces at work is now, I think, a scientifically proven fact" ("A Scientist Caught Between Two Faiths," Interview with Robert Jastrow, *Christianity Today*, August 6, 1982).

Dr. Arthur Compton who was awarded the Nobel Prize for Physics offered this conclusion: "For myself, faith begins with the realization that a supreme intelligence brought the universe into being and created man...for it is incontrovertible that where there is a plan there is intelligence" (Arthur Compton, *Chicago Daily News*, 12 April 1936).

NOT THE *HOW*, BUT THE *WHO*

As we have seen, scientific evidence points to an intelligence, or as one scientist said a *super intellect* and another defined as a *supreme intelligence* which led to the formation of the universe, and ultimately to life itself. But just *WHO* is this intelligence, and what is *he/she/it* like? Does this Creator care about the universe, about life, or even about *me*? There are a variety of religions, namely Islam, Hinduism, Taoism, Mormonism, as well as others, with various views of what God is or is not like and who or what that God is. The facts of the universe prove that there is a God, but to identify that God among the many worshiped requires further investigation.

There are several things, though, that we can know about God, using logic and inference. Does it make sense to believe that a God *without intelligence* could create people *with intelligence*? **NO**. Therefore, God must be intelligent, even incredibly so, to create the universe around us. By sheer observation, we can also surmise that God must be powerful beyond anything we have ever seen. Could a God *without personality* create people *with personality*? The answer again: **NO**. In like manner, could a God who cannot or *will not* communicate create a race of people who can and do communicate? **NO**.

WHAT ABOUT EVIL?

Let me interject one caution at this point. Using this line of reasoning, some wrongly conclude that if there is evil in the world, then God must also be partially evil, which is the Hindu view of God. This is illogical for two reasons. First, if God is all wise and all good, God would know all things, including how things would be if they weren't good. For example, I have never murdered anyone, but that doesn't mean I don't know what murder is. The fact that God should allow evil, as He obviously does, does not mean that He is evil. His allowing the possibility of evil is actually evidence of the highest good. Let me explain.

God created us as choice-makers, with free wills, so that we would not be robots. At stake was whether we would be able to freely love versus whether we would be robotic androids, *machines that look like people yet which do not have free choices*. To illustrate this, what if I told you, "I'll take you out for lunch, and you can have whatever you want. You can have pizza, pizza, or pizza. What do you want?" That's no choice. For real love and goodness to exist, without us merely being robots, there had to be an alternative, a real choice besides love and goodness: evil, or rebellion against the Creator, also known as sin.

The second reason God could not be evil is because He wrote the rule book. By definition, God is the only one who can truly label good *good* and evil *evil*. Whatever He says goes. Our judgments of God matter little. If He created us, who are we to sit in judgment of Him? We would be using brains He created to criticize the One who made us. Nonsense.

A PERSONAL GOD

Therefore, as we return to the original point about what God is like, as popular as is the notion that God is some sort of impersonal *FORCE* who merely set things in motion and then stepped out of the picture, as in deism, fate, or Taoism, such a view does not hold up to reason. God is much more that a FORCE.

Since God is most likely personal (He has created personal beings) and has the ability to communicate (He has created beings who use communication constantly), the next question is whether God has ever communicated with mankind. This would truly be the only way to know what God is like in His character, apart from logically deduced attributes. There are many different religions which claim that God has spoken to them, usually through one of their prophets or founders. One of the first logical steps would be discovering which of the world religions might possibly be true. One simple test would be to determine which of the world religions believe in an all-powerful, personal, moral God who has communicated with mankind.

Only three of the major world religions believe in such a God: Judaism, Islam, and Christianity. The infinitely personal God does not fit the description of the impersonal Brahma who is the World Soul of Hinduism and is both good and evil. Nor does it fit the *Buddha Consciousness* in which Buddhism seeks to suppress human desires as harmful.

COULD ISLAM BE TRUE?

Could Islam be the true religion, just because many of its views of their god Allah seem right and that many of its adherents are very sincere? Logically, Islam cannot be the one true religion as it professes. **WHY?** Because Islam's founder Mohammed said that the Bible is to be *believed*, including the teachings of Jesus. In the Qur'an, Mohammed said, "Say, 'We believed in Allah and in what has been sent down on us and what has been sent down on Abraham and Ishmael and Isaac and Jacob and the tribes and in what was given to Moses and 'Isā and the prophets from their lord. We do not differentiate between any one of them. And to him we are Muslims.'" (Qur'an 3:84. See also Qur'an 4:136; 5:50, 68). Mohammed said that we should *believe* the writings of the Bible, which contain the Law, the Prophets, and the New Testament; yet in reality, Mohammed denied many of the major teachings of the Bible, both Old Testament and New Testament, and doctrines which Jews and Christians have always held to be true. For example, if you read the New Testament, you will discover that the historical crucifixion of Jesus as payment for the sins of the world is the central theme of the entire New Testament (Matthew 27:35, Mark 15:32, Luke 24:20, Acts 2:36, Philippians 2:8, 1 Corinthians 1:23). However, Mohammed denied that Jesus was crucified (Qur'an 4:157).

Another contradiction between the Qur'an and the Bible is that in the New Testament and the Old Testament, Jesus is called the *Son of God* (e.g., John 3:16; Matthew 14:33; John 1:34; and Acts 9:20). Mohammed emphatically taught that Jesus was *not* the Son of God and that anyone who believes that Jesus *is* the Son of God is cursed (Qur'an 9:30); the list of contradictions goes on and on. In the New Testament, Jesus is worshiped as God Who has come in the flesh (John 1:1-14), yet this is condemned and forbidden in the strongest language in the Qur'an.

How could Mohammed say that the teachings of Jesus are to be *believed* and then deny most of the major doctrines of the New Testament? Such irreconcilable contradictions make Islam untrue, definitely not a perfect revelation from a perfect God.

CHRISTIANS OR CHRIST?

Don't judge the Christian faith by hearsay or negative encounters you might have had with Christians. This would be like saying that *all* food is bad because you have experienced bad or rotten food.

Christianity stands or falls based upon *CHRIST*, not *Christians*. God does not ask you to have faith in *Christians*; He asks that you have faith in *CHRIST*. You can read the truth about Jesus Christ in the New Testament of the Bible.

CAN CHRISTIANITY BE PROVEN?

Also, some think of Christianity as *escapism* or as *wishful thinking for those who have a need to imagine a god*. The real issue, of course, is whether or not it is *true*. To say, "There is a tunnel under this prison" may be an escapist idea, but it may also be true. So how can you determine whether Christianity is true? Actually, it is not as hard as you may think. Unlike most other religions which are based upon philosophies and dogmas in which nothing can be proven or disproven, Christianity is a *historical* faith based upon historical facts which can be investigated.

In a spirit of open-mindedness, I urge you to take a fresh look at the history-changing individual known as Jesus. I will show you evidence which proves that Jesus is who He claims to be.

Suppose one day a Man walked this earth claiming to be God, saying, "I am the way, the truth, and the life. No one comes to the Father but by me" (John 14:6). Any person claiming to be the only way to get to God would have to be one of three things: psychotic with delusions of grandeur, a deceiver out to pull off one of the greatest scams of all time, or He might be *GOD*.

C. S. Lewis, once an atheist who studied evidence that eventually led him to become a Christian, wrote, "A man who was merely a man and said the sort of things Jesus said would not be a great moral teacher. He would either be a lunatic on a level with the man who says he is a poached egg or else he would be the Devil of Hell. You must make your choice. Either this man was, and is, the Son of God or else a madman or something worse..." (C.S. Lewis, *Mere Christianity*, New York: Macmillan Publishing, 1978, 56).

Most people do not realize that in the New Testament Jesus is called almost every major name and attribute used to describe God in the Old Testament. For example: Jesus is called *God* (Romans 9:5; John 1:1, 14), *Jehovah* (John 8:58), *Lord* (Acts 10:38) *Creator* (Colossians 1:15-18; Hebrews 1:1), *Savior* (Titus 2:13), *King of kings*

(Revelation 19:16), *the Alpha and the Omega* (Revelation 1:17-18; 22:13), *Holy One* (Acts 3:14), and many more.

You could take Buddha out of Buddhism, and it would remain basically unchanged. You could take Mohammed out of Islam, and it would continue to exist. But, if you took Jesus Christ out of Christianity, it would collapse because Christianity is not merely a *religion* or *philosophy* of life but an encounter with a Person who claimed to be God and who said that He was going to die for us and then rise from the dead to prove His claims: Jesus Christ. Christianity is not an *it* but a *WHO*. Christianity is not a set of rules; it is not a religion of "do this" and "don't do that." It is essentially coming to grips with the claims of Christ and how those relate to you personally.

EVIDENCE FOR JESUS' CLAIMS

Before I go on, some of you are no doubt asking about the evidence for Jesus. Some say: "If you want me to trust Christ, I need to know if there are solid reasons to do so." Absolutely. Let me summarize some of the major reasons that Jesus was telling the truth.

The first is the historical evidence for the resurrection of Jesus. If anyone could disprove the resurrection, they could disprove Christianity. However, to do so, they would have to explain what happened to His mutilated body; how the tomb, which was guarded by Roman soldiers, got empty; how over 500 people saw Him physically alive; and several other equally difficult questions. For further reading, I highly recommend Josh McDowell's book *The Resurrection Factor*.

Another line of evidence involves the trustworthiness of the eyewitnesses themselves. Of the original twelve disciples, excluding Judas the betrayer, history tells us that all but John were *killed* for their belief and bold profession that Jesus had conquered death, that they had seen Him alive after the crucifixion, and that He was the one hope for mankind. Some people such as suicide bombers will die for what they *think* is true, but the apostles would have died for something they *knew* that they made up. In other words, the apostles would have had to die for a lie that *they invented*.

A third piece of evidence is the reliability of the Bible as a historical document. Did you know that there are over 24,600 partial or complete manuscripts of the New Testament? The second-best documented manuscript of antiquity is *The Iliad and The Odyssey* by Homer. It has around 600 manuscripts. Most ancient documents have fewer than ten original copies still in existence. Using standard literary tests, the New Testament we have today is over 99.9 percent reliable. Not one word in a thousand is in question, and no major doctrine is in doubt.

The last and perhaps most conclusive piece of evidence is *fulfilled prophecy*. There were many prophecies in the Bible foretelling Christ's coming, including where He was to be born (Micah 5:2), and that He would die having His hands and feet pierced (Psalm 22:16; cf., Isaiah 53; Zechariah 12:10); it also pinpointed the exact week and year He would die (Daniel 9:25, 26). Read *Daniel's Prophecy of the 70 Weeks* by Alva J. McClain (Winona Lake, IN: BMH Books, 2007) to better understand this prophecy. The Bible also predicted that Jesus would conquer death by being resurrected (Psalm 16:10; cf., Acts 2:22-27). There are, in fact, over 300 prophecies about the coming Messiah in the Old Testament.

How could the Bible predict such astounding things hundreds of years in advance if the Bible wasn't true and Christ wasn't who He claimed to be? It was God's way to be sure we wouldn't mistake His coming. Please refer to our special section about the prophecies of Jesus to read about more of this evidence.

THE REAL PROBLEM

Like a perfect physician, Jesus was very clear when diagnosing our deepest problem; in fact, He said that He was going to die to heal our *disease*. That destructive condition is known as *SIN*. The Bible is clear that, although God created mankind to live in perfect fellowship with Himself, humanity has rebelled against our Creator; this is called sin. God reveals, "For ALL have sinned and have fallen short of the glory of God" (Romans 3:23). In other words, no one is able to reach *His perfect standard*.

Of all the truths of Christianity, the universal sinfulness of mankind is rarely questioned. Why? One word: HISTORY. One does not have to look very far into the annals of human history to witness extreme decadence, hatred, greed, and abuse multiplied millions of times over. But actually, we do not even have to look that far; each one of us is reminded of our own sinfulness every time we honestly look into the mirror.

Take heart. A necessary fact of His justness and goodness is that God hates sin; however, He still loves the *sinner*. That is why God Himself has provided the way for us to be forgiven from our sins. He wants to restore you to a right relationship with Him. But He has left the choice up to you. He has given you a free will to choose or reject His offer of love and salvation.

STEPS TO KNOWING GOD

Principle #1: God is a God of love (I John 4:16). He loves you (John 3:16). What God wants for you is awesome beyond belief (Ephesians 3:14-21). What could be more incredible than a relationship with the Creator of the Universe, knowing that He loves you deeply?

Principle #2: So, what went wrong? Why aren't more people experiencing what God intended? It is because our sin separates us from a holy God (Isaiah 59:2; Romans 6:23). Sin is active or passive rebellion against God. It is missing God's mark of perfection. Because God is *holy*, meaning He's pure and blameless, and totally without sin (Isaiah 6:1-5; I John 1:5), we cannot just come into His presence. We all fall short of God's standard of perfection.

According to the Bible, we all stand guilty before God, no matter whether we have sinned a little or a lot (James 2:10). It is like the man who was caught stealing a car who said to the judge, "But look at all the *other cars* that I didn't steal!" The point? None of us deserves to go to Heaven. Scripture teaches that we have all sinned against an eternal God and committed eternal crimes.

Principle #3: Jesus died to pay the penalty for our sin; therefore, Christ is the only way to a right relationship with God (II Thessalonians 1:8-9; John 3:16; Romans 5:8; Acts 20:28). Jesus is the bridge that connects a holy God with sinful man (I Timothy 2:5).

The Bible says that the penalty for sin is death (Romans 6:23). When we stood condemned before God as the Judge, without hope, deserving death and hell, God, in a very real sense, took off His *judicial robe* of glory, He put on a *humble robe* of humanity, became a man in the person of Jesus Christ, and died for us. The scripture says that God took on human flesh (John 1:1, 14). He lived the perfect life that we could never live, and then He died for us accomplishing what we could never do for ourselves (Romans 5:6).

Principle #4: Just *knowing* the first three principles is not enough. It takes a response on our part. Salvation is something we must *RECEIVE* (John 1:12). The Bible makes it very clear that salvation is a *FREE GIFT*; there is nothing we can do to earn it or deserve it (Ephesians 2:8-9). "For the wages of sin is death, but the *GIFT OF GOD* is eternal life through Jesus Christ our Lord" (Romans 6:23).

How much do you have to pay to get a *FREE* gift? Well, *NOTHING*. A gift is to be received, not earned, not bought, nor bargained for. It is to be received, accepted. But God will not force you to accept His offer of salvation. Many people look at their sinful lives and think that God wants them to first *clean up their act* or to *become worthy* of salvation. NO. He wants you to admit that you *can't* fix your sin problem and then to receive His divine forgiveness in faith, turning away from your sinful rebellion against Him.

Someone once said that we are born with our backs to God; in other words, we are naturally sinful, always turning away and running from God, even if we appear to be outwardly *religious*. We might even be in a church or synagogue nearly every Saturday or Sunday. Maybe we feel like we are living better lives than many other people, but this is missing the entire point. Regularly sitting in a church can't make you a Christian any more than sitting in a garage will make you into a car. Let's face it; we have already blown it. If we are to be saved, then only God can save us.

WHAT MUST I DO TO BE SAVED?

So, now the real question comes: *How* do you receive the gift of salvation? First, you must believe that Jesus really did die for your sins and that He arose from the dead (I Corinthians 15:3-5; Romans 10:9). Some have asked: "*Why* does God require *belief*?" It is because He is asking us to *trust* Him, for that is the essence of faith. He wants us to trust Him.

Since it is your sin which has been keeping you from God, you must acknowledge your sin and be willing to turn away from it as well (Mark 1:14, 15). The Bible calls this *repentance*, which simply means to turn around. If you are headed down a one-way street in the wrong direction, away from God, then turn around. As you turn back to God, ask God to forgive you and receive you back. The Bible says that if you will confess or *admit* your sins, no matter how great or small they are,

God will forgive you (Isaiah 1:18; I John 1:9) based upon what He has done for you on the cross.

The story is told of a man who skillfully walked a tightrope over and back across Niagara Falls with a heavy sack of sand on his shoulders. Upon successfully completing a two-way trip across the falls without even the slightest problem, he turned to a spectator and asked, "Do you believe that I could do that with a person on my back instead of a sack of sand?" The person said, "Of course!" The tightrope walker tossed down the bag of sand and said, "Then climb on my back." *Wow.* Real believing is more than giving mental assent to the claims of Christ. God asks you to *climb on board* and commit yourself to Him. It is more than merely believing something to be true in your head. It is a commitment of the heart.

A TIME OF DECISION

If you feel God speaking to you, deep down, and you have become convinced in your heart and in your mind that what I have shared is true, then you face a decision.

Think about it: some day you will stand before God, either forgiven or unforgiven. Hell is one of those horrible realities we don't like to discuss. However, Jesus talked about it more than all the other Bible writers put together. Not to choose God, and accept His offer of forgiveness, is to choose a life of eternal separation from Him (Revelation 20:11-15; II Thessalonians 1:8-9; Matthew 13:40-43). God is serious when it comes to sin. God is holy, and He judges sin.

But remember: there is no sin too great for God to forgive. He loves you. He died for you. Whatever you have done, whatever guilt you are carrying, God is willing to forgive. God does not lie. He promises to forgive you if you will receive Christ as Savior (Isaiah 1:18; I John 1:9).

This may be a hard decision for you. Much is at stake. If you receive Jesus as Lord, it will cost you. You may be misunderstood. Friends and family members may reject you. *Welcome to the club. Jesus was also misunderstood and rejected. But He was willing to die for you. Are you willing to live for him?*

When you are ready to make your peace with God, perhaps you could pray something like this: "Dear Jesus, I thank you for loving me. I am sorry for the ways that I have sinned against you. I believe that you died on the cross for my sin. As best as I know how, right now, I invite you to come into my life. Please forgive me, and cleanse me from all my sin. Make me the person you want me to be. I need you. Thank you for hearing my prayer. Amen."

May the Lord encourage your heart with His truth and His love.

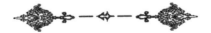

NOW AVAILABLE – Volume Two

In the next volume we will look at the prophets Ezekiel, Elisha, Samuel, Isaiah, Jeremiah, Daniel, Ezra, and we will:

- See how Ibn Kathir fabricated their stories as if there was some record of them in the Qur'an.
- See how, at times, Ibn Kathir used partial and ambiguous references from the Qur'an and applied these same verses to different prophets.
- Examine the stories of David and Solomon, Zacharias and John the Baptist.
- Examine the claimed "Jesus" of the Qur'an.
- Continue to expose the lies of the so-called Muslim scholars regarding the prophets.
- Reveal the truth about these prophets from the true biblical account.

We will contrast in separate chapters the life of our Lord and Savior Jesus Christ (His birth, life, ministry, teaching, death, and resurrection) with the life of Mohammed, the "claimed" prophet of Islam. By this, we will show that *the only truth* can be found in the Gospel of the Holy Scriptures.

ORDER TODAY!

Print Version: http://www.thestraightway.org/booksdvds/

NOW AVAILABLE

Coming Summer 2015
the E-book Version

To order, please visit our website
www.thestraightway.org

Volume 1
In Volume 1 we will look at a range of topics and people such as: Creation, Adam, Noah, Abraham, Ishmael, Isaac, and Moses. We will:
- See how Ibn Kathir fabricated their stories as if there was some record of them in the Qur'an.
- See how, at times, Ibn Kathir used partial and ambiguous references from the Qur'an and applied these same verses to different people and prophets.
- Examine the stories of Satan, Lot, Job, Jonah, and Elijah.
- Expose the lies of the so-called Muslim scholars regarding the topics, people, and prophets in Volume 1.
- Reveal the truth about these topics and prophets from the true biblical account.

Volume 2
In the next volume we will look at the prophets Ezekiel, Elisha, Samuel, Isaiah, Jeremiah, Daniel, Ezra, and we will:
- Continue to see how Ibn Kathir continued to fabricate their stories and use partial and ambiguous references from the Qur'an and applied these same verses to different prophets.
- Examine the stories of David and Solomon, Zacharias and John the Baptist.
- Examine the claimed "Jesus" of the Qur'an.
- Continue to expose the lies of the so-called Muslim scholars regarding the prophets.
- Reveal the truth about these prophets from the true biblical account.

We will contrast in separate chapters the life of our Lord and Savior Jesus Christ (His birth, life, ministry, teaching, death, and resurrection) with the life of Mohammed, the "claimed" prophet of Islam. By this, we will show that *the only truth* can be found in the Gospel of the Holy Scriptures.

The Generous Qur'an

An Accurate, Modern English Translation of the Qur'an, Islam's Holiest Book

Get Your Copy Today!

The need for a clear understanding of what this ideology/religion of Islam actually teaches is more important at this time than ever before, now that Islam is controlling an increasing portion of the world and dramatically gaining influence in Europe and the United States. Islam is being welcomed with open arms and in general ignorance by the West.

To further assist the reader in understanding Islam, Usama Dakdok, working with a team of scholars around the world, has created an accurate, modern English translation of the Qur'an, Islam's holiest book. This valuable resource combines an accurate verse by verse translation with annotations throughout the text to help the reader better understand what the content actually means and how it relates to relevant biblical verses. Additional exposition and tables further aid the reader in understanding Islam.

Features:
1. Accurate English Translation
2. Study Notes for the Reader
3. Errors and Contradictions
4. Comparison with Biblical Accounts
5. Points to Original Sources
6. Highlights Non-Arabic Words & Idioms in the Qur'an
7. Table of Bible Prophecies about Jesus
8. Gospel Invitation
9. Index

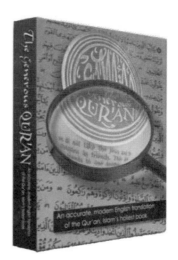

ORDER TODAY!

Print Version: http://www.thestraightway.org/booksdvds/
E-Book Version: https://www.smashwords.com/books/view/491841